江苏省高等学校重点教材(编号：2021-2-09)

国际投资学

(双语)

主　编　黄志勇
副主编　张　成　刘敏楼

更多教学资源请扫码

南京大学出版社

图书在版编目(CIP)数据

国际投资学:双语:汉、英 / 黄志勇主编. —南京:南京大学出版社,2022.3
ISBN 978-7-305-25464-2

Ⅰ.①国… Ⅱ.①黄… Ⅲ.①国际投资-汉、英 Ⅳ.①F831.6

中国版本图书馆 CIP 数据核字(2022)第 039114 号

出版发行	南京大学出版社	
社　　址	南京市汉口路 22 号　　邮　　编	210093
出 版 人	金鑫荣	

书　　名 国际投资学(双语)
主　　编 黄志勇
责任编辑 王日俊

照　　排	南京开卷文化传媒有限公司	
印　　刷	常州市武进第三印刷有限公司	
开　　本	787×1092　1/16　印张 23.25　字数 605 千	
版　　次	2022 年 3 月第 1 版　2022 年 3 月第 1 次印刷	
ISBN	978-7-305-25464-2	
定　　价	62.00 元	

网　　址:http://www.njupco.com
官方微博:http://weibo.com/njupco
微信服务号:njuyuexue
销售咨询热线:025-83594756

* 版权所有,侵权必究
* 凡购买南大版图书,如有印装质量问题,请与所购图书销售部门联系调换

前　　言

　　国际投资学是目前很多高校的专业必修课程，国内目前也有很多国际投资学的教材，但是这些教材都存在以下一些问题：

　　一是语言方面的问题。国际投资学作为一门国际化程度较高的课程，很多高校都采用了双语或全英文的方式进行授课。这种授课方式一般来说采用英文教材或双语教材较好。但目前国内还没看见有学者出版国际投资学的英文教材或双语教材。国外引进版中，主要就是 Bruno Solnik 和 Fennis Mcleavey 合著的 *International Investments*，但该教材引进到第六版（2010 年）就停止了，比较旧。

　　二是内容方面的问题。Bruno Solnik 和 Fennis Mcleavey 的教材只是讲述国际组合投资，不牵涉国际直接投资。一般国外教材中国际直接投资的内容都是放在国际经济学的跨国公司和国际金融中的跨国融资中讲述，所以引进的国际投资教材一般都缺少国际直接投资方面的内容。而国内教材则相反，因为我国的对外开放主要是直接投资，证券投资至今仍没有完全开放，因此国内教材以国际直接投资为主，对于国际组合投资都只是进行简单的原理介绍，没有实践。因此，目前国际投资学方面的教材可以说很不完整。

　　本教材对以上两个方面做了改进，一是采用双语进行编写，教材的正文部分采用英文，旁边重点和难点的地方备注有中文，方便英语偏差的同学进行对照学习；二是教材以国际组合投资和国际直接投资相结合进行，其中更偏重于国际组合投资，这和国际上关于国际投资的理念是一致的，同时，更着重于市场实践。

　　全书共包括四大部分十一章，第一部分的第一章是对国际投资进行概览，对一些基本概念进行阐述;第二部分是国际组合投资,包括第二、三、四、五、六共五章,第二章介绍组合的风险和收益的计算方法;第三章介绍CAPM和国际CAPM;第四章介绍国际分散化投资的实践;第五章和第六章分别介绍了国际股票投资和国际债券投资的具体情况;第三部分为国际直接投资部分,包括第七、八和第九章,第七章对国际直接投资的一些概念和理论进行阐述;第八章对国际直接投资中的外汇风险进行分析;第九章则对国际直接投资中的政治风险进行了介绍;第四部分是介绍中国的国际投资状况,包括第十章的中国国际直接投资和第十一章的中国国际组合投资状况。

  本教材由南京财经大学金融学院国际投资学课程组编写,主编黄志勇教授负责全书初稿和统稿,副主编张成教授负责整体编排,副主编刘敏楼副教授负责外联和润色,郭平、吴珊、胡君等老师负责查遗补漏以及反馈教学效果。

Contents

Part I Overview on International Investment

Chapter 1 Overview on International Investment 3
  The requirement of Learning 3
  1 The conception and the types 3
    1.1 The conception 3
    1.2 The types 5
  2 International Investments and Balance of Payments 5
    2.1 Basic structure 5
    2.2 The reconciliation of BOP and IIP 7
  3 The difference of FDI and IPI 7
  4 Development of International Investment 10
    4.1 Before 1914 10
    4.2 During the period of the world wars 11
    4.3 From the end of world war II to 1979 11
    4.4 From 1980s to 2000s 12
    4.5 From 2000s to 2010 14
    4.6 The Latest development of International investment 17
  Summary 19
  Exercises 20

Part II International Portfolio Investment (IPI)

Chapter 2 Diversification and Portfolio Theory 23
  The requirement of Learning 23
  1 Why a Diversified Portfolio Investment is Important 23
    1.1 Avoiding Disaster 23
    1.2 Portfolio: Reduce Risk 24
  2 The Modern Portfolio Theory 30
    2.1 The Emergence of Modern Portfolio Theory 30
    2.2 The Theory of Security Portfolio 31

Summary ·· 55
Exercises ··· 56

Chapter 3 CAPM and International CAPM ····························· 58
The requirement of Learning ··· 58
1 Capital Assets Pricing Model (CAPM) ····························· 58
   1.1 Assumptions ·· 59
   1.2 The capital market line ·· 60
   1.3 The market portfolio ··· 61
   1.4 The efficient set ··· 63
   1.5 The security market line ······································ 64
   1.6 Market and Non-Market Risk ································ 68
2 International CAPM ·· 69
   2.1 Real exchange rate ··· 69
   2.2 Foreign Currency Risk Premiums ···························· 71
   2.3 Separation Theorem and Risk-pricing relation ············ 72
Summary ·· 75
Exercises ··· 75

Chapter 4 The Practice for International Diversification ············ 78
The requirement of Learning ··· 78
1 Traditional Case International Diversification ···················· 80
   1.1 Risk Reduction through Attractive Correlations ·········· 80
   1.2 Portfolio Return Performance ································ 92
   1.3 Forward-Looking Optimization ································ 96
   1.4 Currency Risk Not a Barrier to International Investment ····· 97
2 The Case Against International Diversification ··················· 99
   2.1 Increase in Correlations ······································· 99
   2.2 Past Performance Is a Good Indicator of Future Performance ······ 102
   2.3 Barriers to International Investments ······················· 103
3 The Case for Emerging Markets ····································· 108
   3.1 The Basic Case ·· 108
   3.2 Volatility, Correlations, and Currency Risk ············· 109
   3.3 Portfolio Return Performance ································ 110
   3.4 Investability of Emerging Markets ························· 111
   3.5 Segmentation versus Integration Issue ····················· 112
Summary ·· 113
Exercises ··· 113

Chapter 5 International Equity Investment ······························ 115
The requirement of Learning ··· 115
1 Market Differences: A Historical Perspective ···················· 115

1.1	Historical Differences in Market Organization		116
1.2	Historical Differences in Trading Procedure		117
2	Global Market Statistics		118
2.1	Market Size		118
2.2	Liquidity		120
2.3	Concentration		121
3	Market Practical Aspects		121
3.1	Tax Aspects		121
3.2	Stock Market Indexes		123
4	Investing in foreign Equity Securities		127
4.1	Investing the Shares of foreign Listing		127
4.2	Depository Receipt		128
4.3	Closed-end Country Funds		133
4.4	An Exchange-Traded Fund (ETF)		136
5	Analysis Methods		138
5.1	The information Problem		139
5.2	A vision of the world		140
5.3	Differences in National Accounting Standards		140
5.4	The effects of Accounting Principles on Earnings and Stock Prices		144
6	Global Analyses		145
6.1	Country Analysis		145
6.2	Industry Analysis		148
7	Equity Analyses		151
7.1	Global financial ratio analysis		151
7.2	Valuation Models		152
7.3	The effects of inflation on Stock prices		153
Summary			155
Exercises			156

Chapter 6 International Bond Investment 160

The requirement of Learning			160
1	The Introduction of Global Bond Market		160
1.1	The various Segments		160
1.2	World market size		162
1.3	Bond Indexes		162
1.4	The Eurobond Market		164
1.5	Emerging Markets and Brady Bonds		168
2	Major Differences among Bond Markets		169
2.1	Types of Instruments		170
2.2	Quotations, Day Count, and Frequency of Coupons		170

3　A Refresher on Bond Valuation ……………………………………………… 172
　　3.1　Zero-Coupon Bonds ……………………………………………………… 172
　　3.2　Bond with Coupons ……………………………………………………… 173
　　3.3　Duration and Interest Rate Sensitivity …………………………………… 174
　　3.4　Credit Spreads …………………………………………………………… 175
　　3.5　The return and risk on foreign bond investment ………………………… 176
4　Floating Rate Notes and Structured Notes ……………………………………… 178
　　4.1　Floating-Rate Notes (FRNs) …………………………………………… 178
　　4.2　Bull FRN ………………………………………………………………… 181
　　4.3　Bear FRN ………………………………………………………………… 182
　　4.4　Dual-Currency Bonds …………………………………………………… 182
　　4.5　Currency-Option Bonds ………………………………………………… 183
Summary …………………………………………………………………………… 185
Exercises …………………………………………………………………………… 186

Part Ⅲ International Direct Investment

Chapter 7　FDI: Conception and Theories ……………………………………… 193
The requirement of Learning ……………………………………………………… 193
1　The Definition and Measurement ……………………………………………… 193
　　1.1　The "lasting interest" *vs.* Control ……………………………………… 194
　　1.2　Classification of FDI …………………………………………………… 195
2　Theories ………………………………………………………………………… 196
　　2.1　Theory of Monopolistic Competition …………………………………… 197
　　2.2　Internalization Theory …………………………………………………… 199
　　2.3　Theory of International Product Cycle …………………………………… 200
　　2.4　The Eclectic Paradigm …………………………………………………… 202
3　The Decision Sequence of FDI ………………………………………………… 205
4　Foreign Direct Investment Originating in Developing Countries ……………… 206
Summary …………………………………………………………………………… 207
Exercises …………………………………………………………………………… 208

Chapter 8　The Risks of Foreign Exchange Rate ……………………………… 209
The requirement of Learning ……………………………………………………… 209
1　Transaction Exposure …………………………………………………………… 210
　　1.1　Purchasing or Selling on Open Account ………………………………… 211
　　1.2　Borrowing and Lending ………………………………………………… 211
　　1.3　Other Causes of Transaction Exposure ………………………………… 212
　　1.4　Contractual Hedges ……………………………………………………… 212
　　1.5　Management of an Account Payable …………………………………… 223

2	Operating Exposure	225
	2.1 Attributes of Operating Exposure	226
	2.2 Illustrating Operating Exposure: Trident	228
	2.3 Strategic Management of Operating Exposure	234
	2.4 Proactive Management of Operating Exposure	237
3	Translation Exposure	246
	3.1 Overview of Translation	246
	3.2 Translation Methods	247
	3.3 Translation Example: Trident Europe	250
	3.4 Comparing Translation Exposure with Operating Exposure	255
	3.5 Managing Translation Exposure	256
Summary		260
Exercises		262

Chapter 9 FDI: Political Risks 263

The requirement of Learning		263
1	Defining Political Risk	263
2	Assessing Political Risk	264
	2.1 Predicting Firm-specific Risk (Micro Risk)	265
	2.2 Predicting Country-Specific Risk (Macro Risk)	265
	2.3 Predicting Global-Specific Risk	266
3	Firm-Specific Risks	266
	3.1 Governance Risks	267
4	Country-Specific Risks	272
	4.1 Transfer Risk: Blocked Funds	272
	4.2 Country-Specific Risks: Cultural and Institutional Risks	276
5	Global-Specific Risks	280
	5.1 Terrorism and War	280
	5.2 Crisis Planning	281
	5.3 Cross-Border Supply Chain Integration	281
	5.4 Anti-globalization Movement	283
	5.5 Environmental Concerns	283
	5.6 Poverty	284
	5.7 Cyber Attacks	284
	5.8 Corporate Social Responsibility	285
Summary		285
Exercises		286

Part IV International Investment in China

Chapter 10 International Direct Investment in China ········· 291
  The requirement of Learning ········· 291
  1 FDI in China ········· 291
    1.1 Why study FDI in China? ········· 292
    1.2 FDI Inflows into China between 1979 and 2009 ········· 293
    1.3 China's FDI Inflows in Global Perspective ········· 296
    1.4 The Regional Distribution of FDI within China ········· 298
    1.5 Who are the Major Investors in China? ········· 299
    1.6 Sectoral Distribution of FDI in China ········· 301
    1.7 The Contribution of FDI to China's Economy ········· 303
    1.8 The Evolution of China's Opening Policies to FDI ········· 305
  2 OFDI in China ········· 312
    2.1 Introduction ········· 312
    2.2 Phases of Chinese OFDI ········· 316
    2.3 The latest development of Chinese OFDI ········· 320
    2.4 International Investment Strategy of China's OFDI ········· 331
  Summary ········· 333
  Exercises ········· 334

Chapter 11 International Portfolio Investment in China ········· 335
  Learning requirements ········· 335
  1 Overview ········· 335
  2 Foreign investors invest in Chinese stocks ········· 337
    2.1 Investing in overseas-listed stocks of Chinese companies ········· 338
    2.2 QFII and RQFII ········· 345
    2.3 Interconnection mechanism ········· 346
    2.4 Foreign investor invest in China's Bond ········· 350
  3 China's Indirect Investment abroad ········· 353
    3.1 QDII ········· 353
    3.2 Sovereign wealth funds ········· 357
  Summary ········· 359
  Exercises ········· 360

REFERENCES ········· 362

Part I

Overview on International Investment

Chapter 1
Overview on International Investment

The requirement of Learning
- Knowing the conceptions of investment and international investment.
- Knowing the difference between the international investment and the domestic investment.
- Familiar with the reconciliation from BOP and IIP.
- Understanding the difference between FDI and FPI.
- Knowing the developmental history of international investment.
- Knowing the latest development of international investment.

1 The conception and the types

1.1 The conception

Simply stated, Investment is an activity in which funds can be used with the expectation that they will be preserved or will increase in value or will generate positive returns. The term investment can cover a wide range of activities. In theoretical economics, investment means the purchase of capital goods which are not consumed but instead used in future production. For example, It includes building a railroad, or a factory, clearing land, or putting oneself through college etc. In finance, investment means buying monetary or paper assets, for example equity investment or real estate investment or bonds. These investments may then provide a future income and increase in value. Idle cash is not an investment, since its value is likely to be eroded by inflation and it fails to provide any type of return. The same cash placed in a bank savings account would be considered as an investment, because the account provides a positive return. The various types of investments can be differentiated on the basis of a few factors, such as short term, medium term and long term investment, public investment and private Investment, domestic and international, etc.

> 简单地说，投资是指目前投入资金，未来预期可以保值或增值产生正收益的一种活动。

> 国际投资是指跨国公司、跨国金融机构、官方和半官方投资者以及个人投资者投入资金到境外以期获得正收益的投资行为。

投资主体不同

投资环境不同

International investment refers to any economic behaviors through which investors such as transnational corporations（TNCs）, transnational financial institutions; official and semi-official institutions; and individuals invest their assets in countries other than their own with the expectation of positive return. Although international investments cover almost the same varieties of domestic investments, they are extensively regarded more complicated and difficult than domestic ones due to its internationalization. The differences between them lie mainly in:

- The differences of investors. International investors are mainly multinational companies and international banks, Domestic investors are primarily levels of government, various types of economic entities and individuals. There exist many differences in the size of investment, financial strength, technological and management experience, etc.

- The differences of investment environment. Firstly, Political environment is different. Domestic investors are familiar and easy to understand the country's political environment. The international investors face the diversity political environment, such as the host country can be either a socialist country or a capitalist country, a developed country or a developing country, a treaty of friendship concluded with the investor's country or no official contacts with the investor's country, a open and welcome country or a close and exclusive country, and so on. Secondly, Economic environment is different. Domestic investors are more familiar with their own investment environment, but international investors face the types of economic environment, Such as whether the investment activities are in line with the economic policies, or whether the host country's infrastructure can ensure the smooth process of investment. Thirdly, Legal environment is different. In international investment, the legal environment is much more complex owing to the different policy. In addition, there exist great differences in language, geographical environment, customs, etc.

投资目标不同

- The differences of investment targets. Investment objective can be divided into the direct target and the ultimate goal. Domestic and international investments may have the same ultimate goal, that is to pursue the maximization of profit, but the direct target may be quite different. Generally speaking, it is almost the same in the direct and final goals of domestic investment, but international investment may have the diversification of direct target, such as developing and keeping the share of oversea markets, reducing the cost of production and labor, diversifying the risks, learning advanced foreign technology, access to host resources, developing economic assistance to host countries, improving the bilateral economic or political relationship and so on.

- The differences of investment factors. The flow of some factors is limited in the international investment. Such as the human capital or some advanced technology. Moreover, there exist the diversification of currency and monetary system in the different countries. So it makes the international investment more complicated than the domestic investment.

投资要素不同

- The use of Monetary is different. Domestic investment generally use the home currency, but international investment may use many different currencies.

使用货币不同

1.2 The types

International investment can be divided into many types according to different factors. For example, according to the period, we have long-term investments and short-term investments; According to different investors, there are official investors and private investors; According to whether investors own control right in the management of a firm or not, it can be divided into the international direct investment and the international indirect investment. In the international direct investment, there are inward foreign direct investments (FDI inflow) and outward foreign direct investments (FDI outflow) according to the direction of the fund's flow. The international indirect investment is also called the international portfolio investments (IPI).

2 International Investments and Balance of Payments

2.1 Basic structure

For a better understanding of international investment, it is necessary to gain knowledge of the components in the balance-of-payments (BOP) framework. The BOP is a statistical statement that

为了更好地理解国际投资,有必要了解国际收支框架。国际收支

> 平衡表是一种统计报表,它系统地记录了一个经济体在特定时期内与世界其他地区的经济交易。国际收支账户包括三个子账户:经常账户、资本和金融账户、错误和遗漏。

systematically summarizes, for a specific time period, the economic transactions of an economy with the rest of the world. The BOP comprises three accounts: the current account, capital and financial account, error and mission. A simplified BOP statement of a country (e.g. Table 1.1, Babylonia) can be presented.

Table 1.1 A simplified FA statement of a country

```
B. Financial account
1. Direct investment
   1.1  Abroad
        Equity capital
            Claims on affiliated enterprises
            Liabilities to affiliated enterprises
        Reinvested earnings
        Other capital
            Claims on affiliated enterprises
            Liabilities to affiliated enterprises
   1.2  In the reporting economy
        Equity capital
            Claims on direct investors
            Liabilities to direct investors
        Reinvested earnings
        Other capital
            Claims on direct investors
            Liabilities to direct investors
2. Portfolio investment
3. Other investment
4. Reserve assets
```

The IIP is a statement of an economy's stock of external financial assets and liabilities at a particular point in time. The classification scheme used for the IIP is similar to that used for the financial account, and reflects the close relationship between the IIP statement, shown in table 1.2 (only for FDI components), and the external financial assets and liabilities of the BOP as indicated in table 1.1.

Table 1.2 IIP: components in the direct Investment category

```
Assets
   Direct investment abroad
      Equity capital and retained earnings
         Claims on affiliated enterprises
         Liabilities to affiliated enterprises
      Other capital
         Claims on affiliated enterprises
         Liabilities to affiliated enterprises
```

```
    Liabilities
    Direct investment in reporting economy
        Equity capital and retained earnings
            Claims on direct investors
            Liabilities to direct investors
        Other capital
            Claims on direct investors
            Liabilities to direct investors
```

2.2 The reconciliation of BOP and IIP

It is important to note the close relationship between the BOP flow-oriented framework, particularly of the financial account, and the IIP stock-oriented framework. Reconciliation of the flow activities in the financial account with a change in stocks made during a defined period is the responsibility of the BOP compiler. The BOP accounts record reflects only transactions; on the other hand, a change in stocks appearing in the IIP can be attributable to transactions (financial account flows), to valuation changes due to changes in exchange rates and prices, and to other adjustments.

Measurement errors can have an impact on reconciliation of the BOP and IIP statements. This is particularly true when, for example, different sources are used to measure flows and stocks of financial assets and liabilities. Measurement errors can also arise as a result of faulty reporting by respondents and the use of sampling to collect inputs.

Retained (reinvested) earnings, which are an intrinsic component of shareholders' equity, are used in conjunction with the value of the shares for determining the value of the stock of direct investment. For countries that do not record reinvested earnings accruing to foreign direct investors in the BOP, it may be necessary to add reinvested earnings as an additional item for reconciliation of FDI flows and stocks.

3 The difference of FDI and IPI

Two key elements need to be emphasized in the definition of FDI and in distinguishing it from IPI. FDI can be defined as an investment made by a resident of one economy in another economy, and it is of a long-term nature or of "lasting interest." It should be noted in this context that country of residence is different from nationality or citizenship. The second element is that the investor has a "significant degree of influence" on the management of the enterprise.

For operational purposes, 10 per cent of the voting shares or voting power is the level of ownership necessary for a direct investment interest to exist (IMF, 1993, p362; OECD, 2008, p117). This 10 per cent limit is recommended to enhance international comparability.

For countries new to BOP compilation or FDI statistics, it is an international criterion to be followed. Nevertheless, countries that do not adhere to the 10 percent rule should identify, where possible, the aggregate value of transactions which deviate from the rule in order to facilitate international comparability. Moreover, from a practical aspect, it is preferable to have an objective rule rather than relying on subjective judgment.

The following two examples shed light on the differences between FDI and FPI.

> **Example 1-1**
>
> ABC Ltd. is a wholly-owned affiliate of ABC Corporation, a United States TNC. The investment by ABC Corporation is typical of a direct investment where the direct investor owns the majority of the voting shares or voting power of an enterprise located in another country. In this case the foreign direct investor controls the operations of the direct investment enterprise and has a "significant degree of influence" on the management of the enterprise. The foreign direct investor is represented on the board of directors of the direct investment enterprise and participates in its policy-making process. This is a case of FDI.

> **Example 1-2**
>
> An investment made by a United States individual who owns 100 shares of Babylonian Telecommunication Corporation. The company is listed on the stock exchange and has issued one million shares. This is a typical example of a portfolio investor.

尽管国际组合投资像直接投资一样也可以是长期投资，但这两种投资在视角和前景上有相当大的不同。国际组合投资通常持有两到三年，但持有的股票可以在任何时候轻松出售。

The two examples of international investments involve the issue of equity ownership, they are nonetheless different: apart from the 10 percent ownership threshold that distinguishes them, they also differ in terms of investment intentions and expectations. The objectives and the purposes of the two investments are also very different.

Although portfolio investment can also be a long-term investment, like direct investment, there is a considerable difference in perspective and outlook between the two investments. Portfolio investment in the securities of a foreign enterprise tends to be held for two or three years. But it is considered to be just that: a holding of shares that can be easily sold in the stock market at any time.

Direct investment, however, is considered to be investment in nuts and bolts in the foreign country. It is not viewed as a holding of shares of a foreign enterprise but as an investment in the fixed assets, personnel and management of the enterprise. The portfolio investor is a holder of shares amounting to less than 10 per cent equity of an enterprise in a foreign country, whereas a direct investor either wholly or partially owns an enterprise domiciled in a foreign country. The direct investor, views the investment as ownership of the company's property, plant(s) and equipment rather than of equity and debt securities.

Foreign investors that own between 10 and 50 per cent of the shares of foreign affiliates, with the intention of a long-term investment, also fall into the category of FDI. These investments, although constituting less than majority ownership, nevertheless comprise relatively sizeable and significant investments in the enterprises. The investments are large enough for the investor to have a role in the management of the associate companies, and hence can be classified as direct investments rather than portfolio investments. Based strictly on ownership of voting shares or voting power, the direct investor may not control the direct investment enterprise, but is nevertheless considered to be entitled to exercise a significant degree of influence on the management of the enterprise.

> 出于长期投资的目的,持有外国子公司10%至50%股份的国际投资者也属于国际直接投资类别。

Box 1. FDI versus foreign portfolio and other investment flows

FDI have different investment motives from investors in portfolio and other investments. In supplying long-term capital to a foreign entity, a direct investor is interested in establishing a lasting relationship with that company. The investment could be made to provide access to natural resources and markets for products; gain access to labor supply, technology and other assets; ensure security of supplies; and control the quality of a certain product or service etc.

> Investors in portfolio or other investment, on the other hand, have either invested relatively small amounts in the voting shares of the foreign companies or have acquired other types of claims, such as debt, on the foreign entity.

4 Development of International Investment

Emerged early in the late 18th century, International investment has been developing into the most active driving force in the world economy today. After more than two hundred years, International investments have experienced great changes in many aspects. According to the investment size and the modes, it can be divided into the following phases:

4.1 Before 1914

International investments appeared because production surplus resulted from the second industrial revolution. And the indirect investment dominated in the international investment during that period. The history of multinational firms, and of the cross-border capital flows associated with them, foreign direct investment, goes back a long time.

Early foreign investment went mainly into government securities, probably thought of as relatively safe, although some of them proved riskier than was expected. Later investment went heavily into railroads. A common feature, aside from lending to the federal government during the Civil War, was that foreign portfolio investment went to large, lumpy, social overhead capital projects—railroads, canals, and later public utilities—relatively safer investments and less dependent on local knowledge than the typically much smaller, and on that account, riskier enterprises in agriculture or manufacturing, which were left mainly to local financing.

Many manufacturing enterprises were set up by foreign craftsmen or entrepreneurs with special skills. Since transportation and communication were so slow that it was impossible to manage these enterprises from abroad, the investment was therefore often accompanied by the migration of children or other relatives of the foreign investors to manage the enterprise. Although these enterprises were a form of direct investment, they were different from most direct investment now in that they were not controlled by parent firms as an outgrowth of their businesses, but by individual investors.

4.2 During the period of the world wars

It was a slowly developing period. Due to the two world wars, international investments were held back heavily. The value of international investment by major investor countries dropped to US $38 billion in 1945 when the Second World War ended. Indirect investment was still the main mode.

The period of World War I saw the first major U.S. portfolio investment abroad, including large loans to foreign governments that outweighed total private financing. By the end of 1919, direct investment had been reduced to a little over half of U.S. private investment abroad but to less than a quarter of total foreign investment including inter-government loans.

The 1920s were characterized by rapid growth in both direct and portfolio private investment abroad but were unlike the earlier periods in that portfolio investment became the predominant avenue for U.S. investment, tripling in value while direct investment only doubled, and accounting for over 60 percent of the growth in private U.S. investment abroad. By 1929, the value of U.S. private portfolio investment exceeded that of direct investment for the first time.

The Great Depression reversed the change in the composition of the U.S. private foreign investment portfolio that had taken place in the 1920s. Half of the foreign loans extended in the late 1920s went into default. U.S. holdings of securities, even valued at par, were reduced by almost 30 percent (almost 50 percent with defaulted bonds at market value), and short-term credits were cut almost in half (Lewis, 1938). By 1940, direct investment was back to 60 percent of U.S. private outward investment. It was a little more than that in 1950 and remained between 60 percent and two-thirds through 1970.

> 这段时期,国际投资发展缓慢,由于两次世界大战的影响,国际投资受到严重阻碍。1945年第二次世界大战结束时,主要投资国的国际投资额下降到380亿美元,国际组合投资仍是主要投资方式。

4.3 From the end of world war II to 1979

International investments started to develop again. During this period, international investments increased rapidly, the value from

> 在此期间,国际投资迅速增加,发达国家的

> 投资额从 1945 年的 510 亿美元增加到 1978 年的 6 000 亿美元。另一个明显的特点是，国际直接投资取代国际间接投资，在国际投资中占据主导地位。例如，1978 年国际直接投资达到 3 693 亿美元，占投资总额的 61.6%，而 1945 年为 200 亿美元。

developed countries reaching US$600 billion in 1978 from US$51 billion in 1945. And another obvious feature is that direct investment replaced indirect investment to dominate in international investment. For example, FDI reached US$369.3 billion in 1978, accounting for 61.6% of the total from the US$20.0 billion in 1945. Please see Table 1.3 for detailed increase.

Table 1.3 Private FDI from Main Capitalist countries, billion US $

Year	1960	1967	1971	1973	1975	1979
Amount	53.7	106.3	158	196.5	259	447.2

Source: Abstract of American Statistics 1985, US Commercial Department.

U.S. government loans to foreign countries had expanded further during World War II and by 1950 were almost twice the total of all private investment stocks. Thus the restored dominance of direct investment in 1950 applied only to private investment. After 1950, U.S. government loans did not increase greatly, and by 1970, more than 70 percent of U.S. international assets were private and almost half were direct investment.

The United States not only had much or most of its international investment in the form of direct investment but also accounted for a large part of the world's stock of direct investment. In 1960, almost half of all the outward direct investment was owned by investors based in the United States. No other country came close; the next ranking holder of direct investment was the United Kingdom at 18 percent, followed by the Netherlands at 10 percent and France at 6 percent (United Nations, 1988).

4.4 From 1980s to 2000s

> 这是一个国际投资快速发展的阶段。技术进步、金融创新和全球化促进了国际直接投资和国际组合投资的发展，其速度超过了世界生产总值和世界贸易的发展。

There was a rapid development phase. Technological progress, financial innovations and globalization facilitate international investment both in FDI and indirect investment and the development speed exceeds that of GDP and of the world trade. Please refer to Figure 1.1 and Table 1.4 for the great change. Table 1.5 is given the comparison between FDI and some production indices and Table 1.6 is given the FPI of developed countries.

Chapter 1　Overview on International Investment

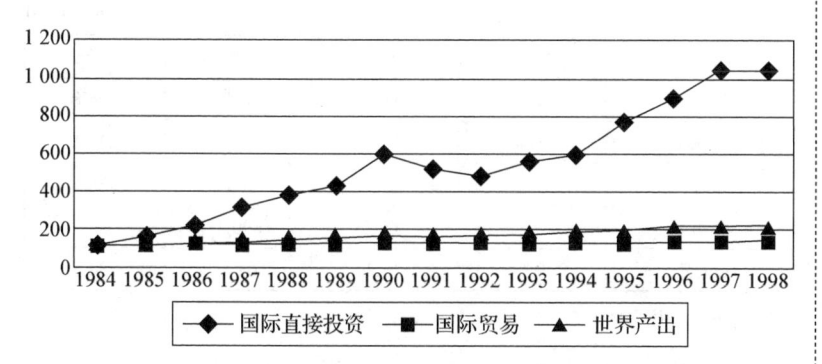

Figure 1.1　The Growth of FDI, International Trade and Global Output (1984—1998)

国际直接投资　国际贸易　世界产出

Table 1.4　International Investments in 1989 and 1999 (as per the share in GDP)

Countries	Total Invested 1989	Total Invested 1999	Total FDI 1989	Total FDI 1999	Total FPI 1989	Total FPI 1999
The world	8.5	18.3	2.0	4.6	6.5	13.7
Low-income countries	0.8	1.2	0.2	0.3	0.6	0.9
middle-income countries	1.9	4.9	0.4	1.6	1.5	3.3
high-income countries	12.7	29.2	2.9	7.2	9.8	22.0

Source: World Bank, World Development Indicators. 2001

Table 1.5　FDI and Related Production Indices (US $1billion, %)

Items	1982	1990	2000	1986—1990	1991—1995	1996—1999
Inward FDI flows	57	202	1 271	23.0	20.8	40.8
Outward FDI flows	37	235	1 150	26.2	16.3	37.0
Inward FDI stock	719	1 889	6 314	16.2	9.3	18.4
Outward FDI stock	568	1 717	5 976	20.5	10.8	16.4
Transnational M&A	—	151	1 144	26.4	23.3	50.0
Exports of Goods & Services	2 124	4 381	7 036	15.4	8.6	1.9

Source: UNCTAD. WIR, 2001.

Table 1.6　Transnational transactions in Bonds and Stocks by Main DCs (% of GDP)

countries	1980	1985	1990	1996
USA	9.0	35.1	89.0	151.5
Japan	7.7	63.0	120.0	82.8

continued

countries	1980	1985	1990	1996
Germany	7.5	33.4	57.3	196.8
France	8.4	21.4	53.6	229.2
Italy	1.1	4.0	26.6	435.4
British	—	367.5	690.1	—
Canada	9.6	26.7	64.4	234.8

Source: IMF. 1997 6b.

The United States was by far the major source of direct investment outflows in the early 1970s, but Europe soon caught up and Japan almost did before fading out in the 1990s. Hong Kong became a major investor in the 1990s, investing heavily in China. The United States shifted from being the world's largest net supplier of direct investment to being a large absorber of such investment from other countries, especially in 1985—1989, and then reverted to its earlier net supplier role. Latin America and Southeast Asia have been continuous net recipients of direct investment. Portfolio capital has been supplied to the world steadily by Japan. The United States, at times, particularly in 1985—1989, has absorbed much of this capital, on net balance, and Southeast Asia and Latin America have also been major borrowers.

The different forms of international investment flows not only vary in importance among regions but have different characteristics in other ways. Direct investment flows have been the least volatile among the different types in most countries, the chief exception being the United States, which has flipped back and forth from being the dominant net supplier to dominant net recipient and back to dominant net supplier. For other countries, and particularly for developing countries, direct investment has been the most dependable source of foreign investment.

4.5 From 2000s to 2010

There exists some characteristics from the figure 1.2. Firstly, Global FDI reached new records high in 2000 and 2007 respectively, and the inflows record set in 2000 is $1,400 billion and the record set in 2007 is $1,833 billion, the previous record set in 2000 was surpassed by some $400 billion. Secondly, FDI in developed countries is dominant, but the difference is reduced between the developed countries and the developing countries after

2000. Thirdly, FDI of the transition economies become more after 2000.

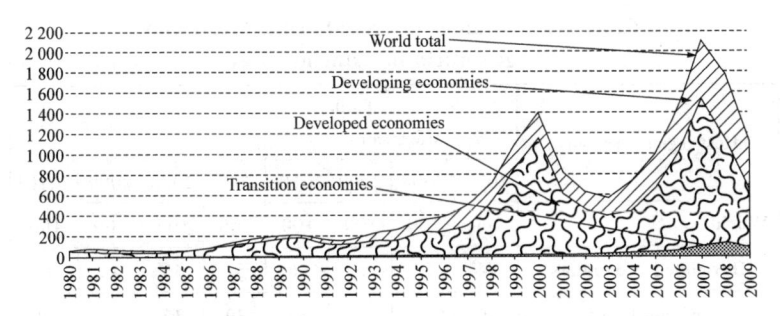

国际直接投资以发达国家为主,但2000年后,发达国家和发展中国家之间的差距缩小了。第三,2000年后,转型经济体的国际直接投资逐渐增加。

Source: UNCTAD, based on annex table 1 and the FDI/TNC database (http://www.unctad.org/fdistatistics)

Figure 1.2 FDI inflows: global and by groups of economies, (Billions of dollars)

In global rankings of the largest FDI recipients, there are three developing and transition economies ranked among the six largest foreign investment recipients in the world in 2009, and China was the second most popular destination, While the United States maintained its position as the largest host country in 2009, a number of European countries saw their rankings slide.

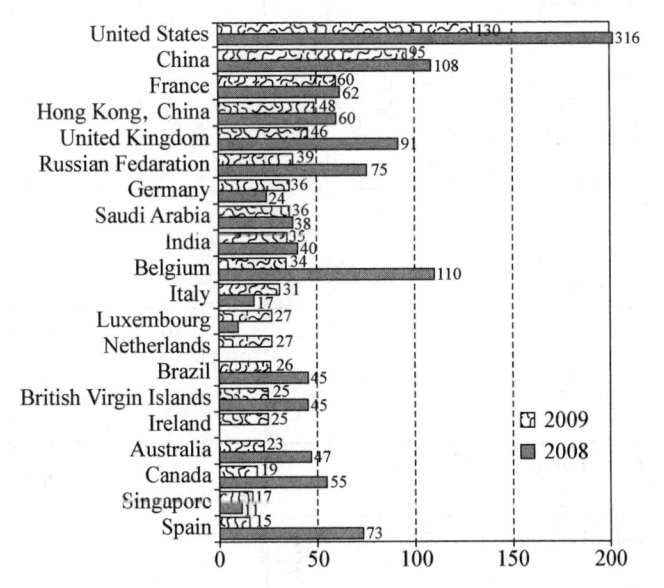

Source: UNCTAD, based on annex table 1 and the FDI/TNC database (http://www.unctad.org/fdistatistics)

Figure 1.3 Global FDI inflows, top 20 host economies, 2008—2009

Developing and transition economies attracted more greenfield investments than developed countries in 2008—2009 (Table 1.7). Although the majority of cross-border M&A deals still take place in developed regions, the relative share of such transactions in developing and transition economies has been on the rise.

Table 1.7 Number of cross-border M&A and greenfield investment cases

Host region/economy	Net Cross-border M&A sales[b]				Greenfield Investments			
	2007	2008	2009	2010[a]	2007	2008	2009	2010[a]
World	100	100	100	100	100	100	100	100
Developed economies	74	72	69	66	52	46	46	49
European Union	39	38	32	32	39	34	30	31
France	3	3	2	3	5	4	3	3
Germany	6	5	4	4	4	4	3	3
United Kingdom	10	10	7	9	6	5	8	7
United States	18	17	17	16	7	6	9	10
Japan	2	2	2	2	1	1	1	1
Developing economies	22	23	23	25	42	47	48	45
Africa	2	2	1	2	3	5	5	5
South Africa	1	1	1	—	—	1	1	1
Latin America and the Canbbean	6	6	5	8	7	7	9	9
Brazil	2	2	1	2	1	2	2	2
Mexico	1	1	1	1	2	2	2	2
Asia	14	16	16	16	32	35	34	32
West Asia	2	2	2	2	5	7	7	7
South East and South-East Asia	13	14	15	14	27	28	27	26
China	3	4	3	3	10	9	8	8
Hong Kong, China	2	1	2	2	1	1	2	1
India	2	2	2	2	6	6	5	6
South-East Europe and the CIS	4	5	8	9	6	7	6	6
Russian Federation	2	3	4	6	3	4	3	3
Memorandum								
Total number of cases	7 018	6 425	4 239	1 802	12 210	16 147	13 727	4 104

Source: UNCTAD cross-border M&A database and information from the Financial Times Ltd, fdi Markets (www.fDimarkets.com). a 2010 data cover January to May for M&As and January to April for greenfield investments. b Net sales by the region/economy of the immediate acquired company.

4.6 The Latest development of International investment

4.6.1 Global trends

Global foreign direct investment (FDI) flows continued their slide in 2018, falling by 13 per cent to $1.3 trillion from a revised $1.5 trillion in 2017 (figure 1.4). The decline—the third consecutive fall in FDI—was mainly due to large repatriations of accumulated foreign earnings by United States multinational enterprises (MNEs) in the first two quarters of 2018, following tax reforms introduced at the end of 2017, and insufficient compensation from upward trends in the second half of the year.

FDI flows declined sharply in developed countries and economies in transition while those to developing countries remained stable, rising by 2 per cent. As a result, developing economies accounted for a growing share of global FDI, at 54 per cent, from 46 per cent in 2017.

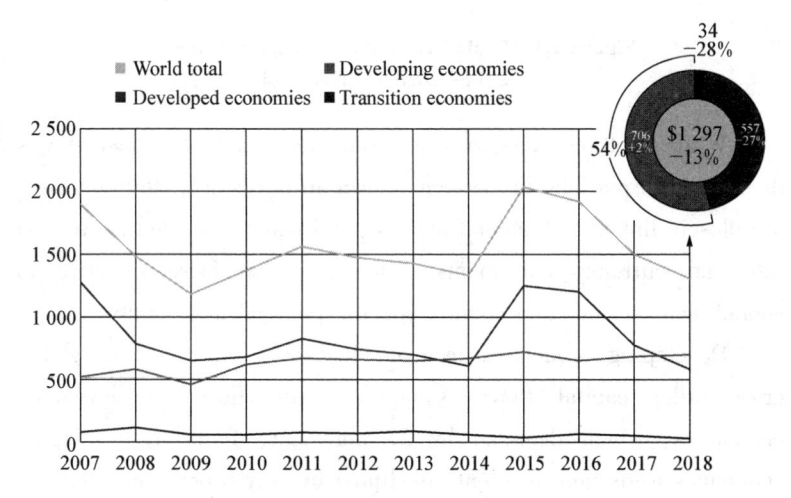

> 全球国际直接投资流量近年来持续下滑，2018年的国际直接投资流量从2017年的1.5万亿美元下降到1.3万亿美元，降幅为13%。

Source: UNCTAD, FDI/MEN database (www.unctad.org/fdistatistics).

Figure 1.4 FDI inflows (Billions of dollars and per cent)

Repatriations of United States multinationals' foreign earnings abated in the second half of 2018. The lifting of tax liabilities on accumulated foreign earnings of United States MNEs may have contributed to the M&A boom recorded in the last quarter, limiting the global FDI decline for the year, after projections based on the first six months had estimated that annual inflows would be down by more than 40 per cent.

4.6.2 FDI and other cross-border capital flows

The decline in global FDI flows was in line with the trend in

> 全球国际直接投资流量的下降与其他跨境资本流动的趋势一致。

> 2018年,国际直接投资、证券投资和其他投资(主要是银行贷款)合计达5万亿美元,占全球国内生产总值的5.9%,比2017年下降了20%以上(图1.5)。

other cross-border capital flows. Together FDI, portfolio flows and other investment (mostly bank loans) amounted to $5 trillion, or 5.9 per cent of global GDP in 2018, a decline of more than 20 per cent from 2017 (figure 1.5).

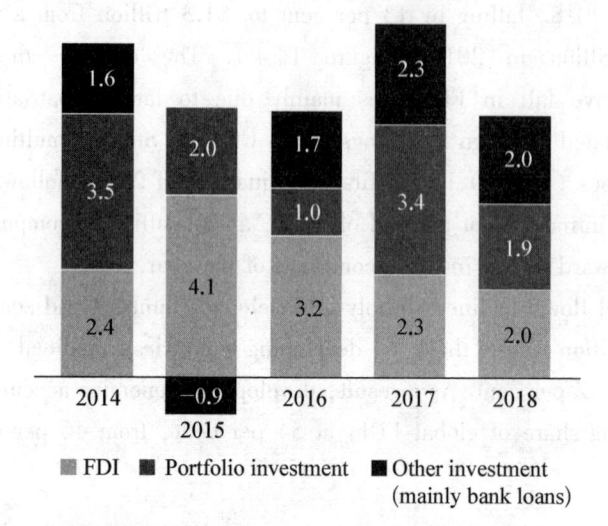

Figure 1.5 Global cross-border capital flows, 2014—2018 (Per cent of GDP)

While all three categories of capital flows fell, the decline was the largest in portfolio investment (down 40 per cent). Portfolio flows are closely linked to financial market performance, as well as interest rate and currency movements. They are also more sensitive to geopolitical tensions and country-specific political uncertainty.

Developing economies received just over one third of global cross-border capital flows. Compared with flows to developed economies, which declined by 27 per cent, flows to developing economies were more resilient, declining by only 8 per cent, because FDI—the more stable type of finance—represents a larger share of their capital inflows. Portfolio inflows and other investment in developing economies declined by 30 per cent and 14 per cent, respectively. Declines in portfolio flows were particularly large in Latin America and in West Asia. Policy uncertainty and currency instability in major regional recipients of portfolio flows, including Argentina, Mexico and Turkey, contributed to the declines. In those countries, too, FDI inflows proved more stable and actually increased in 2018.

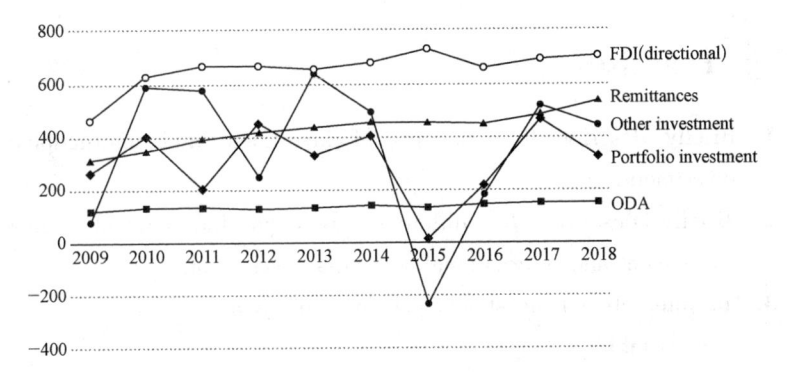

Figure 1.6 Developing economies: sources of external finance (Billions of dollars)

The size and relative stability of FDI makes it the most importance source of external finance for developing economies (figure 1.6). Preliminary data for official development assistance (ODA) (bilateral and multilateral) show an increase of 1.5 per cent to $149 billion. Preliminary data for remittances show an increase of 9.6 per cent to $529 billion.

Summary

- Simply stated, Investment is an activity in which funds can be used with the expectation that they will be preserved or will increase in value or will generate positive returns.
- International Investment refers to any economic behaviors through which investors such as TNCs, transnational financial institutions, official and semi-official institutions and individuals invest their assets in countries other than their own with the expectation of positive return.
- For a better understanding of international investment, it is necessary to gain knowledge of the components in the balance-of payments (BOP) framework.
- For operational purposes, 10 per cent of the voting shares or voting power is the level of ownership necessary for a direct investment interest to exist.
- According to the investment size and the modes, International investment can be divided into the difference phases.

Exercises

1. Briefly describe the concepts of investment and international investment.
2. Briefly describe the difference between international direct investment and international securities investment.
3. The international investment position table is a (   ).
    A. Flow table
    B. Stock table
    C. Foreign investment stock table
    D. Foreign investment flow statement
4. The fifth Edition of the IMF's Balance of Payment Manual defines the owner of (   ) or more of a company's capital as a direct investor.
    A. 15%   B. 10%   C. 20%   D. 1%
5. The aim of FDI may be (   ).
    A. gain access to labor supply, technology and other assets
    B. access to natural resources and markets for products
    C. control the quality of a certain product or service
    D. ensure security of supplies
6. According to whether investors own control right in the management of a firm or not, international investment can be divided into (   ).
    A. Long-run and short-run investments
    B. official and private investments
    C. Foreign direct investment and international indirect investment
    D. Domestic investment and international investment
7. Before 1914, (   ) is the main investors of international investment.
    A. American   B. European   C. Asian   D. African
8. According to the latest statistics, the gap between international direct investment in developed and developing countries (   ).
    A. became bigger   B. became smaller
    C. keeps unchanged   D. uncertain

Part II

International Portfolio Investment (IPI)

Chapter 2
Diversification and Portfolio Theory

> **The requirement of Learning**
> - Understanding why a diversified portfolio perspective is important.
> - Knowing the Markowitz approach to portfolio selection.
> - Knowing how to calculate the expected return and standard deviation of portfolio.
> - Knowing the matrix.
> - Knowing how to select the optimal portfolio.

1 Why a Diversified Portfolio Investment is Important

One of the biggest challenges faced by investors is to decide how to invest for future needs. For individual investors, the goal might be to fund retirement needs. For institutional investors such as insurance companies, the goal is to fund future liabilities in the form of insurance claims. Regardless of the ultimate goal, all face the same set of challenges that extend beyond just the choice of what asset classes to invest in. They ultimately center on formulating basic principles that determine how to think about investing. One important question is: Should we invest in individual securities, evaluating each in isolation, or should we take a portfolio approach? By "portfolio approach", we mean evaluating individual securities in relation to their contribution to the investment characteristics of the whole portfolio. In the following section, we illustrate a number of reasons why a diversified portfolio perspective is important.

1.1 Avoiding Disaster

Portfolio diversification helps investors avoid disastrous investment outcomes. This benefit is most convincingly illustrated by examining what may happen when individuals have not diversified.

Let's see an example. During the 1990s, Enron Corporation was

> 投资者面临的最大挑战之一是决定如何为未来投资。对单个投资者来说，其目标可能是考虑退休后的资金需求；对诸如保险公司的机构投资者来说，其目的是保证对未来以保险权益而存在的负债资金需求。

> 组合分散可以帮助投资者避免灾难性的投资结果。这个结论可以通过灾难发生时，如果没有进行分散化的后果而令人信服地展示出来。

one of the most admired corporations in the United States. A position in Enron shares returned over 27 percent per year from January 1990 to September 2000, Compared to 13 percent for the S&P 500 Index for the same time period. But between January 2001 and January 2002, Enron's share price fell from about US$90 per share to zero.

A typical investor, for instance, who had invested all or most of his savings in Enron shares, experienced financial ruin. The bankruptcy of Enron resulted in the closing of its operations, the dismissal of thousands of employees, and its shares becoming worthless. Hence, the failure of Enron was disastrous to the typical Enron employee. Apparently, the hard lesson from this experience was to "not put all your eggs in one basket."

Thus, by taking a diversified portfolio approach, investors can spread away some of the risk. All rational investors are concerned about the risk-return tradeoff of their investments. The portfolio approach provides investors with a way to reduce the risk associated with their wealth without necessarily decreasing their expected rate of return.

1.2 Portfolio: Reduce Risk

In addition to avoiding a potential disaster associated with overinvesting in a single security, portfolios also generally offer equivalent expected returns with lower overall volatility of returns—as represented by a measure such as standard deviation.

Consider this simple example: Suppose you wish to make an investment in companies listed on the Shanghai Stock Exchange and you start with a sample of five companies.

The individual quarterly returns for each of the five shares are shown in table 2.1. The annualized means and annualized standard deviations for each are also shown.

Table 2.1 Quarterly Returns (in percent) for Sample of Listed Shares

	A	B	C	D	E	Equally Weighted
Q3 2004	−11.1%	−2.3%	0.6%	−13.2%	−1.1%	−5.4%
Q4 2004	−0.5	−5.4	10.8	1.7	21.0	5.5
Q1 2005	5.7	6.8	19.1	13.8	15.5	12.2
Q2 2005	5.3	4.6	−2.1	16.9	12.4	7.4
Q3 2005	17.2	2.4	12.6	14.5	−7.9	7.8

continued

	A	B	C	D	E	Equally Weighted
Q4 2005	−17.6	−10.4	−0.9	4.4	−16.7	−8.2
Q1 2006	12.6	7.4	4.2	−10.9	15.4	5.7
Q2 2006	7.5	−0.4	−3.6	29.2	21.9	10.9
Q3 2006	−7.9	1.3	−5.1	−2.0	−1.6	−3.1
Q4 2006	8.2	27.5	0.1	26.0	−10.1	10.3
Q1 2007	18.3	24.5	16.5	22.8	25.7	21.5
Q2 2007	0.1	−2.6	−6.7	−0.4	0.3	−1.8
Q3 2007	−6.2	−4.2	16.7	11.9	11.1	5.8
Q4 2007	−8.0	17.9	−1.8	12.4	8.4	5.8
Q1 2008	3.5	−20.1	−8.5	−20.3	−31.5	−15.4
Q2 2008	2.1	−11.8	−2.6	24.2	−6.1	1.2
Mean annual return	7.3%	8.7%	12.3%	32.8%	14.2%	15.1%
Annual standard deviation	20.2%	25.4%	18.1%	29.5%	31.3%	17.9%
Diversification ratio						71.0%

Source: Datastream.

1.2.1 The selection of one security

Suppose you want to invest in one of these five securities next year. There is a wide variety of risk-return trade-off for the five shares selected. If you believe that the future will replicate the past, then choosing the D firm would be a good choice. For the prior four years, D firm provided the best trade-off between return and risk. In other words, it provided the most return per unit of risk. However, if there is no reason to believe that the future will replicate the past, it is more likely that the risk and return on the one security selected will be more like selecting one randomly. When we randomly selected one security each quarter, we found an average annualized return of 15.1 percent and an average annualized standard deviation of 24.9 percent, which would now become your expected return and standard deviation, respectively.

1.2.2 An equally weighted portfolio

Alternatively, you could invest in an equally weighted portfolio of the five shares, which means that you would invest the same money in

假设你明年想投资这五种证券中的一种。对于所选的五种股票，有各种各样的风险回报权衡。

each security for each quarter. The quarterly returns on the equally weighted portfolio are just the average of the returns of the individual shares.

As reported in table 2.1, the equally weighted portfolio has an average return of 15.1 percent and a standard deviation of 17.9 percent. As expected, the equally weighted portfolio's return is the same as the return on the randomly selected security. However, the same does not hold true for the portfolio standard deviation. That is, the standard deviation of an equally weighted portfolio is not simply the average of the standard deviations of the individual shares. In a later chapter we will demonstrate in greater mathematical detail how such a portfolio offers a lower standard deviation of return than the average of its individual components due to the correlations or interactions between the individual securities.

Because the mean return is the same, a simple measure of the value of diversification is calculated as the ratio of the standard deviation of the equally weighted portfolio to the standard deviation of the randomly selected security. This ratio may be referred to as the diversification ratio. In this case, the equally weighted portfolio's standard deviation is approximately 71 percent of that of a security selected at random. The diversification ratio of the portfolio's standard deviation to the individual asset's standard deviation measures the risk reduction benefits of a simple portfolio construction method, equal weighting. Even though the companies were chosen from a similar industry grouping, we see significant risk reduction. An even greater portfolio effect (i.e., Lower diversification ratio) could have been realized if we had chosen companies from completely different industries.

This example illustrates one of the critical ideas about portfolios: Portfolios affect risk more than returns. In the prior section portfolios helped avoid the effects of downside risk associated with investing in a single company's shares. In this section we extended the notion of risk reduction through portfolios to illustrate why individuals and institutions should hold portfolios.

1.2.3 Better portfolio than the equally weighted portfolio

In the previous section we compared an equally weighted portfolio to the selection of a single security. In this section we examine additional combinations of the same set of shares and observe the trade-offs between portfolio volatility of returns and expected

在前一节中,我们将同等权重的投资组合与单一证券的选择进行了比较。本节我们将考察同一组股票的额外组合,并观察投资组合回报率波动性和预期回报率之间的比率(简而言之,风险回报比)。

Chapter 2 Diversification and Portfolio Theory

return (for short, their risk return trade-offs). If we select the portfolios with the best combination of risk and return (taking historical statistics as our expectations for the future), we produce the set of portfolios shown in Figure 2.1.

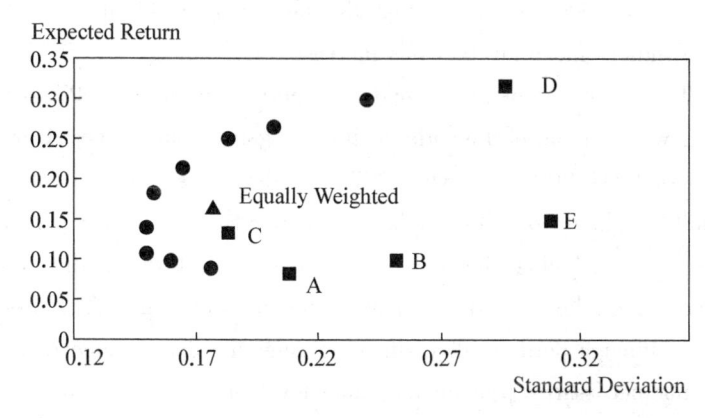

Figure 2.1 Optimal Portfolio for Sample of Listed Shares

In addition to illustrating that the diversified portfolio approach reduces risk, Figure 2.1 also shows that the composition of the portfolio matters. For example, an equally weighted portfolio (20 percent of the portfolio in each security) of the five shares has an expected return of 15.1 percent and a standard deviation of 17.9 percent. Alternatively, a portfolio with 25 percent in A, 3 percent in B, 52 percent in C, 20 percent in D, and 0 percent in E produces a portfolio with an expected return of 15.1 percent and a standard deviation of 15.6 percent. Compared to a simple equally weighted portfolio, this provides an improved tradeoff between risk and return because a lower level of risk was achieved for the same level of return.

A major reason that portfolios can effectively reduce risk is that combining securities whose returns do not move together provides diversification. Sometimes a subset of assets will go up in value at the same time that another will go down in value. The fact that these may offset each other creates the potential diversification benefit we attribute to portfolios. However, an important issue is that the co-movement or correlation pattern of the securities' returns in the portfolio can change in a manner unfavorable to the investor. We use historical return data from a set of global indices to show the impact of changing co-movement patterns.

投资组合能够有效降低风险的一个重要原因是,将回报率不一致的证券组合在一起可以提供多样化。

1.2.4 Ineffective Diversification

When we examine the return of a set of global equity indices from the Q4 of 1993 to Q1 of 2009, we observe a reduction in the diversification benefit due to a change in the pattern of global indices for two different time periods. Comparing the first time period, from Q4 1993 through Q3 2000, with the last time period, from Q1 2006 through Q1 2009, we show that the degree to which these global equity indices move together has increased over time.

The latter part of the second time period, from Q4 2007 to Q1 2009, was a period of dramatic declines in global share prices. During the period Q4 2007 through Q1 2009, the average return for the equally weighted portfolio, including dividends, was −48.5 percent. Other than reducing the risk of earning the return of the worst performing market, the diversification benefits were small. The lesson is that although portfolio diversification generally does reduce risk, it does not necessarily provide the same level of risk reduction during times of severe market turmoil as it does when the economy and markets are operating "normally". In fact, if the economy or markets fail totally (which has happened numerous times around the world), then diversification is a false promise. In the face of a worldwide contagion, diversification was ineffective, as illustrated at the end of 2008.

Table 2.2 Returns to Global Equity Indices

Global Index	Q4 1993 – Q3 2000 mean1	standard deviation	Q1 2006 – Q1 2009 mean2	standard deviation	Q4 2007 – Q1 2009 mean3	standard deviation
S&P 500	20.5	13.9	−6.3	21.1	−40.6	23.6
MSCI EAFE US$	10.9	14.2	−3.5	29.4	−48.0	35.9
Hang Seng	20.4	35.0	5.1	34.2	−53.8	34.0
Nikkei 500	3.3	18.0	−13.8	27.6	−48.0	30.0
MSCI AC EAFE + EM US$	7.6	13.2	−4.9	30.9	−52.0	37.5
Randomly selected index	12.6	18.9	−4.7	28.6	−48.5	32.2
Equally weighted portfolio	12.6	14.2	−4.7	27.4	−48.5	32.0
Diversification ratio			75.1		95.8		99.4

Source: Datastream.

1.2.5 Domestic Diversification and International Diversification

Figure 2.2 presents portfolio risk reduction for the U.S.

economy. It shows that a fully diversified U.S. portfolio is only about 27% as risky as a typical individual stock. This relationship implies that about 73% of the risk associated with investing in a single stock is diversifiable in a fully diversified U.S. portfolio. Although we can reduce risk substantially through portfolio diversification, it is not possible to eliminate it totally because security returns are affected by a common set of factors—a set we characterize as the market.

The total risk of any portfolio is therefore composed of systematic risk (the market) and unsystematic risk (the individual securities). Increasing the number of securities in the portfolio reduces the unsystematic risk component leaving the systematic risk component unchanged.

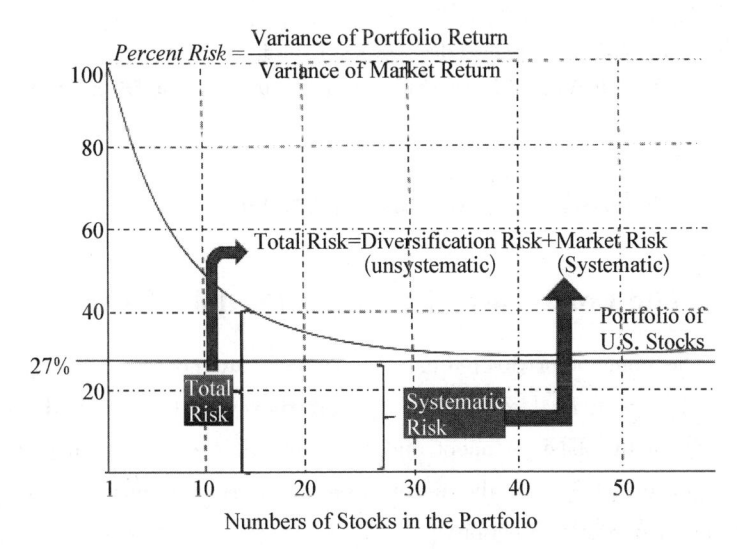

> 投资组合的总风险由系统风险(市场)和非系统风险(单个证券)组成。增加投资组合中的证券数量会减少非系统风险部分,而系统风险保持不变。

$$Percent\ Risk = \frac{Variance\ of\ Portfolio\ Return}{Variance\ of\ Market\ Return}$$

Note: When the portfolio is diversified, the variance of the portfolio's return relative to the variance of the market return (beta) is reduced to the level of systematic risk—the risk of the market itself.

Figure 2.2 Portfolio Risk Reduction through Diversification

Figure 2.3 illustrates the incremental gains of diversifying both domestically and internationally. The lowest line in Figure 2.3 (portfolio of international stocks) represents a portfolio in which foreign securities have been added. It has the same overall risk shape as the U.S. stock portfolio, but it has a lower portfolio beta. This means that the international portfolio's market risk is lower than that of a domestic portfolio. This situation arises because the returns on the foreign stocks are closely correlated not with returns on U.S. stocks, but rather with a global beta.

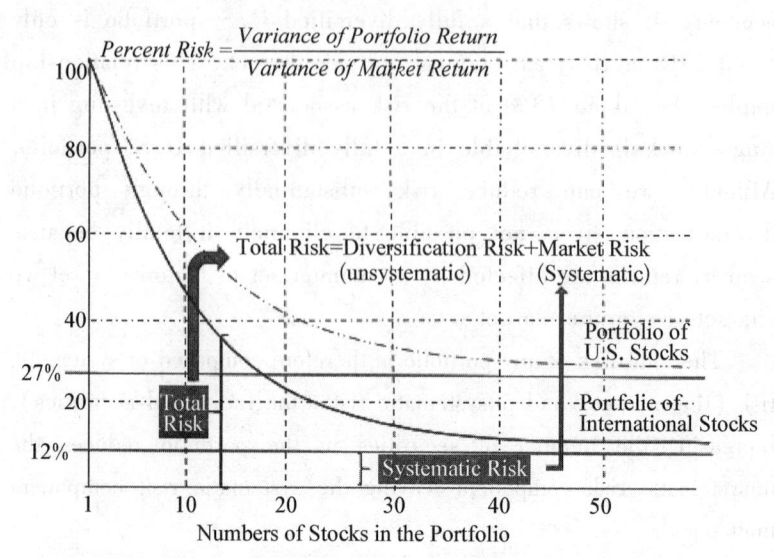

$$\text{Percent Risk} = \frac{\text{Variance of Portfolio Return}}{\text{Variance of Market Return}}$$

Note: When the portfolio is diversified internationally, the portfolio's beta—the level of systematic risk that can not be diversified away—is lowered.

Figure 2.3 Portfolio Risk Reduction through International Diversification

2 The Modern Portfolio Theory

2.1 The Emergence of Modern Portfolio Theory

> 分散化的概念古已有之,并且有很强的直觉吸引力。

The concept of diversification has been around for a long time and has a great deal of intuitive appeal. However, the actual theory underlying this basic concept and its application to investments only emerged in 1952 with the publication of Harry Markowitz's classic article on portfolio selection.

The article provided the foundation for what is now known as modern portfolio theory (MPT). The main conclusion of MPT is that investor should not only hold portfolios but should also focus on how individual securities in the portfolios are related to one another.

In addition to the diversification benefits of portfolios to investors, the work of William Sharpe (1964), John Lintner (1965), and Jack Treynor (1961) demonstrated the role that portfolios play in determining the appropriate individual asset risk premium (i.e., the return in excess of the risk-free return expected by investors as compensation for the asset's risk). According to capital market theory, the priced risk of an individual security is affected by holding it in a well-diversified portfolio.

The early research provided the insight that an asset's risk should be measured in relation to the remaining systematic or non-diversifiable risk, which should be the only risk that affects the asset's price. This view of risk is the basis of the capital asset pricing model, or CAPM. Although MPT has limitations, the concepts and intuitions illustrated in the theory continue to be the foundation of knowledge for portfolio managers.

2.2 The Theory of Security Portfolio

In 1952, Harry M. Markowitz published a landmark paper that is generally viewed as the origin of the modern portfolio theory approach to investing. His approach begins by assuming that an investor has a given sum of money to invest at the present time. This money will be invested for a particular length of time known as the investor's holding period. At the end of the holding period, the investor will sell the securities that were purchased at the beginning of the period and then either spend the proceeds on consumption or reinvest the proceeds in various securities (or do some of both). So his approach can be viewed as a single-period approach, where the beginning of the period is denoted $t=0$ and the end of the period is denoted $t=1$. At $t=0$ the investor must make a decision on what particular securities to purchase and hold until $t=1$. Because a portfolio is a collection of securities, this decision is equivalent to selecting an optimal portfolio from a set of possible portfolios. Hence it is often referred to as the portfolio selection problem.

In making this decision at $t=0$, the investor should recognize that security returns (and thus portfolio returns) over the forthcoming holding period are unknown. Nevertheless, the investor could estimate the expected (or mean) returns on the various securities under consideration, and then invest in the one with the highest expected return. Markowitz notes that this would generally be an unwise decision because the typical investor, although wanting "returns to be high," also wants returns to be as certain as possible." This means that the investor, in seeking to both maximize expected return and minimize uncertainty (that is risk), has two conflicting objectives that must be balanced against each other when making the purchase decision at $t=0$. One interesting consequence of having these two conflicting objectives is that the investor should diversify by purchasing not just one security but several.

1952年,哈里·马克维茨发表了一篇里程碑式的论文,该论文被普遍认为是现代投资组合理论方法的起源。

2.2.1 The single security: Expected return and risk

Expected value (or mean) can be viewed as a measure of the potential reward associated with any portfolio, and standard deviation can be viewed as a measure of the risk.

The expected return and risk of the single security can be calculated by the following equations:

$$\bar{r} = \sum_{i=1}^{n} r_i \times p_i$$

$$\sigma = \sqrt{\sum_{i=1}^{n} (r_i - \bar{r})^2 \times p_i}$$

Where p_i denotes the probability, r_i denotes the predicted return in the p_i, $\bar{r}$ denotes the expected return (or mean), σ denotes the standard deviation.

Example 2 - 1

A stock has the following probability distribution of returns:

Return	Probability
-10%	0.50
0	0.15
20%	0.35

Based on this estimate, calculate the expected return and standard deviation of A stock.

Solution:

$$\bar{r} = \sum_{i=1}^{n} r_i \times p_i$$
$$= -10\% \times 0.50 + 0 \times 0.15 + 20\% \times 0.35$$
$$= 2\%$$

$$\sigma = \sqrt{\sum_{i=1}^{n} (r_i - \bar{r})^2 \times p_i}$$
$$= \sqrt{(-10\% - 2\%)^2 \times 0.50 + (0 - 2\%)^2 \times 0.15 + (20\% - 2\%)^2 \times 0.35}$$
$$\approx 13.6\%$$

2.2.2 The Portfolio security: Expected return and risk

The expected return and risk of the portfolio security can be calculated by the following equations:

$$\bar{r}_P = \sum_{i=1}^{n} x_i \times \bar{r}_i$$

$$\sigma_P^2 = \sum_{i=1}^{n} \sigma_i^2 x_i^2 + \sum_{i=1}^{n} \sum_{\substack{j=1 \\ j \neq i}}^{n} x_i x_j \sigma_{ij} \text{ or } \sigma_P = \Big[\sum_{i=1}^{n} \sum_{j=1}^{n} x_i x_j \sigma_{ij} \Big]^{1/2}$$

Where $\overline{r_P}$ denotes the expected return of portfolio, x_i denotes the ratio of security i in the portfolio, $\overline{r_i}$ denotes the expected return of security i. σ_p denotes the standard deviation of portfolio, σ_{ij} denotes the covariance of the returns between security i and security j. Closely related to covariance is the statistical measure known as correlation.

Example 2-2

Assume there is a portfolio including A, B, and C stock which expected returns are 16.2%, 24.6%, and 22.8%, respectively. The number of A, B, and C Shares in Portfolio is 100, 200 and 100. Initial Market price per Share is: A for 40 $, B for 35 $ and C for 62 $. Suppose that the investor has a one-year holding period, calculate the expected return of this portfolio. If given the following variance-covariance matrix for the stocks of A, B, and C, Calculate the standard deviation of this portfolio.

$$\begin{pmatrix} 146 & 187 & 145 \\ 187 & 854 & 104 \\ 145 & 104 & 289 \end{pmatrix}$$

Solution:

$$x_A = \frac{100 * 40}{100 * 40 + 200 * 35 + 100 * 62} = 0.2325$$

$$x_B = \frac{200 * 35}{100 * 40 + 200 * 35 + 100 * 62} = 0.4070$$

$$x_C = \frac{100 * 62}{100 * 40 + 200 * 35 + 100 * 62} = 0.3605$$

$$\overline{r_P} = \sum_{i=1}^{n} x_i \times \overline{r_i}$$

$$= 0.2325 \times 16.2\% + 0.4070 \times 24.6\% + 0.3605 \times 22.8\% = 22\%$$

$$\sigma_P^2 = \sum_{i=1}^{n} \sigma_i^2 x_i^2 + \sum_{i=1}^{n} \sum_{\substack{j=1 \\ j \neq i}}^{n} x_i x_j \sigma_{ij} \text{ or } \sigma_P = \Big[\sum_{i=1}^{n} \sum_{j=1}^{n} x_i x_j \sigma_{ij} \Big]^{1/2}$$

$$\begin{aligned}\sigma_P &= [X_1X_1\sigma_{11} + X_1X_2\sigma_{12} + X_1X_3\sigma_{13} + X_2X_1\sigma_{21} + X_2X_2\sigma_{22} + \\ &\quad X_2X_3\sigma_{23} + X_3X_1\sigma_{31} + X_3X_2\sigma_{32} + X_3X_3\sigma_{33}]^{1/2} \\ &= [0.2325^2 \times 146 + 0.4070^2 \times 854 + 0.3605^2 \times 289 + 2 \times \\ &\quad 0.2325 \times 0.4070 \times 187 + 2 \times 0.2325 \times 0.3605 \times 145 + 2 \times \\ &\quad 0.3605 \times 0.4070 \times 104]^{1/2} \\ &= [277.13]^{1/2} = 16.65\%\end{aligned}$$

In fact, the covariance between two random variables is equal to the correlation between the two random variables times the product of their standard deviations:

$$\sigma_{ij} = \rho_{ij}\sigma_i\sigma_j$$

Where ρ_{ij} denotes the correlation coefficient between the return on security i and security j. Correlation coefficients always lie between -1 and $+1$. A value of -1 represents perfect negative correlation, and a value of $+1$ represents perfect positive correlation. Most cases lie between these two extreme values.

2.2.3 The Selection of Portfolio

In a set of N securities, there are many possible portfolios. How does the investor evaluate all these portfolios?

Consider the following two securities. Security 1, the Shipping Company, has an expected return of 5% and standard deviation of 20%. Security 2, the Gold company, has an expected return of 15% and standard deviation of 40%. Now consider some possible portfolios that an investor could purchase by combining these two securities such as the following Table 2.3.

Table 2.3 The expected return and standard deviation

X_1	X_2	$\bar{r}_p$	$\sigma_P(\rho=-1)$	$\sigma_P(\rho=1)$	$\sigma_P(\rho=0)$
1.00	0.00	5.0%	20%	20.0%	20%
0.83	0.17	6.70	10.0	23.33	17.94
0.67	0.33	8.30	0.00	26.67	18.81
0.50	0.50	10.0	10.00	30.00	22.36
0.33	0.67	11.70	20.00	33.33	27.60
0.17	0.83	13.30	30.00	36.67	33.37
0.00	1.00	15.0	40.00	40.00	40.00

$\bar{r}_p = (X_1 \times 5\%) + (X_2 \times 15\%)$
$\sigma_P = [(X_1^2 \times 20^2) + (X_2^2 \times 40^2) + 2X_1X_2\sigma_{12}]^{1/2}$, $\sigma_{12} = \rho_{12} \times \sigma_1 \times \sigma_2 = 800\rho_{12}$

In order to consider these seven portfolios for possible investment, their expected returns and standard deviations must be calculated. And the standard deviation depends upon the size of the correlation coefficient. Note that the value of σ_p will be at a minimum when the correlation coefficient is at a minimum (that is $\rho = -1$), and the value of σ_p will be at a maximum when the correlation coefficient is at a maximum (that is $\rho = +1$). These values are shown in Figure 2.4.

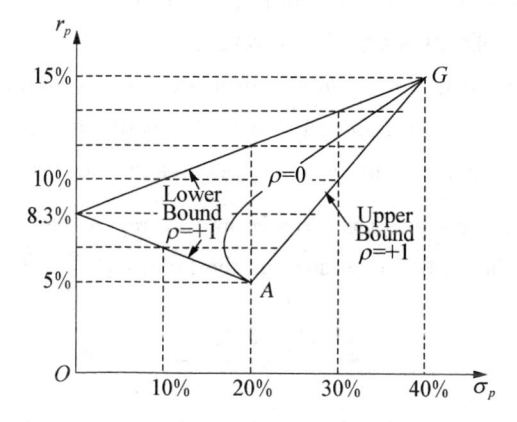

Figure 2.4 Upper and Lower Bounds of Combinations of Securities

Interestingly, the upper bounds all lie on a straight line connecting points A and G. This means that any portfolio consisting of these two securities cannot have a standard deviation that plots to the right of a straight line connecting the two securities. This observation suggests a motivation for diversifying a portfolio. Namely, *diversification generally leads to risk reduction.*

Another observation is that the lower bounds all lie on one of two line segments that go from point A to a point on the vertical axis corresponding to 8.30% and then to point G. This means that any portfolio consisting of these two securities cannot have a standard deviation that plots to the left of either of these two line segment.

In sum, any portfolio consisting of these two securities will lie within or on the boundary of the triangle shown in Figure 2.4, with its actual location depending on the magnitude of the correlation coefficient between the two securities.

When the correlation coefficient is zero, as it can be seen, these portfolios lie on a line that is curved or bowed to the left. While not shown here, if the correlation were less than zero, the line would curve more to the left. If the correlation were greater than zero, it would not curve quite as much to the left. The important point about this figure is that as long as the correlation is less than +1 and greater than −1, the line representing the set of portfolios consisting of various combinations of the two securities will have some degree of curvature to the left. Furthermore, the "northwest" portion will be concave.

Similar analysis can be applied to a situation where there are more than two securities under consideration. According to this analysis, we can get the location of the feasible set.

2.2.4 Portfolio of Many Risky Assets

To examine how a portfolio with many risky assets works and the ways in which we can reduce the risk of a portfolio, assume that the portfolio has equal weights for all N assets. In addition, assume that $\overline{\sigma^2}$ and $\overline{Cov}$ are the average variance and average covariance. Now we can rewrite the portfolio variance as the following.

$$\sigma_P^2 = \sum_{i=1}^{n} \sigma_i^2 x_i^2 + \sum_{i=1}^{n} \sum_{\substack{j=1 \\ j \neq i}}^{n} x_i x_j \sigma_{ij}$$

$$= \frac{\overline{\sigma^2}}{N} + \frac{(N-1)}{N} \overline{Cov}$$

The equation shows that as N becomes large, the first term with the denominator of N becomes smaller and smaller, implying that the contribution of one asset's variance to portfolio variance gradually becomes negligible. The second term, however, approaches the average covariance as N increase. It is reasonable to say that for portfolios with a large number of assets, covariance among the assets accounts for almost all of the portfolio's risk.

Now we assume that all assets in the portfolio have the same variance and the same correlation among assets. In that case, the portfolio risk can then be rewritten as:

$$\sigma_P^2 = \frac{\sigma^2}{N} + \frac{(N-1)}{N} \rho \sigma^2$$

The first term becomes negligible as the number of assets in the portfolio increases leaving the second term (correlation) as the main determining factor for portfolio risk. If the assets are unrelated to one another, the portfolio can have close to zero risk.

2.2.5 Minimum-Variance Portfolios
2.2.5.1 The feasible set: Investment Opportunity Set

If two assets are perfectly correlated, the risk-return opportunity set is represented by a straight line connecting those two assets. The line contains portfolios formed by changing the weight of each asset invested in the portfolio. If the two assets are not perfectly correlated, the portfolio's risk is less than the weighted average risk of the components and the portfolio formed from the two assets bulges on the left as shown by curves with the correlation coefficient less than 1.0 in Figure 2.4. All of the points connecting the two assets are achievable (or feasible). The addition of new assets to this portfolio creates more and more portfolios that are either a liner combination of the existing portfolio and the new asset or a curvilinear combination depending on the correlation between the existing portfolio and the new asset.

> 如果两种资产完全相关,风险收益的机会集由连接这两种资产的直线表示。

As the number of available assets increases, the number of possible combinations increases rapidly. When all investment assets are considered, and there are hundreds and thousands of them, we can construct an opportunity set of investments. The opportunity set will ordinarily span all points within a frontier because it is also possible to reach every possible point within that curve by judiciously creating a portfolio from the investment assets.

Figure 2.5 provides an illustration of the location of the feasible set, from which the efficient set can be identified. It simply represents all portfolios that could be formed from a group of N securities. That is, all possible portfolios that could be formed from the N securities lie either on or within the boundary of the feasible set. In general, this

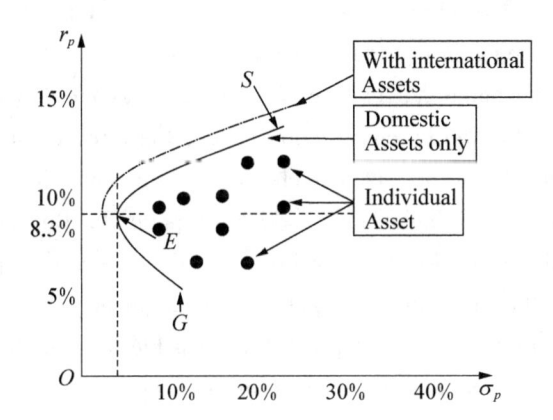

Figure 2.5 Investment Opportunity Set

set will have an umbrella-type shape similar to the one shown in the figure. Depending on the particular securities involved, it may be more to the right or left, or higher or lower, or fatter or skinnier than indicated here.

Figure 2.5 also shows the effect of adding a new asset class, such as international assets. As long as the new asset class is not perfectly correlated with the existing asset class, the investment opportunity set will expand out further to the northwest providing a superior risk-return trade-off.

The investment opportunity set with international assets dominates the opportunity set that includes only domestic assets. Adding other asset classes will have the same impact on the opportunity set. Thus, we should continue to add asset classes until they do not further improve the risk-return trade-off. The benefits of diversification can be fully captured in this way in the construction of the investment opportunity set, and eventually in the selection of the optimal portfolio.

2.2.5.2 The Efficient Set: Minimum-Variance Frontier

The investment opportunity set consisting of all available investable sets is shown in Figure 3.2. There are a number of portfolios available for investment, but we must choose a single optimal portfolio.

Firstly, let's look at the efficient set theorem: An investor will choose his or her optimal portfolio from the set of portfolios that

Offer maximum expected return for equaling levels of risk.

Offer minimum risk for equaling levels of expected return.

> 等风险水平下提供最大的预期收益。
> 等预期收益水平下提供最小的风险。

The set of portfolios meeting these two conditions is known as the efficient set. The efficient set can now be located by applying the efficient set theorem to the feasible set.

Consider points X, A, B in Fig. 2.6, and assume they are on the same horizontal line by construction. Thus, the three points have the same expected return. Given a choice, an investor will choose the point with the minimum risk, which is point X. But point X is unattainable because it does not lie within the investment opportunity set. Thus, the minimum risk that we can attain is point A. Point B and all points to the right of point A are feasible but they have higher risk. Therefore, a risk-averse investor will choose only point A in preference to any other portfolio with the same return.

Similarly, point C is the minimum variance point for the return earned at *C*. Points to the right of *C* have higher risk. We can extend the proceeding analysis to all possible returns. In all cases, we find that the minimum variance portfolio is the one that lies on the solid curve drawn in Figure 2.6. The entire collection of these minimum-variance portfolios is referred to as the minimum-variance frontier. The minimum-variance frontier defines the smaller set of portfolios in which investors would want to invest. Note that no risk-averse investor will choose to invest in a portfolio to the right of the minimum-variance frontier because a portfolio on the minimum-variance frontier can give the same return but at a lower risk.

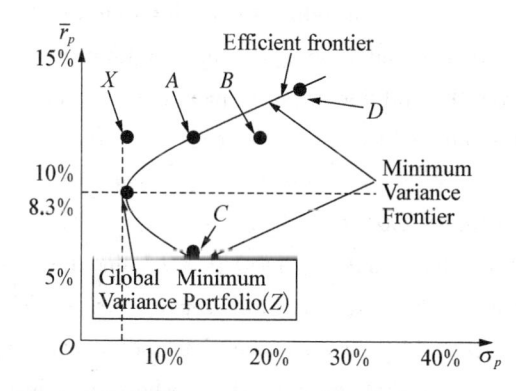

Figure 2.6 Minimum-Variance Frontier or the efficient set

2.2.5.3 Global Minimum-Variance Portfolio

The left-most point on the minimum-variance frontier is the portfolio with the minimum variance among all portfolios of risky assets, and is referred to as the global minimum variance portfolio. An investor cannot hold a portfolio consisting of risky assets that has less risk than that of the global minimum-variance portfolio. Note the emphasis on "risky" assets. Later, the introduction of a risk-free asset will allow us to relax this constraint.

最小方差边界上最左边的点是所有风险资产组合中方差最小的组合,称为全局最小方差组合。

2.2.5.4 Efficient Frontier of Risky Assets

Now let's consider points *A* and *C* in Fig. 2.6. Both of them have the same risk. Obviously, an investor will choose portfolio *A* because it has a higher return. The same analysis applies to all points on the minimum-variance frontier that lie below the global minimum variance portfolio. Thus, portfolios on the curve below the global minimum variance portfolio and to the right of the global minimum variance portfolio are not beneficial and are inefficient portfolios for an investor.

The curve that lies above and to the right of the global minimum variance portfolio is referred to as the Markowitz efficient frontier because it contains all portfolios of risky assets that rational, risk-averse investors will choose.

An important observation that is often ignored is the slope at various points on the efficient frontier. As we move right from the global minimum variance portfolio in Fig. 2.6, there is an increase in risk with a concurrent increase in return. The increase in return with every unit increase in risk, however, keeps decreasing as we move from left to the right because the slope continues to decrease. The slope at point D is less than the slope at point A, which is less than the slope at point Z. The increase in return by moving from point Z to point A is the same as the in return by moving from point A to point D. It can be seen that the addition risk in moving from point A to point D is different from the additional risk in moving from point Z to point A. Thus, investors obtain decreasing increases in return as they assume more risk.

2.2.6 Indifference Curves

The method that should be used in selecting the most desirable portfolio involves the use of indifference curves. These curves represent an investor's preferences for risk and return, and thus can be drawn on a two-dimensional figure where the horizontal axis indicates risk as measured by standard deviation (denoted σ_p) and the vertical axis indicates reward as measured by expected return (denoted r_p).

The following figure illustrates a "map" of indifference curves. Each curved line indicates one indifference curve for the investor and represents all combinations of portfolios that provide the investor with a given level of desirability. For example, the investor with the indifference curves would find portfolios A and B (the same two portfolios) equally desirable, even though they have different expected returns and standard deviations, because they both lie on the same indifference curve, I_2. Portfolio B has a higher standard deviation (20%) than portfolio A (10%) and is therefore less desirable on that dimension.

However, exactly offsetting this loss in desirability is the gain in desirability provided by the higher expected return of B (12%) relative to A (8%). This example leads to the first important feature of indifference curves: all portfolio that lie on a given indifference curve are equally desirable to the investor. An implication of this feature is that indifference curves cannot intersect. Although the investor represented in figure 2.7 would find portfolios A and B equally desirable, he or she would find portfolio C, with an expected return of 11% and a standard deviation of 14%, preferable to both of them. This is because portfolio C happens to be on an indifference curve, I_3, that is located to the "northwest" of I_2. Now C has a sufficiently larger expected return relative to A to more than offset its higher standard deviation and, on balance, make it more desirable than A. Equivalently, C has a sufficiently smaller standard deviation than B to more than offset its smaller expected return and, on balance, make it more desirable than B. This leads to the second important feature of indifference curves: An investor will find any portfolio that is lying on an indifference curve that is "further northwest" to be more desirable than any portfolio lying on an indifference curve that is "not as far northwest".

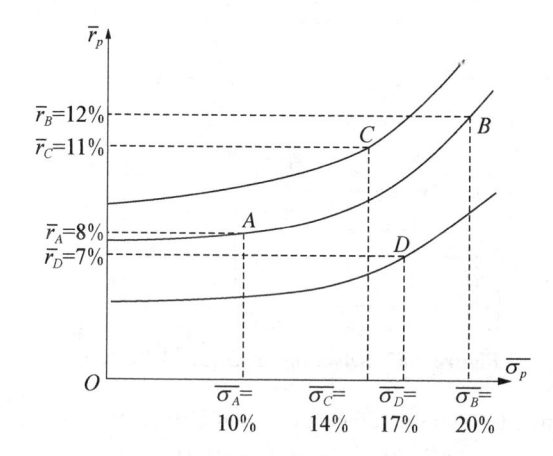

Figure 2.7　Indifference Curves

Lastly, it should be noted that an investor has an infinite number of indifference curves. This simply means that whenever there are two indifference curves that have been plotted on a graph, it is possible to plot a third indifference curve that lies between them.

Plot the indifference curves on the same figure as the efficient set and then proceed to choose the portfolio that is on the indifference curve that is "further northwest".

This portfolio will correspond to the point where an indifference curve is just tangent to the efficient set.

2.2.7 Selection of the optimal portfolio

How will the investor select an optimal portfolio? First, we give the following two Assumptions:

> 不满足:投资者被认为更喜欢较高水平的最终财富,而不是较低水平的最终财富。
>
> 风险厌恶:投资者会选择标准差较小的投资组合。

Non-satiation: Investors are assumed to prefer higher levels of terminal wealth to lower levels of terminal wealth.

Risk Aversion: The investor will choose the portfolio with the smaller standard deviation.

As shown in Figure 2.8, the investor should plot his or her indifference curves on the same figure as the efficient set and then proceed to choose the portfolio that is on the indifference curve that is "furthest northwest." This portfolio will correspond to the point where an indifference curve is just tangent to the efficient set. As can be seen in the figure, this is portfolio O^* on indifference curve I_2. Although the investor would prefer a portfolio on I_3, no such feasible portfolio exists.

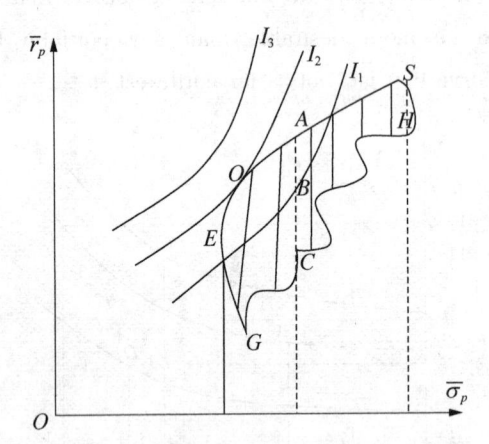

Figure 2.8 Selecting an Optimal Portfolio

The investor should select the portfolio that put him or her on the indifference curve "furthest northwest." The efficient set theorem, stating that the investor need not be concerned with portfolios that do not lie on the "northwest" boundary of the feasible set, is a logical.

Now it will be shown that the efficient set is generally positively sloped and concave, meaning that if a straight line is drawn between any two points on the efficient set, the straight line will lie below the efficient set. This feature of the efficient set is important because it means that there will be only one tangent point between the investor's indifference curves and the efficient set.

2.2.8 Markowitz approach's expended

The Markowitz approach assumes that the assets considered for investment are risky and all the portfolios also have uncertain returns over the investor's holding period and thus are risky. Furthermore, the investor is not allowed to use borrowed money to purchase a portfolio of assets. This means that the investor is not allowed to use financial leverage, or margin.

The following is the Markowitz approach's expansion by first allowing the investor to consider investing in not only risky assets but also in a risk-free asset. Second, the investor is allowed to borrow money but has to pay a given rate of interest on the loan. Now we consider the effect of adding a risk-free asset to the set of risky assets.

2.2.8.1 Defining the risk-free asset

What exactly is a risk-free asset? It means that the return is certain. If the investor purchases a risk-free asset at the beginning of a holding period, then he or she knows exactly what the value of the asset will be at the end of the holding period. As there is no uncertainty about the terminal value of the risk-free asset, the standard deviation is zero.

In turn, this means that the covariance between the rate of return on the risk-free asset and the rate of return on any risky asset is zero. This can be seen by remembering that the covariance between the returns on any two assets I and J is equal to the product of the correlation coefficient between the assets and the standard deviations of the two asses: $\sigma_{ij} = \rho_{ij}\sigma_i\sigma_j$. Given that $\sigma_i = 0$ if i is the risk-free asset, it follows that $\sigma_{ij} = 0$.

Because a risk-free asset has by definition a certain return, this type of asset must be some kind of fix-income security with no possibility of default. As all corporate securities in principle have some chance of default, the risk-free asset cannot be issued by a corporation. Instead it must be a security issued by the government. However, not just any security issued by the government qualifies as a risk-free security.

Consider an investor with a three-month holding period who purchases a Treasury security maturing in 20 years. Such a security is risky because the investor does not know what this security will be worth at the end of his or her holding period. As interest rates will very likely change in an unpredictable manner during the investor's holding period, the market price of the security will likewise change in an unpredictable manner. Because the presence of such interest-rate risk makes the value of the Treasury security uncertain, it cannot qualify as a risk-free asset. Indeed, any Treasury security with a maturity date greater than the investor's holding period cannot qualify as a risk-free asset.

Next consider a Treasury security that matures before the end of the investor's holding period, such as a 30-day Treasury bill in the case of the investor with the three-month holding period. In this situation, the investor does not know at the beginning of the holding period what interest rates will be in 30 days, this means that the investor does not know the interest rate at which the proceeds from the maturing Treasury bill can be reinvested for the remainder of the holding period. The presence of such reinvestment-rate risk in all Treasury securities of shorter maturity than the investor's holding period means that these securities do not qualify as risk free assets.

This leaves only one type of Treasury security to qualify as a risk-free asset: a Treasury security with a maturity that matches the length of the investor's holding period would find that a Treasury bill with a three-month maturity date had a certain return. Because this security matures at the end of the investor's holding period, it provides the investor with an amount of money at the end of the holding period that is known for certain at the beginning of the holding period when an investment decision has to be made.

Investing in the risk-free asset is often referred to a risk-free lending, because such an investment involves the purchase of Treasury bills and thus involves a loan by the investor to the government.

2.2.8.2 Allowing for risk-free lending

With the introduction of a risk-free asset, the investor is now able to put part of his or her money in this asset. Adding these new opportunities expands the feasible set significantly and, more importantly, changes the location of a substantial part of Markowitz's efficient set. The nature of these changes needs to be analyzed, since investors are concerned with selecting a portfolio from the efficient set. In so doing, consideration is given initially to determining the expected return and standard deviation for a portfolio that consists of combining an investment in the risk-free asset with an investment in a single risky security.

(1) Investing in Both a Risk-Free Asset and a Risky Asset

Assuming the companies of L, M and K have expected returns, variances, and co-variances as indicated in the following expected return vector and variance-covariance matrix:

$$E(r) = \begin{pmatrix} 16.2 \\ 24.62 \\ 22.8 \end{pmatrix} \quad VC = \begin{pmatrix} 146 & 187 & 145 \\ 187 & 854 & 104 \\ 145 & 104 & 289 \end{pmatrix}$$

Chapter 2 Diversification and Portfolio Theory

Defining the risk-free asset as security number 4, consider all portfolios that involve investing in just the common stock of company L and the risk-free asset. Let X_1 denote the proportion of the investor's funds invested in company L and $X_4 = 1 - X_1$ denote the proportion invested in the risk-free asset. If the investor put all his or her money in the risk-free asset, then $X_1 = 0$ and $X_4 = 1$. Alternatively, the investor could put all his or her money in just L, in which case $X_1 = 1$ and $X_4 = 0$. A combination of 0.25 in A and 0.75 in the risk-free asset is also possible, as are respective combinations of 0.50 and 0.50 or 0.75 and 0.25. While there are other possibilities, the focus here will be on these five portfolios:

	Portfolio A	Portfolio B	Portfolio C	Portfolio D	Portfolio E
X_1	0.00	0.25	0.50	0.75	1.00
X_4	1.00	0.75	0.50	0.25	0.00

Assuming that the risk-free asset has a rate of return (often denoted r_f) of 4%, all the necessary information for calculating the expected returns and standard deviations for these five portfolios is at hand. It can be calculated for the following equation.

$$\overline{r}_p = \sum_{i=1}^{N} X_i \overline{r}_i = \sum_{i=1}^{4} X_i \overline{r}_i$$

Portfolios A, B, C, D, and E do not involve investing in the second and third securities (that is, M and K companies), meaning that $X_2 = 0$ and $X_3 = 0$ in these portfolios. Thus, the previous equation reduces to:

$$\overline{r}_p = \sum_{i=1}^{N} X_i \overline{r}_i = X_1 \overline{r}_1 + X_4 \overline{r}_4 = (X_1 \times 16.2\%) + (X_4 \times 4\%)$$

Where the risk-free rate is now denoted r_4.

For portfolios A and E this calculation is trivial because all the investor's funds are being placed in just one security. Thus, their expected returns are just 4% and 16.2%, respectively. For portfolios B, C, and D, the expected returns are respectively:

$$\overline{r}_B = \sum_{i=1}^{N} X_i \overline{r}_i = X_1 \overline{r}_1 + X_4 \overline{r}_4 = (0.25 \times 16.2\%) + (0.75 \times 4\%)$$
$$= 7.05\%$$

$$\overline{r}_C = \sum_{i=1}^{N} X_i \overline{r}_i = X_1 \overline{r}_1 + X_4 \overline{r}_4 = (0.50 \times 16.2\%) + (0.50 \times 4\%)$$

$$= 10.10\%$$

$$\overline{r_D} = \sum_{i=1}^{N} X_i \overline{r_i} = X_1 \overline{r_1} + X_4 \overline{r_4} = (0.75 \times 16.2\%) + (0.25 \times 4\%)$$
$$= 13.15\%$$

The standard deviations of portfolios A and E are simply the standard deviations of the risk-free asset and able, respectively. Thus $\sigma_A = 0$ and $\sigma_E = 12.08\%$. In calculating the standard deviations of portfolios B, C, and D, The following equation must be utilized:

$$\sigma_p = \left[\sum_{i=1}^{N} \sum_{j=1}^{N} X_i X_j \sigma_{ij} \right]^{1/2} = \left[\sum_{i=1}^{4} \sum_{j=1}^{4} X_i X_j \sigma_{ij} \right]^{1/2}$$

As $X_2 = 0$ and $X_3 = 0$ in these portfolios, this equation reduces to:

$$\sigma_p = [X_1 X_1 \sigma_{11} + X_1 X_4 \sigma_{14} + X_4 X_1 \sigma_{41} + X_4 X_4 \sigma_{44}]^{1/2}$$
$$= [X_1^2 \sigma_1^2 + X_4^2 \sigma_4^2 + 2 X_1 X_4 \sigma_{14}]^{1/2}$$

This equation can be reduced even further, because security number 4 is the risk-free security that, by definition, has $\sigma_4 = 0$ and $\sigma_{14} = 0$. Accordingly, it reduces to:

$$\sigma_p = [X_1^2 \sigma_1^2]^{1/2} = [X_1^2 \times 146]^{1/2} = X_1 \times 12.08\%$$

Thus, the standard deviations of portfolios B, C, and D are:

$$\sigma_B = 0.25 \times 12.08\% = 3.02\%$$
$$\sigma_C = 0.50 \times 12.08\% = 6.04\%$$
$$\sigma_D = 0.75 \times 12.08\% = 9.06\%$$

In summary, the five portfolios have the following expected returns and standard deviations:

Portfolio	X_1	X_4	Expected Return	Standard Deviation
A	0.00	1.00	4.00%	0.00%
B	0..25	0.75	7.05%	3.02%
C	0.50	0.50	10.10%	6.04%
D	0.75	0.25	13.15%	9.06%
E	1.00	0.00	16.20%	12.08%

These portfolios are plotted in Figure 2.9. It can be seen that they all lie on a straight line connecting the points representing the location of the risk-free asset and A.

Although only five particular combinations of the risk-free asset and L company have been examined here, it can be shown that any combination of the risk-free asset and L will lie somewhere on the straight line connecting them; the exact location will depend on the relative proportions invested in these two assets. Furthermore, this observation can be generalized to combinations of the risk-free asset and any risky asset. This means that any portfolio consisting of a combination of the risk-free asset and a risky asset will have an expected return and standard deviation such that it plots somewhere on a straight line connecting them.

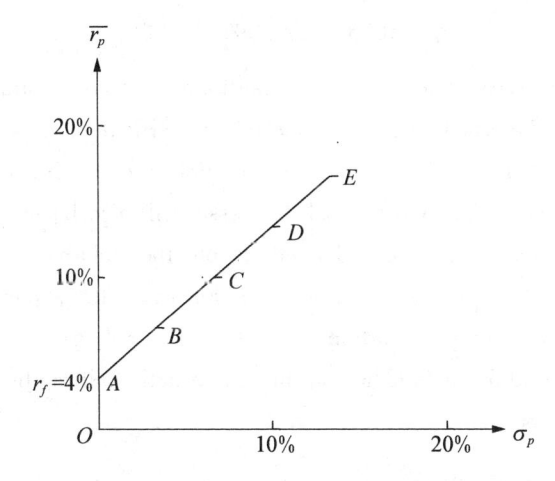

Figure 2.9 Combining Risk-free lending with a risky asset

(2) Investing in Both the Risk-Free Asset and a Risky Portfolio

Next consider what happens when a portfolio consisting of more than just one risky security is combined with the risk-free asset. For example, consider the risky portfolio PLK that consists of L and K in proportions of 0.80 and 0.20, respectively. Its expected return $\overline{r_{PLK}}$ and standard deviation (denoted σ_{PLK}) are equal to:

$$\overline{r_{PLK}} = (0.80 \times 16.2\%) + (0.20 \times 22.8\%) = 17.52\%$$

$$\sigma_{PLK} = [(0.80 \times 0.80 \times 146) + (0.20 \times 0.20 \times 289) + (2 \times 0.80 \times 0.20 \times 145)]^{1/2} = 12.30\%$$

Any portfolio that consists of an investment in both PLK and the risk-free asset will have an expected return and standard deviation that can be calculated in a manner identical to that previously shown for combinations of an individual asset and the risk-free asset. A portfolio that has the proportion X_{PLK} invested in the portfolio PLK and the proportion $X_4 = 1 - X_{PLK}$ in the risk-free asset will have an expected return and standard deviation that are equal to. Respectively:

$$\overline{r_P} = (X_{PLK} \times 17.52\%) + (X_4 \times 4\%)$$

$$\sigma_P = X_{PLk} \times 12.30\%$$

For example, consider investing in a portfolio consists of *PLK* and the risk-free asset in proportions of 0.25 and 0.75, respectively. This portfolio will have an expected return of:

$$\overline{r_P} = (0.25 \times 17.52\%) + (0.75 \times 4\%) = 7.38\%$$

$$\sigma_P = 0.25 \times 12.30\% = 3.08\%$$

Figure 2.10 shows that this portfolio lies on a straight line connecting the risk-free asset and *PAC*. In particular, it is indicated by the point P on this line, other portfolios consisting of various combinations of *PLK* and the risk-free asset will also lie on this line, with their exact locations depending on the relative proportions invested in *PLK* and the risk-free asset. For example, a portfolio that involves investing a proportion of 0.50 in the risk free asset and a proportion of 0.50 in *PLK* lies on this line exactly halfway between the two endpoints.

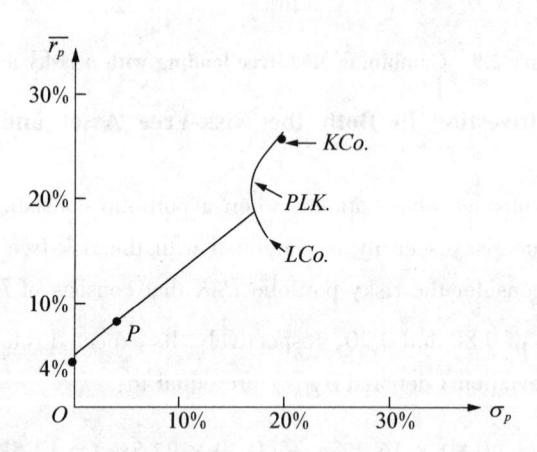

Figure 2.10 Combining Risk-free lending with a risky portfolio

In summary, combining the risk-free asset with any risky portfolio can be viewed as being no different from combining the risk-free asset with an individual risky security, in both cases, the resulting portfolio has an expected return and standard deviation such that it lies somewhere on a straight line connecting the two endpoints.

(3) The Effect of Risk-Free Lending on the Efficient Set

The feasible set is changed significantly as a result of the introduction of risk-free lending.

Figure 2.11 shows how it changes the feasible set for the example at hand. Here all risky assets and portfolios, not just L company and PLK, are considered in all possible combinations with the risk-free asset. In particular, note that there are two boundaries that are straight lines emanating from the risk-free asset. The bottom line connects the risk-free asset with M company. Thus, it represents portfolios formed by combining M and the risk-free asset.

The other straight line emanating from the risk-free asset represents combinations of the risk-free asset and a particular risky portfolio on the efficient set of the Markowitz model. It is a line that is just tangent to this efficient set, with the tangent point being denoted T. This tangent point represents a risky portfolio consisting of L, K, and M companies in proportions equal to, respectively, 0.12, 0.19, and 0.69. And the expected return and standard deviation of T are 22.4% and 15.2%, respectively.

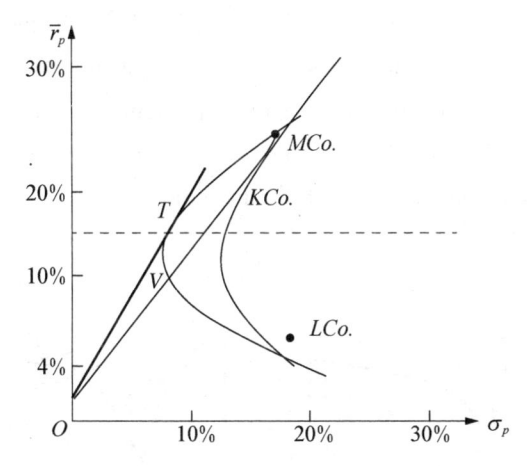

Figure 2.11 Feasible and Efficient Sets with the Risk-free lending

Although other risky efficient portfolios from the Markowitz model can also be combined with the risk-free asset, portfolio T deserves special attention. Why? Because there is no other portfolio consisting purely of risky assets that, when connected by a straight line to the risk-free asset, lies northwest of it. In other words, of all the lines that can be drawn emanating from the risk-free asset and connecting with either a risky asset or risky portfolio, none has a greater slope than the line that goes to T.

This is important because part of the efficient set of the Markowitz model is dominated by this line. In particular, the portfolios on the Markowitz model efficient set going from the minimum risk portfolio, denoted V, to T are no longer efficient when a risk-free asset is made available for investment. Instead the efficient set now consists of a straight-line segment and a curved segment. The straight-line segment is the straight line going from the risk-free asset to T and thus consists of portfolios made up of various combinations of the risk-free asset and the curved segment consists of those portfolios to the northeast of T on the Markowitz model efficient set.

(4) The Effect of Risk-Free Lending on Portfolio Selection

Figure 2.12 shows how an investor would go about selecting an optimal efficient portfolio when there is a risk-free asset available for investment in addition to a number of risky assets.

If the investor's indifference curves look like those shown in panel (a), the investor's optimal portfolio O^* will involve investing part of his or her initial wealth in the risk-free asset and the rest in T because his or her indifference curves are tangent to the efficient set between the risk-free asset and T. Alternatively, if the investor is less risk averse and has indifference curves that look like those shown in panel (b), then the investor's optimal portfolio O^* will not involve any risk-free lending because his or her indifference curves are tangent to the curved segment of the efficient set that lies to the northeast of T.

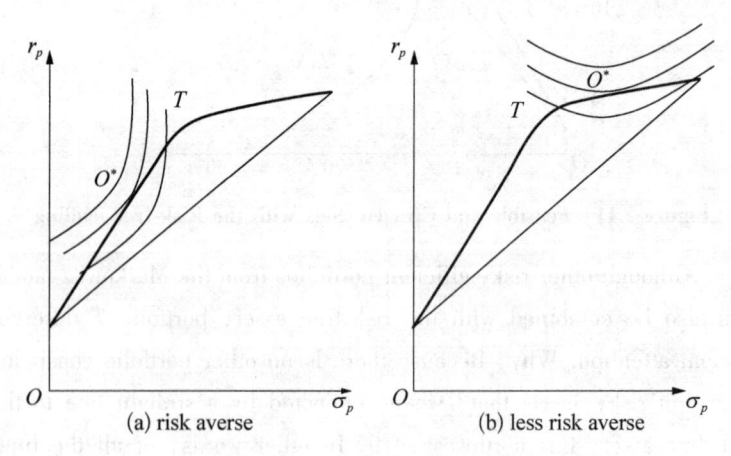

Figure 2.12 Portfolio Selections with Risk-Free Lending

2.2.8.3 Allowing for Risk-Free Borrowing

The analysis that was presented in the previous section can be expanded by allowing the investor to borrow money. This means that the investor is no longer restricted to his or her initial wealth when it comes time to decide how much money to invest in risky assets. However, if the investor borrows money, then interest must be paid on the loan, Since the interest rate is known and there is no uncertainty about repaying the loan, it is often referred to as risk-free borrowing.

It will be assumed that the rate of interest charged on the loan is equal to the rate of interest that could be earned from investing in the risk-free asset. In the earlier example, this means that the investor now has not only the opportunity to invest in a risk-free asset that earns a rate of return of 4% but alternatively may borrow money, for which the investor must pay a rate of interest equal to 4%. Earlier the proportion invested in the risk-free asset was denoted X_4, and this proportion was constrained to be a non-negative number between zero and one. Now with the opportunity to borrow at the same rate, X_4 will no longer be so constrained. In the earlier example, the investor had initial wealth of \$17,200. If the investor borrows money, then he or she will have in excess of \$17,200 to invest in the risky securities of A, B and C.

For example, if the investor borrows \$4,300, then he or she will have a total of \$21,500 (= \$17,200 + \$4,300) to invest in these securities. In this situation, X_4 can be viewed as being equal to -0.25 (= $-$ \$4,300/ \$17,200). However, the sum of the proportions must still equal one. This means that if the investor has borrowed money, the sum of the proportions invested in risky assets would be greater than one. For example, borrowing \$4,300 and investing \$21,500 in A share means that the proportion in A share, X_1, equals 1.25 (= \$21,500/ \$17,200). In this case $X_1 + X_2 = 1.25 + (-0.25) = 1$.

(1) **Borrowing and Investing in a Risky Security**

To evaluate the effect that the introduction of risk-free borrowing has on the efficient set, the example presented in the previous section will expanded. In particular, consider portfolios F, G, H, and I where the investor will invest all the borrowed funds as well as his or her own funds in A share. Thus the proportions for these portfolios can be summarized as follows:

	Portfolio F	Portfolio G	Portfolio H	Portfolio I
X_1	1.25	1.50	1.75	2.00
X_4	-0.25	-0.50	-0.75	-1.00

The expected returns of these portfolios are calculated in the same manner as was shown in the previous section.

$$\overline{r_p} = \sum_{i=1}^{N} X_i \overline{r_i} = \sum_{i=1}^{4} X_i \overline{r_i} = X_1 \overline{r_1} + X_4 \overline{r_4}$$
$$= (X_1 \times 16.2\%) + (X_4 \times 4\%)$$

Thus portfolios F, G, H and I have the following expected returns:

$$\overline{r_F} = \sum_{i=1}^{N} X_i \overline{r_i} = X_1 \overline{r_1} + X_4 \overline{r_4} = (1.25 \times 16.2\%) + (-0.25 \times 4\%) = 19.25\%$$

$$\overline{r_G} = \sum_{i=1}^{N} X_i \overline{r_i} = X_1 \overline{r_1} + X_4 \overline{r_4} = (1.50 \times 16.2\%) + (-0.50 \times 4\%) = 22.30\%$$

$$\overline{r_H} = \sum_{i=1}^{N} X_i \overline{r_i} = X_1 \overline{r_1} + X_4 \overline{r_4} = (1.75 \times 16.2\%) + (-0.75 \times 4\%) = 25.35\%$$

$$\overline{r_I} = \sum_{i=1}^{N} X_i \overline{r_i} = X_1 \overline{r_1} + X_4 \overline{r_4} = (2.00 \times 16.2\%) + (-1.00 \times 4\%) = 28.40\%$$

Similarly, the standard deviations of these portfolios are calculated:

$$\sigma_p = \left[\sum_{i=1}^{N} \sum_{j=1}^{N} X_i X_j \sigma_{ij} \right]^{1/2} = \left[\sum_{i=1}^{4} \sum_{j=1}^{4} X_i X_j \sigma_{ij} \right]^{1/2}$$

Which was shown to reduce to:

$$\sigma_p = [X_1^2 \sigma_1^2]^{1/2} = [X_1^2 \times 146]^{1/2} = X_1 \times 12.08\%$$

Thus the standard deviations of the four portfolios are:

$$\sigma_F = 1.25 \times 12.08\% = 15.10\%$$
$$\sigma_G = 1.50 \times 12.08\% = 18.12\%$$
$$\sigma_H = 1.75 \times 12.08\% = 21.14\%$$
$$\sigma_I = 2.00 \times 12.08\% = 24.16\%$$

In summary, these four portfolios, as well as the five portfolios that involve risk-free lending, have the following expected returns and standard deviations:

Portfolio	X_1	X_4	Expected return %	Standard Deviation
A	0.00	1.00	4.00	0.00
B	0.25	0.75	7.05	3.02

continued

Portfolio	X_1	X_4	Expected return %	Standard Deviation
C	0.50	0.50	10.10	6.04
D	0.75	0.25	13.15	9.06
E	1.00	0.00	16.20	12.08
F	1.25	−0.25	19.25	15.10
G	1.50	−0.50	22.30	18.12
H	1.75	−0.75	25.35	21.14
I	2.00	−1.00	28.40	24.16

It can be seen that the four portfolios that involve risk-free borrowing (F, G, H, and I) all lie on the same straight line that goes through the five portfolios that involve risk-free lending (A, B, C, D and E). Furthermore, the larger the amount of borrowing, the further out on the line the portfolio lies; equivalently, the smaller the value of X_4, the further out on the line the portfolio lies.

Although only four particular combinations of borrowing and investing in A share have been examined here, it can be shown that any combination of borrowing and investing in A share will lie somewhere on this line with the exact location generalized to combinations of risk-free borrowing and an investment in any particular risky asset. This means that borrowing at the risk-free rate and investing all the borrowed money and the investor's own money in a risky asset will result in a portfolio that has an expected return and standard deviation such that it lies on the extension of the straight line connecting the risk-free rate and the risky asset.

(2) Borrowing and Investing in a Risky Portfolio

Next consider what happens when a portfolio of more than one risky asset is purchased with both the investor's own funds and borrowed funds. Earlier it was shown that the portfolio having proportions invested in L and K shares equal to 0.80 and 0.20, respectively, had an expected return of 17.52% and a standard deviation of 12.30%. This portfolio was referred to as *PLK*. Any portfolio that involves borrowing money at the risk-free rate and then investing these funds and the investor's own funds in *PLK* will have an expected return and standard deviation that can be calculated in a manner identical to that which was previously shown when borrowing was incurred and L share was purchased. A portfolio the involves borrowing the proportion X_4 and investing these funds and all the investor's own funds in *PLK* will have an expected return and standard deviation that are equal to, respectively:

$$\overline{r_{PLK}} = (X_{PLK} \times 17.52\%) + (X_4 \times 4\%)$$
$$\sigma_{PLK} = X_{PLK} \times 12.30\%$$

For example, consider borrowing an amount of money equal to 25% of the investor's initial wealth and then investing all the investor's own funds and these borrowed funds in *PLK*. Thus, $X_{PLK} = 1 - X_4 = 1 - (-0.25) = 1.25$. This portfolio will have an expected return of:

$$\overline{r_P} = (1.25 \times 17.52\%) + (-0.25 \times 4\%) = 20.90\%$$

And a standard deviation of:

$$\sigma_P = 1.25 \times 12.30\% = 15.38\%$$

It can be seen that this portfolio (denoted *P*) lies on the extension of the line that connects the risk-free rate with *PLK*. Other portfolios consisting of *PLK* and borrowing at the risk-free rate will also lie somewhere on this extension with their exact location depending on the amount of the borrowing to purchase an individual risky asset. In both cases, the resulting portfolio lies on an extension of the line connecting the risk-free rate with the risky investment.

2.2.8.4 Allowing for both Risk-Free Borrowing and Lending

(1) The effect of risk-free borrowing and lending

Figure 2.12 shows how the feasible set is changed when both borrowing and lending at the same risk-free rate are allowed. Here all risky assets and portfolios, not just *L* company and *PLK*, are considered. The feasible set is the entire area between the two lines emanating from the risk-free rate that go through the location of *M* share and the portfolio denoted *T*. These two lines extend indefinitely to the right if it is assumed that there is no limit to the amount of borrowing that the investor can incur.

The straight line that goes through portfolio *T* is of special importance because it represents the efficient set. This means that it represents the set of portfolios that offer the best opportunities as it represents the set of feasible portfolios lying furthest northwest. Portfolio *T*, as was mentioned earlier, consists of investments in *L*, *M*, and *K* in proportions equal to, respectively, 0.12, 0.19, and 0.69.

As before, the line going through *T* is just tangent to the

Markowitz model efficient set. None of the portfolios, except for T, that were on the Markowitz model efficient set are efficient when risk-free borrowing and lending are introduced. This can be seen by noting that every portfolio (except T) that lies on the Markowitz model efficient set is dominated by a portfolio on this straight line having the same standard deviation along with a higher expected return.

(2) **The effect of risk-free borrowing and lending on portfolio selection**

Given the opportunity to either borrow or lend at the risk-free rate, an investor would proceed to identify the optimal portfolio by plotting his or her indifference curves on this graph and noting where one of them is tangent to the linear efficient set. Figure 2.12 shows two alternative situations. If the investor's indifference curves look like the ones in panel (a), then the investor's optimal portfolio O^* will consist of an investment in the risk-free asset as well as in T. Alternatively, if the investor is less risk averse and has indifference curves that look like those shown in panel (b), then the investor's optimal portfolio O^* will consist of borrowing at the risk free rate and investing these funds as well as his or her own funds in T.

Summary

- The Markowitz approach to portfolio selection assumes that investors seek both maximum expected return for a given level of risk and minimum uncertainty (risk) for a given level of expected return.
- Expected return serves as the measure of potential reward associated with a portfolio. Standard deviation is viewed as the measure of a portfolio's risk.
- An indifference curve represents the various combinations of risk and return that the investor finds equally desirable.
- Investors are assumed to consider any portfolio lying on an indifference curve "further to the northwest" more desirable than any portfolio lying on an indifference curve that is "not as far northwest."
- The assumptions of investor non-satiation and risk aversion cause indifference curves to be positively sloped and convex.
- The expected return on a portfolio is a weighted average of the expected returns of its component securities, with the relative

portfolio proportions of the component securities serving as weights.
- Covariance and correlation measure the extent to which two random variables "move together."
- The standard deviation of a portfolio depends on the standard deviations and proportions of the component securities as well as their co-variances with one another.
- The efficient set contains those portfolios that offer both maximum expected return for varying levels of risk and minimum risk for varying levels of expected return.
- Investors are assumed to select their optimal portfolios from among the portfolios lying on the efficient set.
- An investor's optimal portfolio is identified as the tangent point between the investor's indifference curves and the efficient set.
- Diversification usually leads to risk reduction, because the standard deviation of a portfolio generally will be less than a weighted average of the standard deviations of the component securities.
- The market's index's return does not completely explain the return on a security. The unexplained elements are captured by the random error term of the market model.
- According to the market model, the total risk of a security consists of market risk and unique risk.
- Diversification leads to an averaging of market risk. And it can substantially reduce unique risk.
- The return on a riskfree asset is certain. The riskfree asset's standard deviation is zero as is its covariance with other assets.
- With riskfree lending, the efficient set becomes a straight line from the risk free rate to a point tangent to the curved Markowitz efficient set, in addition to the portion of the Markowitz efficient set that lies northeast of this tangent point.
- Introducing riskfree borrowing permits an investor to engage in leverage. The investor may use all of his or her money, plus money borrowed at the riskfree rate, to purchase a portfolio of risky assets.
- Investors with higher levels of risk aversion will engage in less borrowing (or more lending) than investor with less risk aversion.

❓ Exercises

1. Considering an investment in A stock, if you estimated the

following probability distribution of returns for A stock:

Return	-10%	0%	10%	20%	30%
Probability	10%	25%	40%	20%	5%

Based on this estimates, calculate the expected return and standard deviation of A stock.

2. Given the following variance-covariance matrix for three securities, as well as the percentage of the portfolio that each security comprises, calculate the portfolio's standard deviation.

	Security A	Security B	Security C
Security A	459	-211	112
Security B	-211	312	215
Security C	112	215	179
	$X_A = 0.50$	$X_B = 0.30$	$X_C = 0.20$

3. You owns three stocks and has estimated the following joint probability distribution of returns:

Outcome	Stock A	Stock B	Stock C	Probability
1	-10%	10%	0%	0.30
2	0	10	10	0.20
3	10	5	15	0.30
4	20	-10	5	0.20

Calculate the portfolio's expected return and standard deviation if you invest 20% in stock A, 50% in stock B, and 30% in Stock C. Assume that each security's return is completely uncorrelated with the returns of the other securities.

4. If you own a risky portfolio with a 15% expected return, the riskfree return is 5%. What is the expected return on the total portfolio if you invest the following proportions in the risky portfolio and the remainder in the riskfree asset?
   a. 120%   b. 90%   c. 75%

5. Consider a risky portfolio with an expected return of 18%. With a riskfree return of 5%, how could you create a portfolio with a 24% expected return?

6. If a portfolio is composed of an investment in a risky portfolio (with a 12% expected return and a 25% standard deviation) and a riskfree asset (with a 7% return). If the total portfolio has a 20% standard deviation, what is its expected return?

Chapter 3
CAPM and International CAPM

> **The requirement of Learning**
> - Knowing the assumption of CAPM
> - Understanding the implication of the CML and the SML
> - Understanding the implication of the β value
> - Understanding the difference between the market risk and non-market risk
> - Knowing the assumption of International CAPM
> - Understanding the real exchange rate and the nominal exchange rate
> - Understanding the exchange rate risk and exchange risk premium
> - Understanding the separation theorem and the risk-pricing relation of International CAPM

1 Capital Assets Pricing Model (CAPM)

马科维茨模型提出了一种识别投资者最优投资组合的方法。使用这种方法,投资者需要估计所有考虑中的证券的预期收益和方差。此外,需要估计这些证券之间的所有协变量,并确定无风险利率。

The Markowitz model presented a method for identifying an investor's optimal portfolio. With this method, the investor needs to estimate the expected returns and variances for all securities under consideration. Furthermore, all the co-variances among these securities need to be estimated and the risk-free rate needs to be determined. Once this is done, the investor can identify the composition of the tangent portfolio as well as its expected return and standard deviation. At this juncture the investor can proceed to identify the optimal portfolio by noting where one of his or her indifference curves touches but does not intersect with the efficient set. This portfolio involves an investment in the tangent portfolio along with a certain amount of either risk-free borrowing or lending because the efficient set is linear (that is, a straight line).

Such an approach to investing can be viewed as an exercise in normative economics, where investors are told what they should do. Thus, the approach is prescriptive in nature. In this chapter the realm of positive economics is entered, share a descriptive model of how assets are priced is presented. The model assumes among other things that all investors use the approach to investing given in the model. The major implication of the model is that the expected return of an asset will be related to a measure of risk for that asset known as beta. The exact manner in which expected return and beta are related is specified by the Capital Asset Pricing Model. This model provides the intellectual basis for a number of the current practices in the investment industry. Although many of these practices are based on various extensions and modifications of the CAPM, a sound understanding of the original version is necessary in order to understand them. Accordingly, this presents the original version of the CAPM.

1.1 Assumptions

To see how assets are priced, a model (that is, a theory) must be constructed. This requires simplification in that the model builder must abstract from the full complexity of the situation and focus only on the most important elements. The way this is achieved is by making certain assumptions about the environment. These assumptions need to be simplistic in order to provide the degree of abstraction that allows for some success in building the model. The reasonableness of the assumptions (or lack thereof) is of little concern. Instead the test of a model is its ability to help one understand and predict the process being modeled.

为了了解资产是如何定价的，必须构建一个模型（即理论）。这需要简化，因为模型构建者必须从情况的全部复杂性中抽象出来，并且只关注最重要的元素。

Some of the assumptions behind the CAPM are also behind the normative approach to investing described in the previous three chapters. These assumptions are as follows:

- ➢ Investors evaluate portfolios by looking at the expected returns and standard deviations of the portfolios over a one-period horizon.
- ➢ Investors are never satiated.
- ➢ Investors are risk-averse.
- ➢ Individual assets are infinitely divisible, meaning that an investor can buy a fraction of a share if he so desires.
- ➢ There is a risk-free rate at which an investor may either lend (that is, invest) money or borrow money.
- ➢ Taxes and transaction costs are irrelevant.
- ➢ All investors have the same one-period horizon.
- ➢ The risk-free rate is the same for all investors.
- ➢ Information is freely and instantly available to all investors.
- ➢ Investors have homogeneous expectations.

1.2 The capital market line

Having made these ten assumptions, the resulting implications can now be examined. First, investors would analyze securities and determine the composition of the tangent portfolio. In so doing, every would obtain in equilibrium the same tangent portfolio. However, this is not surprising because there is complete agreement among investors on the estimates of the securities expected returns, variances, and covariances, as well as on the size of the risk-free rate. This also means that the linear efficient set is the same for all investors because it simply involves combinations of the agreed upon tangent portfolio and either risk-free borrowing or lending.

As all investors face the same efficient set, the only reason they will choose different portfolios is that they have different indifference curves. Thus different investors will choose different portfolios from the same efficient set because they have different preferences toward risk and return. For example, as was shown in Figure 9.8, the investor in panel (a) will choose a different portfolio than the investor in panel (b). Note, however, that although the chosen portfolios will be different, each investor will choose the same combination of risky securities, denoted T in Figure 9.8. This means that each investor will spread his or her funds among risky securities in the same relative proportions, adding risk-free borrowing or lending in order to achieve a personally preferred overall combination of risk and return. This feature of the CAPM is often referred to as the separation theorem:

The optimal combination of risky assets for an investor can be determined without any knowledge of the investor's preferences toward risk and return.

In other words, the determination of the optimal combination of risky assets can be made without determining the shape of an investor's indifference curves.

The reasoning behind the separation theorem involves a property of the linear efficient set. It was shown that all portfolios located on the linear efficient set involved an investment in a tangent portfolio combined with varying degrees of risk-free borrowing or lending. With the CAPM each person faces the same linear efficient set, meaning that each person will be investing in the same tangent portfolio (combined with a certain amount of either risk-free borrowing or lending that depends upon that person's indifference curves). It

> 无需了解投资者风险与收益的偏好就能确定该投资者的风险资产最优组合。

therefore follows that the risky portion of each person's portfolio will be the same.

In the former example, three securities were considered, corresponding to the stock of L, K, and M companies. With a risk-free rate of return of 4%, the tangent portfolio T was shown to consist of investments in L, K, and M in proportions equal to 0.12, 0.19, and 0.69, respectively. If the ten assumptions of the CAPM are made, then the investor shown would invest approximately half of his or her money in the risk-free asset and the remainder in T. The investor, on the other hand, would borrow an amount of money equal to approximately half the value of his or her initial wealth and proceed to invest these borrowed funds as well as his or her own funds in T. Thus, the proportions invested in the three stocks would be equal:

$$(0.5) \times \begin{pmatrix} 0.12 \\ 0.19 \\ 0.69 \end{pmatrix} = \begin{pmatrix} 0.060 \\ 0.095 \\ 0.345 \end{pmatrix} \qquad (a)$$

$$(1.5) \times \begin{pmatrix} 0.12 \\ 0.19 \\ 0.69 \end{pmatrix} = \begin{pmatrix} 0.180 \\ 0.285 \\ 1.035 \end{pmatrix} \qquad (b)$$

Although the proportions to be invested in each of these three risky securities for the (a) investor (0.060, 0.095, 0.345) can be seen to be different in size from their values for the (b) investor (0.180, 0.285, 1.035), note how the relative proportions are the same, being equal to 0.12, 0.19, and 0.69, respectively.

1.3 The market portfolio

Another important feature of the CAPM is that in equilibrium each security must have a nonzero proportion in the composition of the tangent portfolio.

This means that no security can in equilibrium have a proportion in T that is zero. The reasoning behind this feature lies in the previously mentioned separation theorem, where it was asserted that the risky portion of every investor's portfolio is independent of the investor's risk-return preferences. The justification for the theorem was that the risky portion of each investor's portfolio is simply an investment in T. If every investor is purchasing T and T does not involve an investment in each security, then nobody is investing in those securities with zero proportions in T. This means that the prices of these zero-proportion securities must fall, thereby causing the expected returns of these securities to rise until the resulting tangent portfolio has a non-zero proportion associated with them.

In the previous example, *M* Corp. had a current price of $62 and an expected end of period price of $76.14. This meant that the expected return for *M* Corp. was 22.8%. Now imagine that the current price of *M* Corp. is $72, not $62, meaning that its expected return is 5.8%. If this were the case, the tangent portfolio associated with a risk-free rate of 4% would involve just able and *K* Corp. in proportions of 0.90 and 0.10, respectively. Because *M* Corp. has a proportion of zero, nobody would want to hold shares of *M* Corp.. Consequently, orders to sell would be received in substantial quantities with virtually no offsetting orders to buy being received. As a result, *M* Corp.'s price would fall as brokers would try to find someone to buy the shares. However, as *M* Corp.'s price falls, its expected return would rise because the same end of period price of $76.14 would be forecast for *M* Corp. as before and it would now cost less to buy one share. Eventually, as the price falls, investors would change their minds and want to buy shares of M Corp.. Ultimately, at a price of $62 investors will want to hold shares of *M* Corp. so that in aggregate the number of shares demanded will equal the number of shares outstanding. Thus in equilibrium *M* Corp. will have a non-zero proportion in the tangent portfolio.

Another interesting situation could also arise, what if each investor concludes that the tangent portfolio should involve a proportionate investment in the stock of *K* Corp. equal to 0.40, but at the current price of *K* Corp. there are not enough shared outstanding to meet the demand? In this situation orders to buy *K* Corp. will flood in, and brokers will raise the price in search of sellers. This will cause the expected return of *K* Corp. to fall, making it less attractive and thereby reducing its proportion in the tangent portfolio to a level where the number of shares demanded equals the number of shares outstanding.

Ultimately, everything will balance out, when all the price adjusting stops. The market will have been brought into equilibrium. First, each investor will want to hold a certain positive amount of each risky security. Second, the current market price of each security will be at a level where the number of shares demanded equals the number of shares outstanding. Third, the risk-free rate will be at a level where the total amount of money borrowed equals the total amount of money lent. As a result, in equilibrium the proportions of the tangent portfolio will correspond to the proportions of what is known as the market portfolio, defined as follows:

The market portfolio is a portfolio consisting of all securities where the proportion invested in each security corresponds to its relative market value. The relative market value of a security is simply equal to the aggregate market value of the security divided by the sum of the aggregate market values of all securities.

The reason the market portfolio plays a central role in the CAPM is that the efficient set consists of an investment in the market portfolio, coupled with a desired amount of either risk-free borrowing or lending. Thus, it is common practice to refer to the tangent portfolio as the market portfolio and to denote it as M instead of T. In theory, M consists not only of common stocks but also such other kinds of investments as bonds, preferred stocks, and real estate. However, in practice some people restrict M to just common stocks.

> 市场投资组合是由所有证券组成的投资组合,其中投资于每种证券的比例与其相对市场价值相对应。证券的相对市场价值等于证券的总市场价值除以所有证券的总市场价值之和。

1.4 The efficient set

In the world of the CAPM, it is a simple matter to determine the relationship between risk and return for efficient portfolios. In the previous figure, Point M represents the market portfolio and r_f represents the risk-free rate of return. Efficient portfolios plot along the line starting at r_f and going through M and consist of alternative combinations of risk and return obtainable by combining the market portfolio with risk-free borrowing or lending. This linear efficient set of the CAPM is known as the CML. All portfolios other than those employing the market portfolio and risk-free borrowing or lending would lie below the CML, although some might plot very close to it.

The slope of the CML is equal to the difference between the expected return of the market portfolio and that of the risk-free security ($\overline{r}_M - r_f$) divided by the difference in their risks ($\delta_M - 0$) or ($\overline{r}_M - r_f$)/$\delta_M - 0$, because the vertical intercept of the CML is r_f, the straight line characterizing the CML has the following equation:

$$\overline{r}_p = r_f + \left[\frac{\overline{r}_M - r_f}{\sigma_M}\right]\sigma_p$$

Where $\overline{r}_p$ and σ_p refer to the expected return and standard deviation of an efficient portfolio. In the previous example, the market portfolio associated with a risk-free rate of 4% consisted of companies L, M, and K (these stocks are assumed to be the only ones that exist) in the proportions of 0.12, 0.19, and 0.69, respectively. The expected return and standard deviation for a portfolio with these proportions was 22.4% and 15.2%, respectively, the equation for the resulting CML is:

$$\overline{r}_p = 4 + \left[\frac{22.4 - 4}{15.2}\right]\sigma_p = 4 + 1.21\sigma_p$$

Equilibrium in the security market can be characterized by two key numbers. The first is the vertical intercept of the CML (that is, the risk-free rate), which is often referred to as the reward for waiting. The second is the slope of the CML, which is often referred to as the reward per unit of risk borne. In essence, the security market provides a place where time and risk can be traded with their prices determined by the forces of supply and demand. Thus the intercept and slope of the CML can be thought of as the price of time and the price of risk, respectively. In the example, they are equal to 4% and 1.21, respectively.

1.5 The security market line

The capital market line represents the equilibrium relationship between the expected return and standard deviation for efficient portfolios. Individual risky securities will always plot below the line because a single risky security is an inefficient portfolio. The Capital Asset Pricing Model does not imply any particular relationship between the expected return and the standard deviation (that is, total risk) of an individual security, to say more about the expected return of an individual security, deeper analysis is necessary.

The following equation was given for calculating the standard deviation of any portfolio:

$$\sigma_p = \left[\sum_{i}^{N}\sum_{j}^{N} X_i X_j \sigma_{ij}\right]^{1/2}$$

Where X_i and X_j denoted the proportions invested in securities i and j, respectively, and σ_{ij} denoted the covariance of returns between security i and j, Now consider using this equation to calculate the standard deviation of the market portfolio:

$$\sigma_M = \left[\sum_i^N \sum_j^N X_{iM} X_{jM} \sigma_{ij} \right]^{1/2}$$

Where X_{iM} and X_{jM} denote the proportions invested in securities i and j in forming the market portfolio, respectively. It can be shown that another way to write equation is as follows:

$$\sigma_M = \left[X_{1M} \sum_{j=1}^N X_{jM} \sigma_{1j} + X_{2M} \sum_{j=2}^N X_{jM} \sigma_{2j} + \cdots X_{NM} \sum_{j=N}^N X_{jM} \sigma_{Nj} \right]^{1/2}$$

At this point a property of covariance can be used: the covariance of security i with the market portfolio (σ_{iM}) can be expressed as the weighted average of every security's covariance with security i:

$$\left[\sum_{j=1}^N X_{jM} \sigma_{ij} \right] = \sigma_{iM}$$

This property, when applied to each one of the N risky securities in the market portfolio, results in the following:

$$\sigma_M = \left[X_{1M} \sigma_{1M} + X_{2M} \sigma_{2M} + \cdots + X_{NM} \sigma_{NM} \right]^{1/2}$$

Where σ_{1M} denotes the covariance of security 1 with the market portfolio, σ_{2M} denotes the covariance of security 2 with the market portfolio, and so on. Thus, the standard deviation of the market portfolio is equal to the square root of a weighted average of the covariances of all the securities with it, where the weights are equal to the proportions of the respective securities in the market portfolio.

At this juncture an important point can be observed. Under the CAPM, each investor holds the market portfolio and is concerned with its standard deviation because this will influence the slope of the CML and hence the magnitude of his or her investment in the market portfolio. The contribution of each security to the standard deviation of the market portfolio can be seen in equation to depend on the size of its covariance with the market portfolio. Accordingly, each investor will note that the relevant measure of risk for a security is its covariance with the market portfolio, σ_{iM}. This means that securities with larger values of σ_{iM} will be viewed by investors as contributing more to the risk of the market portfolio. It also means that securities with larger standard deviations should not be viewed as necessarily adding more risk to the market portfolio than those securities with smaller standard deviations.

From this analysis it follows that securities with larger values provide proportionately larger expected returns to interest investors in purchasing them. To see why, consider what would happen if such securities did not provide investors with proportionately larger levels of expected return. In this situation, these securities would contribute to the risk of the market portfolio while not contributing proportionately to the expected return of the market portfolio. This means that deleting such securities from the market portfolio would cause the expected return of the market portfolio relative to its standard deviation to rise. Because investors would view this as a favorable change, the market portfolio would no longer be the optimal risky portfolio to hold. Thus, security prices would be out of equilibrium.

The exact form of the equilibrium relationship between risk and return can be written as follows:

$$\overline{r_i} = r_f + \left[\frac{\overline{r_M} - r_f}{\sigma_M^2}\right]\sigma_{iM}$$

The equation represents a straight line having a vertical intercept of r_f and a slope of $(\overline{r_M} - r_f)/\sigma_M^2$. As the slope is positive, the equation indicates that securities with larger co-variances with the market (σ_{iM}) will be priced so as to have larger expected returns (r_i). This relationship between co-variance and expected return is known as the Security Market Line (SML).

Interestingly, a risky security with $\sigma_{iM} = 0$ will have an expected return equal to the rate on the risk-free security, r_f. Why? Because this risky security, just like the risk-free security, doer not contribute to the risk of the market portfolio. This is so even though the risky security has a positive standard deviation whereas the risk-free security has a standard deviation of zero.

It is even possible for some risky securities (meaning securities with positive standard deviations) to have expected returns less than the risk-free rate. According to the CAPM, this will occur if $\sigma_{iM} < 0$, thereby indicating that they contribute a negative amount of risk to the market portfolio (meaning that they cause the risk of the market portfolio to be lower than it would be if less money were invested in them).

Also of interest is the observation that a risky security with σ_{iM} will have an expected return equal to the expected return on the market portfolio, $\overline{r_M}$. This is because such a security contributes an average amount of risk to the market portfolio.

Another way of expressing the SML is as follows:

$$\overline{r_i} = r_f + (\overline{r_M} - r_f)\beta_{iM}$$

Where the term β_{iM} is defined as:

$$\beta_{iM} = \frac{\sigma_{iM}}{\sigma_M^2}$$

The term β_{iM} is known as the beta coefficient (or simply the beta) for security i, and is an alternative way of representing the covariance of a security. This equation is a different version of the SML. Although having the same intercept as the earlier version, r_f, it has a different slope. The slope of this version is $(\overline{r_M} - r_f)$, whereas the slope of the earlier version was $[(\overline{r_M} - r_f)/\sigma_M^2]$.

One property of beta is that the beta of a portfolio is simply a weighted average of the beta of its component securities, where the proportions invested in the securities are the respective weights. That is, the beta of a portfolio can be calculated as:

$$\beta_{pM} = \sum_{i=1}^{N} X_i \beta_{iM}$$

Earlier it was shown that the expected return of a portfolio is a weighted average of the expected returns of its component securities, where the proportions invested in the securities are the weights. This means that because every security plots on the SML, so will every portfolio. To put it more broadly, not only every security but also every portfolio must plot on an upward sloping straight line in a diagram with expected return on the vertical axis and beta on the horizontal axis. This means that efficient portfolios plot on both the CML and the SML, although inefficient portfolios plot on the SML but below the CML.

Also of interest is that the SML must go through the point representing the market portfolio itself. Its beta is 1 and its expected return is $\overline{r_M}$, so its coordinates are $(1, \overline{r_M})$. Because risk-free securities have beta values of 0, the SML will also go through a point with an expected return of r_f and coordinates of $(0, r_f)$. This means that the SML will have a vertical intercept equal to r_f and a slope equal to the vertical distance between these two points $(\overline{r_M} - r_f)$ divided by the horizontal distance between these two points $(1-0)$ or $(\overline{r_M} - r_f)/(1-0) = (\overline{r_M} - r_f)$. Thus these two points suffice to fix the location of the SML, indication of the SML, indicating the appropriate expected returns for securities and portfolios with different beta values.

The equilibrium relationship shown by the SML comes to exist through the combined effects of investors' adjustments in holdings and the resulting pressures on security prices. Given a set of security prices, investors calculate expected returns and co-variances and then determine their optimal portfolios. If the number of shares of a security collectively desired differs from the number available, there will be upward or downward pressure on its price. Given a new set of prices, investors will reassess their desires for the various securities. The process will continue until the number of shares collectively desired for each security equals the number available.

For the individual investor, security prices and prospects are fixed while the quantities held can be altered. For the market as a whole, however, these quantities are fixed (at least in the short run), and prices are variable. As in any competitive market, equilibrium requires the adjustment of each security's price until there is consistency between the quantity desired and the quantity available.

It may seem logical to examine historical returns on securities to determine whether or not securities have been priced in equilibrium as suggested by the CAPM. However, the issue of whether or not such testing of the CAPM can be done in a meaningful manner is controversial. For at least some purposes, affirmative test results may not be necessary to make practical use of the CAPM.

1.6 Market and Non-Market Risk

The total risk of a security σ_i^2 could be partitioned into two components as follows:

$$\sigma_i^2 = \beta_{i1}^2 \sigma_I^2 + \sigma_{\varepsilon i}^2$$

Where the components are:

$$\beta_{i1}^2 \sigma_I^2 = \text{market risk, and}$$
$$\sigma_{\varepsilon i}^2 = \text{unique risk.}$$

Because beta, or covariance, is the relevant measure of risk for a security according to the CAPM, it is only appropriate to explore the relationship between it and the total risk of the security. It turns out that the relationship is identical *except that the market portfolio is involved instead of a market index*:

$$\sigma_i^2 = \beta_{iM}^2 \sigma_M^2 + \sigma_{\varepsilon i}^2$$

As with the market model, the total risk of security, measured by its variance and denoted σ_i^2, is shown to consist of two parts. The first component is the portion related to moves of the market portfolio. It is equal to the product of the square of the beta of the stock and the variance of the market portfolio, and also often referred to as the market risk of the security. The second component is the portion not related to moves of the market portfolio. It is denoted $\sigma_{\varepsilon i}^2$ and can be considered non-market risk. Under the assumptions of the market model, it is also unique to the security in question and hence is termed unique risk.

2 International CAPM

2.1 Real exchange rate

Firstly, we assume the purchasing power parity holds exactly at any point in the international CAPM, so exchange rates would simply mirror inflation differentials between two countries.

$$X = e \times (P_f / P_d)$$

where

X is the real exchange rate (direct quotation); e is the nominal exchange rate; P_f is the foreign country price level; P_d is the domestic country price level.

Real exchange rate movements are defined as movements in the exchange rates that are not explained by the inflation differential between the two countries. If x and F are the percentage movement in the real and nominal exchange rates. π_d and π_f are the inflation rates in the domestic and foreign countries, then

$$x = F + \pi_f - \pi_d = F - (\pi_d - \pi_f)$$

If PPP holds, the real exchange rate is constant ($x = 0\%$), and the nominal exchange rate movement is equal to the inflation rate differential. For example, assume that there is a one-month inflation rate of 1% in the dollar and 0% Swiss Franc. For the real exchange rate to stay constant over the month, the franc has to appreciate by 1% against the dollar. If the franc turned out to appreciate by 5% during that month, then there would be a real appreciation of 4% of the franc. Any such real exchange rate movement would violate the assumptions supporting the domestic CAPM extension. To summarize, in the absence of real foreign currency risk, the extended CAPM would hold.

Example 3-1 Constant real exchange rate

An investor considers investing in the securities of a foreign country. The direct exchange rate between the two countries is currently two domestic currency units for one foreign currency unit. The price level of the typical consumption basket in domestic country relative to the price level of the typical consumption basket in foreign country is also 2 to 1, which means that the real exchange rate is 1 to 1. A year later the inflation rate has been 3 percent in domestic country and 1 percent in foreign country. The foreign currency has appreciated and the exchange rate is now 2.04. What is the new real exchange rate?

Solution:

$$\frac{P_{f1} - P_{f0}}{P_{f0}} = 1\% \Rightarrow \frac{P_{f1}}{P_{f0}} = 1.01 \qquad \frac{P_{d1} - P_{d0}}{P_{d0}} = 3\% \Rightarrow \frac{P_{d1}}{P_{d0}} = 1.03$$

$$\frac{P_{f1}}{P_{d1}} = \frac{1.01 \times P_{f0}}{1.03 \times P_{d0}} = \frac{1.01}{1.03} \times \frac{1}{2} = \frac{1.01}{2.06}$$

$$X = e \times (P_{f1}/P_{d1}) = 2.04 \times 1.01/2.06 = 1$$

So, the new real exchange rate is equal to 1.

Example 3-2 foreign currency risk

An investor considers investing one-year bonds of a foreign country. The expected inflation rate has been 3 percent in domestic country and 1 percent in foreign country. Inflation rates are totally predictable over the next year. The exchange rate between the two countries is currently two domestic currency units for one foreign currency unit. The price level of the typical consumption basket in domestic country relative to the price level of the typical consumption basket in foreign country is also 2 to 1, the real exchange rate is 1 to 1. The one-year interest rate is 5% in domestic country and 3% in foreign country. The investor expects the real exchange rate to remain constant over time.

Questions:

1. What are the expected exchange rate and the expected return on the foreign bond in domestic currency?

> 2. If a year later the inflation rates have indeed been 3% in DC and 1% in FC. The foreign exchange rate has been very volatile over the year, and the foreign currency has depreciated with an end-of-the-year exchange rate of 1.80. What is the real exchange rate at the end of the year and the *ex post* return on the foreign bond?
>
> **Solutions**:
>
> 1. According to the Example 1, we know the expected exchange rate is equal to 2.04, and the expected return on the foreign bond is equal to
>
> $$(1+3\%) \times 2.04/2 - 1 = 5.06\%$$
>
> 2. the new real exchange rate is $X = S \times (P_{f1}/P_{d1}) = 1.8 \times 1.01/2.06 = 0.88$ the *ex post* return on the foreign bond is $(1+3\%) \times 1.8/2 - 1 = -7.3\%$

2.2 Foreign Currency Risk Premiums

Deviations from PPP can be a major source of exchange rate variation, and consumption preferences can differ among countries. The risk that real prices of consumption goods might not be identical in every country is called *real foreign currency risk*, *real exchange rate risk*, or *purchasing power risk*.

Foreign Currency Risk Premiums: The risk premium on any investment is simply equal to its expected return in excess of the domestic risk-free rate:

$$RP = E(R) - R_0$$

And the foreign Currency Risk Premiums (SRP) is defined as the expected return on a foreign investment minus the domestic currency risk-free rate:

$$SRP = E[(S_1 - S_0)/S_0] - (r_{DC} - r_{FC}) - [E(S_1) - f]/S_0$$

> **Example 3 – 3 Foreign currency risk premium**
>
> The one-year risk-free interest rates are 5% in *DC* and 3% in *FC*. The exchange rate between the two countries is currently 2 *DC* units for 1 *FC* unit. The expected exchange rate appreciation of *FC* is 3%. What is the foreign currency risk premium? What is the expected *DC* return on the foreign investment?

Solution:

The foreign currency risk premium is

$$SRP = E[(S_1 - S_0)/S_0] - (r_{DC} - r_{FC})$$
$$= E(S) - (r_{DC} - r_{FC}) = 3\% - (5\% - 3\%) = 1\%$$

The expected DC return on the foreign investment is $3\% + 3\% = 6\%$ or $5\% + 1\% = 6\%$

Example 3-4 The Foreign Currency Risk Premium

Suppose the one-year risk-free interest rates are 5% in America and 3% in England. The exchange rate is 1 GBP = 2 USD. The expected exchange rate appreciation of the GBP is 3%. The expected return on England stocks is 6% in GBP.

1. What is the expected return on England stocks in dollars if there is no currency hedging?

2. What is the expected return on England stocks in dollars with full currency hedging?

3. What is the foreign currency risk premium on the GBP and who pays/receives it?

Solutions:

1. If there is no currency hedging, the expected return on England stocks in dollars is: $6\% + 3\% = 9\%$

2. With full currency hedging, the forward premium is equal to the interest rate differential of 2%, so the expected return on England stocks in dollars is $6\% + 2\% = 8\%$

3. The foreign currency risk premium on the GBP is $3\% - (5\% - 3\%) = 1\%$, This risk premium is "paid" by Americans and "received" by England.

2.3 Separation Theorem and Risk-pricing relation

In the international CAPM, as in the domestic CAPM, all investors determine their demand for each asset by a mean-variance optimization (expected-utility maximization), using their domestic currency as base currency. The demand from each investor is aggregated and set equal to the supply of assets, their market capitalization. The net supply of borrowing and lending (the risk-free asset) in each currency is assumed to be zero, two conclusions emerge from this international CAPM:

分离定理

Separation Theorem: The optimal investment strategy for an

investor should hold a combination of the risk-free asset in his own currency, and the world market portfolio optimally hedged against foreign currency risk. This world market portfolio is the same for each investor and is the only portfolio of risky assets that should be held, partly hedged against foreign currency risk. However, it must be stressed that the optimal currency hedge ratio needs not be unitary and will generally be different for different assets and currencies. The optimal hedge ratios depend on variables such as differences among countries in relative wealth, foreign investment position, and risk aversion. Unfortunately, these variables cannot be observed or inferred from market data. The international CAPM does not provide simple, clear-cut, operational conclusions about the optimal currency-hedge ratios.

Risk-pricing relation: The descriptive conclusion of the international CAPM is an international equilibrium risk-pricing relation that is more complex than in the domestic CAPM. In the presence of exchange rate risk, additional risk premiums must be added to the risk-pricing relation to reflect the covariance of the asset with the various exchange rates (the currencies' betas). If there are $k+1$ countries, there will be k additional currency risk premiums. Hence, the expected return on an asset depends on the market risk premium plus various foreign currency risk premiums:

风险定价关系

$$E(r_i) = r_f + \beta_{im} \times RP_m + \gamma_{i1} \times SRP_1 + \gamma_{i2} \times SRP_2 + \cdots + \gamma_{ik} \times SRP_k$$

Where

r_f is the domestic currency risk-free interest rate.

β_{im} is the sensitivity of asset i domestic currency returns to market movements (market exposure).

RP_m is the world market risk premium equal to $E(R_m) - R_0$,

γ_{i1} toar γ_{ik} e the currency exposures, the sensitivities of asset i domestic currency returns to the exchange rate on currencies 1 to k, and SRP_1 to SRP_k are the foreign currency risk premiums on currencies 1 to k.

In Equation, all returns are measured in the investor's domestic currency, it indicates that the foreign investment return in domestic currency equals (a) the domestic risk-free rate, plus (b) a world market risk premium, times the asset's sensitivity to the world market, plus (c) foreign currency risk premiums times the investment's currency exposures.

The ICAPM differs from a domestic CAPM in two respects. First, the relevant market risk is world market risk, not domestic market risk. This is not surprising. Second, additional risk premiums are linked to an asset's sensitivity to currency movements. The different currency exposures of individual securities would be reflected in different expected returns.

> **Example 3-5 International Asset Pricing**
>
> You are a European investor considering investing in a foreign country. The world market risk premium is estimated at 5%, the foreign currency offers a 1% risk premium the current risk-free rates are equal to 5% in euros and 3% in FC units. Your broke provides you with some statistics:
>
> | Securities | Stock A | Stock B | Stock C | Stock D |
> |---|---|---|---|---|
> | World Beta | 1.0 | 1.0 | 1.2 | 1.4 |
> | Currency exposure | 1.0 | 0.0 | 0.5 | -0.5 |
>
> 1. According to the ICAPM, what should be the expected returns on the four stocks, in euros?
>
> 2. Stocks A and B have the same world beta, but different expected returns. Give an intuitive explanation for this difference.
>
> **Solutions:**
>
> 1. According to the ICAPM:
>
> $$E(r_i) = r_f + \beta_{iM} \times RP_M + \gamma_i \times SRP_F$$
>
> We can get:
>
> | Securities | Stock A | Stock B | Stock C | Stock D |
> |---|---|---|---|---|
> | Theoretical $\overline{r_i}$ (euro) | 11.0% | 10.0% | 11.5% | 11.5% |
>
> 2. The difference is explained by their different exposure to currency movements. The euro value of B is insensitive to unexpected movements in the exchange rare. As far as foreign currency risk is concerned, B is less risky than A, so its expected return should be different from that of A. Because the currency risk premium is equal to +1%, the difference in expected return between A and B should be 1%.

Chapter 3 CAPM and International CAPM

Summary

- CAPM is based on a specific set of assumptions about investor behavior and the existence of perfect security markets.
- The linear efficient set of the CAPM is known as the Capital Market Line (CML). The CML represents the equilibrium relationship between the expected return and standard deviation of efficient portfolios.
- The linear relationship between market covariance and expected return is known as the Security Market Line (SML).
- Under the CAPM, the total risk of a security can be separated into market risk and non-market risk. Under the market model, each security's non-market risk is unique to that security and hence is termed its unique risk.

Exercises

1. Assume that two securities constitute the market portfolio. Those securities have the following expected returns, standard deviations, and proportions:

Security	Expected return	Standard Deviation	Proportion
A	10%	20%	0.40
B	15%	28%	0.60

Based on this information, and given a correlation of 0.30 between the two securities and a risk-free rate of 5%, specify the equation for the Capital Market Line.

2. The market portfolio is assumed to be composed of four securities. Their covariances with the market and their proportions are shown below:

Security	Covariance with Market	Proportion
A	242	0.20
B	360	0.30
C	155	0.20
D	210	0.30

Given this data, calculate the market portfolio's standard deviation.

3. You own a portfolio composed of three securities. The betas of those

securities and their proportions are shown on the table. What is the beta of the portfolio?

Security	beta	Proportion
A	0.90	0.30
B	1.30	0.10
C	1.05	0.60

4. Given that the expected return on the market portfolio is 10%, the risk free rate of return is 6%, the beta of stock A is 0.85, and the beta of stock B is 1.20.

   a. Draw the SML;

   b. What is the equation for the SML?

   c. What are the equilibrium expected returns for stocks A and B?

   d. Plot the two risky securities on the SML.

5. Consider an asset that has a beta of 1.25. If the risk-free rate is 3.25% and the market risk premium is 5.5%, calculate the expected return on the asset.

6. An asset has a beta of 0.9. The variance of return on a market index, $\sigma_m^2 = 90$. If the variance of returns for the asset is 120, what proportion of the asset's total risk is systematic, and what proportion is residual risk?

7. A portfolio consists of three assets. Asset 1 has a beta of 0.85, Asset 2 has a beta of 1.3, and Asset 3 has a beta of 0.9. Asset 1 has an allocation of 50%, while Asset 2 and Asset 3 each have an allocation of 25%. The variance of returns on a market index, σ_m^2, is 120, calculate the variance of portfolio returns, assuming that the specific risk of the portfolio is negligible.

8. A Canadian investor is considering the purchase of U.K. securities. The current exchange rate is C\$1.46 per pound. Assume that the price level of a typical consumption basket in Canada is 1.46 times the price level of a typical consumption basket in the United Kingdom.

   a. Calculate the real exchange rate.

   b. One year later, price levels in Canada have risen 2%, while price levels in the United Kingdom have risen 4%. The new exchange rate is C\$1.4308 per pound. What is the new real exchange rate?

   c. Did the Canadian investor experience a change in the real exchange rate?

9. Suppose that you are an investor based in Switzerland, and you expect the U.S dollar to depreciate by 2.75% over the next year. The interest rate on one-year risk-free bonds is 5.25% in the United States and 2.75% in Switzerland. The current exchange rate is SFR1.62 per U.S. dollar.

   a. Calculate the foreign currency risk premium from the Swiss investor's viewpoint.

   b. Calculate the return on the U.S. bond from the Swiss investor's viewpoint, assuming that the Swiss investor's expectations are met.

10. Assume you are a U.S investor who is considering investments in the French (Stocks A and B) and Swiss (Stocks C and D) stock markets. The world market risk premium is 6%. The currency risk premium on the Swiss franc is 1.25%, and the currency risk premium on the euro is 2%. The interest rate on one-year risk-free bonds is 3.75% in the United States. In addition, you are provided with the following information:

	Stock A	Stock B	Stock C	Stock D
Country	France	France	Switzerland	Switzerland
β_m	1.0	0.9	1	1.5
γ_{euro}	1.0	0.8	−0.25	−1.0
γ_{SFr}	−0.25	0.75	1.0	−0.5

   a. Calculate the expected return for each of the stocks. The U.S. dollar is the base currency.

   b. Explain the differences in the expected returns of the four stocks in terms of β_m, γ_{euro} and γ_{SFr}.

Chapter 4
The Practice for International Diversification

> **The requirement of Learning**
> - Risk Reduction through Attractive Correlations.
> - Calculate the expected return and standard deviation for a two-asset portfolio containing a domestic asset and a foreign asset.
> - Demonstrate how changes in currency exchange rates can affect return and risk that investors earn on foreign security investments.
> - Discuss global equity market correlations and global bond market correlations.
> - The case for investing in emerging markets.

International portfolio investment is currently showing a strong trend. In the early 1970s, US pension funds basically held no foreign assets, but the percentage of foreign assets approached 15 percent of total assets by 2000; Some Dutch pension funds have more than half of their assets invested abroad.

In fact, it's the development of global securities market that result in the increase of international investment. As shown in Figure 4.1, in 1974, the New York Stock Exchange was the only significant market in the world, representing 60 percent of a world market capitalization of less than a trillion dollars. The size of the world market multiplied by a factor of 30 in the next 25 years, and the share of U.S. equity moved from 60 percent to less than 30 percent in 1988, and back to 50 percent by the end of 2000. At the end of 2001, the world stock market capitalization was around $25 trillion. The Pacific region, which made up a big third of the world stock market in the early 1990s, shrank to 15 percent at the end of 2001.

Figure 4.1 covers only developed markets; the share of the Asian markets would be somewhat increased if emerging markets were included. Europe makes up one-third of the world market. The Bank for International Settlements estimated the world market capitalization of publicly issued bonds to be around $37 trillion at the end of 2001. U.S. dollar bonds accounted for roughly 50 percent of the world bond market, while yen bonds accounted for somewhat less than 20 percent and bonds denominated in European currencies accounted for some 30 percent.

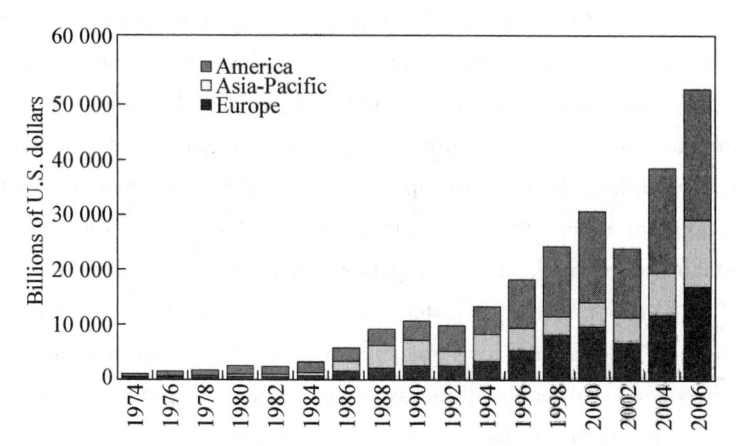

Source: Data from World Federation of Stock Exchanges.

Figure 4.1 Stock Market Capitalization—Developed Markets

In a fully efficient, integrated, global capital market, buying the world market portfolio would be the natural passive strategy. In theory, an American investor should hold half of the portfolio in international securities. But, even if not believe in a perfect, integrated world market, the case for diversifying in international securities is strong. The basic argument in favor of international diversification is that foreign investments allow investors to reduce the total risk of the portfolio, while offering additional profit potential. By expanding the investment opportunity set, international diversification helps to improve the risk-adjusted performance of a portfolio.

Domestic securities tend to move up and down together because they are similarly affected by domestic conditions, such as monetary announcements, movements in interest rates, budget deficits, and national growth. This creates a definite positive correlation among nearly all stocks traded in the same national equity market. The correlation applies equally to bonds; bond prices on the same national market are very strongly correlated. Investors have searched for methods to spread their risks and diversify away the national market risk. In their variety, foreign capital markets provide good potential for diversification beyond domestic instruments and markets.

1 Traditional Case International Diversification

> 全球化投资有两点理由。

There are two motivations for global investment. All else being equal, a low international correlation allows reduction of the volatility, or total risk, of a global portfolio. A low international correlation also provides profit opportunities for an active investor: Because markets do not move up or down together, an expert investor can hope to adjust the international asset allocation of the global portfolio toward markets with superior expected returns. This should lead to a superior risk adjusted performance. On the other hand, barriers to international investments also exist. Hence, we will discuss risk reduction through attractive correlations, superior expected returns, and trends in barriers.

1.1 Risk Reduction through Attractive Correlations

The objective of risk diversification is to reduce the total risk of a portfolio. Of course, one hopes simultaneously to achieve high expected returns. The total risk of most stock markets is larger than that of the U.S. market when the dollar is used as the base currency. In part, this is caused currency risk, which adds to the risk of a foreign investment, even though the volatility of national markets is often comparable when measured in their local currency. Nevertheless, the addition of more risky foreign assets to a purely domestic portfolio still reduces its total risk as long as the correlation of the foreign assets with the domestic market is not large. This can be shown mathematically.

Let's consider a portfolio partly invested in domestic assets (e.g, a U.S. stock index for a U.S. investor) and partly invested in foreign assets (e.g, a French stock index). The proportions invested in each asset class is denoted w_d for domestic assets and w_f for foreign assets they sum to 100 percent. The returns are denoted R_p for the portfolio, R_d for the domestic assets, and R_f for the foreign assets. All returns are measured in the base currency (e.g, the U.S. dollar for a U.S. investor). So, the return on foreign assets is subject to currency risk. The domestic and foreign assets have standard deviations denoted σ_d and σ_f, respectively. The total risk of the portfolio is its standard deviation σ_p. The correlation between the two asset classes is denoted $\rho_{d,f}$. Remember that the variance of the portfolio is the square of its standard deviation, and that the covariance between the two asset classes is given by

$$\text{cov}_{d,f} = \rho_{d,f}\sigma_d\sigma_f$$

First note that the expected return on the portfolio is simply equal to the average expected return on the two asset classes:

$$E(R_p) = w_d E(R_d) + w_f E(R_f) \qquad (4.1)$$

A well-known mathematical result is that the variance of the portfolio is equal to

$$\sigma_p^2 = w_d^2\sigma_d^2 + w_f^2\sigma_f^2 + 2w_d w_f \text{cov}_{d,f}$$

or

$$\sigma_p^2 = w_d^2\sigma_d^2 + w_f^2\sigma_f^2 + 2w_d w_f \rho_{d,f}\sigma_d\sigma_f$$

The standard deviation is simply equal to the square root:

$$\sigma_p = (w_d^2\sigma_d^2 + w_f^2\sigma_f^2 + 2w_d w_f \rho_{d,f}\sigma_d\sigma_f)^{1/2} \qquad (4.2)$$

The portfolio's total risk (σ_p) will always be less than the average of the two standard deviations: $w_d\sigma_d + w_f\sigma_f$. The only case in which it will be equal is when the correlation is exactly equal to 1.0 (perfect correlation between the two assets). Otherwise diversification benefits will show, and the lower the correlation, the bigger the risk reduction.

Example 4-1 International Risk Diversification Benefits

Assume that the domestic and foreign assets have standard deviations of $\sigma_d = 15\%$ and $\sigma_f = 17\%$, respectively, with a correlation of $\rho_{d,f} = 0.4$. (1) What is the standard deviation of a portfolio equally invested in domestics and foreign assets? (2) What is the standard deviation of a portfolio with a 40 percent investment in the foreign asset? (3) What is the standard deviation of a portfolio equally invested in domestic and foreign assets if the correlation is 0.5? What if the correlation is 0.8?

Solution:

(1) $\sigma_p^2 = 0.5^2[\sigma_d^2 + \sigma_f^2 + (2\rho_{df}\sigma_d\sigma_f)]$

$= 0.5^2[225 + 289 + (2 \times 0.4 \times 255)] = 179.5$

Hence, the standard deviation is given by $\sqrt{179.5}$, or 13.4%

(2) $\sigma_p^2 = (0.6^2 \times \sigma_d^2) + (0.4^2 \times \sigma_f^2) + (2 \times 0.4 \times 0.6\rho_{d,f}\sigma_d\sigma_f)$

$= 176.2$

The standard deviation is 13.27%

> (3) If the correlation is 0.5 instead of 0.4, the risk of the portfolio equally invested becomes $\sigma_p = 13.87\%$. If the correlation is 0.8, the risk of the portfolio equally invested becomes $\sigma_p = 15.18\%$. The risk of the portfolio increases with the level of correlation.

1.1.1 Currency Considerations

The return and risk of an asset depend on the currency used. For example, the return and risk of a French asset will be different if measured in the euro or in the dollar. The dollar value of the asset is equal to its euro value multiplied by the exchange rate (number of dollars per euro):

$$V^\$ = V \times S \tag{4.3}$$

where V and $V^\$$ are, respectively, the values in the local currency (euro) and in the dollar, and S is the exchange rate (number of dollars per euro). The rate of return in dollars from time 0 to time 1 is given by

$$r^\$ = \frac{V_1^\$ - V_0^\$}{V_0^\$} = \frac{V_1 S_1 - V_0 S_0}{V_0 S_0} = \frac{V_1 - V_0}{V_0} + \frac{S_1 - S_0}{S_0} + \frac{V_1 - V_0}{V_0} \times \frac{S_1 - S_0}{S_0}$$
$$= r + s + (r \times s) \tag{4.4}$$

where r is the return in local currency, $r^\$$ is the return in dollars, and s is the percentage exchange rate movement.

For example, if the return on a French asset is 5% in euros and the euro appreciates by 1 percent, the return in dollar is 6.05 percent. This is slightly different from the sum of the euro return and of the currency movement, because the currency appreciation applies not only to the original capital, but also to the capital gain. This cross-product is equal to $5\% \times 1\% = 0.05\%$.

It is easy to compare the risks of an asset measured in different currencies. To simplify notations, it is usually assumed that the cross-product $r \times s$ is small relative to r and s and can be ignored for risk calculations. Hence, the variance of the dollar return is simply equal to the variance of the sum of the local currency return and of the exchange rate movement:

$$var(r^\$) = var(r + s) = var(r) + var(s) + 2cov(r, s)$$

or

$$\sigma_f^2 = \sigma^2 + \sigma_s^2 + 2\rho\sigma\sigma_s \tag{4.5}$$

where, σ_f^2 is the variance of the foreign asset measured in dollars, σ^2 is its variance in local currency, σ_s^2 is the variance of the exchange rate (number of dollars per local currency), and ρ is the correlation between the asset return, in local currency, and the exchange rate movement. As the correlation is never greater than 1.0, the asset and currency risks are not additive, and we have:

$$\sigma_f \leqslant \sigma + \sigma_s$$

The difference between σ_f and σ is called the contribution of currency risk.

Example 4-2 Currency Risk Contribution

Suppose that we have a foreign investment with the following characteristics $\sigma = 15.5\%$, $\sigma_s = 7\%$ and $\rho = 0$. What is the risk in domestic currency and the contribution of currency risk?

Solution:

We have:

$$\sigma_f^2 = \sigma^2 + \sigma_s^2 + 0 = (15.5)^2 + (7.0)^2 = 289.25$$

Hence the standard deviation σ is given by $\sqrt{289.25}$, or 17 percent. Note that this number is well below the sum of the risk of the asset measured in the local currency ($\sigma = 15.5\%$) and the risk of the currency ($\sigma_s = 7\%$). Currency risk only Increases the asset risk from 15.5 percent in the local currency to 17 percent in domestic currency. Hence the difference between σ_f and σ is the contribution of currency risk, here $\sigma_f - \sigma = 1.5\%$.

1.1.2 Efficient Portfolios

A portfolio is mean-variance efficient if it has the highest level of expected return for a given level of risk. The set of all efficient portfolios is called the efficient frontier.

Example 4-3 Risk-Return Trade-off of International Diversified Portfolios

Assume that the domestic and foreign assets have standard deviations of $\sigma_d = 15\%$ and $\sigma_f = 17\%$, respectively, with a correlation of $\rho_{d,f} = 0.4$. The expected returns of the domestic and foreign assets are equal, respectively, to $E(R_d) = 10\%$ and $E(R_f) = 12\%$. Draw the set of all portfolios combining these two assets with positive weights in a risk-return graph.

Solution:

We can use equations 4.1 and 4.2 to derive the set of portfolios invested in various proportions in the two assets. Their representation in a risk-return graph is given in Figure 4.2, in which D and F represent the domestic and foreign assets respectively.

Of course, one can invest in many different domestic and international assets. Combining all domestic stocks in an efficient mean-variance fashion, we derive the domestic efficient frontier represented in Figure 4.3. Combining all domestic and international stocks in an efficient mean-variance fashion, we derive the global mean-variance-efficient frontier represented on the same Figure. The global efficient frontier is to the left of the domestic efficient frontier, showing the increased return opportunities and risk diversification benefits brought by the enlarged investment universe. For example, portfolio A is on the domestic efficient frontier. Portfolio B on the global efficient frontier has the same return but less risk than portfolio A; portfolio C on the global efficient frontier has the same risk but more return than portfolio A.

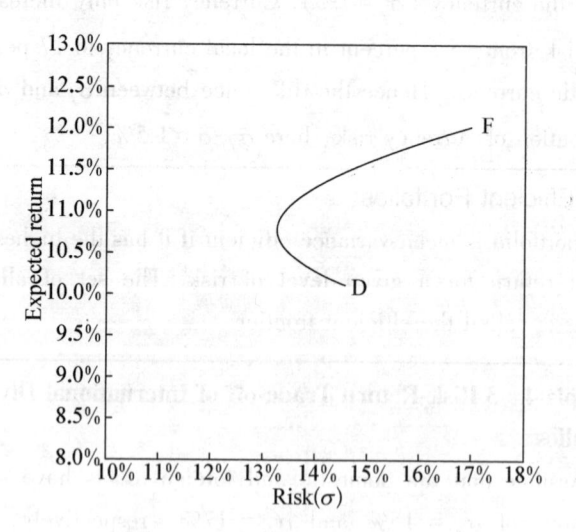

Figure 4.2 Risk-Return trade-off of Internationally Diversified Portfolios

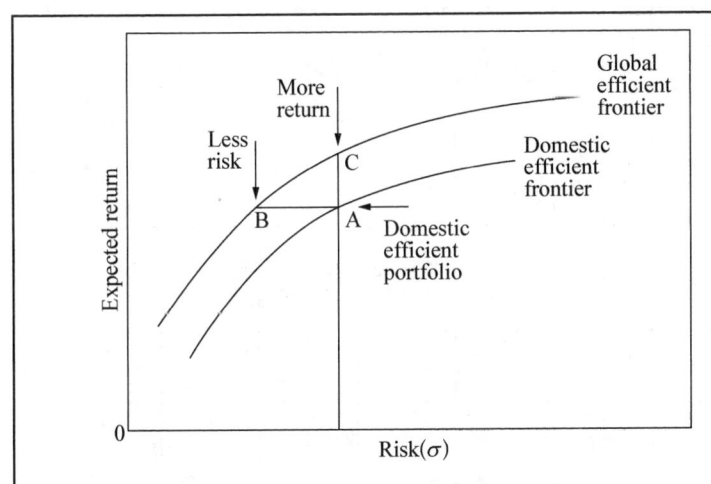

Figure 4.3 Risk-Return trade-off of Internationally Diversified versus Domestic-only Portfolios

A prerequisite for this argument is that the various capital markets of the world have somewhat independent price behaviors. If the Paris Bourse and the London Stock Exchange moved in parallel with the U.S. market, diversification opportunities would not exist. So, we start by an empirical investigation of the level of international correlation.

The correlations between various stock and bond markets are systematically monitored by major international money managers. Although the correlation coefficients between markets vary over time, they are always far from unity. For the portfolio manager, this means that there is ample room for successful risk diversification. Following is a discussion of some recently estimated correlations, as illustration. Correlation estimates change somewhat over time, and the issue of stability in the correlation is discussed in the next sections of this chapter.

1.1.3 Equity

Table 4.1 gives the correlations across selected national stock markets with returns measured in two different currencies over the 10-year period January 1992 to January 2002. The bottom left part of the matrix gives the correlation when all returns are measured in U.S. dollars. The top right part of the matrix gives the correlation when the foreign investments are fully hedged against currency risk; in other words, the foreign currency is assumed to be sold forward for an amount equal to that of the foreign stock investment. Let's first examine the correlations when no currency hedging is undertaken (U.S. dollar returns).

Table 4.1 Correlation of Stock Markets, 1997—2007 Monthly returns in U.S. dollars (bottom left) and currency hedged (top right)

	United States	Canada	United Kingdom	France	Germany	Italy	Switzerland	Japan	Hong Kong	Europe	EAFE	World	Emerging Markets
United States	1.00	0.73	0.74	0.71	0.73	0.55	0.66	0.41	0.51	0.77	0.77	0.91	0.67
Canada	0.72	1.00	0.60	0.65	0.61	0.51	0.56	0.47	0.54	0.67	0.70	0.77	0.70
United Kingdom	0.73	0.62	1.00	0.76	0.72	0.66	0.73	0.40	0.46	0.86	0.83	0.82	0.59
France	0.70	0.66	0.77	1.00	0.87	0.78	0.77	0.45	0.39	0.91	0.88	0.83	0.59
Germany	0.73	0.63	0.73	0.86	1.00	0.72	0.71	0.42	0.39	0.88	0.85	0.83	0.61
Italy	0.52	0.51	0.62	0.78	0.71	1.00	0.65	0.36	0.26	0.80	0.75	0.68	0.50
Switzerland	0.57	0.51	0.70	0.72	0.64	0.62	1.00	0.45	0.37	0.81	0.80	0.76	0.54
Japan	0.43	0.50	0.40	0.35	0.30	0.23	0.40	1.00	0.31	0.47	0.66	0.56	0.56
Hong Kong	0.51	0.55	0.48	0.41	0.41	0.28	0.37	0.43	1.00	0.45	0.50	0.54	0.66
Europe	0.76	0.69	0.86	0.91	0.88	0.78	0.78	0.40	0.48	1.00	0.92	0.88	0.65
EAFE	0.76	0.74	0.83	0.85	0.81	0.70	0.76	0.65	0.57	0.90	1.00	0.90	0.72
World	0.91	0.78	0.81	0.81	0.81	0.64	0.69	0.56	0.57	0.87	0.90	1.00	0.74
Emerging Markets	0.66	0.72	0.58	0.60	0.62	0.49	0.47	0.52	0.68	0.65	0.73	0.74	1.00

For example, Table 4.1 indicates that the correlation between the Japanese and U.S. stock markets is 0.43. The square of this correlation coefficient, usually called R^2, indicates the percentage of common variance between the two markets. Here only 18 percent ($R^2 = 0.43^2$) of stock-price movements are common to the Japanese and U.S. markets. Note that, on the average, the common variance between the U.S. and other markets is 37 percent (average R of 0.61). The correlation with Canada is, of course, quite strong (0.71), because the two economies are closely linked. Other groups of countries are also highly correlated, indicating strong regional links. Germany and France tend to have high correlations because their economies are interrelated. Conversely, Japan shows little correlation with European or U.S. markets. This result confirms that the Japanese business cycle has been somewhat disconnected from the rest of the world.

The last four rows and columns in Table 4.1 give the correlation of each national market with four international indexes. The first three indexes are computed in U.S. dollar terms by Morgan Stanley Capital International for developed equity markets. The world index is a market capitalization-weighted index of all the major stock markets of the world. The Europe, Australasia, and Far East (EAFE) index is the non-American world index and is made up of stock markets from those parts of the world. The Europe index is made up of stock markets from Western Europe. The correlation of the U.S. market with the EAFE index is only 0.76. Therefore, the overall common variance between U.S. and non-US. stock indexes is 58 percent ($R^2 = 0.76^2$). This implies that any well-diversified portfolio of non-U.S. stocks provides an attractive risk-diversification vehicle for a domestic U.S. portfolio.

The correlation of the U.S stock market with the world index is much larger ($R^2 = 0.91^2 = 83\%$) than it is for the EAFE index. But this should not be surprising, because the U.S. market accounts for a significant share of the world market.

In general, the low correlation across countries offers risk-diversification and return enhancement opportunities. It allows naive investors to spread risk, because some foreign markets are likely to go up when others go down. This also provides opportunities for expert international investors to time the markets by buying those markets that they expect to go up and neglecting the bearish ones.

The degree of independence of a stock market is directly linked to the independence of a nation's economy and governmental policies. To some extent, common world factors affect expected cash flows of all firms and therefore their stock prices. However, purely national or regional factors seem to play an important role in asset prices. leading to sizable differences in the degrees of independence among markets. It is clear that constraints and regulations imposed by national governments, technological specialization, independent fiscal and monetary policies, and cultural and sociological differences all contribute to the degree of a capital market's independence. On the other hand, when there are closer economic and governmental policies, as among the euro countries, one observes more commonality in capital market behavior. In any case, the covariation between markets is still far from unity, leaving ample opportunities for risk diversification.

The last row/column of Table 4.1 reports the correlation with a diversified index of emerging markets. Emerging markets present a positive but rather low correlation with developed markets; the correlation with the world index of developed markets is around 0.66.

Let's now examine the correlation across stock markets when full currency hedging is undertaken. The correlation coefficients in the top right part of the matrix are very similar to those in the bottom left part. For example, the correlation between the U.S. and French markets remains the same, the correlation between the U.S. and Italian markets increases slightly to 0.34; but some other correlations are slightly smaller such as the correlation between the China Hong Kong and Japanese markets (0.17 versus 0.24). There is little difference between stock market correlations when we look at hedged and unhedged returns.

1.1.4 Bonds

Similar conclusions can be reached for bonds, as can be seen in Table 4.2, which is presented in a fashion similar to that of Table 4.1. Let's first look at the correlation of the various bond markets when returns are all expressed in U.S. dollars (the bottom left part of the Table 4.2). For example, the correlation of U.S. dollar returns of U.S. and French bonds is only 0.38, or an average percentage of common variance of less than 15 percent (the square of 0.38). The correlation of U.S. bonds with every foreign bond market is below 0.50. Canadian dollar bonds are most strongly correlated with U.S. dollar bonds. In general, long-term return variations are not highly correlated across countries.

Chapter 4 The Practice for International Diversification

Table 4.2 Correlation of Bond Markets, January 1992–2002 Monthly Returns in U.S. Dollar (bottom right) and Currency Hedged (top right)

	United States	Canada	United Kingdom	France	Germany	Italy	Switzerland	Netherlands	Japan	U.S. Equity
United States	1.00	0.64	0.51	0.49	0.55	0.33	0.67	0.57	0.23	0.19
Canada	0.49	1.00	0.47	0.37	0.36	0.28	0.23	0.38	0.16	0.26
United Kingdom	0.49	0.30	1.00	0.68	0.74	0.50	0.51	0.75	0.05	0.19
France	0.38	0.11	0.61	1.00	0.85	0.71	0.63	0.83	0.09	0.09
Germany	0.40	0.13	0.62	0.92	1.00	0.58	0.68	0.94	0.25	0.07
Italy	0.27	0.23	0.54	0.61	0.53	1.00	0.34	0.57	0.08	0.21
Switzerland	0.32	0.05	0.50	0.88	0.89	0.43	1.00	0.71	0.24	-0.05
Netherlands	0.40	0.14	0.59	0.96	0.96	0.55	0.90	1.00	0.24	0.12
Japan	0.17	0.06	0.23	0.42	0.46	0.12	0.50	0.48	1.00	-0.09
U.S. Equity	0.19	0.41	0.17	-0.01	0.00	0.08	-0.14	0.01	0.11	1.00

Regional blocs do appear. European bond markets tend to be quite correlated. This is especially true of countries from the Eurozone, because a common currency was progressively introduced over the period under study. The Eurozone bond markets now Figure a correlation close to 1.0 for government bonds.

The general observation is that national monetary/budget policies are not fully synchronized. For example, the growing U.S. budget deficit in the mid-1980s, associated with high U.S. interest rates and a rapid weakening of the dollars, was not matched in other countries. The relative independence of national monetary/budget policies, influencing both currency and interest rate movements, leads to a surprisingly low correlation of U.S. dollar returns on the U.S. and foreign bond markets. Hence, foreign bonds allow investors to diversify the risks associated with domestic monetary/budget policies.

Finally, the last asset class in Table 4.2 is U.S. equity. The correlation of foreign bonds with the U.S. stock market is quite small. This is not surprising, given the independence between U.S. and foreign national economic and monetary policies. Foreign bonds offer excellent diversification benefits to a U.S. stock portfolio manager.

Let us now examine the correlation across bond markets when full currency hedging is undertaken. The correlation coefficients in the top-right part of the matrix are somewhat different from the U.S. dollar correlations. This is because there exists a correlation between currency movements and bond yield movements (and hence bond returns). For example, some countries practice a "leaning against the wind" policy, whereby they raise their interest rates to defend their currencies. So the correlation of two national bond markets would be different if we look at hedged returns or at currency-adjusted returns.

1.1.5 Leads and Lags

So far, we have talked about the contemporaneous correlation across markets taking place when an event or factor affects two or more markets simultaneously. Some investigators have attempted to find leads or lags between markets. For example, they studied whether a bear market in February on Wall Street would lead to a drop in prices on other national markets in March. No evidence of a systematic delayed reaction of one national market to another has ever been found, except for daily returns, as outlined later. The existence of such simple market inefficiencies is, Indeed, unlikely, because it would be easy to exploit them to make an abnormal profit.

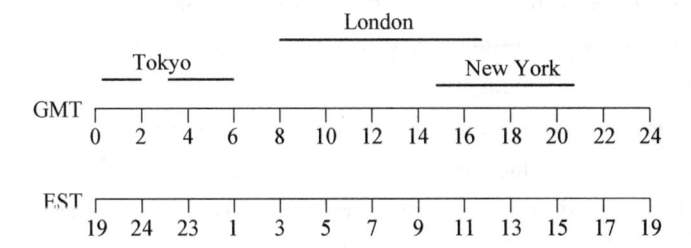

```
                    London
          Tokyo     ─────────
         ─────             New York
                                ─────
GMT ┌──┬──┬──┬──┬──┬──┬──┬──┬──┬──┬──┐
    0  2  4  6  8  10 12 14 16 18 20 22 24

EST ┌──┬──┬──┬──┬──┬──┬──┬──┬──┬──┬──┐
    19 24 23 1  3  5  7  9  11 13 15 17 19
```

Figure 4.4 Stock Exchange Trade Hours in Greenwich Mean Time and Eastern Time Clocks

One must take into account the time differences around the world, however, before assessing whether a given national market leads or lags other markets. The stock exchanges in New York and Tokyo are not open at the same time. If important news hits New York prices on a Tuesday, it will affect Tokyo prices on Wednesday. If important news hits London prices on a Tuesday, it will affect New York prices the same day, because New York generally lags London by five hours. Indeed, when it is Tuesday noon in New York, it is already Tuesday 17:00 (or 5 P.M.) local time in London and Wednesday 02:00 (or 2 A.M.) in Tokyo. The opening and closing times of the three major stock markets are depicted in Figure 4.4, in which the trading hours are indicated using both the universal GMT (Greenwich Mean Time) and the American EST (Eastern Standard Time). It can be seen that New York and Tokyo official trading hours never overlap. London and New York trading hours generally overlap for two hours. If the markets are efficient, international news should affect all markets around the globe simultaneously, with markets closed at that hour reflecting the news immediately on opening. For example, important news is revealed after noon EST, it can be impounded in Japanese and British stock prices only the next day; because of the time differences involved, we should not be surprised to find a lagging correlation of Tokyo and London with New York when returns are measured from closing price to closing price. This lagged correlation can be explained by the difference in time zones, not by some international market inefficiency that could be exploited to make a profit. This effect gets drastically reduced when looking at correlation of longer-period return, for example, monthly returns.

1.2 Portfolio Return Performance

We have devoted so much attention to the risk-reduction benefits of international investment because risk diversification is the most established and frequently invoked argument in favor of foreign investment, justifying foreign investment even to the naive investor. However, risk reduction is not the sole motive for international investment. Indeed, mere risk reduction could more easily be achieved by simply investing part of one's assets in domestic risk-free bills. Unfortunately, although the inclusion of risk-free bills lowers the portfolio risk, it also lowers expected return.

In the traditional framework of the capital asset pricing model (CAPM), the expected return on a security is equal to the risk-free rate plus a risk premium. In an efficient market, reducing the risk level of a portfolio by adding less-risky investments implies reducing its expected return.

> 国际投资的风险降低效应是非常值得重视的,因为风险分散是支持国际投资强有力的证据,甚至对普通投资者来说也是如此。

Example 4-4 Sharpe Ratio

Assume that the domestic and foreign assets have standard deviations of $\sigma_d = 15\%$ and $\sigma_f = 17\%$, respectively, with a correlation of $\rho_{d,f} = 0.4$. The risk-free rate is equal to 4% in both countries. (1) If $E(R_d) = E(R_f) = 10\%$. Calculate the Sharpe ratios for the domestic asset, the foreign asset, and an internationally diversified portfolio equally invested in the domestic and foreign assets. What do you conclude? (2) Assume now that the expected return on the foreign asset is higher than on the domestic asset, $E(R_d) = 10\%$ but $E(R_f) = 12\%$. Calculate the Sharpe ratio for an internationally diversified portfolio equally invested the domestic and foreign assets, and compare your findings to those in question 1.

Solution:

(1) The domestic asset:

$$Shape\ Ratio = \frac{E(R) - riskfree\ rate}{\sigma} = \frac{10\% - 4\%}{15\%} = 0.4$$

The foreign asset: Sharpe ratio = (10%−4%)/17% = 0.353

A portfolio equally invested in the domestic and foreign asset:

$$\sigma_p^2 = 0.5^2[\sigma_d^2 + \sigma_f^2 + (2\rho_{df}\sigma_d\sigma_f)]$$
$$= 0.5^2[225 + 289 + (2 \times 0.4 \times 255)] = 179.5$$

Hence, the standard deviation is given by $\sqrt{179.5}$, or 13.4%.

The Sharpe ratio of the portfolio is equal to:

$$ShapeRatio = \frac{E(R_p) - riskfree\ rate}{\sigma_p} = \frac{10\% - 4\%}{13.4\%} = 0.448$$

The foreign asset has a lesser Sharpe ratio than the domestic asset because it has the same expected return but a larger standard deviation. However, the equally weighted portfolio benefits from risk diversification and a lower standard deviation. Hence its Sharpe ratio is better than the ratios of both the domestic and the foreign assets.

(2) A portfolio equally invested in the domestic and foreign asset has now an expected return of 11 percent ($0.5 \times 10\% + 0.5 \times 12\% = 11\%$), Hence the Sharpe ratio is equal to ($11\% - 4\%$)/$13.4\% = 0.522$. The portfolio's Sharpe ratio is now better than that of the domestic asset (0.4), both because of risk-diversification benefits and because of the superior expected return of the foreign asset [new Sharpe ratio of ($12\% - 4\%$)/$17\% = 0.471$].

International diversification, however, implies no reduction in expected return. Such diversification lowers risk by eliminating nonsystematic volatility without sacrificing expected return. A traditional way to evaluate a portfolio's risk-adjusted performance is to evaluate its Sharpe ratio. This is the ratio of the return on a portfolio, in excess of the risk-free rate, divided by its standard deviation. Money managers attempt to maximize this Sharpe ratio, which gives the excess return per unit of risk. Global investing should increase the Sharper ratio because of the reduction in risk investing in foreign assets allows a reduction in portfolio risk (the denominator of the Sharpe ratio), without necessarily sacrificing expected return (the numerator of the Sharpe ratio). Both domestic and foreign investors can see their Sharpe ratio increase if they diversify away from purely local assets. As long as the expected returns on domestic and foreign are comparable, both types of investors would benefit from international risk reduction compared to a portfolio of purely local assets. The second argument for an increase in the Sharpe ratio is that more profitable investments are possible in an enlarged investment universe. Higher expected returns may arise from faster-growing economies and firms located around the world, or simply from currency gains. These advantages can be obtained by optimizing the global asset allocation.

It is easy to derive the global asset allocation that would have been optimal from a risk-return viewpoint over some past period, but the results depend on the period selected. To illustrate such an analysis, Figure 4.5 shows optimal global stock allocations for different risk levels and for a U.S. investor, as reported by Odier and Solnik (1993). This is the efficient frontier based on returns for the period 1980—1990. No investment constraints other than no short selling are applied; results do not reflect any currency hedging. The mean annual return is given on the Y axis, and the asset volatility (standard deviation) is given on the X axis. Each asset or portfolio is represented by one point on the graph (a few selected markets are plotted on the graph). The U.S. stock market has a risk of 16.2 percent and an annualized total return of 13.3 percent. Other stock markets are more volatile, partly because of currency risk. By combining the various national stock markets, we get diversified portfolios whose returns and risks can be calculated. because we know the returns and covariances of all the assets. Investors select asset allocations that lie on the efficient frontier depicted in Figure 4.5. The best achievable risk-return trade-offs—the optimal asset allocations—lie on the efficient frontier.

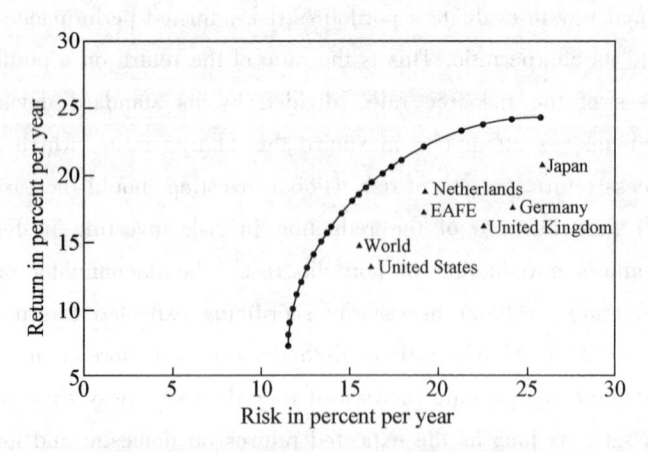

Figure 4.5 Efficient Frontier for Stocks (U.S. dollar, 1980—1990)

As Figure 4.5 shows, international diversification of a pure U.S.

stock portfolio would greatly enhance returns without a large increase in risk. A global stock portfolio with the same risk level as the purely U.S. stock portfolio (16.2 percent per year) would achieve an annualized total return above 19 percent, compared with 13.3 percent for the U.S. portfolio.

Can bonds help improve the risk-adjusted performance of globally diversified portfolios? The question here is not whether investors should prefer portfolios made up solely of bonds or solely of stocks, but whether bonds should be added to a stock portfolio in a global investment strategy. Figure 4.6 gives the efficient frontier for a global asset allocation allowing for bonds and stocks, foreign and domestic. To keep the figure readable, we did not plot individual bond and stock markets, but only the U.S. bond and stock indexes, as well as the world stock index. Their relative positions are consistent with theory. The U.S. bonds have a lower risk and a lower return. Over the long run, riskier stock investments are compensated by a risk premium. The global asset allocations on the efficient frontier strongly dominate U.S. investments. The global efficient asset allocation with a return equal to that of the U.S. stock market (13.3 percent per year) has a risk equal to only half that of the U.S. stock market. Conversely, a global efficient allocation with the same risk as the U.S. stock market outperforms the U.S. stock market by 8 percent per year. Similarly, any domestic U.S. stock/bond strategy is strongly dominated by a global stock/bond strategy. A domestic portfolio of U.S.

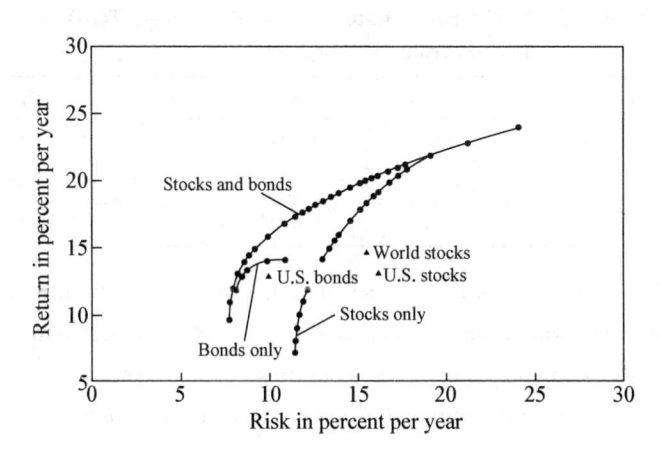

Source: P. Odier and B. Solnik. Adapted from "Lessons for International Asset Allocation," *Financial Analysis Journal*, March/April 1993. Copyright © 2007 CFA institute. All Rights Reserved.

Figure 4.6　Global Efficient Frontier for Stocks and Bonds (U.S. dollar, 1980—1990)

stocks and bonds tends to have half the return of that on a global efficient allocation with the same risk level. Adding foreign bonds in a global asset allocation can be attractive from a risk-return viewpoint because of their low correlation with domestic bond and stock investments as outlined previously.

Figure 4.6 also shows the global efficient frontier for stocks only (same as Figure 4.5), as well as the efficient international frontier for bonds only. Clearly, stocks offer a strong contribution to a bond portfolio in terms of risk-return trade-off; the bond-only efficient frontier is also dominated by a global strategy.

1.3 Forward-Looking Optimization

> 尽管事后事件得出一些有趣的经验,但投资组合管理需要有前瞻性。

Although ex post exercises yield some interesting general lessons, portfolio management needs to be forward looking. An adequate global asset allocation should be based on market forecasts, not on past returns. Several factors can help formulate expectations.

In the long run, the performance of stock markets can be explained by national economic factors. This can be seen in Table 4.3, which gives the mean annual growth rate in GDP for successive 10-year periods for the United States, Japan, Europe, and the average of all OECD countries. For example, real growth was much higher in Japan than in the United States in the 1970s and 1980s, and much lower in the 1990s. The stock markets' performance followed the same pattern.

Table 4.3　Real Growth Rate of Selected Regions, Ten-Year Periods from 1971 to 2000

GDP Growth	United States	Japan	Europe	OECD
1971—1980	2.76%	4.51%	2.95%	3.13%
1981—1990	2.48%	4.15%	2.34%	2.71%
1991—2000	3.40%	1.30%	2.50%	2.30%

Economic flexibility is also an important factor in investment performance, which may explain differences between past and future performances among emerging countries. Wage and employment rigidity are bad for the national economy. In countries such as France, Canada, and Sweden, corporations have a difficult time adjusting to slowing activity; on the other hand, they do not take full advantage of growth opportunities, because they are reluctant to hire new employees, whom they cannot fire if activity slows.

Economic forecasting is a useful exercise, but it should be stressed that scenarios that are widely expected to take place should already be impounded in current asset prices. For example, if a Country X is widely expected to experience higher economic growth than other countries, it should be reflected in higher stock prices in country X. If future growth develops according to expectations, there is no reason to have higher future returns for stocks of Country X. So, investors forecasting economic growth rates must take into account the market consensus about future growth rates.

It should be stressed that there is no guarantee that the past will repeat itself. Indeed, over any given period, one national market is bound to outperform the other, and if an investor had perfect foresight, the best strategy would be to invest solely in the top-performing market, or even in the top-performing security in that market. But because of the great uncertainty of forecasts, it is always better to spread risk in the fund by diversifying globally across markets with comparable expected returns. This ensures a favorable risk-return trade-off or, in the jargon of theory, higher risk-adjusted expected returns. If managers believe that they have some relative forecasting ability, they will engage in active investment strategies that reap the benefits of international risk diversification while focusing on preferred markets. For example, a U.S. investor may concentrate on U.S. and European stocks if she is bullish on those markets and may avoid Japan for political or currency reasons.

Some emerging economies offer attractive investment opportunities. The local risks (volatility, liquidity, political environment) are higher, as illustrated by numerous crises, but the expected profit is large. Furthermore, those risks get partly diversified away in a global portfolio. Hence, emerging markets and alternative investments can have a positive contribution in terms of risk-return trade-offs.

1.4 Currency Risk Not a Barrier to International Investment

Currency fluctuations affect both the total return and the volatility of any foreign currency-denominated investment. From time to time, in fact, the effects of currency fluctuations on the investment return may exceed that of capital gain or income, especially over short periods of time. Empirical studies indicate that currency risk, as measured by the standard deviation of the exchange rate movement, is

货币波动会影响任何外币计价投资的总回报和波动性。

smaller than the risk of the corresponding stock market (roughly half). On the other hand, currency risk is often larger than the risk (in local currency) of the corresponding bond market (roughly twice). In a global portfolio, the depreciation of one currency is often offset by the appreciation of another. Indeed, several points are worth mentioning regarding currency risk.

First, market and currency risks are not additive. This would be true only if the two were perfectly correlated. In fact, there is only a weak, and sometimes negative correlation between currency and market movements. This point was stressed in the previous section. In Example 6.2, the exchange rate standard deviation is 7% compared with a local-currency standard deviation of 15.5 percent for the foreign stock. However, the contribution of currency risk to total risk is only 1.5 percentage points. So, currency risk only adds some 10 percent (1.5 percent as a fraction of 15.5 percent) to the risk of a foreign asset. This is a typical figure. The correlation between changes in the exchange rate and the asset price is an important element in assessing the contribution of currency risk. The lower the correlation, the smaller the contribution of currency risk to total risk.

Second, the exchange risk of an investment may be hedged for major currencies by selling futures or forward currency contracts, buying put currency options, or even borrowing foreign currency to finance the investment. So, currency risk can easily be eliminated in international investment strategies. But currencies can also provide some attractive profit opportunities.

Third, the contribution of currency risk should be measured for the total portfolio rather than for individual markets or securities, because part of that risk gets diversified away by the mix of currencies represented in the portfolio. As stressed by Jorion (1989), the contribution of currency risk to the total risk of a portfolio that includes only a small proportion of foreign assets (say, 5 percent) is insignificant. The contribution of currency risk is larger if one holds the world market portfolio and, hence, a large share of foreign assets actually holding some foreign currency assets can provide some diversification to domestic fiscal and monetary risks. A lax domestic monetary policy can be bad for domestic asset prices and lead to a home-currency depreciation. Foreign currencies help diversify that risk.

Fourth, the contribution of currency risk decreases with the length of the investment horizon. Exchange rates tend to revert to fundamentals over the long run (mean reversion). Hence, an investor with a long time horizon should care less about currency risk than should an investor who is concerned about monthly fluctuations in the portfolio's value. Froot (1993) shows that currency risk can disappear over very long term horizons (over one or several decades).

2 The Case Against International Diversification

Several impediments to international portfolio investing are often mentioned. First, the case for international diversification presented earlier has been attacked basis that it strongly overstates the risk benefits of international investing. Second, skeptics also look at the historical performance of their domestic market relative to other foreign markets. Third, there are numerous physical barriers to international investing.

2.1 Increase in Correlations

It is often argued that the benefits of international diversification are overstated because markets tend to be more synchronized than suggested previously. There is no reason for the correlation between two equity markets to remain constant over a long period of time. Indeed, it has been observed that international correlations have trended upward over the past decade. It has also been observed that international correlation increases in periods of high market volatility.

2.1.1 Correlations Have Increased over Time

Economies and financial markets are becoming increasingly integrated, leading to an increase in international correlation of asset prices. Economic and financial globalization observed at the turn of the millennium can be witnessed in many areas.

- Capital markets are being deregulated and opened to foreign players. Markets that used to be segmented are moving toward global integration.
- Capital mobility has increased, especially among developed countries. International capital flows have dramatically increased since the 1950s. The success of international investing means that foreign institutional investors, such as pension funds, are now major players on most domestic markets.
- National economies are opening up to free trade, in part under the pressure of the World Trade Organization and of regional

agreements such as NAFTA, ASEAN, and the European Union. Hence, national economies are becoming more synchronized.

- As the economic environment becomes global, corporations become increasingly global in their operations. They achieve this global strategy through increased exports, international organic growth, and foreign acquisitions. A simple indicator is provided by the amount of cross-border mergers and acquisition (M&As) shown in Figure 4.7. The amount of cross-border M&As has risen dramatically from 1991 to 2000, both in dollar amount and in percentage of world GDP. Cross-border M&As were few in the early nineties, but they have become an increasing proportion of total M&As. While the economic slowdown of the early 2000s has slowed down M&As, the share of cross-border M&As among total M&As is still on the rise.

As corporations become more global, it is not surprising to see the correlation between their stock prices increase. The legal nationality of a corporation becomes less important. As a firm competes globally and derives a significant part of its cash flows from abroad, its value is affected by global factors, not primarily by the location of its headquarters. Hence, it is not surprising to find that country factors become less important and that the correlation among national stock markets tends to increase.

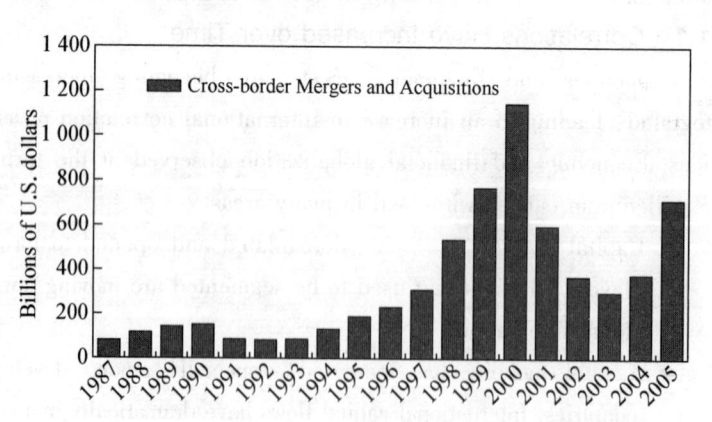

Figure 4.7   Value of Cross-Border M&As, 1987—2005

International correlations move over time, as can be seen on Table 4.3. Correlation is high in periods when global shocks affect all countries (e.g, the oil shock of the early 1970s) and lower in other periods. However, Table 4.3 suggests that the correlation between the

U.S. and other stock markets has been trending upward since 1975.

2.1.2 Correlation Increases When Markets Are Volatile

A major criticism addressed to the mean-variance framework used to present the case for international diversification is that it assumes "normality". In statistical terms, all returns are supposed to have a "joint multivariate normal distribution." In real life, returns are not exactly drawn from normal probability tables with constant correlations across assets. Three deviations from market "normality" are most often mentioned:

- Distributions of returns tend to have fat tails (leptokurtic distribution). In other words, the occurrence of large positive or negative returns is more frequent than expected under normal distributions.
- Market volatility varies over time, but volatility is "contagious". In other words, high volatility in the U.S. stock market tends to be associated with high volatility in foreign stock markets, as well as in other financial markets (bond, currency).
- The correlation across markets increases dramatically in periods of high volatility, for example, during major market events such as the October 1987 crash.

The fact that there are fat tails or that volatility tends to move up or down together on all markets is not a direct attack on global risk diversification. It simply says that a static mean-variance analysis is a simplified view of the world and that more sophisticated quantitative methods could be used; but it does not negate the advantage of international risk reduction. Correlation moves over time for obvious reasons. There are tranquil periods during which domestic factors dominate and markets are not strongly correlated across countries. There are times during which global shocks affect simultaneously all economies, and business cycles move in sync. The oil shock of 1974 provides an example, as shown in Table 4.3, and the correlation measured from 1971 to 1975 was much higher than in the next five years. The correlation estimated over a long period of time is simply an average over these various market cycles. For reasons mentioned previously, correlation of developed stock markets tends to increase slowly over time. But what is really troubling is that correlation seems to increase dramatically in periods of crises, so that the benefits of international risk diversification disappear when they are most needed. This phenomenon is sometimes referred to as "correlation breakdown."

If all markets crash when your domestic market is crashing, there is little risk benefit to be internationally diversified. While it might be beneficial in "normal" times, it becomes useless in the exceptional times when there is a huge loss on domestic investments. And remember, that fat tails mean that the occurrence of such crashes is more frequent than expected under "normality."

2.2 Past Performance Is a Good Indicator of Future Performance

Another criticism of international investing is country-specific, as it is typically formulated by investors whose markets have enjoyed a prolonged period of good performance. Skeptics point to the fact that, in recent periods, their domestic markets have generated greater returns than most other markets, and hence, that there is no need for international investments in the future. As can be seen on Table 4.3, the Japanese equity market had a superb performance relative to the rest of the world in the 1970s and 1980s. International investing was not in favor in Japan in 1990. A similar attitude has been adopted recently in the United States: U.S. equity yielded greater returns than overseas equity markets, especially Japan, in the 1990s and early 2000s. After a few years of poor performance of their foreign investments relative to domestic equities, U.S. investors were less inclined toward international investing.

Simply extrapolating past performance to forecast future expected returns is questionable. It is unlikely that one country will always outperform all others. Just as one domestic sector is unlikely to continually outperform all other domestic sectors. It could be that one economy is deemed to be more efficient than others, but this should be reflected in higher equity prices. Let's assume, for example, that the U.S. economy is indeed more flexible and competitive than all others in the foreseeable future. In a global context, in which foreign investors extensively invest in the United States and vice versa, this forecast should be discounted today in higher U.S equity prices. If investors share the vision that the U.S. economy will be superior to other economies forever, that forecast should be reflected immediately into higher U.S. stock prices today, not by higher future returns forever. Future outperformance of U.S. stocks must be caused by "surprise," the unexpected news that the U.S. economy is doing even better than expected. To justify continuing outperformance the future, we must go from positive surprise to positive surprise.

2.3 Barriers to International Investments

The relative size of foreign capital markets would justify extensive foreign investment by investors of any nationality. Empirical studies build a strong case for international diversification, However, international investment, although rapidly growing, is still not widespread in several countries and is certainly far from what it should be according to the world market portfolio weights. This conservative behavior may be explained by the prevalence of potential barriers to foreign investment.

> 外国资本市场的相对规模将证明任何国籍的投资者进行大规模外国投资是合理的。

2.3.1 Familiarity with Foreign Markets

Culture differences are a major impediment to foreign investment. Investors are often unfamiliar with foreign cultures and markets. They feel uneasy about the way business is done in other countries: the trading procedures, the way reports are presented, different languages, different time zones, and so on, Many investors, especially Americans, feel more comfortable investing in domestic corporations. In turn, these local corporations provide some international exposure through their exports, foreign subsidiaries, or acquisitions of foreign corporations, Foreign markets and corporations are perceived as more risky simply because they are unfamiliar.

2.3.2 Political Risk

Some countries run the risk of being politically unstable. Many emerging markets have periodically suffered from political, economic, or monetary crises that badly affected the value of local investments. For example, a currency crisis could curtail the dollar value of local investments. Simply looking at a statistical measure of risk based on recent past stock price behavior can be misleading and underestimate the risk of a crisis. A statistician would say that the distribution of return on such investments is not "normal" and that the standard deviation of return is not a good proxy of the risk borne.

2.3.3 Market Efficiency

A first question in market efficiency is that of liquidity. Some markets are very small; others have many issues traded in large volume, Of course, some issues on the major markets, as well as some of the smaller national markets, trade on little volume. Large institutional investors may wish to be careful and invest only a small part of their portfolios in these small-capitalization, less-liquid shares. Indeed, it may be difficult to get out of some national markets on a large scale. An excellent performance on a local index may not translate into a similarly good performance on a specific portfolio because of the share price drop when liquidating the portfolio. Another liquidity risk is the imposition of capital controls on foreign portfolio investments. Such capital control prevents the sale of a portfolio of foreign assets and the repatriation of proceeds. This has never happened on any of the major capital markets of the world; the cost of such a political decision would be very high for any government, because it would reduce its borrowing capacity on the international capital market. However, it is a definite risk for investments in many emerging countries. Such capital controls may be imposed in an extreme financial or political crisis, and international money managers need to carefully monitor a few high-risk countries.

In some countries, corporations do not provide timely and reliable information on their activity and prospects. Foreign investors tend to avoid such corporations. The rapid growth in international investing has put intense pressure on these corporations to live up to the transparency that is the norm in major developed markets.

Another issue in market efficiency is price manipulation and insider trading. If foreign markets were too affected by these problems, a manager would probably not run the risk of investing in these markets to benefit the domestic speculators. Many studies have established that all major stock markets are nearly efficient in the usual sense. Some countries, however, have historically been quite lax in terms of price manipulation, insider trading, and corporate governance. In some countries, majority stockholders can take advantage of their controlling interest to the detriment of minority stockholders. The globalization of financial markets leads to a rapid improvement in national regulations to control this type of behavior. Some U.S. pension plans, notably CalPERS, have been very active in inciting corporations worldwide to improve their corporate governance.

2.3.4 Regulations

In some countries. regulations constrain the amount of foreign investment that can be undertaken by local investors. For example, institutional investors are sometimes constrained on the proportion of foreign assets they can hold in their portfolios. Such quotas can be found in some European countries and even among U.S. public pension plans.

Some countries limit the amount of foreign ownership in their national corporations. This is typically the case for emerging countries, which tend to limit foreign ownership to a maximum percentage of the capital of each firm. This is also the case for some developed countries. For example, Swiss corporations tend to issue special shares to foreign owners, and these shares trade at a premium over those available solely to Swiss nationals. Again, the trend is toward progressive removal of these constraints. For example, the European Union prohibits any ownership discrimination among its members. Such constraints are rarely found for bond investments. All governments are happy to have foreign investors subscribe to their bond issues, financing their budget deficit. Conversely, they often force their national institutional investors to hold domestic bonds. This limits the scope of international investing by these institutional investors.

2.3.5 Transaction Costs

The transaction costs of international investments can be higher than those of domestic investments. It is difficult to calculate the average transaction cost on a typical trade. A first component of transaction costs is the brokerage commission, and it varies in the way it is charged (fixed or negotiable commission, variable schedule, or part of the bid-ask spread). However, brokerage commissions on stocks tend to be low in the United States (typically 0.10 percent for large transactions) and higher in foreign countries (ranging from 0.10 percent to 1.0 percent). In a few countries, commissions are fixed, and a stamp tax applies. However, the deregulation of capital markets is lowering these commissions worldwide. A large component of transaction costs is the price impact of a trade. For example, a large buy order will raise the price. This is a function of the size of the order. Liquidity can be limited on many national stock markets, inducing high transaction costs. However, this effect is present in any country. For example, transaction costs on the Nasdaq can be large, because of the limited liquidity on most issues.

It is even more difficult to quote a so-called average commission for bonds. On most of the major bond markets (including the Eurobond market), prices are quoted net, so that the commissions have to be inferred from the bid-ask spread, which depends on the volume of transactions on a specific bond. In general, commissions on bonds tend to be very low on all markets.

Custody costs tend to add to the costs of international investments. Custody costs tend to be higher for international investments because, here, investors engage in a two-level custodial arrangement, in which a master custodian deals with a network of sub-custodians in every country. Higher costs are also incurred because of the necessity of a multicurrency system of accounting, reporting, and cash flow collection. Some countries have a very inexpensive and efficient centralized custodial system with a single clearinghouse, and local costs tend to be less than in the United States. However, the need for the international network may raise the annual cost to more than 0.10 percent of assets.

Management fees charged by international money managers tend to be higher than those charged by domestic money managers. This is justified by the higher costs borne by the money managers in terms of

- International database subscriptions,
- data collection,
- research,
- the international accounting system,
- communication costs (international telephone, computer links, and travel).

Management fees for foreign portfolios typically run a few basis points higher than fees on similar domestic portfolios. Some investors believe that they can limit costs by simple buying foreign firms listed on their domestic markets (called American Depositary Receipts, or ADRs, in the United States). Although this may be a practical alternative for the private investor, it is a questionable strategy for larger investors. A growing number of companies have multiple listings, but these companies tend to be large multinational firms that provide fewer foreign diversification benefits than a typical foreign firm. Also, the foreign share price of a corporation (e.g, the U.S. dollar ADR price of a French firm) is often determined by its domestic market price adjusted by the exchange rate. When a large order to buy an ADR is received, brokers will generally arbitrage between the prices in New York and the local market. This means that on most ADRs, the execution will be made at a high price compared with the local price (adjusted for the exchange rate). The commission seems low, but the market impact on the price tends to be high. It is often in the best interest of a large customer to deal on the primary market, where there is the largest transaction volume for the shares. However, there are significant exceptions. Several Dutch and British companies have a very large transaction volume on U.S. markets.

2.3.6 Taxes

Withholding taxes exist on most stock markets. The country where a corporation is headquartered generally withholds an income tax on the dividends paid by the corporation. This tax can usually be reclaimed after several months; this time lag creates an opportunity cost. In a very few cases, part of the tax is completely lost, according to the tax treaty between the two countries. Alternatively, a taxable investor may claim this amount as a tax credit in his home country, but this is not possible for a nontaxable investor, such as a pension plan. However, the withholding tax (generally 15 percent) applies only to the dividend yield. For a yield of 2 percent, a total loss of withholding tax on common stocks would imply a 0.30 percent reduction in performance. There are also a few countries (e. g, Australia and France) where investors benefit from some tax credit for the tax that the local corporation has paid on its profits distributed as dividends. This tax credit is not available to nonresidents. Withholding taxes have been progressively eliminated on bonds.

2.3.7 Currency Risk

As discussed, currency risk can be a major cause of the higher volatility of foreign assets, but is often overstated. Furthermore, it is a risk that need not be borne, because it can be hedged with derivatives. Nevertheless, currency hedging leads to additional administrative and trading costs.

2.3.8 Conclusions

Altogether, foreign investment may not seem more costly for a resident from a high-cost country, such as Switzerland, but it is clearly more expensive for a U.S. resident for a U.S. investor, a ballpark estimate of the increase in total costs (management fee, taxes, commissions, custody) is on the order of 0.10 percent to 0.50 percent for stocks and 0 percent to 0.20 percent for bonds. The difference would be less for a passively managed fund. These Figures are still small compared with the risk-return advantage of foreign investment, as presented in the first part of this chapter. However, they could explain why an investor would want to overweigh the domestic component of the portfolio compared with the world market portfolio weights. Information and transaction costs, differential taxes, and sometimes political or transfer risk give a comparative advantage to the domestic investor on the home market. This does not imply that foreign investment should be avoided altogether.

3 The Case for Emerging Markets

3.1 The Basic Case

Emerging economies offer attractive investment opportunities. The local risks (volatility, liquidity, and political risk) are higher, as illustrated by numerous crises, but the expected profit is large.

Figure 4.8 plots the value of the MSCI indexes of developed stock markets ("World") and of emerging stock markets ("Emerging") over the period December 1987 to August 2002. Although the higher volatility of emerging markets is apparent, they also had a significantly larger return over the long run. While most emerging markets were still in their infancy, they had an excellent performance in the early 1980s.

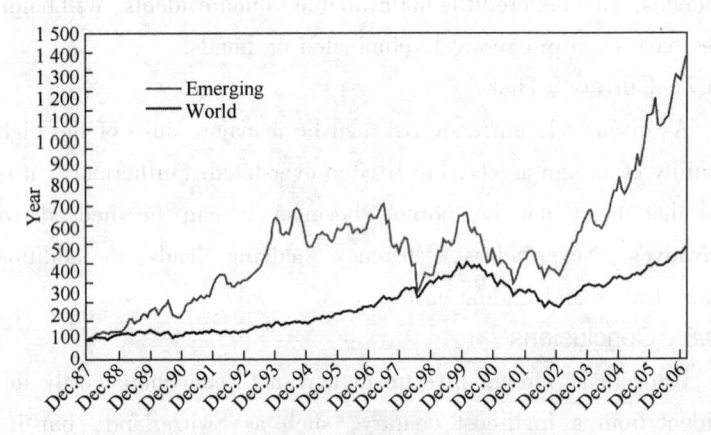

Figure 4.8 Performance of World Developed Markets and Emerging Markets

Emerging markets also present a positive but moderate correlation with developed markets (see Table 4.1); the correlation with the world index of developed markets is around 0.6. Because of the low correlation between emerging and developed markets, the risks of investing in emerging markets get partly diversified away in a global portfolio. Hence, emerging markets can have a positive contribution in terms of risk-return trade-offs. Let's review the main factors affecting expected returns and risks that should be taken into account when including emerging markets in a global asset allocation.

3.2 Volatility, Correlations, and Currency Risk

3.2.1 Volatility

The volatility of emerging markets is much larger than that of developed markets. Furthermore, the distribution of returns is not symmetric, and the probability of a shock (a large price movement) is higher than would be the case if the distribution of returns measure of market risk. Investment risk in emerging economies often comes from the possibility of a crisis.

> 新兴市场的波动性比发达市场大得多。

The development of many emerging markets stems from the winds of political reform. Problems can easily materialize, however. Some emerging countries do not have a fully stable political and social situation. The explosive social transformation serious imbalances, causing social and political unrest.

The infrastructure can limit growth. Thailand, for example, have stretched the limit of their existing road infrastructures. Education structures are often insufficient to train a large number of workers and managers in modern international techniques. Multilateral development banks have made education a priority, but improvements are very slow, as local teachers must first be trained but are then tempted to leave the education system after their training. The quality of goods produced may be below international standards because of a lack of training and quality standards different from those required in developed countries.

Corruption is a rampant problem everywhere but may be more so in some emerging countries. Family ownership tends to favor family and friends at the detriment of other stockholders, especially foreign ones. Links between politicians and company managers sometimes go beyond what would be in the best interest of stockholders. The banking sector is sometimes poorly regulated, unsupervised, undercapitalized for the lending risks assumed, and lacking in the sophistication required by modern financial operations.

3.2.2 Correlation

International correlation tends to increase in periods of crises, and emerging markets are subject to periodic large crises. Patel and Sankar (1998) find that crises on emerging markets tend to be more prolonged than crises on developed markets, and tend to spread to all emerging markets in the region. It is often the case, however, that a

> 在危机时期,国际相关性往往会增加,而新兴市场也容易受到周期性大危机的影响。

crisis affecting one emerging country does not spread to other emerging countries, especially outside of its region. This is the case when the crisis is caused primarily by domestic political problems, many examples can be found in the recent past. An emerging market boom or crisis does not necessarily spread to developed markets, explaining the rather low correlation between developed and emerging markets. Spread depends on whether the factors creating the boom or crisis are primarily local or global.

3.2.3 Currency Risk

Another observation is the correlation between stock and currency returns. Developed markets sometimes exhibit a negative correlation with the value of their currencies. Namely, the local stock market tends to appreciate when the value of the local currency depreciates; the argument is based on an improvement in the international competitiveness of the local firms. This is not the case for emerging stock markets. Both the stock market and the currency are affected by the state of the economy. In periods of crisis, both drop significantly. For example, the Korean won lost more than 50 percent of its value in 1997. and the Seoul stock market also dropped. Both went up significantly in 1998, when the Korean situation showed some encouraging signs. Numerous similar examples could be found in Asia or Latin America. This positive correlation means that foreign investors suffer doubly from currency risk in emerging markets.

3.3 Portfolio Return Performance

Emerging markets have a vocation to become developed markets. To emerge, an equity market has to move from an embryonic stage to that of a truly active market attracting international investors. If successful, the market will grow, become more mature, and reach the stage of becoming a developed market. This process should lead to high returns.

Clearly, a major argument for investing in emerging economies is their prospective economic growth. Portfolio managers want to find countries that will exhibit in the future the type of growth witnessed by Japan between the 1960s and the 1980s. Most analysts expect emerging economies to grow at a higher rate than developed nations, given the liberalization of international trade. Arguments frequently mentioned are lower labor costs, lower level of unionization and social rigidities, delocalization of production by high-cost developed countries, and rapid growth in domestic demand. The arrival of foreign capital helps those countries develop at a rapid pace and to compete on the world goods market. The transition to a more democratic political system with less corruption, more efficient regulation of the financial industry and other sectors, promotion of free enterprise, and application of the rule of law should strongly benefit local stock markets. Some specific factors could also affect the local stock markets. For example, pension funds have recently been created in many Latin American countries and are likely to invest heavily in their local stock markets. Many countries are pursuing an active program of privatization, and more local firms are attracted by the financing potential of stock markets. Under pressure from international investors, emerging markets are becoming more efficient, providing more rigorous research on companies and progressively applying stricter standards of market supervision. Accounting standards that conform with international accounting standards (IAS) have been adopted in many countries and are progressively implemented. Most of these markets have automated their trading and settlement procedures, using computer software tested on developed markets. High returns can be expected in emerging economies that are successful in achieving this transition.

3.4 Investability of Emerging Markets

Foreign investors face restrictions when investing on many emerging markets. Although many emerging countries are very liberal toward foreign capital, investability is somewhat restricted in other countries. Restrictions can take many forms:

- Foreign ownership can be limited to a maximum percentage of the equity capital of companies listed on the emerging market. This limit can be zero for "strategic" companies, and a fixed percentage for all other companies.
- Free float is often small because the local government is the primary owner of many companies. Even though the total market cap of a company looks large, the float available to foreign or domestic private investing is limited.
- Repatriation of income or capital can be somewhat constrained. Such capital flows have been liberalized in most emerging countries, but controls are periodically applied in periods of severe crisis. For example, this happened in

> 外国投资者在许多新兴市场投资时面临限制。

Malaysia during the 1997 crisis.
- Discriminatory taxes are sometimes applied to foreign investors, although this is becoming exceptional.
- Foreign currency restrictions are sometimes applied.
- Authorized investors are the only investors allowed to invest in some emerging countries. These authorized foreign investors are typically institutional investors, not private ones.

The pace of liberalization of emerging markets is rapid, and investability regulations are undergoing continual change. However, there is always the risk of an imposition of constraints in periods of crisis.

Another major problem with investing in emerging market is the lack of liquidity. Any sizable transaction can have a very large price impact. So, there could be a significant performance difference between a "paper" portfolio, such as a passive index, and an actual portfolio.

Providers of emerging-market stock indexes have tried to reflect the investability of markets by constructing "investable" or "free" indexes. In building global emerging-market indexes, foreign ownership restrictions, and free float strongly affect the weight of a given emerging country in the index.

3.5　Segmentation versus Integration Issue

在一体化的市场中,具有相同风险的资产应该获得相同的回报,无论其位于何处。

In integrated markets, assets with identical risk should command identical return, regardless of location. In segmented markets, the expected returns on similar assets from different countries should not be related. In practice, emerging markets are somewhat segmented from the international market. Segmented asset pricing is attractive to the global investor. It implies that assets are mispriced relative to their "international" value.

Despite all the problems of emerging economies, which create higher investment risks, emerging stock markets are an attractive asset allocation opportunity. Again, the idea is that investors should be willing to buy emerging markets, which are inherently very volatile, because some of them are likely to produce very high returns. Altogether, the contribution of emerging markets to the total risk of the global portfolio is not very large, because of their low correlation with developed markets.

Summary

- International investing reduces risk because the correlations between country markets are less than 1.0.
- The domestic rate of return on a foreign asset is the rate of return of that asset in the foreign currency plus the rate of return on the exchange rate plus the product of the rate of return in the foreign currency times the rate of return on the exchange rate.
- International diversification provides an efficient frontier that dominates the domestic-only efficient frontier because the domestic-only frontier is more constrained.
- The factors causing equity market correlations across countries to be relatively low are the independence of different nations, economies and government policies, technological specialization, independent fiscal and monetary policies, and cultural and sociological differences.
- The factors causing bond market correlations across countries to be relatively low are the differences in national monetary and budgetary policies.
- An increased Sharpe ratio from international investing is possible because of risk reduction and the increase in profitable investment opportunities in an enlarged investment universe.
- Currency risk may only slightly magnify the volatility of foreign currency denominated investments, because market and currency risks are not additive exchange risk can be hedged.
- The increase in correlations between national markets reduces diversification benefits.
- Emerging markets tend to be somewhat segmented, and mispricing is evident.

Exercises

1. The estimated volatility of a domestic asset is $\sigma_d = 15\%$ (annualized standard deviation of returns). A foreign asset has a volatility of $\sigma_f = 18\%$, and a correlation of $\rho = 0.5$ with the domestic asset. What is the volatility of a portfolio invested 80 percent in the domestic asset and 20 percent in the foreign asset?
2. Consider the correlations (in U.S. dollars) of worldwide bond

markets presented in Table 4.2. Explain the reasons for the correlations observed between the United States and other countries, and indicate the motivations for diversifying a U.S. dollar bond portfolio into foreign-currency bonds.
3. Explain whether there are any benefits to adding bonds to a stock portfolio in a global investment strategy.
4. What factors can be used to explain differences in the long-run performance of equity markets of different countries?
5. Is currency risk a barrier to international investment?

Chapter 5
International Equity Investment

The requirement of Learning
- Discuss the major differences in national accounting standards, as well as between national standards and international accounting standards.
- Understand how neoclassical growth theory and endogenous growth theory can be used to explain trends in economic growth
- Know how to conduct a global industry analysis by analyzing return potential and risk characteristics.
- Know how to conduct global financial analysis, including DuPont analysis.
- Know how to analyze the effects of inflation for valuation purposes.
- Discuss the major differences in national accounting standards, as well as between national standards and international accounting standards.
- Understand how neoclassical growth theory and endogenous growth theory can be used to explain trends in economic growth.
- Know how to conduct a global industry analysis by analyzing return potential and risk characteristics.
- Know how to conduct global financial analysis, including DuPont analysis.
- Know how to analyze the effects of inflation for valuation purposes.

1 Market Differences: A Historical Perspective

Financial paper, in the form of debt obligations, has long been traded in Europe, whereas trading in company shares is relatively recent. The Amsterdam Bourse is usually considered the oldest stock market. The first common stock to be publicly traded in the Netherlands was the famous East Indies Trading Company in the 17th century, but organized stock markets really started in the mid to late 18th century. In Paris, a stock market was started on a bridge. In London, the stock market originated in a tavern; churches and open-air markets were also used as stock markets on the Continent. Most of these European exchanges became recognized as separate markets and were regulated around 1800. The same holds for the United States. However, stock exchanges in Japan and other countries in Asia and most of the Americas are more recent creations.

Historical and cultural differences explain most of the significant differences in stock-trading practices around the world. Rather than engage in a detailed analysis of each national market, this section looks at the major differences in terms of market structures and trading procedures. Many of these differences are being eliminated. But some historical perspective helps gain a better understanding of the current working of those markets.

1.1 Historical Differences in Market Organization

Each stock exchange has its own unique characteristics and legal organization, but broadly speaking, all exchanges have evolved from one of three market organization types.

Private Bourses: founded by private individuals and entities for the purpose of securities trading. Several private stock exchange may compete within the same country, as in the United States, Japan, and Canada. In other countries, one leading exchange has emerged through either attrition or absorption of its competitors. Although these bourses are private, they are not free of public regulation. But the mix of self-regulation and government supervision is oriented more toward self-regulation than in the public bourses. Historically, these private bourses developed in the British sphere of influence.

Public Bourses: Its origin is in the legislative work of Napoleon I. He designed the bourse to be a public institution, with brokers appointed by the government and enjoying a monopoly over all transactions. Commissions are fixed by the state. Brokerage firms are private, but their number is fixed and new brokers are proposed to the state for nomination by the brokers' association. The Paris Bourse followed this model until 1990. Belgium, France, Spain, Italy, Greece and some Latin American countries used this model. But most have moved toward a private bourse model.

Bankers' Bourses: Bankers' Bourses were found in the German sphere of influence: Austria, Switzerland, Scandinavia, and the Netherlands. In this market organization, the Banking Act granted a brokerage monopoly to banks, banks are the major, or even the only, securities trades. Bankers' Bourses maybe either private or semi-public organizations, but their chief function is to provide a convenient place for banks to meet. Sometimes trading takes place directly between banks without involving the official bourse at all. Most banker's bourses moved to a private bourse model in the 1990s to allow foreign financial intermediaries to become brokers.

1.2 Historical Differences in Trading Procedure

Apart from legal structure, other historical differences are found in the operation of national stock markets. The most important differences are in the trading procedures.

Cash versus Forward Markets: In most markets, stocks are traded on a cash basis, and transactions must be settled within a few days. To allow more leveraged investment, margin trading is available on most cash market.

现金市场与远期市场

In contrast, some stock markets were organized as a forward market. In Paris, the settlement date was the end of the month for all transactions made during the month (London settled accounts every two weeks). This is a periodic settlement system. Of course, a deposit is required guarantee a position, as on most forward markets. Moreover, the transaction price is fixed at the time of the transaction and remains at this value even if the market price has changed substantially by the settlement time, settling all accounts once a month greatly simplifies the security clearing system.

Price-Driven versus Order-driven Markets: Price-Driven markets are that market makers (also called dealers) ensure market liquidity at any point in time. Market makers adjust their quotes continuously to reflect supply and demand for the security as well as their own inventory. This type of market is also known as a dealer market or a quote-driven market. Nasdaq is a dealer market.

价格驱动与订单驱动市场

In many other markets and countries, however, active market makers do not exist, and the supply and demand for securities are matched directly in an auction market. An auction market is also known as an order-driven market because all traders publicly post their orders, and the transaction price is the result of the equilibrium of supply and demand. Although a single call auction provides excellent liquidity at one point in time, it makes trading at other times difficult. Hence, the market-making function is being developed on all call auction markets (e.g. Paris, Tokyo, or Frankfurt) to allow the possibility of trading throughout the day.

Example 5-1 Order-driven market

LVMH is a French firm listed on the Paris Bourse, You can access the central limit order book directly on the internet and find the following information (the limit Prices for sell orders are ask prices and those for buy orders are bid prices. You wish to buy 1,000 shares and enter a market order to buy those shares. A Market order will be executed against the best matching order, At what Price will you buy the shares?

Sell Orders		Buy Orders	
Quantity	Limit	Quantity	Limit
1,000	58	2,000	49
3,000	54	500	48
1,000	52	1,000	47
1,000	51	2,000	46
500	50	10,000	44

Solution:

Unless a new sell order is entered at a price below 51 before your order is executed, you will buy 500 shares at 50 and 500 shares at 51.

2 Global Market Statistics

2.1 Market Size

Relative national market capitalizations give some indication of the importance of each country for global investors. Market-capitalization weights are used in the commonly used global benchmarks; hence, market sizes guide global investment strategies.

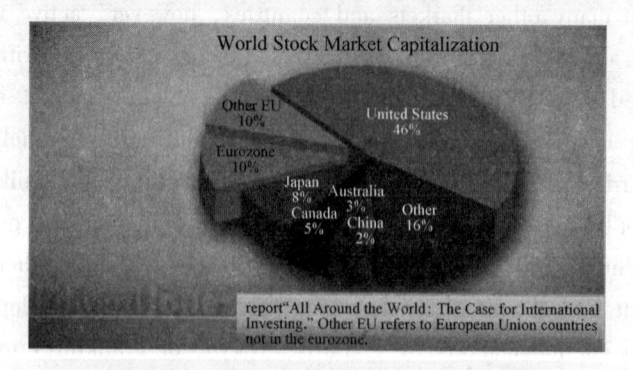

Figure 5.1 World Stock Market Capitalization

The U.S. stock exchanges are the largest exchanges in the world. The U.S. stock market capitalization is much larger than the annual U.S. GDP. Britain also has a market cap almost double its GDP, but the corresponding figure for France or Germany is below 80%. This difference has several reasons:

Firstly, Most U.S. firms prefer to go public, whereas in France, as well as in the rest of Europe, tradition calls for maintaining private ownership as much as possible.

Secondly, in many European countries, corporations are undercapitalized and rely heavily on bank financing. Germany is a typical example because banks finance corporations extensively, thereby reducing the need for outside equity capital. Furthermore, it is common for European banks to own shares of their client companies.

Thirdly, in other countries, many large firms are nationalized and, therefore, not listed on the capital markets. In France, for example, large portions of telecommunication, arms manufacturing, automobile, banking, and transportation industries are partly owned by the government.

Annualized Total Returns		
	S&P 500	MSCI World ex-U.S.
1970s	5.9%	10.9%
1980s	17.6	21.5
1990s	18.2	7.4
2000s	−1.0	2.0
2009	26.5	34.4
2010	15.1	9.4
2011	2.1	−11.8

The MSCI World Excluding U.S. Index is a free float-adjusted market capitalization weighted index that is designed to measure the equity market performance of developed markets.

Figure 5.2 Annualized Total Returns

Japan and the United Kingdom have the largest markets outside of the United States. The size of the world stock market grew steadily in the 1970s and 1980s and neared the $30 trillion at the end of 2000. It has multiplied by approximately 30 since the end of 1974. Currency movements induce changes in the total size and geographical breakdown of the world market. The figure for Japan is somewhat inflated by the practice of cross-holding of stocks among publicly traded Japanese companies and financial institutions.

In emerging markets, the 1980s saw the emergence and rapid growth of stock markets in many developing countries. In Africa, stock markets opened in Egypt, Morocco, and the Ivory Coast, but with limited growth. Growth has been somewhat faster in Latin America, especially in Brazil and Mexico. The most spectacular change has been witnessed in Asia. Stock markets have grown rapidly in India, Indonesia, Malaysia, Thailand, South Korea, and China Taiwan. But the total capitalization of emerging markets represents less than 10 percent of the world stock market cap. Taken together, all emerging markets have a market size somewhere between that of Great Britain and that of France or Germany.

2.2 Liquidity

> 交易量可用来代表市场的流动性。

Transaction volume gives indications on the liquidity of each market. In a liquid market, investor can be more active and design various arbitrage strategies. Illiquidity tends imply higher transaction costs.

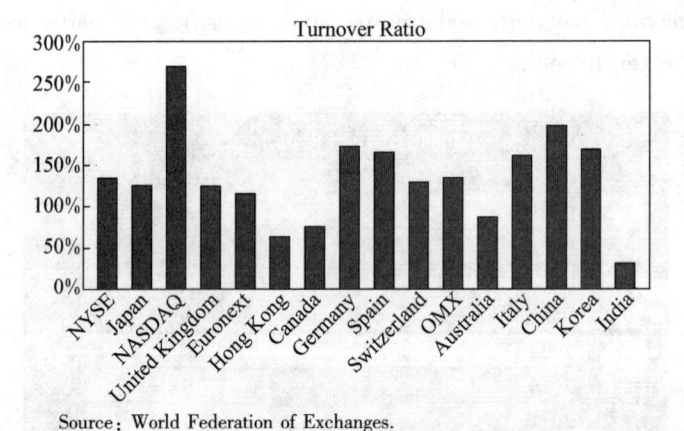

Figure 5.3 Annual Turnover on Major Stock Markets

Source: World Federation of Exchanges.

The turnover ratio varies significantly over time. For example, the transaction volume in Japan soared in the late 1980s to surpass that of the NYSE, and the Japanese turnover ratio became a multiple of the U.S. ratio, but it dropped dramatically in the 1990s. Therefore, comparison of national market liquidity based on this variable could lead to different conclusions, depending on the years observed.

In addition, the transaction volume on some emerging markets is very large relative to their size. Transaction volumes in South Korea or China Taiwan are sometimes larger than that of any developed market except the United States, but this is not the case for many other emerging markets that are quite illiquid.

2.3 Concentration

It is important that investors know whether a national market is made up of a diversity of firms or concentrated in a few large firms. Institutional investors are reluctant to invest in small firms, fearing that they offer poor liquidity. On the other hand, A market dominated by a few large firms provides fewer opportunities for risk diversification and active portfolio strategies.

In 2002, the U.S. stock exchange is a diverse market in which the top 10 firms represent less than 20 percent of total market cap. In the United States, the largest firm represents less than 3 percent of the capitalization for the NYSE. At the other end of the spectrum, the top 10 Swiss multinational firms account for more than 70 percent of the Swiss stock exchange. Nokia is larger than the sum of all other Finnish firms.

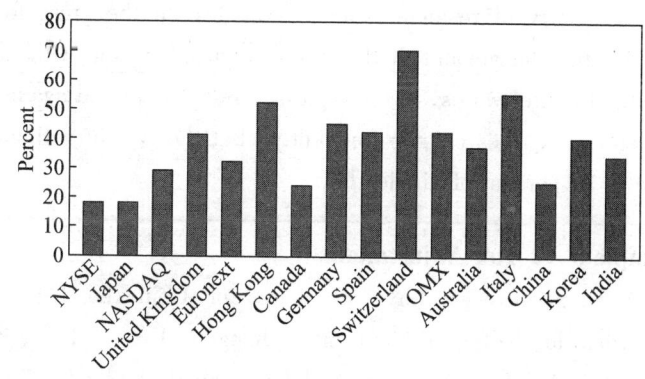

Source: World Federation of Exchanges.

Figure 5.4 Share of the Ten Largest Listed Companies in the National Market Capitalization

3 Market Practical Aspects

3.1 Tax Aspects

Taxes can add to the cost of international investment. Foreign investments may be taxed in two locations: the investor's country and the investment's country, Taxes are applied in any of three areas: Transactions, capital gains and income (dividends, etc.).

Transactions: some countries impose a tax on transactions. The United Kingdom has retained a stamp tax of 0.5 percent on purchases of domestic securities (but not on sales). Most countries have

> 税收会增加国际投资的成本。国际投资可能在两个地点征税：投资者所在国和投资对象国，税收有以下三种：交易税、资本利得税和收入税（股息等）。

eliminated, or drastically reduced, such transaction taxes.

Capital gains are normally taxed where the investor resides, regardless of the national origin of the investment. In other words, domestic and international investments are taxed the same way.

Income (dividends, etc.): Income on foreign stocks is paid from the legal entity of one country to a resident of another country. This transaction often poses a conflict of jurisdiction, because both countries may want to impose a tax on that income. The international convention on taxing income is to make certain that taxes are paid by the investor in at least one country, which is why **withholding taxes** are levied on dividend payments. Because many investors are also taxed on income received in their country of residence, double taxation can result from this practice but is avoided through a network of international tax treaties. An investor receives a dividend net of withholding tax plus **a tax credit** from the foreign government. The investor's country of residence imposes its tax on the gross foreign dividends, but the amount of this tax is reduced by the withholding tax credit. In other words, the foreign tax credit is applied against the home taxes. Tax rules change frequently, but the typical withholding tax rate is 15 percent of dividends.

Example 5-2 Tax Adjustments

A U.S. investor buys 100 shares of Heineken listed in Amsterdam for 40 €s, the current exchange is 1 € = 1.1 $, Her total cost is $4,400. three months later, a gross dividend of 2 € is paid (15 percent withholding tax), and she decides to sell the shares for 38 € per share, the current exchange rate is 1 € = 1.2 $, what are the cash flows received in U.S. dollar?

Solution:

The cash flow are as follows

Net Dividend is (2−0.3)×1.2×100 = 204 $

Tax credit is 0.3×1.2×100 = 36 $

Capital gains is (38×1.2×100−4,400) = 160 $

So, the investor has made a capital gain of $160, which will be taxed in the U.S at the U.S. capital gains tax rate. She will also declare a total gross dividend of $240 as income, which will be taxed at her income tax rate, she can deduct from her income tax a tax credit of $36, however, thanks to the United States-Netherlands tax treaty.

3.2 Stock Market Indexes

A wide variety of Stock Market Indexes exist, including broad market, multimarket, sector, and style indices.

3.2.1 Broad Market Indexes

A broad stock market index represents an entire given equity market and typically includes securities representing more than 90 percent of the selected market. For example, the Shanghai Stock Exchange Composite Index (SSE) is a market capitalization weighted index of all shares that trade on the Shanghai Stock Exchange. In the United States, the Wilshire 5000 Total Market Index is a market capitalization weighted index that includes more than 6,000 equity securities and is designed to represent the entire U.S. equity market[①]. The Russell 3,000, consisting of the largest 3,000 stocks by market capitalization, represents 99 percent of the U.S. equity market.

3.2.2 Multimarket Indexes

Multimarket indexes usually comprise indexes from different countries and are designed to represent multiple security markets. Multimarket indexes may represent multiple national markets, geographic regions, economic development groups, and in some cases, the entire world. World indexes are of importance to investors who take a global approach to equity investing without any particular bias toward a particular country or region. A number of index providers publish families of multimarket equity indexes.

Morgan Stanley Capital International (MSCI) has published international market cap weighted indexes since 1970. They now publish country indexes for all developed as well as numerous emerging markets. They also publish a variety of regional and global indexes.

The World index includes only developed markets, while the All Country World index includes both developed and emerging markets. Their index of non-U.S. stock markets has been extensively used as a benchmark of foreign equity portfolios by U.S. investors; it is called EAFE (Europe/Australasia/Far East). Besides market cap-weighted indexes, it also publishes indexes with various weighting schemes (e. g. GDP weights) and with full currency hedging. Global industry indexes are also available.

---

① Despite its name, the Wilshire 5,000 has no constraint on the number of securities that can be included, it included approximately 5,000 securities at inception.

Besides MSCI, FTSE, created as a joint venture of the Financial Times and the London Stock Exchange, has published international indexes since 1987. The most important international indexes are the world index, the Europe index, the pacific Basin index, and the Europe and Pacific Index. Country, industrial, regional and Global indexes are available.

Other series of global indexes are also available. **Salomon Smith Barney** publishes a series of global indexes that cover developed and emerging markets. In 2000, **Dow Jones** started to publish a series of global indexes. **S&P** publishes an S&P Global 1200 index of developed markets, as well as various sub-indexes.

Some index providers weight the securities within each country by market capitalization and then weight each country in the overall index in proportion to its relative GDP, effectively creating fundamental weighting in multimarket indices. GDP-weighted indices were some of the first fundamentally weighted indices created. Introduced in 1987 by MSCI to address the 60 percent weight of Japanese equities in the market capitalization weighted MSCI EAFE Index at the time, GDP-weighted indices reduced the allocation to Japanese equities by half.

All these global indexes are widely used by international money managers for asset allocation decisions and performance measurements.

3.2.3 Sector Indices

Sector indices represent and track different economic sectors—such as consumer goods, energy, finance, health care, and technology—on either a national, regional, or global basis. Because different sectors of the economy behave differently over the course of the business cycle, some investors may seek to overweight or underweight their exposure to particular sectors.

Sector indices are organized as families; each index within the family represents an economic sector. Typically, the aggregation of a sector index family is equivalent to a broad market index. Economic sector classification can be applied on a global, regional, or country specific basis, but no universally agreed upon sector classification method exists.

Sector indices play an important role in performance analysis because they provide a means to determine whether a portfolio manager is more successful at stock selection or sector allocation. Sector indices also serve as model portfolios for sector specific ETFs

and other investment products.
3.2.4 Style Indices

Style indices represent groups of securities classified according to market capitalization, value, growth, or a combination of these characteristics. They are intended to reflect the investing styles of certain investors, such as the growth investor, value investor, and small cap investor.

Market capitalization indices represent securities categorized according to the major capitalization categories: large cap, midcap, and small cap. With no universal definition of these categories, the indices differ on the distinctions between large cap and midcap and between midcap and small cap, as well as the minimum market capitalization size required to be included in a small cap index. Classification into categories can be based on absolute market capitalization (e.g., below $100 million) or relative market capitalization (e.g., the smallest 2,500 stocks).

Large-cap value	Large-cap growth
Mid-cap value	Mid-cap growth
Small-cap value	Small-cap growth

Some indices represent categories of stocks based on their classifications as either value or growth stocks. Different index providers use different factors and valuation ratio (low price to book ratios, low price to earning ratios, high dividend yield, etc.) to distinguish between value and growth equities.

Combining the three market capitalization groups with value and growth classifications results in six basic style index categories:

Because indices use different size and valuation classifications, the constituents of indices designed to represent a given style, such as small cap value, may differ—sometimes substantially.

Because valuation ratios and market capitalizations change over time, stocks frequently migrate from one style index category to another on reconstitution dates. As a result, style indices generally have much higher turnover than do broad market indices.

3.2.5 Which Index to Use?

Domestic investors usually prefer indexes that are calculated and published locally. Most of these are broadly based, market value weighted indexes. They are true market portfolio indexes in the sense that when the index portfolio is held by an investor, it truly represents movements in the market. But this is not true of equal-weighted indexes, such as U.S. Dow Jones 30 Industrial Average (DJIA) or the Japanese Nikkei 225 Stock Average.

Many stock exchanges have introduced indexes based on a small number of large stocks. There are two reasons for this. First, Meaningful market indicators must be computed using the most actively traded stocks, not those that trade infrequently. Second, exchanges have introduced derivatives (futures, options) on these stock indexes. Dealers in those derivative markets prefer to have an index that is based on a small number of actively traded stocks, because it makes it much easier to hedge their derivatives exposure in the cash stock market.

Because some stocks are listed on several exchanges, some companies appear in different national indexes. For example, the S&P 500 used to include some very large non-U.S. companies.

Local indexes are widely used by domestic investors. Private investors often prefer local indexes for several reasons:

- In most cases, the local indexes have been used for long time.
- Local indexes are used for derivative contracts traded in that country.
- Local indexes can be calculated immediately and available at the same time as stock market quotations on all electronic price services.
- Local indexes are available every morning in all the newspapers throughout the world.
- The risk of error in prices and capital adjustment is possibly minimized in Local indexes by the fact that all calculations are done locally.

Institutional investors prefer to use the MSCI, FTSE, or other international indexes for the following reasons:

- The pension funds do not need up-to-the minute indexes.
- The indexes on all stock markets are available in a central location, whereas local indexes must be drawn from several locations.
- All international indexes are calculated by in a single consistent manner. Allowing for direct comparisons between markets.
- They provide global or regional indexes which international money managers need to measure overall performance.
- They also provide indexes cum-dividends.

4　Investing in foreign Equity Securities

Technological innovations and the growth of electronic information exchanges (electronic trading networks, the Internet, etc.) have accelerated the integration and growth of global financial markets. As we know, global capital markets have expanded at a much more rapid rate than global GDP in recent years. Increased integration of equity markets has made it easier and less expensive for companies to raise capital and to expand their shareholder base beyond their local market.

Moreover, there may be some motivations for a company's multiple listing. First, multiple listing gives them more access to foreign ownership, allowing a better diversification of their capital and access to a larger amount of funds than is available from smaller domestic equity markets. Second, diversified ownership in turn reduces the risk of a domestic takeover. Third, it can raise the profile of a firm in foreign markets. Fourth, it allows access to a wider capital base and increases the business visibility of the firm.

A danger of foreign listing may be the increased volatility of the firm's stock due to a stronger response in foreign versus domestic markets to domestic economic news. Bad political and economic (domestic) news in the Scandinavian countries, for example, has frequently been followed by an immediate negative impact from shares cross-listed on foreign markets. Scandinavian shareholders display less volatile behavior than foreign investors for two reasons: They are not as shaken by bad domestic news, and they tend to keep their capital invested at home anyhow.

4.1　Investing the Shares of foreign Listing

Investors can use a variety of methods to invest in the equity of companies outside of their local market. The most obvious is to buy and sell securities directly in foreign markets. However, this means that all transactions—including the purchase and sale of shares, dividend payments, and capital gains—are in the company's, not the investor's, domestic currency. In addition, investors must be familiar with the trading, clearing, and settlement regulations and procedures of that market. Investing directly often results in less transparency and more volatility because audited financial information may not be

> 技术创新和电子信息交易所(电子交易网络、互联网等)的增长加速了全球金融市场的一体化和增长。

> 投资者可以使用各种方法投资于本国市场以外的公司股权。最明显的是直接在国外市场买卖证券。

provided on a regular basis and the market may be less liquid. Alternatively, investors can use such securities as depository receipts and global registered shares, which represent the equity of international companies and are traded on local exchanges and in the local currencies. With these securities, investors have to worry less about currency conversions (price quotations and dividend payments are in the investor's local currency), unfamiliar market practices, and differences in accounting standards.

4.2 Depository Receipt

A depository receipt (DR) is a security that trades like an ordinary share on a local exchange and represents an economic interest in a foreign company. It allows the publicly listed shares of a foreign company to be traded on an exchange outside its domestic market. A DR is created when the equity shares of a foreign company are deposited in a bank (i.e., the depository) in the country on whose exchange the shares will trade.

A DR can be sponsored or unsponsored. A sponsored DR is when the foreign company whose shares are held by the depository has a direct involvement in the issuance of the receipts. Investors in sponsored DRs have the same rights as the direct owners of the common shares (e.g., the right to vote and the right to receive dividends). In contrast, with an unsponsored DR, the underlying foreign company has no involvement with the issuance of the receipts. Instead, the depository purchases the foreign company's shares in its domestic market and then issues the receipts through brokerage firms in the depository's local market. In this case, the depository bank, not the investors in the DR, retains the voting rights. Sponsored DRs are generally subject to greater reporting requirements than unsponsored DRs. In the U.S., for example, sponsored DRs must be registered (meet the reporting requirements) with the U.S. Securities and Exchange Commission (SEC).

4.2.1 Global Depositary Receipts (GDRs)

Some firms have issued Global Depositary Receipts (GDRs) that are simultaneously listed on several national markets. These GDRs give the firms access to a larger base to raise new capital.

A GDR is issued outside of the company's home country and outside of the United States. The depository bank that issues GDRs is generally located (or has branches) in the countries on whose exchanges the shares are traded. A key advantage of GDRs is that they are not subject to the foreign ownership and capital flow restrictions that may be imposed by the issuing company's home country because they are sold outside of that country. The issuing company selects the exchange where the GDR is to be traded based on such factors as investor's familiarity with the company or the existence of a large international investor base. The London and Luxembourg exchange were the first ones to trade GDRs. Other stock exchange trading GDRs are the Dubai International Financial Exchange, the Singapore Stock Exchange, and the Hong Kong Stock Exchange. Currently, the London and Luxembourg exchanges are where most GDRs are traded because they can be issued in a more timely manner and at a lower cost. Regardless of the exchange they are traded on, the majority of GDRs are denominated in U.S. dollars, although the number of GDRs denominated in pound sterling and €s is increasing. Note that although GDRs cannot be listed on U.S. exchanges, they can be privately placed with international investors based in the United States.

4.2.2 American Depository Receipts (ADRs)

An American Depositary Receipts (ADRs) is a U.S. dollar denominated security that trades like a common share on U.S. exchanges. First created in 1927, ADRs are the oldest type of depository receipts and are currently the most commonly traded depository receipts. They enable foreign companies to raise capital from U.S. investors.

> 美国存托凭证（ADRs）是以美元计价的证券,在美国交易所交易时就像普通股一样。

There are four primary types of ADRs, with each type having different levels of corporate governance and filing requirements.

- Level Ⅰ: the company does not comply with SEC registration and reporting requirements, and Sponsored ADRs can be traded only on the OTC market (but not NASDAQ)
- Level Ⅱ: The company registers with the SEC and complies with its reporting requirements. The Sponsored ADRs can be listed on an official U.S. stock exchange (e.g., NYSE, NASDAQ, and American Stock Exchange).
- Level Ⅲ: The company's ADRs are traded on a U.S. stock exchange or NASDAQ and the company may raise capital in the United States through a public offering of the ADRs.
- The fourth type of ADR, an SEC rule 144A or a Regulation S depository receipt, does not require SEC registration. Instead,

foreign companies are able to raise capital by privately placing these depository receipts with qualified institutional investors or to offshore non-U.S. investors. Table 5.1 summarizes the main features of ADRs.

Table 5.1 Summary of the Main Features of ADRs

	Level (Unlisted)	Level listed	Level listed	Rule 144A (Unlisted)
Objectives	Develop and broaden U.S. investor base with existing shares	Develop and broaden U.S. investor base with existing shares	Develop and broaden U.S. investor base with existing or new shares	Access qualified institutional buyers (QIBs)
Raising capital on U.S. markets?	No	No	Yes, through public offerings	Yes, through Private placements to QIBs
SEC registration	Form F-6	Form F-6	Form F-1 Form F-6	None
Trading	Over the counter	NYSE, NASDAQ or AMEX	NYSE, NASDAQ or AMEX	Private offerings, resales, and trading through automated linkages such as PORTAL
Listing fees	Low	High	High	Low
Size and earnings Requirements	None	Yes	Yes	None

Source: Boubakri, Cosset, and Samet (2008): Table 1.

More than 2,000 DRs from over 80 countries, currently trade on U.S. exchanges. Based on current statistics, the total market value of DRs issued and traded is estimated at approximately US $2 trillion, or 15 percent of the total dollar value of equities traded in U.S. markets.

Example 5-3

An investor would like to purchase 100 shares of A company which is trades on the Paris Bourse, the London stock exchange and the NYSE as an ADR. At the NYSE, One Depositary Receipt is equivalent to one-fourth of a share, the investor asks its brokers to quote net prices, without any commissions, in the three trading venues, there is no stamp tax in London on foreign shares listed there.

> The stock quotes are as follows:
> New York: $24.07—24.37
> London: £66.31—67.17
> Paris: €85.40—86.30
> The exchange rate quotes from banks are:
> GBP/USD = 1.4575—1.4580
> EUR/USD = 1.0691—1.0695
> Compare the dollar costs of purchasing 10,000 Shares.
> **Solution:**
> The cost of purchasing 10,000 shares in NYSE is
> $$24.37 * 4 * 10,000 = \$974,800$$
> The cost of purchasing 10,000 shares in London is
> $$67.17 * 1.4580 * 10,000 = \$979,338.6$$
> The cost of purchasing 10,000 shares in Paris is
> $$86.30 * 1.0695 * 10,000 = \$922,978.5$$
> So, it is the cheapest to buy the shares in Paris.

4.2.3 Global Registered Share

A Global registered share (GRS) is a common share that is traded on different stock exchange around the world in different currencies. Currency conversions are not needed to purchase or sell them, because identical shares are quoted and traded in different currencies. Thus, the same share purchased on the Swiss exchange in Swiss francs can be sold on the Tokyo exchange for Japanese yen. As a result, GRSs offer more flexibility than depository receipts because the shares represent an actual ownership interest in the company that can be traded anywhere and currency conversions are not needed to purchase or sell them. GRSs were created and issued by Daimler Chrysler in 1998.

全球注册股票(GRS)是一种普通股,以不同的货币在世界各地的证券交易所进行交易。

4.2.4 Basket of Listed Depository Receipts

Another type of global security is a basket of listed depository receipts (BLDR), which is an exchange-traded fund (ETF) that represents a portfolio of depository receipts. An ETF is a security that tracks an index but trades like an individual share on an exchange. An equity ETF is a security that contains a portfolio of equities that tracks an index. It trades throughout the day and can be bought, sold, or sold short, just like an individual share. Like ordinary shares, ETFs can also be purchased on margin and used in hedging or

另一种类型的全球证券是一篮子存托凭证,这是一种交易所交易基金(ETF),代表存托凭证的一种组合。ETF是跟踪指数但可以像单个股票一样进行交易的证券。

arbitrage strategies. The BLDR is a specific class of ETF security that consists of an underlying portfolio of DRs and is designed to track the price performance of an underlying DR index. For example, the Asia 50 ADR Index Fund is a capitalization weighted ETF designed to track the performance of 50 Asian market based ADRs.

4.2.5 Compare the Valuation

Multiple listing implies that the share values of a company are linked on several exchanges. One company should sell at the same share price all over the world, once adjustments for exchange rates and transactions costs have been made. Arbitrage among markets ensures that this is so. An important question is: What is the dominant-satellite market relationship the home market is the dominant force, and the price in the foreign market (the satellite) simply adjusts to the home market price. This is clearly the case for many dual-listed stocks of which only a very small proportion of capitalization is traded abroad. For most ADRs, the price quoted by market makers is simply the home price of the share adjusted by the exchange rate. But, because the ADR market is less liquid, a large bid-ask spread can be observed because the arbitrage costs between the ADR and the original share can be sizable. The answer is less obvious, however, for a few large European companies that have a very active market in other countries (especially the United States). The volume of trading of a few European multinationals is sometimes bigger in New York and London than on their home market. This also applies to a few Latin American firms and to many of the GDRs.

The influence of time zones should also be noted. Because stock trading takes place at different times around the world, U.S. stocks listed on the Paris Bourse are traded before the opening of the U.S. markets. Their French prices reflect not only the previous close in New York and the current exchange rate, but also anticipation about the current day's new price, based on new information released following the U.S. close.

4.2.6 The Advantages/Disadvantages of ADRs (or GDRs)

ADRs (or GDRs) allow an easy and direct investment in some foreign firms. Although buying ADRs (or GDRs) is an attractive alternative for retail investors, it is usually more costly than a direct purchase abroad for a large investor. On the other hand, some ADRs issued by companies from emerging countries tend to have larger trading volumes in New York than in their home markets, and the execution costs are lower in New York. Whereas the small investor may find it more convenient to trade in foreign shares listed on the home market, the large investor may often find the primary market of overseas companies to be more liquid and cheaper. In all cases, price levels, transaction costs, taxes, and administrative costs should be major determinants of whichever market the investor chooses.

Another disadvantage of ADRs (or GDRs) is that only a limited number of companies have issued ADRs, and they represent only a small proportion of foreign market capitalization. They tend to be large companies in each country, so they do not offer full international diversification benefits.

4.3 Closed-end Country Funds

A country fund is a mutual fund that invests in one country. A country fund holds a portfolio of securities, generally stocks, of companies located exclusively in a given country. Also called a "single-country fund."

国家基金是在一个国家投资的共同基金。

A single-country fund for Russia, for example, will only invest in assets based in that country, such as the stocks of Russian companies, Russian government debt and other Russia-based financial instruments.

Country funds can demonstrate fantastic results because of their concentrated holdings. However, along with this type of performance also comes a high level of risk and price volatility, especially in developing countries, which are usually categorized as emerging markets. In emerging markets, a fund's portfolio may be concentrated in a small number of issues with very low market liquidity.

Even in some developed markets, putting investment funds in a single-country fund means that you are subjecting your risk-return expectations to a relatively narrow market environment.

4.3.1 Example of a Country Fund

The Voya Russia A fund seeks long-term capital appreciation through investment primarily in equity securities of Russian companies. It normally invests at least 80% of its assets in equity securities of Russian companies, is not constrained by investment style or market capitalization and seeks companies undervalued by the market because their pace of development or earnings growth has been underestimated.

It had $83 million in assets under management, as of May 22, 2018. It had a one-year annualized return of 16.94% and a 10-year annualized return of −3.94%.

4.3.2 Global Funds vs. Country Funds

Country funds and global funds can be used to add geographic diversification to a portfolio. A global fund is a fund that invests in companies located anywhere in the world, including the investor's own country. A global fund often seeks to identify the best investments from a global universe of securities.

A global fund provides investors with a diversified portfolio of global investments. Investing in international securities can often increase an investor's potential return with some additional risks. A global fund can help to mitigate some of the risks and fears investors may have when considering international investments through its diversified portfolio structure.

An investor could, in theory, construct a geographically diverse portfolio using individual country funds. This would require a great deal of research and effort and could be accomplished simply by selecting a global fund. However, country funds can easily be used to supplement a global portfolio and concentrate a bet on a region, in effect overweighting a single country, while the global fund maintains diversification.

4.3.3 NAV and Market Price

A country Fund is a closed-end fund whose assets consist primarily of stocks of the country for which the fund is named. Numerous country funds are listed in the United States, the United Kingdom, and major stock markets.

A closed-end fund is an investment vehicle that buys stocks in the market and can be traded in the stock market at a price determined by supply and demand. The numbers of shares usually remains fixed and shares cannot be redeemed. The fund's market price can differ from the value of the assets held in its portfolio, which is called the Net asset value (NAV):

$$NAV = Market\ price - Premium$$

The advantage of a closed-end fund for the investment manager is that she does not have to worry about redemptions; once a closed-end fund is initially subscribed, the investment manager keeps the money under management.

> 国家基金和全球基金都可用于增加投资组合的地域多样性。

> 国家基金是一种封闭式基金,其资产主要由该基金命名国家的股票组成。

Example 5-4

Paf is an emerging country with severe foreign investment restrictions but an active stock market open mostly to local investors. A closed-end country fund, its net asset value is 100 dollars and trades in New York with a premium of 30 percent. The exchange rate is: 1 pif/ $.

a. Give some intuitive explanations for this Positive Premium.
b. Paf Unexpectedly announces that it will lift all foreign investment restrictions, which has two effects. First, stock prices in Paf go up by 20 percent because of the expectation of massive foreign investment. Second, the premium on the country fund drops to zero. What would be your total gain on the shares of Paf Country fund?

Solutions:

a. There is no alternative to investing in the closed-end fund for foreign investors. Foreign investors may find Paf shares attractive from a risk-return viewpoint so that they compete and bid up the price.
b. The net result can be calculated for 100 of original NAV. Before the lifting of restrictions, the fund was worth 130 for 100 of NAV. After the lifting of restrictions, the NAV moves up to 120 and the fund is now worth its NAV, or 120. The rate of return for the foreign investor is (120−130)/130 = −7.7%

The motivation for investing is twofold: First, they offer a simple way to access the local market and benefit from international diversification. Second, some countries and regions traditionally restricted foreign investment. Country funds, approved by the local government, are a way to overcome foreign investment restrictions.

4.3.4　The pricing of Country Funds

The price of a country fund is seldom equal to its NAV. The change in market price of a country fund is equal to the change in NAV plus the change in the premium (discount).

国家基金的价格很少等于其资产净值。

Some country funds provide a unique way to invest in emerging countries with foreign investment restrictions. When these foreign investment restrictions are binding, one would expect the country fund to sell at a premium over its NAV. When the lifting of a foreign investment restriction is announced, the premium on a local-country fund should drop, as local shares will be more widely available to foreign investors. The liberalization in Brazil and Korea has indeed led to large drops in the premium of closed-end funds invested in those countries.

4.3.5 Advantages/Disadvantages

Advantages: allow investors access to a portfolio invested in some foreign region, the portfolio is better diversified than a collection of a few ADRs of that region.

Disadvantages: owing to the costs and volatility, it is an inferior substitute for direct investment in foreign stock markets, even for most emerging markets.

4.4 An Exchange-Traded Fund (ETF)

An exchange-traded fund (ETF) is a type of security that involves a collection of securities—such as stocks—that often tracks an underlying index, although they can invest in any number of industry sectors or use various strategies. ETFs are in many ways similar to mutual funds; however, they are listed on exchanges and ETF shares trade throughout the day just like ordinary stock.

4.4.1 Feature of ETFs

Some well-known example is the SPDR S&P 500 ETF (SPY), which tracks the S&P 500 Index. ETFs can contain many types of investments, including stocks, commodities, bonds, or a mixture of investment types. An exchange-traded fund is a marketable security, meaning it has an associated price that allows it to be easily bought and sold.

- An exchange-traded fund (ETF) is a basket of securities that trade on an exchange, just like a stock.
- ETF share prices fluctuate all day as the ETF is bought and sold; this is different from mutual funds that only trade once a day after the market closes.
- ETFs can contain all types of investments including stocks, commodities, or bonds; some offer U.S. only holdings, while others are international.
- ETFs offer low expense ratios and fewer broker commissions than buying the stocks individually.

An open-end mutual fund is publicly offered and its shares can be purchased and redeemed at the NAV of the assets owned by the fund. Typically investors must announce their decision to buy/redeem their shares before the NAV is calculated. For example, investors must notify their decision before noon, and the NAV is calculated at the end of the day. For open-end funds invested in foreign shares, the lag between notification and determination of the NAV that will be used to execute the transaction can be a couple of days. A large bid-ask spreads on the fund's price can also be imposed. Many of open-end funds take the form of index funds. Such as ETFs.

An ETF is an open-end fund with special characteristics. it traded on a stock market like shares of any individual company. But ETFs are shares of a portfolio, not of an individual company. ETFs are generally designed to closely track the performance of a specific index. Many ETFs are listed on the major stock markets. ETFs on some emerging markets are also offered, so they can be used for international diversification strategies.

A major feature of ETFs is the redemption in-kind process. Creation/redemption units are created in large multiples of individual ETF shares, for example 50,000 shares.

Example 5-5

An ETF is Indexed on a Japanese stock Indexes and is listed in New York, Its NAV is computed based on closing Prices in Tokyo. When it is 9 A.M. in New York, It is already 11 P.M. in Tokyo, On the same day, The NAV based on Tokyo Closing prices is 10,000 yen, the exchange rate at 9 A.M. EST is 1 dollar = 100 yen.

a. What is the dollar NAV of this EFT at the opening of trading in New York?

b. When New York close at 4 P.M. EST, Tokyo is still closed (6 a.m. local time), but the exchange rate is now 99 yen per dollar. What is the dollar NAV at closing time?

c. Bad international news hit after the Tokyo closing, European and U.S. stock markets dropped by 5 percent. Should the ETF Price have remained at its NAV? Assuming that the Tokyo market is strongly correlated with the U.S. market (at least for this type of international news). Give an estimate of the ETF price at the New York closing.

Solution:

a. The Dollar NAV is $100

b. The closing dollar NAV is $101.01

> c. The price of the ETF should reflect expectations that the Tokyo stock index will drop in reaction to the news, so its price should be below the NAV computed on past closing prices in Tokyo. If the markets are strongly correlated, we could estimate that Tokyo will also drop by 5%. Hence, we should have an estimated market value for the dollar NAV equal to 1,0000×(1−0.05)/99 = $95.96. This is an estimate of the current price of the ETF. It will trade at a 5% discount from its "official" NAV.

4.4.2 Advantages/Disadvantages

ETFs are attractive to individual investors because they offer the benefits of international diversification with excellent liquidity at a low cost. They are also designed to be tax efficient. ETFs are useful in an international portfolio strategy. They can be purchased in the home market while offering a diversified play on a foreign market or region. They are well designed to be used in active asset allocation. On the other hand, they usually are designed to match a benchmark and will not provide active return above that benchmark. To add active return, investors can combine them with the direct purchase of specific companies or ADRs.

5　Analysis Methods

There is nothing unique to financial analysis in an international context. Analysts must already take foreign variables into account in evaluating domestic firms. After all, Product markets in which many domestic industrial companies compete are international.

Large domestic firms tend to export extensively and head a network of foreign subsidiaries, these companies must be analyzed as global firms, not purely domestic ones. In many sectors, the competition is fully global. The methods and data required to analyze international manufacturers are quite similar. In brief, research on a company should produce two pieces of information:

❖ *Expected return.* The expected return on an investment can be measured by a rate of return, including potential price appreciation, over some time period, or by some other quantified form of buy-or-sell.

❖ *Risk exposure.* Risk sensitivity, or risk exposure, measures how much a company's value responds to certain key factors, such as economic activity, energy costs, interest rates, currency volatility, and general market conditions. Risk analysis enables a manager or investment policy committee to simulate the performance of an investment in different scenarios. It also helps the manager to design more diversified portfolios.

The overall purpose of analysis is to find securities with superior expected returns, given current domestic and international risks.

5.1 The information Problem

Information on foreign firms is often difficult to obtain; Even if it is obtained, it is often difficult to interpret and analyze using domestic methods.

In the United States, companies publish their quarterly earnings, which are publicly available within just a couple of weeks after the close of the quarter. In contrast, certain European and Far Eastern firms publish their earnings only once a year and with a considerable reporting time lag. French companies, for example, follow this pattern and don't actually publish their official earnings until two to six months after the end of their fiscal years. As a result, official earnings figures are outdated before they become public. To remedy this lack of information, most corporations with significant foreign ownership have begun announcing quarterly or semiannual earnings estimates a short time after the close of the quarter. This is true worldwide for large international corporations. As do U.S. firms, British firms publish detailed financial information frequently. Similarly, Japanese firms have begun publishing U.S.-style financial statements, though sometimes only once a year.

Other problems arise from the language and presentation of the financial reports. Many reports are available only in a company's domestic language. Whereas multinational firms tend to publish both in their domestic language and in English, many smaller but nevertheless attractive firms do not. In general, financial reports vary widely from country to country in format, degree of detail, and reliability of the information disclosed. Therefore, additional information must sometimes be obtained directly from the company.

As international investment has grown, brokers, banks and information services have started to provide more financial data to meet investors' needs. In fact, today, many large international brokerage houses and banks provide analysts' guides covering companies from a large number of countries. Similarly, several data services, such as Bloomberg, Reuters, Thomson Financial, Factset, and Moody's, are extending their international coverage on companies and currently feature summary financial information on an increasing number of international corporations. Some financial firms, such as Thomson First Call, have specialized in collecting earnings forecasts from financial analysts worldwide.

Despite these developments, to get the most timely information possible, financial analysts may have to visit international corporations. This, of course, is a time-consuming and expensive process. Moreover, the information obtained is often not homogeneous across companies and countries.

5.2 A vision of the world

Traditionally, investment organizations use one of three major approaches to international research, depending on their vision of the world:

- If a portfolio manager believes that the value of companies worldwide is affected primarily by global industrial factors, her research effort should be structured according to industrial sectors.
- If a portfolio manager believes that all securities in a national stock market are influenced primarily by domestic factors, her research effort should be structured on a country-by-country basis.
- If a portfolio manager believes that some particular attributes of firms are valued worldwide, she will engage in style investing.

In general, an organization must structure its investment process based on some vision of the major common factors influencing stock returns worldwide.

5.3 Differences in National Accounting Standards

Each country follows a set of accounting principles that are usually prepared by the accounting profession and the national authorities. These sets of accounting principles are sometimes called national GAAP (generally accepted accounting principle). Two distinct models can describe the preparation of these national accounting principles:

- In the Anglo-American model, it often gives the financial statements a true and fair position, and there are large differences between accounting statements and tax statements.
- In the Continental model, the financial statements are geared to satisfy legal and tax provisions and may not give a true and fair view of the firm.

5.3.1 International Harmonization of Accounting Practices

The International Accounting Standards Committee (IASC) was set up in 1973 by leading professional accounting organizations in nine countries: Australia, Canada, France, German, Japan, Mexico, the Netherlands, the United Kingdom and Ireland, and the United States. It issued the first International accounting standard (IAS) in 1974. In 2001, the IASC was renamed the International Accounting Standards Board (IASB).

Although the IASB is able to propose international accounting standards, it does not have the authority to require companies to follow these standards. In 1995, The international organization of Securities Commissions (IOSCO) stated that it would consider adopting the international accounting standards once the IASB had prepared a comprehensive set of standards covering all the major areas of importance. At the start of 1999, the IASB prepared a core set of standards and submitted them to IOSCO for review and endorsement.

The IASB also received the support of the World Bank. A large number of emerging countries, as well as China Hong Kong, have adopted the IAS as a basis for their accounting standards, Corporations from many developed countries also use the IAS in their financial reporting.

Furthermore, The European Union (EU) is supporting the use of IAS. In 2002, the EU issued a Regulation requiring listed companies to prepare their consolidated financial statements in accordance with IAS from 2005 onward. But the road to global cooperation is never easy, and it will be a long time before full harmonization of financial reporting is achieved.

5.3.2 Differences in global Standards

Several inconsistencies in accounting standards require that the analyst take particular care in making cross-border comparisons. For example, one question to ask is whether all assets and/or liabilities are properly reflected on the balance sheet. If not, these off-balance-

会计准则中的不协调要求分析师在进行跨境比较时特别小心。

企业合并

sheet assets and liabilities must be analyzed and appropriate adjustments made in any valuation exercise.

- **Business Combination.** Under IAS 22 *the purchase method* of accounting is generally used (recording acquired assets and liabilities at fair value at the acquisition date), although the uniting of interest method (recording acquired assets and liabilities at historical book value) is used when the acquirer cannot be identified. Until recently, the United States permitted use of the pooling method (substantially equivalent to uniting of interest) for many acquisitions. Now all new acquisitions in the United States must be accounted for by using the purchase method. Previous acquisitions under the pooling method continue to be reported by using the pooling method. Australia prohibits the pooling/uniting of interest method. In France, Germany, and Italy (at least until 2005), There is a more liberal use of uniting of interests than under IAS. Japan and Switzerland do not have specific rules related to the classification of business combinations.

合并报表

- **Consolidation.** In most countries, corporations publish financial statements that consolidate, to some extent, the accounts of their subsidiaries and affiliates. A full range of consolidation practices exists. In all countries, majority interests in domestic subsidiaries are typically consolidated. This is not always the case when dealing with foreign subsidiaries or with minority interests. In Italy and Japan, certain dissimilar subsidiaries can be excluded. In France, there is considerable leeway in the method used for consolidation. In Japan and Germany, many firms publish separately the financial statements of the various companies belonging to the same group. This can be partly explained by the extent of cross-holdings in these countries. The perimeter of consolidation is often difficult to establish in Japan because of the extent of cross-holding. The practice of publishing (partly) nonconsolidated statements renders the valuation of a company a difficult exercise. IAS 27 imposes consolidation for all subsidiaries with uniform accounting policies. In addition to subsidiaries, there is also the question of non-operating entities created to carry out a special purpose, such as leasing assets or securitizing receivables.

- ❖ Joint ventures. Joint ventures are increasingly used in international business. Most European countries consolidated joint ventures using proportional consolidation, as provided under IAS. In this method, assets, liabilities, and earnings are consolidated line by line, proportional to the percentage of ownership in the subsidiary. U.K. and U.S. corporations use the equity method. A share of the subsidiary profits is consolidated on a one-line basis, proportional to the share of equity owned by the parent. The value of the investment in the subsidiary is adjusted to reflect the change in the subsidiary's equity. The two methods lead to marked differences in the corporation's balance sheet. IAS 31 states that the benchmark treatment should be proportional consolidation, although jointly controlled entities can alternatively be accounted for by using equity consolidation. 〔合资企业〕

- ❖ Goodwill. Goodwill can appear in various ways. Most commonly, goodwill is created when a company engages in an acquisition or merger at a market value different from the book value. Under IAS, goodwill is capitalized and amortized, usually over 20 years or less, and is subject to an impairment test. In Switzerland and Germany, goodwill can be written off against equity immediately and does not affect the income statement. In the United Kingdom, goodwill need not be amortized. In the United States, until recently goodwill and other intangibles without a determinable useful life are no longer amortized, but are subject to impairment tests. 〔商誉〕

- ❖ Financial leases. Financial leases are an indirect way to own an asset and provide the financing for it. In some countries, they are simply carried as off-balance-sheet items. In other countries, these leases are capitalized both as assets and liabilities. This was not common in countries in which accounting systems are driven by tax considerations (e.g., France, Germany, and Italy), but it is progressively implemented in most countries. IAS 17 requires capitalization of financial leases. 〔金融租赁〕

- ❖ Others, such as Asset Revaluation, Provisions, Pensions, Financial Assets and Derivatives, Employee stock Options, there existed differences among IAS and various national GAAP.

5.4 The effects of Accounting Principles on Earnings and Stock Prices

> 同一公司使用不同国家会计准则可能会出现不同收益。有些国家的会计准则比其他国家保守,从而导致报告收益减少。

The same company using different national accounting standards could report different earnings. Some accounting standards are more conservative than others, in the sense that they lead to smaller reported earnings. For example, Radebaugh and Gray (1997) conclude that U. S. accounting principles are significantly more conservative than the U. K. accounting principles but significantly less conservative than Japanese and Continental European accounting principles. If the United States' earnings are arbitrarily scaled at 100. Japanese at 66, German at 87, French at 97, and British at 125. Various studies come up with somewhat different adjustments, so these figures should be interpreted with some caution. Also, recent changes, particularly in the United States and Europe, will impact this assessment in the future.

Example 5 – 5

Japanese company A owns 10 percent of Company B; the initial investment was 10 million yen; Company B owns 20 percent of company A; the initial investment was 10 million yen; both companies value their minority interests at historical cost. The annual net income of company A was 10 million yen, the annual net income of company B was 30 million yen. Assume that the two companies do not pay any dividends, the current stock market values are 200 million yen for company A and 450 million yen for company B.

The questions are:

a. Restate the earnings of the two companies, using the equity method of consolidation.

b. Calculate the P/E ratio, based on non-consolidated and consolidated earnings, how does the non-consolidation of earnings affect the P/E ratios?

Solutions:

a. Company A: 10 million +10% of 30 million = 13 million
Company B: 30 million +20% of 10 million = 32 million

b.

	Company A:	Company B
non-consolidated	200/10 = 20	450/30 = 15
consolidated	200/13 = 15.4	450/32 = 14.1

> Due to non-consolidation, the earnings are understated. Thus, the P/E ratios are overstated due to non-consolidation. As seen here, the consolidation of earnings adjusts the P/E ratios downward.

These national accounting principles also affect the reported book value of equity. Speidell and Bavishi (1992) report the adjustment that should be made to the book value of foreign shareholders' equity if the U.S. GAAP were used, the book value of equity would be increased by 41 percent in Germany and 14 percent in Japan, and would be reduced by 14 percent in the U.K. and 28 percent in France.

Price-earnings (P/E) ratios are of great interest to international investors, who tend to compare the P/E ratios of companies in the same industrial sector across the world. The P/E ratio divides the market price of a share by its current or estimated annual earnings. As of Nov. 30, 1998, P/E ratio ranged from a low of 18.1 in China Hong Kong to a high of 191.0 in Japan, the U.S. market P/E was 28.5. Japanese companies have traditionally traded at very high P/E ratios in comparison with those of U.S. companies. For comparison purposes, these P/E ratios should be adjusted because of the accounting differences in reporting earnings.

6 Global Analyses

The valuation of a common stock is usually conducted in several steps. A company belongs to a global industry and is based in a country. Hence, country and industry analysis is necessary. Companies compete against global players within their industry. Studying a company within its global industry is the primary approach to stock valuation.

6.1 Country Analysis

Companies tend to favor some countries in their business activities. They target some countries for their sales and base their production in only a few countries. Hence, country analysis is of importance in studying a company. In each country, economists try to monitor a large number of economic, social, and political variables, such as

- Anticipated real growth
- Monetary policy

- Fiscal policy
- Competitiveness
- Social and political situations
- Investment climate

In the long run, real economic growth is probably the major influence on a national stock market. Economists focus on economic growth at two horizons:

- long-term sustainable growth
- business cycle

What are favorable country conditions for equity investment? There can be favorable long-term sustainable growth as well as favorable business cycle conditions. If the favorable conditions are a consensus view, however, they will already be priced in the equity markets. The analyst must find a way of discerning these conditions before others do.

A high long-term sustainable growth rate in GDP is favorable, because this translates into high long-term profits and stock returns. In creating GDP and productivity growth rate expectations, the analyst will undoubtedly examine the country's savings rate, investment rate, and total factor productivity (TFP). TFP measures the efficiency with which the economy converts capital and labor into goods and services.

The main factors that interact with the country's investment rate to affect GDP growth are the rate of growth in employment, work hours, education levels, technological improvement, business climate, political stability and the public or private nature of the investment.

In the short term, business cycle conditions can be favorable for investments, but business cycle turning points are so difficult to predict that such predictions should only cause the analyst to make investment recommendations to slightly adjust portfolio. Calverley (2003) classifies the business cycle stages and attractive investment opportunities as:

- *Recovery*: The economy picks up from its slowdown or recession. Good investments to have are the country's cyclical stocks and commodities. Followed by riskier assets as the recovery takes hold.
- *Early Upswing*: Confidence is up and the economy is gaining some momentum. Good investments to have are the country's stocks and also commercial and residential property.

- *Late Upswing*: Boom mentality has taken hold. This is not usually a good time to buy the country's stocks. The country's commodity and property prices will also be peaking. This is the time to purchase the bonds and interest rate sensitive stocks.
- *Economy Slows or Goes into Recession*: The economy is declining, Good investments to have are the bonds and interest rate sensitive stocks.
- *Recession*: Monetary policy will be eased but there will be a lag before recovery. Particularly toward the end of the recession, good investments to make are the stocks and commodities.

6.1.1 Business cycle Synchronization

National business cycles are not fully synchronized. This makes country analysis all the more important. However, economies are becoming increasingly integrated. Growth of major economies is, in part, exported abroad. For example, growth in the U.S. can sustain the activity of an exporting European firm even if demand by European consumers is stagnant. But rigidities in a national economy can prevent it from quickly joining growth in a world business cycle. Studies of rigidities are important here.

Although national economies are becoming increasingly integrated with a world economy, there are so many economic variables involved that the chances of full synchronization are extremely remote. If long-term GDP growth and business cycles were perfectly synchronized among countries, then one would expect a high degree of correlation between markets, especially in periods of crisis. In making investment asset-allocation relations. In the long term, international diversification will always be advantageous until national economies are expected to be perfectly synchronized around the world. It is difficult to imagine such a possibility. Expected returns and expected standard deviations will differ among countries with unsynchronized short-term business cycles and long-term GDP growth rates, even though investors may follow the crowd in their short-term reactions to crises.

各国经济周期不完全同步,这使得国家分析更加重要。

6.1.2 Growth Theory

Growth theory is a branch of economics that examines the role of countries in value creation. Two competing economic theories attempt to shed light on the sustainable long-term growth rate of a nation.

- ❖ Neoclassical Growth theory assumes that the marginal productivity of capital declines as more capital is added. This is the traditional case in economics with diminishing marginal returns to input factors. It predicts that the long-term level of GDP depends on the country's savings rate, but the long-term growth rate in GDP does not depend on the savings rate.

- ❖ Endogenous growth theory assumes that the marginal productivity of capital does not necessarily decline as capital is added. Technological advances and improved education of the labor force can lead to efficiency gains. Any one firm faces diminishing returns, but endogenous growth theory assumes that externalities arise when a firm develops a new technology, Thus, one firm's technical breakthrough, begets another's breakthrough, perhaps through imitation. In this case, the marginal product of capital does not decline with increasing capital per capita. It predicts that the long-term growth rate in GDP depend on the savings rate.

Equity valuation implications are different for countries experiencing these two theories. If a country is experiencing neoclassical growth and its savings rate increases, there would be an increase in dividends as the new level of GDP is reached, but not an increase in the dividend growth rate. For a country experiencing endogenous growth with cascading breakthroughs, however, there would be an increase in both dividends and the dividend growth rate.

6.1.3　The Limitation of the country concept in Financial Analysis

Many companies compete globally, the national location of their headquarters is not a determinant variable. Many multinational corporations realize most of their sales and profits in foreign countries. So, an analysis of the economic situation of the country of their headquarters is not of great importance. Many companies do most of their business outside of their home country, so their valuation should be based on the global competition they face in their industry.

6.2　Industry Analysis

Global industry analysis centers on an examination of sources of growth and sustainability of competitive advantage. An analyst valuing a company within its global industry should study several key elements.

Demand Analysis: Value analysis begins with an examination of demand conditions. Demand is the target for all capacity, location, inventory, and production decisions. Often, the analyst tries to find a leading indicator to help give some forecast of demand.

In the global context, Demand means worldwide demand. A starting point is a set of forecasts of global and country-specific GDP figures. The analyst will want to estimate the sensitivity of sales to global and national GDP changes. So country analysis is important for demand analysis. Because most companies tend to focus on specific regions.

Value creation: Sources of value come from using inputs to produce outputs in the value chain. The value chain is the set of transformations in moving from raw materials to product or service delivery. Within the value chain, each transformation adds value. Value chain analysis can be used to determine how much value is added at each step. The value added is partly a function of four major factors:

- The learning (experience) curve: As companies produce more output, they gain experience, so that the cost per unit produced declines.
- Economies of scale: As a company expands, its fixed costs may be spread over a larger output, and average costs decline over a ranger of output.
- Economies of scope: As a company produces related products, experience and reputation with one product may spill over to another product.
- Network externalities: Some products and services gain value as more consumers use them, so that they are able to share something popular.

Equity valuation implications come from an analysis of the industry's value chain and each company's strategy to exploit current and future profit opportunities within the chain.

Industry Life cycle: Traditionally, the industry life cycle is broken down into stages from pioneering development to decline.

- *Pioneering development* is the first stage and has a low but slowly increasing industry sales growth rate. Substantial development costs and acceptance by only early adopters can lead to low profit margins.
- *Rapid accelerating growth* is the second stage, and the

industry ales growth rate is still modest but is rapidly increasing. High profit margins are possible because firms from outside the new industry may face barriers t entering the newly established markets.

❖ *Mature growth* is the third stage and has a high but more modestly increasing industry sales growth rate. The entry of competitors lowers profit margins, but the return on equity is high.

❖ *Stabilization and market maturity* is the fourth stage and has a high but only slowly increasing sales growth rate. The sales growth rate has not yet begun to decline, but increasing capacity and competition may cause returns on equity to decline to the level of average returns on equity in the economy.

❖ *Deceleration of growth and decline* is the fifth stage with a decreasing sales growth rate. At this stage, the industry may experience overcapacity, and profit margins may be completely eroded.

One would expect that somewhere in stage 2 or 3 the industry sales growth rate would move above the GDP growth rate in the economy, and in stage 5, the industry sales growth rate would fall back to the GDP growth rate and then decline below it.

Competition Structure: One of the first steps in analyzing an industry is the determination of the amount of industry concentration. If the industry is fragmented, many firms compete, and the theories of competition and product differentiation are most applicable. With more concentration and fewer firms in the industry, Oligopolistic competition and game theories become more important. Finally, the case of one firm is the case in which the theory of monopoly applies.

In analyzing industry concentration, two methods are normally used. One is the N firm concentration ratio: the combined market share of the largest N firms in the industry. Another is the Herfindahl index: the sum of the squared market shares of the firms in the industry.

Letting M_i be the market share of an individual firm, the index is $H = M_1^2 + M_2^2 + \cdots + M_N^2$. The Herfindahl index has a value that is always smaller than one. If all firms have an equal share, the reciprocal of the index shows the number of firms in the industry.

When the firms have unequal shares, the reciprocal indicates the "equivalent" number of firms in the industry.

In practice, the equity analyst will see both the N firm concentration ratio and the H index. The advantage of the concentration ratio is that it provides an intuitive sense of industry competition. The H index has the advantage of greater discrimination and it gives greater weight to the companies with larger market shares. An H below 0.1 indicates un-concentration, 0.1—0.18 is moderate concentration and above 0.18 is high concentration.

Suppose the analyst is comparing two industries:

Industry A	Industry B
One firm has 45%	four firms have 15% each
Three firms have 5% each	four firms have 10% each
Ten firms have 4% each	
Four firm concentration ratio is 60%	Four firm concentration ratio is 60%
H index is 0.23	H index is 0.13

Even though the four firm concentration ratios are the same for both industries, the H index indicates that industry A is highly concentrated, but industry B is only moderately concentrated.

Competitive Advantage: In his book, *The competitive Advantage of Nations*, Michael Porter used the notions of economic geography that different locations have different competitive advantages. National factors that can lead to a competitive advantage are:

- ❖ Factor conditions such as human capital, perhaps measured by years of schooling;
- ❖ Demand conditions such as the size and growth of the domestic market;
- ❖ Related supplier and support industries such as the computer software industry to support the hardware industry; and
- ❖ Strategy, structure, and rivalry such as the corporate governance, management practices, and the financial climate.

竞争优势

7 Equity Analyses

7.1 Global financial ratio analysis

The global industry financial analysis examines each company in the industry against the industry average. One well-accepted approach to this type of analysis is the DuPont Model. The basic technique of the DuPont model is to explain ROE or return on assets (ROA) in terms of its contributing elements. The typical de-composition of ROE is given by:

$$\frac{NI}{Equity} = \frac{NI}{EBT} \times \frac{EBT}{EBIT} \times \frac{EBIT}{Sales} \times \frac{Sales}{Assets} \times \frac{Assets}{Equity}$$

where

NI is net income

EBT is earnings before taxes

NI/EBT is one minus the tax rate, or the tax retention rate with a maximum value of 1.0 if there were no taxes (lower values imply higher tax burden).

$EBIT$ is earnings before interest and taxes, or operating income

$EBT/EBIT$ is interest burden, with a maximum value of 1.0 if there are no interest payments (lower values imply greater debt burden).

$EBIT/Sales$ is operating margin

$Sales/Assets$ is asset turnover ratio (a measure of efficiency in the use of assets)

$Assets/Equity$ is leverage (higher values imply greater use of debt)

$NI/Equity$ is return on equity (ROE)

7.2 Valuation Models

Investors often rely on some form of a discounted cash flow analysis (DCF) to estimate the "intrinsic" value of a stock investment. In a dividend discount model (DDM) model, the stock market price is set equal to the stream of forecasted dividends, D, discounted at the required rate of return, r:

$$P_0 = \frac{D_1}{1+r} + \frac{D_2}{(1+r)^2} + \frac{D_3}{(1+r)^3} + \cdots$$

Assume that dividends will grow indefinitely at a constant compounded annual growth rate, g, Hence, it becomes

$$P_0 = \frac{D_1}{r-g}$$

Analysts forecast earnings, and a payout ratio is applied to transform earnings into dividends. Under the assumption of a constant earnings payout ratio, we find

$$P_0 = \frac{E_1(1-b)}{r-g}$$

where

E_1 is next year's earnings;

b is the earnings retention ratio.

r is the required rate of return on the stock

The intrinsic price-to-earnings ratio (P/E) is defined as P_0/E_1:

$$P/E = P_0/E_1 = \frac{1-b}{r-g}$$

> **Example 5-6**
>
> An American corporation whose next annual earnings are expected to be $20 per share, with a constant growth rate of 5 percent per year, and with a 50 percent payout ratio, assume that the required rate of return for an investment in such a corporation is 10 percent. What is the firm's value?
>
> **Solution:**
>
> $$P_0 = \frac{D_1}{r-g} = \frac{10}{0.1-0.05} = \$200$$
>
> A more realistic DDM approach is to decompose the future in three phases. In the near future, earnings are forecasted individually. In the second phase, a general growth rate of the company's earnings is estimated. In the final stage, the growth rate in earnings is assumed to revert to some sustainable growth rate.

7.3 The effects of inflation on Stock prices

Because inflation rates vary around the world and over time, it is important to consider the effects of inflation on stock prices.

Because historical costs are used in accounting, inflation has a distorting effect on reported earnings. These effects show up primarily in replacement, inventories, borrowing costs and capital gains taxes. To analyze the effects of inflation on the valuation process, analysts try to determine what part of inflation flows through to a firm's earnings. A full-flow-through firm has earnings that fully reflect inflation. Thus, any inflation cost increases must be getting passed along to consumers.

由于世界各地的通货膨胀率各不相同,随着时间的推移,考虑通货膨胀对股票价格的影响很重要。

In an inflationary environment, consider a firm that would otherwise have no growth in earnings, a zero-earning retention ratio and full-inflation flow-through. So, earnings only grow because of the inflation rate I, assumed constant over time. For example, we have

$$E_1 = E_0 \times (1 + I)$$

By discounting this stream of inflation-growing earnings at the required rate r, we find that the intrinsic value of such a firm would then be

$$P_0 = \frac{E_1}{r - I} = E_0\left(\frac{1 + I}{r - I}\right)$$

where

I is the annual inflation rate.

r is the nominal required nominal rate of return

Let's now consider a company with a partial-inflation flow-through of λ percent, so that earnings are only inflated at a rate λI:

$$E_1 = E_0 \times (1 + \lambda I)$$

By discounting this stream of earnings at the nominal required rate r, we find

$$P_0 = \frac{E_1}{r - I} = E_0\left(\frac{1 + \lambda I}{r - \lambda I}\right)$$

If we introduce the real required rate of return $\rho = r - I$, we get

$$P_0 = E_0\left(\frac{1 + \lambda I}{\rho + (1 - \lambda)I}\right) = \frac{E_1}{\rho + (1 - \lambda)I}$$

The intrinsic P/E using prospective earnings is now equal to

$$P_0/E_1 = \frac{1}{\rho + (1 - \lambda)I}$$

We can see the higher the inflation flow-through rate, the higher the price of the company. Indeed, a company that cannot pass inflation through its earnings is penalized. Thus, the *P/E* ratio ranges from a high of $1/\rho$ to a low of $1/r$. The higher the inflation rate, the more negative the influence on the stock price if full inflation pass-through cannot be achieved.

This observation is important if we compare similar companies in different countries experiencing different inflation rates. A company operating in a high-inflation environment will be penalized if it cannot pass through inflation.

> **Example 5-7**
>
> Two companies in the same line of business, but with mostly domestic operations. A is based in a country with no inflation, B is based in a country with a 4 percent inflation rate. There is no real growth in earnings for both companies. The real rate of return required by global investors for this type of stock investment is 6 percent. Company B can only pass 80 percent of inflation through its earnings. What should be the P/E of the two companies?
>
> **Solution:**
>
> The P/E of Company A is: $1/\rho = 1/0.06 = 16.67$
>
> The P/E of Company B is: $1/(6\% + 20\% \times 4\%) = 1/6.8\% = 14.71$
>
> In the inflationary environment, Company B's earnings cannot grow as fast as inflation. Penalized by inflation and its inability to pass along inflation, Company B's P/E ratio is below that of Company A.

Summary

- Stock exchanges throughout the world evolved from three models: private bourses, public bourses, and banker's bourses.
- Trading procedures differ in an order-driven market and in a price-driven market.
- ECNs have developed alongside official stock exchanges.
- The relative market capitalization of national equity markets has changed dramatically over time. Many practical aspects must be taken into account in global equity investing: market concentration, liquidity, tax aspects, and transaction costs.
- Numerous stock indexes are available to track country and regional markets and measure performance.
- It is possible to get some of the benefits of international diversification by investing solely in securities or funds listed at home: ADRs, Country funds and ETFs.
- Each country follows a set of accounting principles that are usually prepared by the accounting profession and the national authorities.
- The major differences in accounting standards around the world appear in the treatment of business combinations, consolidation of subsidiary and affiliate information, goodwill etc.
- National accounting principles can affect the reported earnings and

the reported book value of equity and the *P/E* value.
- In the long run, real economic growth is probably the major influence on a national stock market. Economists focus on economic growth at two horizons: long-term sustainable growth and business cycle.
- Global industry analysis centers on an examination of sources of growth and sustainability of competitive advantage. The global industry financial analysis examines each company in the industry against the industry average.
- The basic technique of the DuPont model is to explain ROE or return on assets (ROA) in terms of its contributing elements.
- Investors often rely on some form of a discounted cash flow analysis (DCF) to estimate the "intrinsic" value of a stock investment.
- Because inflation rates vary around the world and over time, it is important to consider the effects of inflation on stock prices.

Exercises

1. Explanation the ratio of the U.S stock market capitalization in the U.S. GDP is larger than that of continental Europe?
2. Taxes are applied for foreign investment in the following areas: (   )
   A. Transactions   B. capital gains
   C. Income   D. tariff
3. Transaction volume gives indications on the (   ) of each market.
   A. liquidity   B. Market Size
   C. Concentration   D. Tax
4. A U.S. investor buys 100 shares of Heineken listed in Amsterdam for 40 €s, the current exchange is 1 € = 1.1 $, Her total cost is $4,400. three months later, a gross dividend of 2 € is paid (15 percent withholding tax), and she decides to sell the shares for 38 € per share, the current exchange rate is 1 € = 1.2 $, what are the cash flows received in U.S. dollar?
5. Stock exchanges throughout the world evolved from the following models: (   )
   A. private bourses   B. public bourses
   D. banker's bourses   D. none of them
6. A U.S. institutional investor with a large portfolio of U.S. and international stocks wants to add 20,000 shares of Daimler/Chrysler to its portfolio. DaimlerChrysler trades as the same global

share on several exchanges in the world. A U.S. broker quotes the NYSE price of DaimlerChrysler as $43.45 - 43.65, net of commissions. The institutional investor is also considering purchasing shares in Germany, where the offer price quoted for DaimlerChrysler's shares on the Frankfurt stock exchange is EUR 44.95, with a 0.10% commission to be paid on the transaction value. Which of the two alternatives is better for the investor? How much would be the total saving by using the better of the two alternatives? The exchange rate is USD/EUR 0.9705 - 0.9710.

7. Which of the following statements about stock markets is not true? ( )
   A. Many of the stock markets are organized as private bourses.
   B. On most markets, stocks are traded on a cash basis, and transactions are settled within a two-to five-day period.
   C. The central electronic limit order book is the hub of those automated markets that are price-driven.
   D. An auction market, such as the Paris Bourse, is also known as an order-driven market.

8. Which of the following statements about stock indexes is true? ( )
   A. Dow Jones 30 Industrial Average (DJIA) is a global stock index.
   B. Dow Jones 30 Industrial Average (DJIA) is a domestic stock index.
   C. The S&P 350 Europe index is a domestic stock index.
   D. Japanese Nikkei 225 Stock Average is a global stock index.

9. A country fund is a closed-end fund whose NAV is equal to ( )
   A. NAV = Fund market price + Premium.
   B. NAV = Fund market price - Premium.
   C. NAV = Premium.
   D. NAV = Fund market price

10. What are the motivations for investing in the country funds?

11. Paf is an emerging country with severe foreign investment restrictions but an active stock market open mostly to local investors. Pif is the local currency and the exchange rate with the U.S. dollar remain fixed at 1 pif/ $. A closed-end country fund, called Paf country Fund, has been approved by Paf. Its net asset value is 100 dollars and It trades in New York with a premium of 30 percent.
   a. Give some intuitive explanations for this Positive Premium.
   b. Paf Unexpectedly announces that it will lift all foreign investment restrictions, which has two effects: First, stock prices in Paf go up by 20 percent because of the expectation of

massive foreign investment. Second, the premium on the country fund drops to zero. What would be your total gain on the shares of Paf Country fund?

12. What are the advantages and disadvantages of a country fund?

13. An ETF is indexed on a Japanese stock Indexes and is listed in New York, Its NAV is computed based on closing Prices in Tokyo. When it is 9 A.M. in New York, It is already 11 P.M. in Tokyo, On the same day. The NAV based on Tokyo Closing prices is 10,000 yen, The exchange rate at 9 A.M. EST is 1 dollar = 100 yen.
   a. What is the dollar NAV of this ETF at the opening of trading in New York?
   b. When New York close at 4 P.M. EST, Tokyo is still closed (6 a.m. local time), but the exchange rate is now 99 yen per dollar. What is the dollar NAV at closing time?
   c. Bad international news hit after the Tokyo closing, European and U.S. stock markets dropped by 5 percent. Should the ETF Price have remained at its NAV? Assuming that the Tokyo market is strongly correlated with the U.S. market (at least for this type of international news). Give an estimate of the ETF price at the New York closing.

14. Explain why a corporation can have a stock market price well above its accounting book value.

15. Consider a U.K. index fund that trades on a U.S. exchange. This fund is indexed on a British stock index based on several stocks that trade on the London stock exchange. The different time zones of the U.K. and the U.S. markets result in four distinct time periods in a 24-hour period:
One, a six-hour time period prior to the U.S. open, when the market in London is open but the market in the United States is not.
Two, a two-hour period between 9:30 A.M. and 11:30 A.M. in New York when both London and New York markets are open.
Three, a 4.5 hour time period between 11:30 A.M. and 4:00 P.M. in New York when the New York market is open but the London market is not. And
Four, the subsequent period when both markets are closed.
For each of these time periods. Discuss how British pound NAV and the U.S. dollar price of the fund would fluctuate.

16. In 1996, a group of securities called the World Equity Benchmark Shares (WEBS) started trading on the American Stock Exchange.

WEBS for a country is a passively managed ETF indexed on the MSCI country benchmark index for that country. What do you think would be the effect of the launch of WEBS for a country on the premium or discount of the closed-end country fund for that country?

17. The annual revenues (in billion dollars) in financial year 2001 for the top five players in the global media and entertainment industry are given in the following table. The top five corporations in this industry include three U.S-based corporations, one French corporation and one Australian corporation. The revenue indicated for Vivendi Universal does not include the revenue from its environmental business. Assume that the total worldwide revenue of all firms in this industry was $250 billion.

Company	Revenue
AOL Time Warner	38
Walt Disney	25
Vivendi Universal	25
Viacom	23
News Corporation	13

a. Compute the three-firm and five-firm concentration ratios.

b. Compute the three-firm and five-firm Herfindahl indexes.

18. You are given the following data about Walt Disney and News Corporation, two of the major corporations in the media and entertainment industry. The data are for the end of the financial year 1999. And are in US$ millions. Though News Corporation is based in Australia. It also trades on the NYSE and its data in the following table, like those for Walt Disney, is according to the U.S. GAAP.

	Walt Disney	News Corporation
Sales	23,402	14,395
EBIT	3,035	1,819
EBT	2,314	1,212
NI	1,300	719
Assets	43,679	35,681
Equity	20,975	16,374

a. Compute the ROE for these two corporations.

b. Use the DuPont model to analyze the difference in ROE between the two companies, by identifying the elements that primarily cause the difference.

Chapter 6
International Bond Investment

The requirement of Learning
- Discuss the difference between domestic bonds, foreign bonds, and Eurobonds.
- Describe the various stages of a Eurobond issue and the various ways to invest in bonds from emerging countries. Describe a Brady bond and bond quotation and day count conventions across the world.
- Describe the basic valuation method for straight fixed-rate bonds and a yield curve based on zero-coupon bonds.
- Describe and contrast the various methods used to report a yield to maturity (simple yield, annual yield, semiannual yield).
- Define the duration, or interest sensitivity, of a bond and compute the expected excess return (risk premium) on a domestic bond as the sum of the yield spread over the cash rate plus the duration adjusted expected yield movement.
- Define the three components of the quality spread (expected loss component, credit-risk premium, liquidity premium) and compare yield curves in various currencies.
- Knowing the implied forward exchange rate from yield curves in different currencies and can conduct an exchange rate break-even analysis.
- Explain the various sources of return and risk from an international bond. Compute the return on a foreign-currency bond and the return on a foreign bond, hedged against currency risk and the expected excess return (risk premium) on a foreign currency bond, hedged and not hedged against currency risk.
- Describe the characteristics and valuation of straight FRNs, bull FRNs, bear FRNs, dual-currency bonds, and currency-option bonds, and the motivation for their issuance

1　The Introduction of Global Bond Market

1.1　The various Segments

Debt certificates have been traded internationally for several centuries. As a matter of fact, organized trading in domestic and foreign debentures took place well before the start of any equity market.

Although debt financing has always been international in nature, there is still no unified international bond market, Instead, the global bond market is divided into three broad groups:

- Domestic Bonds are issued locally by a domestic borrower and are usually denominated in the local currency.
- Foreign Bonds are issued on a local market by a foreign borrower and are usually denominated in the local currency. Foreign bond issues and trading are under the supervision of local market authorities.
- Eurobonds are underwritten by a multinational syndicate of banks and are placed mainly in countries other than the one in whose currency the bond is denominated. These bonds are not traded on a specific national bond market.

Domestic bonds make up the bulk of a national bond market. Different issuers belong to different market segments: government, semi-government, and corporate. Foreign bonds issued on national markets have existed for a long time. They often have colorful names, such as Yankee bonds, Samurai bonds, Rembrandt bonds, Matador bonds, Caravel bonds, and bulldog bonds.

After the world war II, many non-U.S. firms have financing needs in U.S. dollars, they have a strong incentive to issue bonds in New York. But these bonds must satisfy the disclosure requirements of the U.S. GAAP. In 1963, the United States imposed an Interest Equalization Tax (IET) on foreign securities held by U.S. investors. The tax forced non-U.S. corporations to pay a higher interest rate in order to attract U.S. investors. A few years later, the Federal Reserve Board restricted the financing of foreign direct investment by U.S. corporations. These measures made the U.S. bond market less attractive to foreign borrowers and created a need for offshore financing of U.S. corporate foreign activities. Because of the Glass-Steagall Act, U.S. commercial banks were prevented from issuing and dealing in bonds, Such restrictions did not apply to their offshore activities, and foreign subsidiaries of U.S. commercial banks became very active on the Eurobond market. Because of these, it led to the development of the Eurobond market in the early 1960s. The repeal of the IET in 1974, the partial relaxation of the G-S Act, as well as various measures to attract foreign borrowers and issuers on the U.S. domestic market, did not slow the growth of the Eurobond market.

More important, the Eurobond market came to be recognized by borrowers and investors alike as an efficient, low-cost, and most innovative market.

1.2 World market size

The world bond market comprises both the domestic bond markets and the international market. The size of the world bond market was estimated at around $37 trillion at the start of 2002. The world capitalization of bonds is higher than that of equity. Bonds denominated in dollars currently represent roughly half the value of all outstanding bonds, Yen bonds represent roughly 20 percent of the world bond market, and European currencies, 30 percent. Bonds denominated in euros amount to 20 percent of all bonds.

1.3 Bond Indexes

The wide variety of bond, ranging from zero-coupon bonds to bonds with embedded option (i.e., callable or putable bonds), results in a number of different types of bonds indices. Similar to equities, bonds can be categorized according to the issuer's economic sector, the issuer's geographic region, or the economic development of the issuer's geographic region. Bonds can also be classified along the following dimensions:

➢ Type of issuer (government, government agency, corporation);

➢ Type of financing (general obligation, collateralized).

➢ Currency of payments;

➢ Maturity.

➢ Credit quality (investment grade, high yield, credit agency ratings).

➢ Absence or presence of inflation protection.

Bonds indices are based on these various dimensions and can be categorized as follows:

➢ Aggregate or broad market indices;

➢ Market sector indices;

➢ Style indices;

➢ Economic sector indices;

➢ Specialized indices such as high yield, inflation linked, and emerging market indices.

The first bond index created, the Barclays Capital U. S.

Aggregate Bond Index (formerly the Lehman Brothers Aggregate Bond Index), is an example of a single country aggregate index. Designed to represent the broad market of U.S. bonds, it comprises more than 9200 bonds, including U.S. Treasury, government related, corporate, mortgage backed, asset backed, and commercial mortgage backed bonds.

Aggregate indices can be subdivided by market sector (government, government agency, collateralized, corporate); style (maturity, credit quality); economic sector, or some other characteristic to create more narrowly defined indices. A common distinction reflected in indices is between investment grade (e.g., those with a Standard & Poor's credit rating of BBB-or better) and high yield bonds. Investment grade indices are typically further subdivided by maturity (i.e., short, intermediate, or long) and by credit rating (e.g., AAA, BBB, etc.). The wide variety of bonds indices reflects the partitioning of bonds on the basis of a variety of dimensions.

Table 6.1 illustrates how the major types of bonds indices can be organized on the basis of various dimensions.

Table 6.1 Dimensions of Bonds Indices

Market	Global			
	Regional			
	Country or currency zone			
Type	Corporate	Collateralized	Government agency	Government
		Securitized		
		Mortgage backed		
Maturity	For example, 1-3, 3-5, 5-7, 7-10, 10+ years; short term, medium term, or long term			
Credit quality	For example, AAA, AA, A, BBB, etc; Aaa, Aa, A, Baa, etc; Investment grade, high yield			

Source: Michael G. McMillan, etc. *INVESTMENTS Principles of Portfolio and Equity Analysis*. 2010.

All aggregate indices include a variety of market sectors and credit ratings. The breakdown of the Barclays Capital Global Aggregate Bond Index by market sectors and by credit rating is shown in figure 6.1 and figure 6.2, respectively.

Bond indexes used to be less commonly available than stock indexes. However, total-return bond indexes serve many purposes and are increasingly used. A total-return bond index cumulates the price movement with accrued interest; it is a cumulative index of the total return on a bond portfolio.

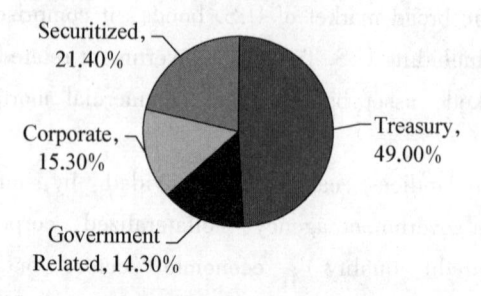

Figure 6.1 Market Sector Breakdown of the Barclays Capital Global Aggregate Bond Index

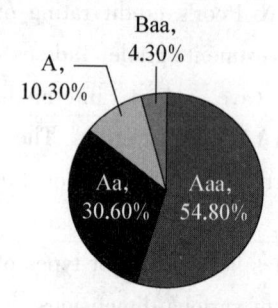

Figure 6.2 Credit Breakdown of the Barclays Capital Global Aggregate Bond Index

These indexes are put to different uses:
- A bond index calculated daily for each bond market allows quick assessment of the direction and magnitude of movements in the market. Such an index must be based on a small but representative sample of actively traded bonds, called a "benchmark" bond, is sometimes used.
- Total-return bond indexes are also required for measuring the performance of a bond portfolio in a domestic or multicurrency setting. This is usually done monthly or quarterly.

Within a national market, the price movements of all fixed-rate bonds tend to be strongly correlated. This is because all bond prices are influenced by movements in the local interest rate.

1.4 The Eurobond Market

Of all the bond markets in the world, the Eurobond market is certainly an attractive one to the international investor, It avoids most national regulations and constraints and provides sophisticated instruments geared to various investment objectives. Because of the important role of Eurobonds in international investment, we will examine in some detail how they are issued and traded.

The figure 6.3 is a Eurobond issued by NKK, a Japanese company. It's a tombstone advertises, it tells: it is a dual-currency bond: issued in yen (20 billion), with interest coupons fixed in yen (8 percent), but its principal repayment is fixed in U.S. dollars. The underwriting syndicate is listed at the bottom of the tombstone.

NEW ISSUE   22nd January, 1994

NKK
Nippon Kokan Kabushiki Kaisha

8 per cent. Dual Currency
Yen/U.S.Dollar Bonds Due 2004
Issue Price: 101 percent of the Issue Amount

Issue Amount: ¥ 20,000,000,000
Redemption Amount at Maturity: U.S. $110,480,000

Nomura International Limited	Mitsubishi Trust & Banking Corporation
Prudential-Bache Securities International	Yamaichi International Limited
Bankers Trust International Limited	Dresdner Bank Aktienge sells chaft
Morgan Stanley International	Morgan Guaranty Ltd

Figure 6.3 A Eurobond issued by NKK

In general, several points distinguish a Eurobond from a domestic bond:

- ❖ The underwriting syndicate is made up of banks from numerous countries.
- ❖ Underwriting banks tend to use subsidiaries established in London or a country with a favorable tax situation.
- ❖ Corporate borrowers sometimes use a subsidiary incorporated in a country with a favorable tax and regulatory treatment.
- ❖ The frequency of coupon payments is annual for fixed rate Eurobonds.
- ❖ A new issue may be placed within three weeks, neither registration formalities nor waiting queues.

1.4.1 The issuing syndicate

Eurobonds are sold in a multistage process. The issue is organized by an international bank called the lead manager. This bank invites several co-managers to form the management group (from 5 to 30 banks, usually). For large issues, there may be several lead managers. The managers prepare the issue, set the final conditions of the bond, and select the underwriters and selling group. One of the managers is appointed as the principal paying agent and fiscal agent. A large portion of the issue is directly subscribed by the management group.

These securities have been sold outside the United States of America and Japan. This announcement appears as a matter of record only. The underwriters are invited to participate in the issue on the basis of their regional placement power. Their number varies from 30 to 300 and comprise international banks from all regions of the world. Together with the management group, the underwriters guarantee final placement of the bonds at a set price to the borrower.

The selling group is responsible for selling the bonds to the public and consists of managers, underwriters, and additional banks with a good selling base. Note that a participant may be, at the same time, manager, underwriter, and seller. Separate fees are paid to compensate for the various services. The total fee ranges from 1% to 2.5%. Unlike their U.S. counterparts, Eurobond underwriters are not obligated to maintain the bond's market price at or above the issue price until the syndicate is disbanded. This means that bonds are often placed at a price below the issue price. There is considerable price discrimination among clients, and selling members may pass along part of their fee to the final buyer of the bond.

1.4.2　The Timetable of a New Issue

Unlike national markets, the Eurobond market has neither registration formalities nor waiting queues. A new issue may be placed within three weeks. A typical timetable is depicted in Figure 6.4.

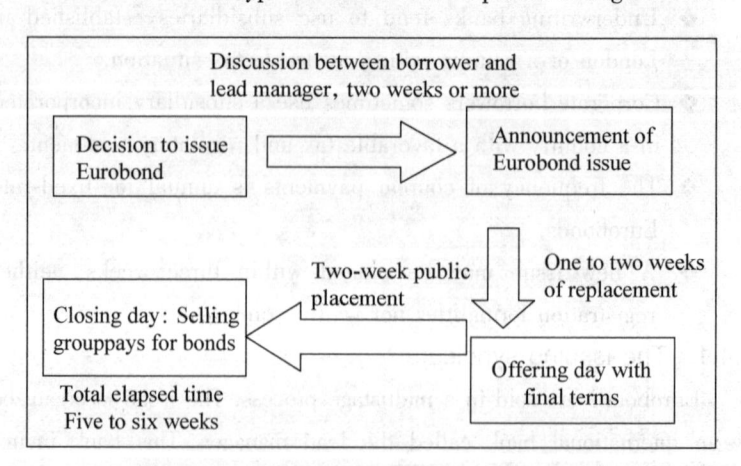

Figure 6.4　Timetable of a New Eurobond Issue

First, the lead manager gets together with borrower to discuss the terms of the bond (amount, maturity, fixed or floating rate, and coupon). The terms generally remain provisional until the official offering date. During this period, the lead manager arranges the management syndicate and prepares various documents, one of which is a preliminary prospectus called, at this stage, a red herring. On the announcement day, the managers send e-mails or faxes describing the proposed bond issue and inviting banks to join the underwriting and selling groups. Potential underwriters are sent the preliminary prospectus. A week or two later, the final prospectus is printed, and the bonds are publicly offered on the offering day. At the end of a public placement period of about two weeks, the subscription is closed on the closing day, and the bonds are delivered in exchange for cash paid to the borrower. A tombstone is later published in international newspapers to advertise the successful issue and to list the participating banks.

After the closing day, the bonds can be publicly traded. However, bond trading actually takes place well before the closing day, A gray market for the bonds starts before the final terms have been set on the offering day; trading is contingent on the final issue price. That is, bonds are traded in the gray market at a premium or discount relative to the future price. For example, a quote of less 1/4 means that the bonds are exchanged at a price of 99.25% if the future issue price is set at 99.5%. This is a form of forward market for bonds that do not yet exist. The gray market is often used by members of the selling group to resell part of their bond allocation at a discount below the issue price, but possibly at a net profit if their fee is large enough.

1.4.3 Dealing in Eurobonds

The Eurobond secondary market is truly international and comprises an informal network of market makers and dealers. A market maker quotes a net price to a financial institution in the form of a bid-ask price. No commissions are charged. Although the Eurobond market has no physical location, most of the bonds are lists on the Luxembourg stock exchange to nominally satisfy the requirement of obtaining a public quotation at least once a year or quarter. However, very few transactions go through the exchange. Instead, Eurobond dealers created an around-the-clock market among financial institutions across the world, forming the *International Securities Market Association* (ISMA), based in Zurich and London. The geographical composition of the ISMA shows the prominent role of

London. But Swiss bands are large investors in the market and the second major force in ISMA.

All market makers and dealers in Eurobonds are part of the ISMA. The ISMA bears some similarities to the U. S. National Association of Securities Dealers (NASD). But, whereas NASD is under the supervision of the SEC, the ISMA is purely self-regulated and is subject to no government intervention.

1.4.4 Eurobond Clearing System

Let's assume that a investment manager wants to buy $100,000 worth of a specific Eurobond. The investment manager calls several market makers to get their best quotations and concludes the deal at the lowest price quoted. The trade is settled in three business days. And the transaction is cleared through one of the two major clearing systems: Euro-clear and Clear-stream. These clearing companies have now joined with major European bond and equity clearing systems.

Euro-clear and Clears-tream collect a transaction fee for each book entry, as well as a custody fee for holding the securities. The custody fees are a function of a client's transaction volume: If the member bank maintains a large bond turnover, the custodial fee and is nil. Euro-clear and Clear-stream also provide security lending facilities.

1.5 Emerging Markets and Brady Bonds

Investors wishing to buy bonds issued by emerging countries have several alternatives:

☙ Directly access the domestic bond markets of some emerging countries.

☙ Foreign bonds issued by these countries.

☙ Eurobonds issued by emerging countries.

☙ Brady bonds on the international capital market.

In the 1980s, many developing countries were hit hard by the drop in commodity prices and other problems, and became unable or unwilling to service their loans from international banks. This led to an international debt crisis that threatened the international financial system. The emerging-country debt often took the form of bank loans, which are non-tradable, as opposed to bonds. Although many emerging countries have not serviced their bank loans, leading to a negotiation to reschedule them. The creditor banks formed the Paris Club to negotiate with emerging countries the rescheduling of their debts. A secondary market for nonperforming loans developed in which these loans traded at a steep discount from their par value, The principles of Brady plans, named after the U. S. Secretary of the Treasury, were implemented from 1990 to provide a satisfactory solution to this debt crisis.

To negotiate its Brady plan, the emerging country must initiate a credible economic reform program that receives approval and funding from the World Bank, the International Monetary Fund, and regional development banks, such as the inter-American development Bank, the African Development Bank, the Asian Development Bank, or the European Bank for Reconstruction and Development. Once the IMF and the World Bank have agreed that the economic reform plan will reduce the risk of new insolvency problems, these organizations provide funding which can be used in part to provide collateral and guarantees in the debt rescheduling. One advantage for creditors is that they exchange commercial loans for tradable bonds. A Brady plan is basically a debt-reduction program whereby sovereign debt is repackaged into tradable Brady bonds, generally with collateral. Close to 20 countries have issued Brady bonds, including Argentina, Brazil, Bulgaria, Costa Rica, Nigeria, Poland, the Philippines, Uruguay, and Venezuela. These bonds are traded in the international capital market, with a total capitalization close to $100 billion.

International commercial banks, which were most active in lending to emerging countries, are the major market makers on the Brady bond market. The bid-ask spread on these bonds averages 25 basis points and is low relative to that of Eurobonds issued by emerging countries, because the issue size of Brady bonds can be very large and their market is quite active.

2 Major Differences among Bond Markets

A through technical knowledge of the various bond markets reduces investors' trading costs and enhances returns; it also helps investors to better understand the risks involved. Because bond markets are still rapidly developing, new types of instruments and issuing techniques appear throughout the world all the time. For this reason, the following description of these markets is bound to become partially outdated over time; it is meant to serve chiefly as a broad overview.

2.1 Types of Instruments

The variety of bonds offered to the international or even the domestic investor is amazing, because of the recent development of bonds with variable interest rates and complex optional clauses. Although the U.S. bond market is among the more innovative markets, the Eurobond market is surely the most creative of all. Investment bankers from many countries bring their expertise to this unregulated market. Each month, new instruments appear or disappear, and the Eurobond market's major difference from domestic markets lies in its multicurrency nature. Many Eurobonds are designed to have cash flows in different currencies.

For example, Japanese firms have frequently issued Swiss franc-denominated bonds convertible into common shares of a Japanese company, This is a bond issued in Swiss francs paying a fixed coupon in Swiss francs, and repaid in Swiss francs, But the bond can also be converted into shares of the Japanese issuing company.

A Swiss investor can benefit from purchasing this bond in any one of three situations:

- A drop in the market interest rate on Swiss franc bonds
- A rise in the price of the company's stock
- A rise in the yen relative to the franc

A non-Swiss investor would also benefit if the franc appreciates relative to the investor's currency. Of course, the reverse scenarios would lead to a loss.

> 由于近年来不同利息和复杂的期权条款类型的债券出现,债券的种类对于投资者来说多得出奇。

2.2 Quotations, Day Count, and Frequency of Coupons

2.2.1 Quotations

Bonds are usually quoted on a price plus accrued interest basis in percentage of face value. The full price, P, is equal to the sum of the quoted, or clean price, Q, plus accrued interest, AI:

$$P = Q + AI$$

Example 6-1

The clean price of a Eurobond is quoted at $Q = 95\%$, The annual coupon is 6%, and we are exactly three months from the past coupon payment. What is the full price of the bond?

> **Solution**: $P = Q + \text{accrued interest} = 95\% + 90/360 \times 6\%$
> $= 96.5\%$

2.2.2 Day Count and Frequency of Coupons

Bonds differ internationally by the frequency of their coupon payments and in the way accrued interest is calculated. The following is coupon characteristics of Major bond markets:

Day Count
- 30/360: the U.S., Eurobonds, Germany, Scandinavia, Switzerland and the Netherlands.
- Actual/actual: U.S. treasury bonds, Australia, United Kingdom, France
- Actual/365: Japan, Canada
- Actual/360: FRNs

Frequency of Coupons
- Semiannual: United States, Japan, Canada, Australia, United Kingdom.
- Annual: Eurobonds, Switzerland, Germany, Netherlands, France.
- Quarter or semiannual: FRNs.

2.2.3 Yield to Maturity (YTMs)

Most financial institutions around the world calculate and publish yields to maturity on individual bonds. But the methods used for the calculation vary among countries. So that yields are not directly comparable. Usually:

- Most Europeans calculate an annual YTM using the ISMA-recommended formula.
- U.S.A (and often British) institutions publish a semiannual actuarial yield.

Suppose A U.S. bond issued at par with 6% coupons will pay a coupon of $3 semiannually per $100 of face value and is reported as having a semiannual YTM of 6%. Europeans would quote this bond as having a 6.09% YTM. In Japan, the financial institutions sometimes report YTM based on a simple-interest calculation. The formula is:

$$YTM = \frac{Coupon}{Current\ Price} + \frac{(100 - Current\ Price)}{Current\ Price} \times \frac{1}{Years\ To\ Maturity}$$

> **Example 6 – 2**
> A three-year bond has exactly three years till maturity, and

> the last coupon has just been paid. The coupon is annual and equal to 6%, The bond price is 95%, what is its simple yield?
> **Solution**: Simple yield = 6/95 + (100−95)/95×1/3 = 8.07%

3 A Refresher on Bond Valuation

3.1 Zero-Coupon Bonds

到期收益率(YTM):

Yield to maturity (YTM): The theoretical value of a bond is determined by computing the present value of all future cash flows generated by the bond discounted at an appropriate interest rate. Conversely, we can calculate the internal rate of return, or (YTM), of a bond on the basis of its current market price and its promised payments.

For example, the interest rate at which P dollars should be invested today in order to realize C_t dollars t years from now.

$$P = \frac{C_t}{(1+r_t)^t}$$

3.1.1 Yield Curve

同一货币不同期限的两种零息债券的到期收益率通常是不同的。

The YTMs of two zero-coupon bonds in the same currency but with different maturities are usually different. Graphing the YTMs on bonds with different maturities allows us to draw a yield curve. The yield curve shows the YTM computed on a given date as a function of the maturity of the bonds. It provides an estimate of the current term structure of interest rates. To be meaningful, a yield curve must be drawn from bonds with identical characteristics, except for their maturity.

The most important yield curve is derived from zero-coupon government bonds. This is a default-free yield curve. Although government bonds are seldom issued without coupons, a common technique for creating zero-coupon bonds is called "stripping". That is, the government lets bankers strip a government coupon bond: Each cash flow of a given government bond is transformed into a separate bond. So there are as many zero-coupon bonds as there are coupon payments and final reimbursement. The government Zero-coupon yield curve is derived from these strips.

收益率曲线也可以用政府有息债券的到期收益率来计算。

A yield curve can also be calculated from the YTM on government coupon bonds. It is usually derived from bonds trading at, or around, par (100 percent) and is called *the par yield curve*.

3.2 Bond with Coupons

Most bonds issued pay a periodic coupon.

3.2.1 Valuing a bond with coupons

In general, we suppose the C_1, $C_2 \cdots$, C_n, is the cash flow paid by the bond at times 1, 2, to n, The last cash flow will generally include a coupon and the principal reimbursement. We then have the pricing formula

$$P = \frac{C_1}{(1+r_1)^1} + \frac{C_2}{(1+r_2)^2} + \cdots + \frac{C_n}{(1+r_n)^n}$$

3.2.2 Yield to Maturity

The YTM of a coupon bond can still be defined as the internal rate of return, r, Which equates the discounted stream of cash flows to the current bond market price. Keep in mind, however, that this is really an average yield provided by cash flows that take place at different times. For an annual coupon bond, the equation is as follows:

$$P = \frac{C_1}{(1+r)^1} + \frac{C}{(1+r)^2} + \cdots + \frac{C_n}{(1+r)^n}$$

In practice, Coupons may be paid at any time during the coupon period. This calls for the more general valuation formula to determine YTM:

$$P = \frac{C_{t_1}}{(1+r)^{t_1}} + \frac{C_{t_2}}{(1+r)^{t_2}} + \cdots + \frac{C_{t_n}}{(1+r)^{t_n}}$$

3.2.3 European versus U.S. YTM

Equation above allows us to determine the annual YTM on a bond if we know its cash flows and observe its market value. This method is used worldwide except in the United States, where the tradition is to calculate a YTM over a six-month period and multiply it by 2 to report an annualized yield. We call this annualized yield a U.S. YTM. This method for computing an annualized semiannual yield r' can be described by the formula:

$$P = \frac{C_{t_1}}{(1+r'/2)^{2t_1}} + \frac{C_{t_2}}{(1+r'/2)^{2t_2}} + \cdots + \frac{C_{t_n}}{(1+r'/2)^{2t_n}}$$

> 如果我们知道未来现金流和市价,那么就可以根据上面的式子计算年到期收益率。

Example 6 – 3 European and U.S.YTM

A three-year bond has exactly three years till maturity, and

> the last coupon has just been paid, the coupon is annual and equal to 6 percent, the bond price is 95 percent. What are its European and U.S.YTM?
>
> **Solution:**
>
> The European YTM is r, given by the formula
>
> $$95 = 6/(1+r)^1 + 6/(1+r)^2 + 106/(1+r)^3$$
>
> Using a spreadsheet, we find $r = 7.94\%$.
>
> The U.S. YTM is r', given by the formula
>
> $$95 = 6/(1+r'/2)^2 + 6/(1+r'/2)^4 + 106/(1+r'/2)^6$$
>
> Hence, $r' = 7.79\%$. We verify that $1.0794 = (1+7.79\%/2)^2$.

3.3 Duration and Interest Rate Sensitivity

There is an inverse relationship between the price of a bond and changes in interest rates. If the bond's cash flows are fixed, the price is solely a function of the market yield. Practitioners usually define *interest rate sensitivity, or duration*, as the approximate percentage price change for a 100 basis points (1% point) change in market yield, mathematically, the duration D can be written as

$$\frac{\Delta P}{P} = -D^* \times \Delta r$$

The Macaulay duration of a standard bond is its weighted-average maturity. Also call it *modified duration*

$$D = \frac{1}{P} \sum_{t=1}^{n} t \frac{C_t}{(1+r)^t}$$

In general,

- ❖ The duration of Zero-coupon is equal to its maturity.
- ❖ The longer the maturity of a bond, the larger its duration.

Strictly speaking, the duration is a good approximation of the bond price reaction to interest rate movements only for small movements in the general level in interest rates. In other words, it gives a good approximation for the percentage price movements only for small parallel shifts in the yield curve. For larger movements in yield, the convexity can be introduced. Also note that the duration of a bond changes over time. To summarize, duration is a simple measure of the sensitivity of a bond, or a portfolio of bonds, to a change in interest rates.

> **Example 6 – 4**
>
> You hold a government bond with a duration of 10. its yield is 5%, you expect yields to move up by 10 basis points in the next few minutes. Give a rough estimate of your expected return.
>
> **Solution:**
>
> Given the very short horizon, the only component of return is the expected capital loss:
>
> $$Return = -10 \times 0.1\% = -1\%$$
>
> The return on a bond is equal to the yield over the holding period plus any capital gain/loss due to movements in the market yield, $\Delta yield$. The bond return can be approximated as
>
> $$Return = Yield - D \times (\Delta yield)$$
>
> Over a short holding period, the risk-free rate is the short-term interest rate or cash rate. Hence, the return on a bond investment can be expressed as the sum of
>
> ○ the cash rate
> ○ The spread of the bond yield over the cash rate
> ○ the percentage capital gain/loss due to a movement in yield.
>
> Or
>
> $$Return = Cashrate + (Yield - Cashrate) - D \times (\Delta yield)$$
>
> The *expected* return on a bond is equal to the risk-free cash rate plus a *risk premium*
>
> $$E(return) = Cashrate + Riskpremium$$

3.4 Credit Spreads

Credit risk is an additional source of risk for corporate bonds. The yield required by the market on a corporate issue is a function of the default risk of the bonds. The greater the risk, the higher the yield the borrower must pay. This implies that the yield reflects a *credit spread*, or *quality spread*, over the default-free yield. The quality spread for a specific bond captures three components:

> ○ **An expected loss component.** Investors expect that the bond will default with some probability. To compensate for that expected loss, the issuer must pay a spread above the default-free yield. If investors were risk-neutral, they would

信用风险是企业债券的一个额外风险。

○ 预期损失部分。

only require that the expected return on the corporate bond, taking into account the probability of default, be equal to the default-free yield.

> **A credit-risk premium.** Investors are risk-averse and cannot easily diversity the risk of default on bonds. Furthermore, when the economy is in recession, the financial situation of most corporations deteriorates simultaneously. This is, in part, systematic market risk (business cycle risk) as the stock market is also affected. So investors require a risk premium to compensate for that risk, on top of the expected loss component.

> **A liquidity premium.** Each corporate bond is a bit different from another one, in part because each issuer has some distinctions in quality from other issuers. All domestic government bonds have the same credit quality within their domestic market (e.g., U.S. Treasury in the United States, British Gilts in the United Kingdom, or JGB in Japan); there is a vast amount issued and excellent trading liquidity. Because of the lack of liquidity on most corporate issues, investors require a compensation in the form of an additional yield, a liquidity premium. In practice, it is difficult to disentangle the liquidity premium and the credit-risk premium.

International rating agencies (Moody's, Standard & Poor's, Fitch) provide a credit rating for most debt issues traded worldwide.

> 信用风险溢价。
>
> 流动性风险。

Example 6-5

You hold a government bond with a duration of 10. its yield is 5 percent, although the cash (one-year) rate is 2 percent. You expect yields to move up by 10 basis points over the year. Give a rough estimate of your expected return. What is the risk premium on this bond?

Solution: *Return* = 5% − 10 × 0.1% = 4%

This is a rough estimate, because the duration is going to move down over the year as the bond's maturity shortens.

Risk premium = 4% − 2% = 2%

3.5 The return and risk on foreign bond investment

The return from investing in a foreign bond has three components:

Return=Foreign yield−D×(Δforeign yield)+percentage currency movement

The risk on a foreign bond investment has two major sources:
- *Interest rate risk*: the risk that the foreign yields will rise.
- *Currency rise*: the risk that the foreign currency will depreciate.

Of course, the two risks could be somewhat correlated. Furthermore, credit risk should also be taken into account for non-government bonds.

Example 6-6

A one-year bond is issued by a corporation with a 1% probability of default by year end. In case of default, the investor will recover nothing. The one-year yield for default-free bonds is 5%. What yield should be required by investors on this corporate bond if they are risk-neutral? What should the credit spread be?

Solution:

Let's call y the yield and m the credit spread, $y=5\%+m$.

The bond is issued at 100% of par. If the bond defaults (1% probability), the investor gets nothing in a year, In case of no default (99% probability), the investor will get $(100+y)$ percent. So, the yield should be set on the bond so that its expected payoff is equal to the expected payoff on a risk-free bond (105%):

$$105 = 99\% \times (100+y) + 1\% \times 0$$

$y=(105-99)/99=6.06\%$. The credit spread is equal to $m=1.06\%$.

Example 6-7 Return on a foreign bond

A British investor hold a U.S. Treasury bond with a full price of 100 and a duration of 10. its yield is 5 percent, the next day, U.S. yields move up by 5 basis points and the dollar depreciates by 1 percent relative to the British pound. Give a rough estimate of your loss in British pounds.

Solution:

The dollar price of the bond should drop by

$$\Delta P/P = -D \times \Delta r = -10 \times 0.05\% = -0.5\%$$

On top to that, there will be a currency loss of 1%, So, the total loss in pounds is approximately equal to 1.5%.

4 Floating Rate Notes and Structured Notes

4.1 Floating-Rate Notes (FRNs)

FRNs are a very active segment of the Eurobond market. They are generally indexed to the LIBOR, which is the short-term deposit rate on Eurocurrencies. The maturity of the LIBOR chosen as index usually matches the coupon period. The coupon to be paid is determined on the reset date, which usually coincides with the previous coupon date. On the reset date, the value of the index is determined by looking at the quotations of a panel of major banks. The coupon to be paid the next period is then set equal to the LIBOR plus a spread that has been fixed at the time of issue.

$$C_t = i_{t-1} + m_0$$

4.1.1 Motivation

FRN prices behave quite differently from fixed-interest straight bond prices, which adjust to fluctuations in the market interest rate. FRNs exhibit great price stability when compared with straight bonds.

- For an investor, buy FRNs is to avoid interest rate risk that could lead to a capital loss in case of a rise in interest rates. Investors have a long-term investment with little interest rate risk.
- For issuers, FRNs are generally issued by financial institutions with short-term lending activities. These institutions wish to have long-term resources but want to index the cost of their funds to their revenues. Because revenues on short-term loans are indexed on LIBOR, FRNs achieve this objective.

4.1.2 Valuing FRNs

NoDefault Risk. From a theoretical viewpoint, we may ask why there is any price variability at all on floating-rate bonds. It turns out that there are several major reasons for this price variability. To study the pricing of FRNs, it is useful to look first at the case in which the borrower carriers no default risk.

On Reset Date. FRN coupons are periodically reset, or rolled over. The rollover may be annual, semiannual, or quarterly. This means that the coupon is fixed at the reset, or rollover, date for the coming period. The first question is to determine the theoretical price of the bond on the reset date, when the previous coupon has just been paid and the new coupon has just been fixed for the coming period. To disentangled the effects, it is useful to start the analysis by assuming that the borrower has, and will have, no default risk and that the index has been chosen as the relevant short-term interest rate for that borrower. For example, assume that an FRN with annual reset is issued by a major bank, which has to pay exactly LIBOR without any spread, in the absence of default risk:

$$C_t = i_{t-1}$$

Remember that all rates and prices are quoted in percent. Under this assumption of no default risk, we can show that the price of the bond should always be 100% on reset dates. There is a future date when we know the exact value of the bond: this is at maturity T. Right after the last coupon payment, the bond will be reimbursed at 100%. Let's now move to the previous reset date $T-1$. We know that the bond contract stipulates that the coupon C_t will be set equal to the one-year LIBOR observed at time $T-1$, Of course, we do not know today (time 0) what this rate will be at $T-1$, but we know that it will be exactly equal, by contractual obligation, to the market rate for a one-year instrument. Hence, a bond with a maturity of one year paying the one-year interest rate must have a price equal to its principal value. This is confirmed by discounting at time $T-1$, the future cash flow received at time T:

$$P_{T-1} = \frac{100\% + C_T}{1 + i_{T-1}} = \frac{1 + i_{T-1}}{1 + i_{T-1}} = 100\%$$

Hence, we know that the price one period before maturity must be equal to 100. We can apply the same reasoning to the price of the bond at time $T-2$ and so on, until time 0. We have therefore shown that the bond price must be equal to 100 at each reset date.

> **Example 6 – 8**
>
> A company without default risk has issued a 10-year FRN at LIBOR. The coupon is paid and reset semiannually. It is certain that the issuer will never have default risk and will always be able to borrow at LIBOR. The FRN is issued on November 1, 2005. when the six-month LIBOR is at 5 percent. On May 1, 2006, the six-month LIBOR is at 5.5 percent.

> The questions are:
>
> 1. What is the coupon paid on May 1, 2006, per $1000 bond?
>
> 2. What is the new value of the coupon set on the bond?
>
> 3. On May 2, 2006, the six-month LIBOR has dropped to 5.4 percent. What is the new value of the FRN?
>
> **Solution:**
>
> 1. The coupon paid on May 1 was set on November 1 at 5% or $25 per $1,000 bond. Remember that rates are quoted on an annual basis, but apply here to a semester period.
>
> 2. The coupon to be paid on November 1, 2006, is set at $27.5.
>
> 3. Neglecting that one day has passed, we discount the known future value of the bond on November 1, 2006, at the new six-month LIBOR of 5.4%: $P = (1,000 + 27.5)/(1 + (5.4/2)\%) = 1,000.49$
>
> To be exact, we should discount with a LIBOR for six months minus one day, to derive the quoted price, we should subtract one day of accrued interest from the full price.

存在支付风险的债券

Default Risk. Two observations have repeatedly been made on the FRN market:

- ❖ FRNs with long maturities tend to sell at a discount relative to those with a short maturity.
- ❖ Long-term FRN prices are more volatile than are short-term FRN prices.

The first observation can be explained by the fact that the default risk premium tends to increase with time to maturity. A 20-year loan to a corporation, rated A, seems more risky than a 3 month loan to the same corporation. The coupon spread on an FRN is fixed over the life of the bond, whereas the market-required spread, which reflects the default-risk premium, tends to decrease as the bond nears maturity. Hence, bond prices, at least on reset dates, should progressively increase.

The second observation can be explained by unexpected changes in the market required spread. FRNs are "protected" against movements in LIBOR by their indexation clause, but they are sensitive to variations in the required spread, because they pay a spread that is fixed at issuance. Hence, the coupon of an FRN is not fully indexed to the market-required yield, because the interest rate component is indexed, but the spread is fixed over the life of the bond. The coupon paid is equal to LIBOR + m_0, while the market requires LIBOR + m_t, If the market-required spread changes over time, the FRN behaves partly like a fixed-coupon bond, precisely because of this feature, And we know that, technically, long-term bonds are more sensitive than are shore-term bonds to changes in market yield. By contrast, short-term bonds are repaid sooner, and this drives their price close to par.

4.2 Bull FRN

4.2.1 Description

Bull FRNs are bonds that strongly benefit investors if interest rates drop. A typical example is a reverse (inverse) floater, whereby the coupon is set at a fixed rate minus LIBOR. Consider a five-year dollar FRN with a semiannual coupon set at 14% minus LIBOR. The coupon cannot be negative, so it has a minimum of 0%, which is attractive to investors if LIBOR moves over 14%. At the time, the yield curve was around 7%.

看涨 FRNs 是指利率下降时对投资者非常有利的债券。

4.2.2 Motivation

For Investor, he can benefit markedly from a drop in market interest rates, which is very attractive, the properties of various bonds are reproduced in figure 6.5.

	Straight Bond	Straight FRN	Bull FRN	Bear FRN
Coupon	→	↓	↑	↓↓
Price	↑	→	↑↑	↓

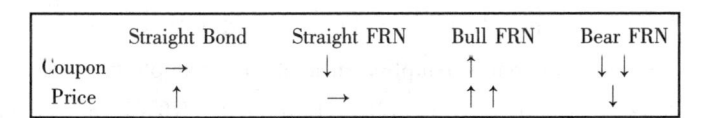

Figure 6.5 Characteristics of bonds, assuming a drop in market interest rates

4.2.3 Valuation

The bull bond could be seen by investors as the sum of three plain-vanilla securities:
- Two straight bonds with a 7 percent coupon
- A short position in a plain-vanilla FRN at LIBOR flat, and
- A 14 percent cap option on LIBOR.

You can verify that the cash flows of this replicating portfolio exactly match those of the bull bond, including at time of redemption. It is straightforward to price the three plain-vanilla securities using quoted prices.

4.3 Bear FRN

4.3.1 Description

看跌债券是指当利率上升时对投资者非常有力的债券。

Bear FRNs are notes that benefit investors if interest rates rise. Plain-vanilla straight bonds or FRNs do not have that property. An example of a bear bond is a note with a coupon set at twice LIBOR minus 7%. Again, the coupon has a floor of 0%, which is attractive to the investor if LIBOR goes below 3.5%.

- ❖ Motivation: The coupon will increase rapidly with a rise in LIBOR.
- ❖ Valuation: the bear could be seen as the sum of
  - Two plain-vanilla FRNs at LIBOR flat.
  - A short position in a straight bond (with a coupon of 7%), and
  - Two 3.5% floor options on LIBOR.

	Straight Bond	Straight FRN	Bull FRN	Bear FRN
Coupon	→	↑	↓	↑↑
Price	↓	→	↓↓	↑

Figure 6.6 Characteristics of bonds, assuming a rise in market interest Rates

4.4 Dual-Currency Bonds

4.4.1 Description

双币债券是指利息用一种货币支付而本金用另一种货币赎回的债券。

A dual-currency bond is a bond issued with coupons in one currency and principal redemption in another. Example 6 - 9 gave the tombstone of such a yen/dollar Eurobond. NKK, a Japanese corporation, issued a 10-year bond for 20 billion yen. During 10 years, it pays an annual coupon of 8% in yen, or 1.6 billion yen. Ten years later, it is redeemed in U.S. dollars for a total of 110,480,000 dollars. The redemption amount in dollars is set so that it is exactly equal to the issue amount using the spot exchange rate prevailing at time of issue, $S_0 = 181.02824$ yen per dollar.

4.4.2 Motivation

For borrowers, issuing this bond is to be able to end up borrowing money in their desired currency but at a lower cost than directly issuing straight bonds in that currency. For investors, buying these dual-currency bonds relies on institutional features and/or market conditions.

4.4.3 Valuation

The value of a yen/dollar dual-currency bond can be broken down into two parts as follows:
- A stream of fixed coupon payments in yen;
- A dollar zero-coupon bond for the final dollar principal repayment

Example 6 – 9

Let's consider the NKK bond. It promises annual coupons of 8% on 20 billion yen and is redeemed in 10 years for $110.480 million. The current spot exchange is ¥181.02824 per dollar, so that $110.480 million is exactly equal to ¥20 billion. The yen yield curve is flat at 4%, and the dollar yield curve is flat at 12%.

a. What is the theoretical value of this dual-currency bond?

b. If the coupon on the bond was set at fair market conditions. What should be its exact value? (A bond is issued at fair market conditions if its coupon is set such that the issue price is equal to its theoretical market value).

Solution:

a. $V = 1.6/(1.04) + 1.6/(1.04)^2 + \cdots + 1.6/(1.04)^{10} + 181.02824 \times \$110.48 \ million/(1.12)^{10} = ¥19.4169 \ billion$

b. $100\% = x\%/(1.04) + x\%/(1.04)2 + \cdots + x\%/(1.04)10 + 100\%/(1.12)10$ or $x = 8.36\%$. this rate is in between the yen and dollar yield on straight bonds.

4.5 Currency-Option Bonds

4.5.1 Description

A currency-option bond is one for which the coupons and the principal can be in two or more currencies, as chosen by the bondholder. For example, a British company issues a five-year pound/euro bond. Each bond is issued at 100 pounds and is repaid 100 pounds or 160 Euros. The annual coupon is 3 pounds, or 4.8 Euros. This particular option gives the bondholder the right to receive principal and interest payments in either pounds or euros. Whichever is more advantageous to the investor. Both the coupon rate and the exchange rate are fixed during the life of the bond.

货币期权债券是利息和本金可以由债券持有人选择的两种或多种货币中的一种。

A currency-option bond benefits the investor who can always select the stronger currency. On the other hand, the interest rate set at issue is always lower than the yields paid on single-currency straight bonds denominated in either currency.

4.5.2 Motivation

Investors select this bond because they offer a long-term currency play with limited risk. Retail investors can directly buy currency options on some options markets, but the maturity of these options is generally limited to a few months. Institutional investors are often prohibited from directly buying derivatives. On the other hand, currency-option bonds are usually issued by good-quality issuers and are therefore available to institutional investors. Investors are willing to receive a lower yield in order to get the currency play.

Issuers pay a lower yield than on straight bonds but run currency risk. They might not wish to retain the currency exposure. For example, the British company might wish to issue a straight pound bond. The bank organizing the issue will then sell to the issuer a long-term currency option to exactly offset the currency exposure. If the sum of the low coupon paid on the currency-option bond and the cost of the option purchased from the bank is less than the coupon rate on a straight bond, the currency-option bond is an attractive low-cost alternative to a straight bond. As with any complex bond, this alternative can only be made possible if a particular category of investors is attracted by the special features of the bond that they cannot access directly.

4.5.3 Valuation

The value of this bond is the sum of
- The value of a straight bond
- The value of currency options.

Example 6 – 10

TATA issues a one-year euro/pound currency-option bond with a coupon rate of 3%. It is issued for 100 pounds, pays a coupon of either 3 pounds or 4.8 euros, and is redeemed for either 100 pounds or 160 euros, at the option of the bondholder. Of course, the bondholder will require payment in euros if the exchange rate is below 1.6 at maturity of the one-year bond. The current spot exchange rate is 1.6 euros/pound, and the one-year interest rates are 6% in euros and 5% in British pounds. A one-year put pound, with a strike price of 1.6 euros per pound, is quoted at 0.015 pound. In other words, investors have to pay a premium of 0.015 pound to get the right to sell one pound at 1.6 euros.

a. What is the fair market value of this currency-option bond?

b. What should have been the fair coupon rate set on this currency-option bond according to market conditions? (A bond is issued at fair market conditions if its coupon is set such that the issue price is equal to its theoretical market value.)

Solution:

a. $V = 103/1.05 + 103 \times 0.015 = 99.64$ pounds

b. $100 \times (1+x\%)/1.05 + 100 \times (1+x\%) \times 0.015 = 100$ pounds

Or $x = 3.37\%$

Summary

- The global bond market comprises domestic bonds, foreign bonds, and Eurobonds.
- The Eurobond market is a dynamic international market without a physical market location.
- Debt from emerging countries can be purchased in many forms: domestic bonds issued in the emerging country, foreign bonds issued on a major bond market, Eurobonds, and Brady bonds.
- Bonds from emerging countries have often been restructured into Brady bonds to make them attractive to global investors.
- Bonds are quoted in the form of a clean price net of accrued interest. So, the full price (or value) of a bond is the sum of its clean price plus accrued interest. The day-count conventions to calculate accrued interest vary across markets and instruments.
- The yield curve based on zero-coupon government bonds is the central tool for valuing individual bonds in each currency.
- The return on a domestic bond is the sum of the yield over the holding period plus any capital gain/loss caused by a movement in the market yield.
- The expected return on a domestic bond is the sum of the cash rate

(the risk-free rate) plus a risk premium.
- Corporate bonds provide a yield equal to the yield on government bonds with similar duration plus a credit spread. This credit spread can be decomposed as the sum of an expected loss component, a credit-risk premium, and a liquidity premium.
- The return from investing in a foreign bond includes three components.
- The risk from investing in a foreign bond has two major components: Interest rate risk and Currency risk.
- The expected return on a foreign bond is equal to the domestic cash rate plus a risk premium.
- Currency hedging allows one to remove currency risk.
- Because currency is a major source of return and risk in global bond management, special attention should be devoted to the currency dimension.
- FRNs are a major segment of the Eurobond market.
- Various complex bonds, often called "structured notes", are issued on the international market.
- The issuer will usually hedge the unusual risks (bets) of a structured note and end up with a plain-vanilla bond at a low all-in cost.
- Some bonds offer plays on interest rates (bull and bear FRNs). Others offer play on currencies (dual-currency bond, currency-option bond).

Exercises

1. If a portfolio manager believes that some particular attributes of firms are valued worldwide, she will engage in (   ).
    a. Style investing
    b. Global industrial investing
    c. investing on a country-by-country basis
    d. none of them

2. A three-year bond has exactly three years till maturity, and the last coupon has just been paid. The coupon is annual and equal to 6 percent, the bond price is 95%, What is its simple yield?

3. Which of the following statements about the global bond market are true?
    a. The international bond market is larger than the domestic bond

market.

   b. The FRN has the biggest share in the market capitalization of Eurobonds by type of instruments.

   c. Euro has the biggest share in the market capitalization of Eurobonds by currency of issuance.

   d. The USA has the biggest share in the market capitalization of domestic bond markets.

4. Consider a newly issued dollar/yen dual-currency bond. This bond is issued in yen. The coupons are paid in yen and the principal will be repaid in dollars. The market price of this bond is quoted in yen. Discuss what would happen to the market price of this dual-currency bond if the following happens:

   a. The market interest rate on yen bonds drops significantly.

   b. The dollar drops in value relative to the yen.

   c. The market interest rate on dollar bonds drops significantly.

5. A European corporation has issued bonds with a par value of SFr 1,000 and an annual coupon of 5 percent, the last coupon on these bonds was paid four months ago. And their current clean price is 90 percent.

   a. If these bonds are Eurobonds, what is their full price?

   b. Would your answer to part(a) be different if the bonds were not Eurobonds, but were issued in the Swiss domestic bond market?

6. a. Compute the yield to maturity of a zero-coupon bond with nine years to maturity and currently selling at 45%.

   b. Compute the YTM of a perpetual bond with an annual coupon of 6 EUR and currently selling at 108 EUR.

7. a. Consider a bond issued at par. The annual coupon is 8% and frequency of coupon is semiannual. How would the YTM of this bond be reported in most of the European markets?

   b. The market price of a two-year bond with annual coupon is 103% of its nominal value. The annual coupon to be paid in exactly one year is 6%. Compute its 1) YTM (European way), and 2) YTM (U.S. way).

8. Bonds A and B are two straight yen-denominated Eurobonds, with the same maturity of four years and the same YTM of 9%, bond A has an annual coupon of 11% and is accordingly price at 106.48%. Bond has an annual coupon of 7% and is accordingly priced at 93.52%.

   a. Compute the simple yield for each of these bonds, as reported sometimes by financial institutions in Japan.

b. What does your answer to part (a) indicate about the potential biases in using the simple yield?

9. You hold a bond with nine years until maturity, a YTM of 4%, and a duration of 7.5, the cash (one-year) rate is 2.5%.

   a. In the next few minutes, you expect the market yield to go up by five basis points. What is the bond's expected percentage price change, and your expected return. Over the next few minutes?

   b. Over the next year, you expect the market yield to go down by 30 basis points. For this period, estimate 1) the bond's expected price change. 2) your expected return, 3) the bond's risk premium.

10. There is a 0.5 percent probability of default by the year-end on a one-year bond issued at par by a particular corporation. If the corporation defaults, the investor will get nothing. Assuming that a default-free bond exists with identical cash flows and liquidity, and the one-year yield on this bond is 4%, what yield should be required by risk-neutral investors on the corporate bond? What should the credit spread be?

11. A French investor has purchased bonds denominated in Swiss francs that have been issued by a Swiss corporation with a mediocre credit rating. Which of the following is a source of risk for this investment?

    a. interest rate risk on Swiss francs.
    b. Currency risk.
    c. Credit risk.
    d. a and b only.

12. An investor is considering investing in one-year zero-coupon bonds, she is thinking of investing in either a British-pound-denominated bond with a yield of 5.2%, or a euro-denominated bond with a yield of 4.5%, The current exchange rate is 1£ = 1.5408 EUR

    a. what exchange rate one year later is the break-even exchange rate, which would make the pound bond and the Eurobond investments equally good?

    b. which investment would have turned out to be better if the actual exchange rate one year later is 1£ = 1.4120 EUR.

13. A Swiss investor has purchased a U.S. Treasury bond priced at 100. Its yield is 4.5%, and the investor expects the U.S. yield to move down by 15 basis points over the year. The duration of the bond is 6. The Swiss franc cash rate is 1% and the dollar cash

rate is 2%. The one-year forward exchange rate is SFr 1.4600/ $.

a. The Swiss investor has come up with his own model to forecast the SFr/$ exchange rate one year ahead. This model forecasts the one-year ahead exchange rate to be SFr 1.3500/$. Based on this forecast, should the Swiss investor hedge the currency risk of his investment using a forward contract?

b. If the Swiss investor decides to hedge using a forward contract, give a rough estimate of his expected return.

c. Verify for the hedged investment that the risk premium in Swiss Francs is the same as the risk premium on the same U. S. Treasury bond for a U.S. investor.

14. A company without default risk has issued a perpetual Eurodollar FRN at LIBOR. The coupon is paid and reset semiannually. It is certain that the issuer will never have default risk. And will always be able to borrow at LIBOR. The FRN is issued on March 1, 2002, when the six-month LIBOR is at 5 percent. The Eurodollar yield curve on September 1, 2002, and December 1, 2002. are as follows:

	Sep. 1, 2002 (%)	Dec. 1, 2002 (%)
One month	4.25	4.00
Three months	4.50	4.25
Six months	4.75	4.50
Twelve months	5.00	4.75

a. What is the coupon paid on September 1, 2002, per $1,000 FRN?

b. What is the new value of the coupon set on the FRN on September 1, 2002?

c. What is the new value of the FRN on December 1, 2002?

15. A perpetual bond is issued by a corporation rated A with an annual coupon set at yearly LIBOR plus a spread of 0.25 percent. Some time later, LIBOR is equal to 5 percent and the market requires a spread of 0.5 percent for such an A corporation. Give an estimate of the bond value on the reset date using the "freezing" method.

Part III

International Direct Investment

Chapter 7
FDI: Conception and Theories

The requirement of Learning
- Knowing the definition and measurement of FDI.
- Understanding the theory of Monopolistic Competition.
- Understanding the internalization theory.
- Understanding the theory of international product cycle.
- Understanding the eclectic paradigm theory.

1 The Definition and Measurement

According to the IMF and OECD definitions, FDI reflects the aim of obtaining a lasting interest by a resident entity of one economy (direct investor) in an enterprise that is resident in another economy (the direct investment enterprise). The "lasting interest" implies the existence of a long-term relationship between the direct investor and the direct investment enterprise and a significant degree of influence on the management of the latter.

FDI involves both the initial transaction establishing the relationship between the investor and the enterprise and all subsequent capital transactions between them and among affiliated enterprises, both incorporated and unincorporated. It should be noted that capital transactions which do not give rise to any settlement, e.g. an interchange of shares among affiliated companies, must also be recorded in the balance of payments.

The definition of direct investment and therefore its measurement have changed considerably over time. Definitions and measurements even now differ among countries despite the efforts of international agencies to push for uniformity.

The current definition of direct investment endorsed by the OECD (1996) and the IMF (1993) avoids the idea of control in favor of a much vaguer concept. "Foreign direct investment reflects the objective of obtaining a lasting interest by a resident entity in one country ('direct investor') in an entity resident in an economy other than that of the investor ('direct investment enterprise').

1.1 The "lasting interest" *vs.* Control

The lasting interest implies "the existence of a long-term relationship between the direct investor and the enterprise and a significant degree of influence on the management of the enterprise" (OECD, 1996). While this concept is a vague one, the recommended implementation is specific. OECD recommends that a direct investment enterprise can be defined as an incorporated or unincorporated enterprise in which a foreign investor owns 10 percent or more of the ordinary shares or voting power of an incorporated enterprise or the equivalent of an unincorporated enterprise. An effective voice in the management, as evidenced by an ownership of at least 10 per cent, implies that the direct investor is able to influence, or participate in the management of an enterprise; it does not require absolute control by the foreign investor (OECD, 1996).

The idea of control, which is behind much of the literature on multinationals, has been specifically abandoned. The fifth edition of the IMF *Balance* of *Payments Manual* points out that the concept of direct investment now used "is broader than the SNA concept of foreign-controlled, as distinguished from domestically controlled resident enterprises" (1993, 86). A single "direct investment enterprise" could be part of several different multinational firms, possibly from several countries. Duplication is avoided in investment flow and stock data, the main areas of concern to the OECD and the IMF, by allocating the financial aggregates to the various owners according to the extent of their ownership. However, data on the activities of multinationals, particularly those collected by home countries on, for example, the sales, employment, or output of their multinational firms or their overseas operations, could easily contain duplication if this 10 percent criterion is used.

The fifth Edition of the IMF's Balance of Payment Manual defines the owner of 10% or more of a company's capital as *a direct investor*. This guideline is not a fast rule, as it acknowledges that smaller percentage may entail a controlling interest in the company (and, conversely, that a share of more than 10% may not signify control). But the IMF recommends using this percentage as the basic dividing

持久利益意味着"直接投资者和企业之间存在长期关系,并对企业的管理产生重大影响"(经合组织,1996年)。

line between direct investment and portfolio investment in the form of shareholdings. Thus, when a non-resident who previously had no equity in a resident enterprise purchases 10% or more of the shares of that enterprise from a resident, the price of equity holdings acquired should be recorded as direct investment. From this moment, any further capital transactions between these two companies should be recorded as a direct investment. When a non-resident holds less than 10% of the shares of an enterprise as portfolio investment, and subsequently acquires additional shares resulting in a direct investment (10% of more), only the purchase of additional shares is recorded as direct investment in the Balance of Payments. The holdings that were acquired previously should not be reclassified from portfolio to direct investment in the Balance of Payments but the total holdings should be reclassified in the IIP.

1.2 Classification of FDI

The classification of direct investment is based firstly on the *direction* of investment both for assets or liabilities; secondly, on the investment instrument used (shares, loans, etc.); and thirdly on the sector breakdown.

As for the direction, it can be looked at it from the home and the host perspectives. From the home one, financing of any type extended by the resident parent company to its nonresident affiliated would be included as *direct investment abroad*. By contrast, financing of any type extended by non-resident subsidiaries, associates or branches to their resident parent company are classified as a decrease in *direct investment abroad*, rather than as a *foreign direct investment*. From the host one, the financing extended by non-resident parent companies to their resident subsidiaries, associates or branches would be recorded, in the country of residence of the affiliated companies, under *foreign direct investment*, and the financing extended by resident subsidiaries, associates and branches to their non-resident parent company would be classified as a decrease in *foreign direct investment* rather than as a *direct investment abroad*. This directional principle does not apply if the parent company and its subsidiaries, associates or branches have cross-holdings in each other's share capital of more than 10%.

As for the instruments, Direct investment capital transactions are made up of three basic components: (i) Equity capital; (ii) Reinvested earnings; (iii) Other direct investment capital:

> 直接投资的分类首先基于资产或负债的投资方向；其次，关于所使用的投资工具（股票、贷款等）；第三是部门分类。

covering the borrowing and lending of funds, including debt securities and trade credits.

2 Theories

Much of the investment theory developed in the past several decades has focused on the efforts of multinational firms to exploit the imperfections in factor and product markets created by governments. The works of Hymer, Kindleberger, and Caves noted that many of the policies of governments create imperfections. These market imperfections cover the entire range of supply and demand of the market: trade policy (tariffs and quotas), tax policies and incentives, preferential purchasing arrangements established by governments themselves, and financial restrictions on the access of foreign firms to domestic capital markets.

- Imperfections in access: Many of the world's developing countries have long sought to create domestic industry by restricting imports of competitive products in order to allow smaller, less competitive domestic firms to grow and prosper—so-called import substitution policies. Multinational firms have sought to maintain their access to these markets by establishing their own productive presence within the country, effectively bypassing the tariff restriction.
- Imperfections in factor mobility: Other multinational firms have exploited the same sources of comparative advantage identified throughout this chapter — the low-cost resources or factors often located in less-developed countries or countries with restrictions on the mobility of labor and capital. However, combining the mobility of capital with the immobility of low-cost labor has characterized much of the foreign direct investment seen throughout the developing world over the past 50 years.
- Imperfections in Management: The ability of multinational firms to successfully exploit or at least manage these imperfections still relies on their ability to gain an "advantage." Market advantages or powers are seen in international markets as in domestic markets: cost advantages, economies of scale and scope, product differentiation, managerial or marketing technique and

knowledge, financial resources and strength.

All these imperfections are the things of which competitive dreams are made. The multinational firm needs to find these in some form or another to justify the added complexities and costs of international investments.

The question that has plagued the field of foreign direct investment is, Why can't all of the advantages and imperfections mentioned be achieved through management contracts or licensing agreements? Why is it necessary for the firm itself to establish a physical presence in the country? What pushes the multinational firm further down the investment decision tree?

The research of Buckley and Casson, and Dunning has attempted to answer these questions by focusing on nontransferable sources of competitive advantage—proprietary information possessed by the firm and its people. Many advantages firms possess center around their hands-on knowledge or producing a good or providing a service. By establishing their own multinational operation they can internalize the production, thus keeping confidential the information that is at the core of the firm's competitiveness. Internalization is preferable to the use of arms-length arrangements such as management contracts or licensing agreements. They either do not allow the effective transmission of the knowledge or represent too serious a threat to the loss of the knowledge to allow the firm to successfully achieve the hoped for benefits of international investment.

2.1 Theory of Monopolistic Competition

The reasons for the growth of multinationals and their decisions to produce abroad were analyzed by S. H. Hymer in 1960. His thesis is based on the following assumption: foreign investors need to exploit market imperfections since investments in overseas manufacturing facilities involve higher risks and costs than productive investments in the home country. Additional investments are required to cover operational and organizational costs of managing foreign subsidiaries from a distance and higher marketing and business development expenses due to language and cultural barriers, and the possibility of discrimination. Therefore, the investing firm must have a specific, in fact a monopolistic advantage, which is derived from market imperfections.

C. P. Kindleberger (1969) expanded Hymer's concept by

defining, on the basis of market imperfections, four key factors that underline the success of TNCs wherever they operate, with or without government intervention and which may alter cost and benefit structures:

- Product-induced imperfections: marketing techniques, brand image, product differentiation.
- Imperfections related to factors of production: exclusive control over manufacturing, proprietary technologies, skills of staff, privileges access to capital market.
- Possibilities of exploiting internal and external economies of scale.
- Government policies and interference.

The application of the theory of monopolistic competition specifically to TNCs led to an exploration of elements such as multi-country access to factors of production and to consumers, as well as economics of scale in international production, distribution and purchasing, This type of analysis has been used to study the factors contributing to the enormous success of TNC operations, both at home and foreign markets. Monopolistic or oligopolistic aspects of TNC activities abroad have provoked specific government policies, although these may not differ greatly from policies towards domestic enterprises.

Subsequent theories, which were based on broader and more up-to-date empirical samples, found out that in most cases a specific advantage was a necessary, but not a sufficient, condition for firms to invest and product abroad. A company may well exploit its specific advantage in the home country and export or simply sell a license, thus avoiding high costs of relocation.

While Hymer emphasized technology and innovation related advantages, other authors after him identified other company-specific advantages as explanatory variables for investing aboard: size of the company, vertical integration, and product differentiation (measured as advertising expenses over turnover). For certain authors, however, the company's size and competitive position in the home market reflect other advantages and are not explanatory variables for FDI. The veracity of this argument is demonstrated by the internalization of an increasing number of medium-size TNCs, which incidentally have become the central target of FDI promotion strategies of certain governments such as Singapore, China and Chile. In these cases, state of the art technologies and know-how controlled by these firms have been crucial elements for global presence. Nevertheless, a critical size is also a decisive factor for investing abroad. This critical size is determined by the number or employees, annual turnover and profit levels.

A number of conclusions can be drawn from this theory for economic and industrial development in a transition country like Russia:

- Foreign investor should be analyzed carefully, particularly their corporate assets and possible contribution to the transfer of superior technologies and know-how; their company-specific advantages determine their readiness to invest and the possible form of investment.
- The success rate placing an investing company in the right sectoral and regional context increases with the amount of information collected by public bodies.
- It is crucial to match the key factors of success of a foreign company with the development strategy of the host country.

These advantages or imperfection-based theorist were later complemented by scholars like Dunning and Porter, whose integrated concepts supply additional elements for targeting potential investors.

2.2 Internalization Theory

The internalization concept establishes a link between FDI by large corporations and their internal organization reflected by the hierarchic integration of business functions. It assumes a situation of market imperfections and was formulated in the second half of the 1970s by P.J. Buckley and M. Casson, two economists of Reading University in the United Kingdom. According to them, large firms are able to expand because of their integrative capacity and the exclusion of competitors from their know-how. The authors reproached previous theories (such as those of Hymer and Kindleberger) for focusing on the production function and neglecting other unique advantages (leadership skills, International organization. Marketing and sourcing capacities, human resource development and sound financial management) that enable companies to maintain their leadership and to expand into other markets and business areas. True international operators derive their competitive advantage not from one specific asset in one determined functional area, but from their capacity to internalize their know-how instead of allowing it to be transferred to other (external) organizations.

Internalization is particularly common in manufacturing business with high R&D costs and capital intensity (e. g. chemicals, automobile), and large-scale flows of intermediary products in the form of components and semi-manufactured goods (e. g. consumer electronics, pharmaceuticals). Progressive FDI agencies (e. g. Singaporean investment development boards) have started establishing a link between high R&D expenditure and transnationalization (FDI) potential: when faced with alternatives, they privilege TNCs that can demonstrate high R&D expenses as a percentage of their turnover. This ratio is also used to canvass new TNCs for the development of specific industrial sectors. The theory may also help understand the internationalization strategies of companies in raw materials and agricultural sectors, and even in services (Buckley and Casson, 1985).

Taxation and other restrictive policies of certain host governments in the form of high import duties, local component content, and non-tariff barriers can also favor the internalization of functions "under one roof". Exports thus become less lucrative than direct investment, especially if the target market is large and of strategic importance (e.g. Brazil, China, India, and Indonesia).

According to A. M. Rugman (1981), the internalization theory is basic to other paradigms on direct investment. Former theories of multinationalization, in particular those developed on the basis of market imperfections, product life-cycle and defensive oligopolistic behavior, can be grouped under the general paradigm of internalization.

2.3　Theory of International Product Cycle

The international product cycle paradigm, which was elaborated in 1966 by the French Scholar R. Vernon, described the dynamic process between international trade and foreign investment. Its empirical setting was the growing trade and investments by US corporations during postwar reconstruction in Europe. The originality of the concept resides in the combination of elements of international economics (trade patterns between countries and reasons for relocation of industries) with those of marketing theory (product life-cycle curve).

According the theory, the natural life-cycle of products and the accompanying cost considerations prompt three types of decisions by corporate leaders: to produce at home, to export or to transfer production to foreign markets. The life of a product consists of three distinct phases: innovation, maturity and standardization. Innovating companies can enjoy temporary monopoly in their home markets during new product launches, enabling them to recover part of the initial R&D and marketing investment. When the products pass on to phases two and three of the cycle, the company has to adopt an internationalization strategy if it wants to survive *vis-à-vis* its competitors. Companies usually seek export markets when their products lose part of their novelty appeal on reaching maturity. At this stage, competition becomes fiercer, resulting in higher unit production costs and lower profit margins. Eventually, during standardization, low-cost production sites have to be identified in other countries, preferably those that also constitute large markets. During product standardization, companies undertake foreign investments to de fend their position as leaders, with a view to later re-export the products to the home country, where the innovation originated.

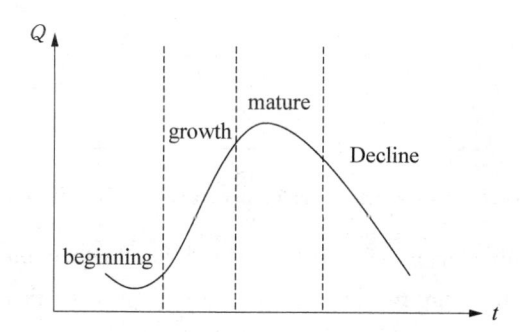

Figure 7.1 Life Cycle of Product

When it was formulated, the theory provided a useful explanation for decisions by US companies to shift their production overseas, since then, the international economic situation has changed dramatically. Competition has spread from home to the global market as corporations and their competitors move to overseas production sites. In the rush for new markets, corporate leaders form strategic alliances or acquire companies abroad to maintain and expand their leadership by gaining access to new markets and technologies. Their decisions are made more by strategic imperatives than by products reaching certain stages of maturity in their respective life-cycles. Government intervention and incentive mechanisms (e.g. the UK FDI promotion strategy to attract Japanese investors in the late 1980s) can also have a significant strategy simultaneously in various countries, which all form links in a complex network of inter-company transactions and cross-shareholdings.

In the 1970s and 1980s, powerful TNCs started emerging outside the United States, especially in Europe; recently, companies in emerging economics of Southeast Asia and Latin America have also joined the league. The US TNCs face tough global competition and in many industries their leadership has vanished. The earlier hierarchical order between countries and national economies suggested by the theory is now blurred, However, the theory incites FDI-oriented governments to observe life cycles at a global level, if not of individual products (this would add to the complexity of the task), then at least of larger product families, industries and technologies.

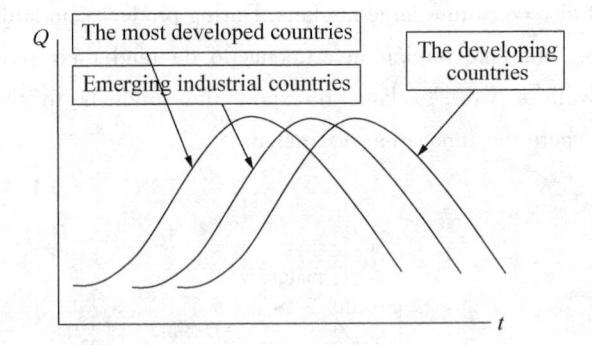

Figure 7.2 Products transfer according to the Life Cycle

The establishment of a research and intelligence unit within a competent FDI authority would serve a useful purpose in this respect as it would study and monitor global life-cycle stages of leading industries (e.g. machinery and equipment, pharmaceuticals, high-tech chemicals, heavy commercial vehicles, aerospace) and state-of-the-art technologies (e.g. micro-electrons, new materials, biotechnologies). Such a unit could, through its research work, easily guide national policy-makers in identifying those TNCs that offer innovative technologies and seek markets and production sites abroad to expand their operations and/or to avoid high factor costs at home.

2.4 The Eclectic Paradigm

The eclectic paradigm theory was formulated for the first time in 1977 by J. H. Dunning. Another well-known economist from the

University of Reading, United Kingdom. The attributive "eclectic" was chosen because, according to the definition of the term, the paradigm (a) aims to select what appears to be best in various methods, doctrines or styles, and (b) is composed of elements drawn from various sources. Dunning has published a number of articles and reference books on the subject and, together with Narula, conceptualized the investment development path paradigm, which fits the eclectic paradigm into a more global context of economic development through FDI.

The paradigm sets out a generalized framework for explaining levels and patterns of FDI activities of companies. It postulates that, at any given point in time, the stock of foreign assets owned and controlled by multinational firms is determined by three conditional elements:

- The extent and nature of ownership-specific or competitive advantages of foreign investors especially compared with national operators (**O-advantages**). 所有权优势
- The extent and nature of location-bound endowments and markets offered by certain countries to investing firms (**L-advantages**) that would add further value to their already existing competitive advantages. 区位优势
- The extent to which companies internationalize (**I-advantages**), or control their competitive advantages, rather than transfer and market them directly to foreign firms, for example through exports or licensing. 内部化优势

The configuration of ownership, location and internalization (OLI) advantages contains objective and subjective components, as it varies with the nature of activity, company-specific characteristics, and expected and real benefits the host country may offer to the foreign investor. The propensity for corporation to invest foreign locations with their comparative (O) advantages, which are to be measured in relation to competition as well as the profits or value accrued to corporations from foreign location (L) advantages.

The eclectic paradigm is a comprehensive theory that can help explain all types of internationalization according to the existing advantages for a foreign investor. A company having both comparative (O) and internalization (I) advantages will decide to invest abroad, if the location-specific (L) advantages exist outside its home territory. Conversely, a company with the same O and I advantages will prefer to export its products and services, if the foreign location offers only low L advantages. In case company-specific advantages cannot be defended, the company may decide to sell licenses to foreign enterprises so that production levels can be maintained at home.

Dunning's eclectic paradigm represents an extension of the internalization theory (through its I-advantage); additionally, it draws on essential elements of business and strategic management theory (through its O-advantages). In this respect, the competitive advantages stressed by business scholars like M. Porter as determinants of internationalization do not differ very much from the O-advantages expounded by Dunning. Both aim to offer a comprehensive and integrated theory for the understanding of FDI.

Table 7.1 All types of internationalization

	O	I	L
FDI	√	√	√
Export	√	√	×
Sell Licenses	√	×	×

Policy-markers in transition countries and their foreign advisors should study and carefully develop essential L-variables so that capital and know-how can be attracted systematically for improving industrial competitiveness and the employment situation. These advantages or disadvantages, depending on the country, have been confirmed by several economic studies as major determinants for inward investment. FDI flows tend to concentrate on those countries that offer comparative advantages not only on terms of natural resources and low factor costs, but also sound economic management, a reliable legal system, and promising perspectives for sustainable growth and development.

Dunning's theory has been adapted by other authors to explain FDI flows from a different perspective. For example, R. Mucchielli (1985) from France designed a synthetic analysis by relating the internationalization strategy of companies to the comparative advantages of their home countries. In this case, FDI decisions by TNCs are mainly determined by factor or market insufficiencies in home markets.

The eclectic paradigm also helps understand how countries move ahead on the investment development path from their initial position as exclusive recipients to their subsequent position as originators of FDI.

3 The Decision Sequence of FDI

The subject of international investment arises from one basic idea: the mobility of capital. Although many of the traditional trade theories assumed the immobility of the factors of production, it is the movement of capital that has allowed foreign direct investments across the global, if there is a competitive advantage to be gained, capital can and will get there.

Consider a firm that wants to exploit its competitive advantage by accessing foreign markets as illustrated in the decision-sequence tree of Figure 7.3.

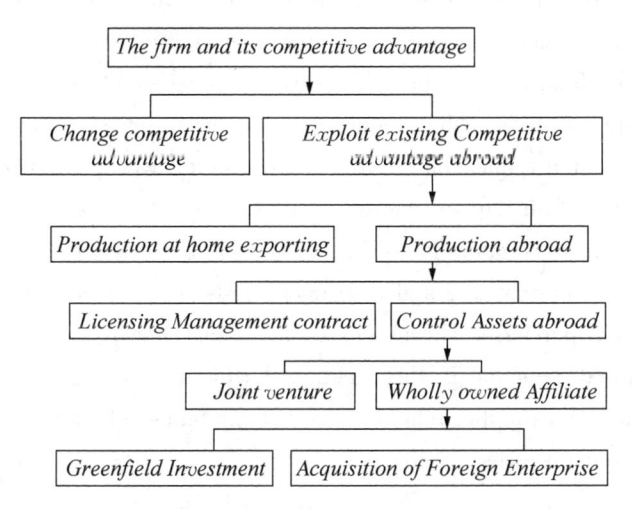

```
                The firm and its competitive advantage
                                │
            ┌───────────────────┴───────────────────┐
    Change competitive              Exploit existing Competitive
        advantage                         advantage abroad
                                                │
                              ┌─────────────────┴─────────────┐
                   Production at home exporting        Production abroad
                                      │                       │
                        ┌─────────────┴────────┐      ┌───────┴────────┐
              Licensing Management contract    Control Assets abroad
                                                      │
                                          ┌───────────┴───────────┐
                                    Joint venture         Wholly owned Affiliate
                                                                  │
                                                  ┌───────────────┴────────────────┐
                                        Greenfield Investment      Acquisition of Foreign Enterprise
```

Figure 7.3 The Decision Sequence of FDI

The first choice is whether to exploit the existing competitive advantage in new foreign markets or to concentrate their resources in the development of new competitive advantages in the domestic market. Although many firms may choose to do both as resources will allow, more and more firms are choosing to go international as at least part of their expansion strategies.

Second, should the firm produce at home and export to the foreign markets, or produce abroad? The firm will choose the path that will allow it to access the resources and markets it needs to exploit its existing competitive advantage. But it will also consider two additional dimensions of each foreign investment decision: (1) the degree of control over assets, technology, information, and operations, (2) the magnitude of capital that the firm must risk.

After choosing to produce abroad, the firm must decide how. The distinctions among different kinds of foreign direct investment, licensing agreements to Greenfield construction, vary by degrees of ownership. The licensing management contract is by far the simplest and cheapest way to produce abroad. Another firm is licensed to produce the product, but with your firm's technology and know-how. The question is whether the reduced capital investment of simply licensing the product to another manufacturer is worth the risk of loss of control over the product and technology.

The firm that wants direct control over the foreign production process next determines the degree of equity control: to own the firm outright, or as a joint investment with another firm. Moreover, many developing countries try to ensure the continued growth of local firms and investors by requiring that foreign firms operate jointly with local firms.

The final decision branch between a "Greenfield investment" — building a firm from the ground up—and the purchase of an existing firm, is often a question of cost. A Greenfield investment is the most expensive of all foreign investment alternatives. The acquisition of an existing firm is often lower in initial cost but may also contain a number of customizing and adjustment costs that are not apparent at the initial purchase. The purchase of a going concern may also have substantial benefits if the existing business possesses substantial customer and supplier relationships that can be used by the new owner in the pursuit of its own business.

4 Foreign Direct Investment Originating in Developing Countries

In recent years, developing countries with large home markets and some entrepreneurial talent have spawned a large number of rapidly growing and profitable MNEs. These MNES have not only captured large shares of their home markets, but also have tapped global markets where they are increasingly competitive.

The Boston Consulting Group has identified six major corporate strategies employed by these emerging market MNES.

- *Taking brands global* means to establish primacy at home, expand in neighboring nations, and then move to the West.
- *Engineering to innovation* means to tap low-cost talent at home, and then develop innovative products.

- Leverage natural resources means to take advantage of domestic oil, mineral, or timber resources to attain a cost edge, and then go global.
- Export business model means to have a management system, and then replicate it globally through acquisitions.
- *Acquire offshore* assets means to become a global player by buying oil and mineral resources or partnering with other developing nation companies.
- *Target a niche* means to focus on an industry, build scale and competence, and then expand globally by acquiring smaller players.

Summary

- The "lasting interest" implies the existence of a long-term relationship between the direct investor and the direct investment enterprise and a significant degree of influence on the management of the latter.
- The classification of direct investment is based firstly on the *direction* of investment both for assets or liabilities; secondly, on the investment instrument used (shares, loans, etc.); and thirdly on the sector breakdown.
- Direct investment capital transactions are made up of three basic components: (i) Equity capital; (ii) Reinvested earnings; (iii) Other direct investment capital: covering the borrowing and lending of funds, including debt securities and trade credits.
- The reasons for the growth of multinationals and their decisions to produce abroad were analyzed by S. H. Hymer in 1960.
- The internalization concept establishes a link between FDI by large corporations and their internal organization reflected by the hierarchic integration of business functions.
- The international product cycle paradigm, which was elaborated in 1966 by the French Scholar R. Vernon, described the dynamic process between international trade and foreign investment.
- The eclectic paradigm was formulated for the first time in 1977 by J.H. Dunning.

Exercises

1. Capital transactions which do not give rise to any settlement, e.g. an interchange of shares among affiliated companies, (   ) recorded in the Balance of Payments.

    A. must be   B. shouldn't be
    C. may be   D. may not be

2. According to the eclectic paradigm, if a company had the ownership-specific advantages and location advantages but no advantages of internalization, it should select (   )

    A. export   B. direct investment
    C. sell licenses

3. According to the eclectic paradigm, if a company had the ownership-specific advantages but had neither location advantages nor advantages of internalization, it should select (   )

    A. export   B. direct investment
    C. sell licenses

4. According to the eclectic paradigm, if a company had the ownership-specific advantages and location advantages and advantages of internalization, it should select (   )

    A. export   B. direct investment
    C. sell licenses

5. (   ) described the dynamic process between international trade and foreign investment.

    A. The eclectic paradigm
    B. The international product cycle paradigm
    C. The internalization theory
    D. Theory of Monopolistic Competition

Chapter 8
The Risks of Foreign Exchange Rate

The requirement of Learning
- Distinguish between the three major foreign exchange exposures experienced by firms.
- Identify foreign exchange transaction exposure.
- Analyze the pros and cons of hedging foreign exchange transaction exposure.
- Identify the alternatives available to a firm for managing a large and significant transaction exposure.
- Evaluate the institutional practices and concerns of conducting foreign exchange risk management.

Foreign exchange exposure is a measure of the potential for a firm's profitability, net cash flow, and market value to change because of a change in exchange rates. An important work of the financial manager is to measure foreign exchange exposure and to manage it so as to maximize the profitability, net cash flow, and market value of the firm. These three components — profits, cash flows, and market value — are the key financial elements of how we view the relative success or failure of a firm. The first two, profits and cash flows, largely give rise to the third, market value.

What happens to a firm when foreign exchange rates change? The effect can be measured in several ways. Figure 8.1 reviews the three main types of foreign exchange exposure—*transaction*, *operating*, and *translation*.

Moment in Time When
Exchange Rate Changes

Translation Exposure	**Operating Exposure**
Changes in reported owners' equity in consolidated financial statements caused by a change in exchange rates	Changes in expected future cash flows arising from an unexpected change in exchange rates

Transaction Exposure
Impact of settling outstanding obligations entered into before change in exchange rates but to be settled after change in exchange rates

Figure 8.1 Conceptual Comparison of Transaction, Operating, and Translation Foreign Exchange Exposure

1 Transaction Exposure

It measures changes in the value of outstanding financial obligations incurred prior to a change in exchange rates but not due to be settled until after the exchange rates change. Thus, it deals with changes in cash flows that result from existing contractual obligations. Transaction exposure arises from the following:

- Purchasing or selling on credit goods or services when prices are stated in foreign currencies.
- Borrowing or lending funds when repayment is to be made in a foreign currency.
- Being a party to an unperformed foreign exchange forward contract.
- Acquiring assets or incurring liabilities denominated in foreign currencies.

> 它衡量在汇率变动之前发生但在汇率变动之后才结算的未偿金融债务的价值变化。

The most common example of transaction exposure arises when a firm has a receivable or payable denominated in a foreign currency.

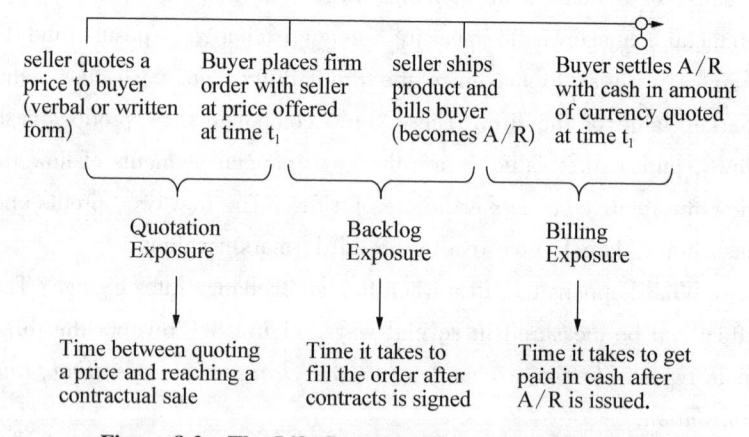

seller quotes a price to buyer (verbal or written form)	Buyer places firm order with seller at price offered at time t_1	seller ships product and bills buyer (becomes A/R)	Buyer settles A/R with cash in amount of currency quoted at time t_1
	Quotation Exposure	Backlog Exposure	Billing Exposure
	Time between quoting a price and reaching a contractual sale	Time it takes to fill the order after contracts is signed	Time it takes to get paid in cash after A/R is issued.

Figure 8.2 The Life Span of a Transaction Exposure

The total transaction exposure consists of quotation, backlog, and billing exposures. A transaction exposure is actually created at the first moment the seller quotes a price in foreign currency terms to a potential buyer (t_1). The quote can be verbal, as in a telephone quote, or written, as in a bid or a printed price list. The placing of an order (t_2) converts the potential exposure created at the time of the quotation (t_1) into actual exposure, called backlog exposure because the product has not yet been shipped or billed. Backlog exposure lasts until the goods are shipped and billed (t_3), at which time it becomes billing exposure. Billing exposure remains until the seller receives payment (t_4).

1.1 Purchasing or Selling on Open Account

Suppose a U.S. firm sells merchandise on open account to a Belgian buyer for €1,800,000, payment to be made in 60 days. The current exchange rate is $1.2/€, and this firm expects to exchange the euros received for €1,800,000 × $1.2/€ = $2,160,000 when payment is received.

Transaction exposure arises because of the risk that this firm will receive something other than the $2,160,000 expected. For example, if the euro weakens to $1.1/€ when payment is received, the firm will receive only €1,800,000 × $1.1/€ = $1,980,000. If the euro should strengthen to $1.3/€, however, the firm received €1,800,000 × $1.3/€ = $2,340,000. Thus exposure is the chance of either a loss or a gain.

The U.S. firm might have avoided transaction exposure by invoicing the Belgian buyer in dollars. Of course, if this firm attempted to sell only in dollars it might not have obtained the sale in the first place. Avoiding transaction exposure by not having a sale is counterproductive to the well-being of the firm! Even if the Belgian buyer agrees to pay in dollars, transaction exposure is not eliminated. Instead, it is transferred to the Belgian buyer, whose dollar account payable has an unknown cost in euros 60 days hence.

1.2 Borrowing and Lending

An example of transaction exposure arises when funds are borrowed or loaned, and the amount involved is denominated in a foreign currency. For example, PepsiCo's largest bottler outside of the United States in 1994 was Group Embotellador de Mexico (Gemex). In mid-Dec. 1994, Gemex had U.S. Dollar debt of $264 million. At that time Mexico's new peso was traded at Ps3.45/US$, a pegged rate that had been maintained with minor variations since January 1, 1993, when the new currency unit was created. On Dec. 22, 1994, the new peso was allowed to float because of economic and political events within Mexico, and in one day it sank to Ps4.65/US$. For most of the following January it traded in a range near Ps5.50/US$.

For Gemex, the increase in the peso amount of its dollar debt was as follows:

> Dollar debt in mid-Dec. 1994: US$264million * 3.45Ps/$ = Ps 910.8 million
> Dollar debt in mid-Jan. 1995: US$264million * 5.5Ps/$ = Ps 1452 million
> Dollar debt increase measured in New Mexico pesos = Ps 541.2 million

The number of pesos needed to repay the dollar debt increased by 59%! In U.S. dollar terms the drop in the value of the pesos caused Gemex to need the peso-equivalent of an additional US$98.4 million to repay. This increase in debt was the result of transaction exposure.

1.3 Other Causes of Transaction Exposure

When a firm buys a forward exchange contract, it deliberately creates a transaction exposure. This risk is usually incurred to hedge an existing transaction exposure.

For example, a U.S. firm might want to offset an existing obligation to purchase ¥100 million to pay for an import from Japan in 90 days. One way to offset this payment is to purchase ¥100 million in the forward market today for delivery in 90 days. In this manner the firm neutralizes any change in value of the Japanese yen relative to the dollar. If the yen increases in value, an unhedged account payable would cost more dollars, a transaction loss. The forward contract, however, has already fixed the amount of dollars needed to buy the ¥100 million. Thus, the potential transaction loss (or gain) on the account payable has been offset by the transaction gain (or loss) on the forward contract.

Note that foreign currency cash balances do not create transaction exposure, even though their home-currency value changes immediately with a change in exchange rates. No legal obligation exists to move the cash from one country and currency to another. If such an obligation did exist, it would show on the books as a payable (for example, dividends declared and payable) or receivable and then be counted as part of transaction exposure. Nevertheless, the foreign exchange value of cash balances does change when exchange rates change.

注意,外币现金余额不会产生交易风险,即使它们的本币价值会随着汇率的变化而发生变化。

1.4 Contractual Hedges

Foreign exchange transaction exposure can be managed by contractual hedge, operating hedge, and financial hedges. The main contractual hedges employ the forward, money, futures, and options markets. Operating and financial hedges use risk-sharing agreements, leads and lags in payment terms, swaps, and other strategies.

The term natural hedge refers to an offsetting operating cash flow, a payable arising from the conduct of business. A financial hedge refers to either an offsetting debt obligation (such as a loan) or some type of financial derivative such as an interest rate swap.

Example 8.1

A U.S. Firm are expected to sell the equipment to a British firm for the value of £ 1 million. The sale is made in March with payment due three months later in June. The following are the financial and market information for the analysis of currency exposure problem:
- Spot exchange rate: $1.7640/£
- Three-month forward rate: $1.7540/£
- U.S. firm's cost of capital: 12.0%
- U.K. Three-month borrowing interest rate: 10.0% (or 2.5% quarter)
- U.K. Three-month investment interest rate: 8.0% (or 2.0% quarter)
- U.S. Three-month borrowing interest rate: 8.0% (or 2.0% quarter)
- U.S. Three-month investment interest rate: 6.0% (or 1.5% quarter
- June put option in the over-the-counter (bank) market for £ 1 million; strike price $1.75 (nearly at-the-money); 1.5% premium.
- U.S. firm's foreign exchange advisory service forecasts that the spot rate in three months will be $1.76/£ .

U.S. firm determined that its minimum acceptable margin was at a sales price of $1,700,000. The budget rate, the lowest acceptable dollar per pound exchange rate, was therefore established at $1.70/£. Any exchange rate below this budget rate would result in U.S. firm actually losing money on the transaction.

The following four options are available to U.S. firm to manage the exposure:
- Remain unhedged
- Hedge in the forward market
- Hedge in the money market
- Hedge in the options market

(1) Unhedged Position

Suppose the U.S. Firm decides to accept the transaction risk, then if the pound fall to, say, $1.65/£, it will receive only $1,650,000 three month later. Of course, exchange risk is not one-side, if the transaction is left uncovered and the pound strengthened even more than forecast. It will receive considerably more than $1,760,000. The essence of an unhedged approach is as follows:

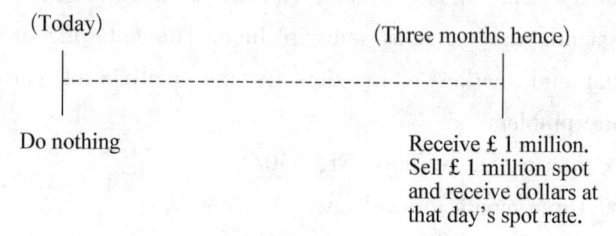

```
(Today)                              (Three months hence)
  |----------------------------------------|

Do nothing                           Receive £ 1 million.
                                     Sell £ 1 million spot
                                     and receive dollars at
                                     that day's spot rate.
```

Figure 8.3　Unhedged Postion

(2) Forward Market Hedge

A "forward hedge" involves a forward (or futures) contract and a source of funds to fulfill that contract. The forward contract is entered into at the time the transaction exposure is created. In this case, that would be in March, when the sale to British firm was booked as an account receivable.

When a foreign currency-denominated sale such as this is made, it is booked at the spot rate of exchange existing on the booking date. In this case, the spot rate on the day it is booked as an account receivable is $1.7640/£, so the sale is recorded on the U.S. firm's books as a sale of $1,764,000. Funds to fulfill the contract will be available in June, when the British firm pays £ 1 million to the U.S. firm. If funds to fulfill the forward contract are on hand or are due because of a business operation, the hedge is considered covered, perfect, or square because no residual foreign exchange risk exists. Funds on hand or to be received are matched by funds to be paid.

In some situations, funds to fulfill the forward exchange contract are not already available or due to be received later, but must be purchased in the spot market at some future date. Such a hedge is open or uncovered. It involves considerable risk because the hedger must take a chance on purchasing foreign exchange at an uncertain future spot rate in order to fulfill the forward contract. Purchase of such funds at a later date is referred to as "covering."

Should the U.S. Firm wish to hedge its transaction exposure in

> 一份"远期对冲"合约包括一笔远期(或期货)合约和一笔履行该合约的资金。

the forward market, it will sell £ 1 million forward today at the three-month forward quotation of $17,540 per pound. This is a covered transaction in which the firm no longer has any foreign exchange risk. In three months, the firm will receive £ 1 million from the British buyer, deliver that sum to the bank against its forward sale, and receive $1,754,000. This certain sum is $6,000 less than the uncertain $1,760,000 expected from the unhedged position because the forward market quotation differs from the firm's three-month forecast. This would then be recorded on the U.S. Firm's books as a foreign exchange loss of %10,000 ($1,764,000 as booked, $1.754,000 as settled).

The essence of a forward hedge is as follows:

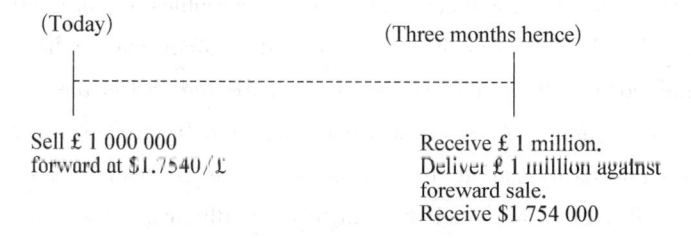

```
(Today)                          (Three months hence)
|--------------------------------|
|                                |
Sell £ 1 000 000                 Receive £ 1 million.
forward at $1.7540/£             Deliver £ 1 million against
                                 foreward sale.
                                 Receive $1 754 000
```

Figure 8.4 Forward Market Hedge

If the U.S. Firm's forecast of future rates were identical to that implicit in the forward quotation, that is, $1.7540, expected receipts would be the same whether or not the firm hedges. However, realized receipts under the unhedged alternative could vary considerably from the certain receipts when the transaction is hedged. Believing that the forward rate is an unbiased estimate of the future spot rate does not prevent us from using the forward hedge to eliminate the risk of an unexpected change in the future spot rate.

(3) Money Market Hedge

Like a forward market hedge, a money market hedge also includes a contract and a source of funds to fulfill that contract. In this instance the contract is a loan agreement. The firm seeking the money market hedge borrows in one currency and exchange the proceeds for another currency. Funds to fulfill the contract—that is, to repay the loan—may be generated from business operations, in which case the money market hedge is covered. Alternatively, funds to repay the loan may be purchased in the foreign exchange spot market when the loan matures. In this instance the money market hedge is uncovered or open.

A money market hedge can cover a single transaction, such as the U.S. Firm's £1 million receivable, or repeated transactions. Hedging repeated transactions is called matching. It requires the firm to match the expected foreign currency cash inflows and outflows by currency and maturity. For example, if the U.S. Firm had numerous sales denominated in pounds to British customers over a long period of time, it would have somewhat predictable U.K. Pound cash in flows. The appropriate money market hedge technique would be to borrow U.K. Pounds in an amount matching the typical size and maturity of expected pound inflows. Then, if the pound depreciated or appreciated, the foreign exchange effect on cash inflows in pounds would be approximately offset by the effect on cash outflows in pounds from repaying the pound loan plus interest.

The structure of a money market hedge resembles that of a forward hedge. The difference is that the cost of the money market hedge is determined by differential interest rates. While the cost of the forward hedge is a function of the forward rate quotation. In efficient markets, interest rate parity should ensure that these costs are nearly the same, but not all markets are efficient at all times. Furthermore, the difference in interest rates facing a private firm borrowing in two separate national markets may not be the same as the difference in risk-free government bill rates or eurocurrency interest rates in these same markets. It is the latter differential that is relevant for interest rate parity.

To hedge in the money market, the U.S. Firm will borrow pounds in London at once immediately convert the borrowed pounds into dollars, and repay the pound loan in three months with the proceeds from the sale. How much should it borrow? It will need to borrow just enough to repay both the principal and interest with the sale proceeds. The borrowing interest rate will be 10% per annum, or 2.5% for three months. Therefore, the amount to borrow now for repayment in three months is

$$\frac{£1,000,000}{1+0.025} = £975,610$$

The U.S. Firm should borrow £975,610 now and in three months repay that amount plus £24,390 of interest from the sale proceeds of the account receivable. It would exchange the £975,610 loan proceeds for dollars at the current spot exchange rate of $1.7640/£, receiving $1,720,976 at once.

The money market hedge, if selected by the U.S. Firm, actually creates a pound denominated liability, that is, a pound bank loan, to offset the pound-denominated asset, the account receivable. The money market hedge works as a hedge by matching assets and liabilities according to their currency of denomination. Using a simple T-account to illustrate the U.S. Firm's balance sheet, we see that the loan (principal and interest payable) in British pounds offsets the pound-denominated account receivable:

Assets		Liabilities and Net Worth	
Account receivable	£ 1 million	Bank loan (Principal)	£ 975,610
		Interest payable	£ 24,390
	£ 1 million		£ 1 million

The loan acts as a balance sheet hedge—a money market hedge in this case—against the pound-denominated account receivable.

To compare the forward hedge with the money market hedge we must analyze how the U.S. Firm's loan proceeds will be utilized for the next three months. Remember that the loan proceeds are received today but the forward contract proceeds are received in three months. For comparison purposes, we must calculate either the future value in three months of the loan proceeds or the present value of the forward contract proceeds. (we will use future value for pedagogical reasons, but the correct use of present value would give the same comparative results.)

Because both the forward contract proceeds and the loan proceeds are relatively certain, it is possible to choose from the two alternatives the one that yields the higher dollar receipts. This result, in turn, depends on the assumed rate of investment of the loan proceeds.

At least three logical choices exist for an assumed investment rate for the loan proceeds for the next three months. First, if the U.S. Firm is cash rich, the loan proceeds might be invested in U.S. Dollar money market instruments that have been assumed to yield 6% per annum. Second, it might simply use the pound loan proceeds to substitute for an equal dollar loan that the U.S. Firm would otherwise have undertaken at an assumed rate 8% per annum. Third, it might invest the loan proceeds in the general operations of the firm, in which case the cost of capital of 12% per annum would be the appropriate rate. The future value of the loan proceeds at the end of three months under each of these three investment assumptions would

因为远期合同收益和贷款收益都是相对确定的,所以有可能从两个选择中选择一个产生更高的美元收益。

be as follows:

Received Today	Invested in	Rate	Future Value in Three Months
$1,720,976	Treasury bill	6%/Yr or 1.5%/quarter	$1,746,791
$1,720,976	Debt cost	8%/Yr or 2.0%/quarter	$1,755,396
$1,720,976	Cost of capital	12%/Yr or 3.0%/quarter	$1,772,605

Because the proceeds in three months from the forward hedge would be $1,754,000, the money market hedge is superior to the forward hedge if the U.S. Firm used the loan proceeds to replace a dollar loan (8%) or to conduct general business operations (12%). The forward hedge would be preferable if the U.S. Firm merely invested the pound loan proceeds in dollar-denominated money market instruments at 6% annual interest.

A break-even investment rate can be calculated that would make the U.S. firm indifferent between the forward hedge and the money market hedge. Assume that r is the unknown three-month investment rate, expressed as a decimal, that would equalize the proceeds from the forward and money market hedges. We have

$$(Loan\ proceeds)(1 + rate) = (forward\ proceeds)$$
$$\$1,720,976(1 + r) = \$1,754,000$$
$$r = 0.0192$$

We can convert this three-month (90-day) investment rate to an annual whole percentage equivalent, the rate is 7.68% (Assuming a 360-day financial year). In other words, if the U.S. firm can invest the loan proceeds at a rate higher than 7.68% per annum, it would prefer the money market hedge. If it can only invest at a rate lower than 7.68%, it would prefer the forward hedge. The essence of the money market hedge is as follows:

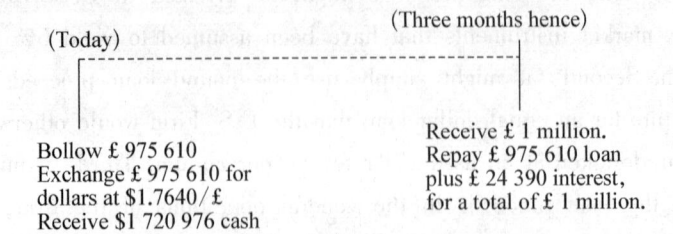

(Today)　(Three months hence)

Bollow £ 975 610
Exchange £ 975 610 for
dollars at $1.7640/£
Receive $1 720 976 cash

Receive £ 1 million.
Repay £ 975 610 loan
plus £ 24 390 interest,
for a total of £ 1 million.

Figure 8.5　Money Market Hedge

The money market hedge results in cash received up front (at the start of the period), which can then be carried forward in time for comparison with the other hedging alternatives.

The Figure 8.6 shows the value of the U.S. firm's £ 1 million account receivable over a range of possible ending spot exchange rates. The value of the receivable is shown uncovered, covered with a forward contract hedge, and covered with a money market hedge. Figure 8.6 makes it clear that the firm's view of likely exchange rate changes aids in the hedging choice. If the firm expects the exchange rate to move against the U.S. firm—to the left of $1.76/£, the money market hedge is the clearly preferred alternative. At a guaranteed value of $1,772,605, the money market hedge is by far the most profitable choice. If the U.S. firm expects the exchange rate to move in the U.S. firm's favor, to the right of $1.76/£, the choice of the hedge is more complex.

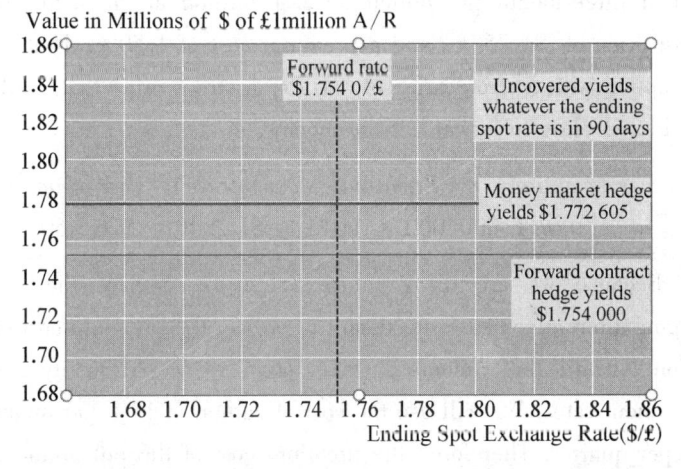

Figure 8.6 Valuation of Cash Flows by Hedging Alternative

Consider the following points:
- If the spot rate is expected to move to the right of $1.77/£, the unhedged alternative always provides the highest U.S. dollar value for the receivable.
- If the U.S. firm worried that its expectations may prove incorrect, the decision to remain unhedged does not assure the U.S. firm of meeting its budgeted exchange rate of $1.70/£. This is an outcome the firm cannot afford. The possibility always exists of a major political or economic event disrupting international currency markets unexpectedly
- If the spot rate is expected to move to the right of $1.77/£, but not far to the right, for example to $1.78/£, the expected

benefits of remaining unhedged are probably outweighed by the risks of remaining unhedged. The money market hedge is still the preferred choice.

Figure 8.5 also helps the U.S. firm focus on exactly what it wishes it could achieve: a position that provides its protection on the downside (to the left of $1.76/£), but still allows it to benefit on the upside (to the right of $1.76/£). This is the basic advantage of an option hedge.

(4) Options Market Hedge

The U.S. firm could also cover its £ 1 million exposure by purchasing a put option. This technique allows it to speculate on the upside potential for appreciation of the pound while limiting downside risk to a known amount.

Given the earlier quote, the U.S. firm could purchase from its bank a three-month put option on £ 1 million at an at-the-money strike price of $1.75/£ and a premium cost of 1.50%. The cost of this option with a strike price of $1.75, a strike price that would be considered close to forward at-the-money, is

$$(Size\ of\ option) \times (Premium) \times (spotrate) = cost\ of\ option$$
$$£\ 1,000,000 \times 0.015 \times \$1.7640 = \$26,460$$

Because we are using future value to compare the various hedging alternatives, it is necessary to project the premium cost of the option forward three months. Once again we could justify several investment rates. We will use the cost of capital of 12% per annum or 3% per quarter. Therefore, the premium cost of the put option as of June would be $26,460 (1.03) = $27,254.

When the £ 1 million is received in June, the value in dollars depends on the spot rate at that time. The upside potential is unlimited, the same as in the unhedged alternative. At any exchange rate above $1.75/£ the firm would allow its option to expire unexercised and would exchange the pounds for dollars at the spot rate. If the expected rate of $1.76/£ materializes, for example, the firm would exchange the £ 1 milion in the spot market for $1,760,000. Net proceeds would be $1,760,000 minus the $27,254 cost of the option, or $1,732,746.

In contrast to the unhedged alternative, downside risk is limited with an option. If the pound depreciates below $1.75/£, the firm would exercise her option to sell (put) £ 1 million at

$1.75/£, receiving $1,750,000 gross, but $1,722,746 net of the $27,254 cost of the option. Although this downside result is lower than the downside of the forward or money market hedges, the upside potential is not limited the way it is with those hedges. Thus, whether the option strategy is superior to a forward or money market hedge depends on the degree to which management is risk averse.

The essence of the at-the-money option market hedge is as follows:

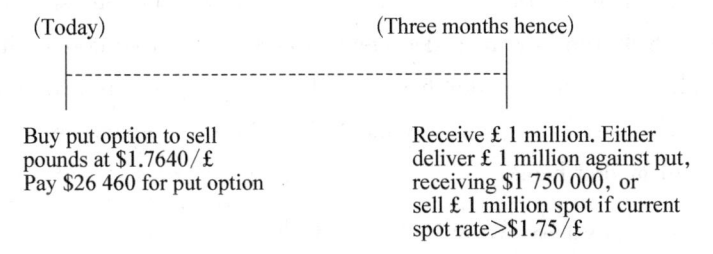

```
(Today)                          (Three months hence)
   |--------------------------------|

Buy put option to sell           Receive £ 1 million. Either
pounds at $1.7640/£              deliver £ 1 million against put,
Pay $26 460 for put option       receiving $1 750 000, or
                                 sell £ 1 million spot if current
                                 spot rate>$1.75/£
```

Figure 8.7 Options Market Hedge

We can calculate a trading range for the pound that defines the break-even points for the option compared with the other strategies. The upper bound of the range is determined by comparison with the forward rate. The pound must appreciate enough above the $1.7540/£ forward rate to cover the $1.0273/£ cost of the option. Therefore, the break-even upside spot price of the pound must be $1.7540 + $0.0273 = $1.7813. If the spot pound appreciates above $1.7813/£, proceeds under the option strategy will be greater than under the forward hedge. If the spot pound ends up below $1.7813/£, the forward hedge would be superior in retrospect.

The lower bound of the range is determined by a comparison with the unhedged strategy. If the spot price falls below $1.75/£, the firm will exercise its put option and sell the proceeds at $1.75/£. The net proceeds per pound will be $1.75/£ less the $0.0273 cost of the option, or $1.7221/£. If the spot rate falls below $1.7221/£, the net proceeds from exercising the option will be greater than the net proceeds from selling the unhedged pounds in the spot market. At any spot rate above $1.7221/£, the spot proceeds from the unhedged alternative will be greater. These rates and values are summarized as follows:

Put Option Strike Price	ATM Option $1,75/£
Option cost (future value)	$27,254
Proceeds if exercised	$1,750,000
Minimum net proceeds	$1,722,746
Maximum net proceeds	Unlimited
Break-even spot rate (upside)	$1.7813/£
Break-even spot rate (downside)	$1.7221/£

(5) Comparison of Alternatives

The four alternatives available to the U.S. firm are shown in Figure 8.8. The forward hedge yields a certain $1,754,000 in three months. The money market hedge, if the loan proceeds are invested at the 12% cost of capital, yields $1,772,605, preferable to the forward market hedge.

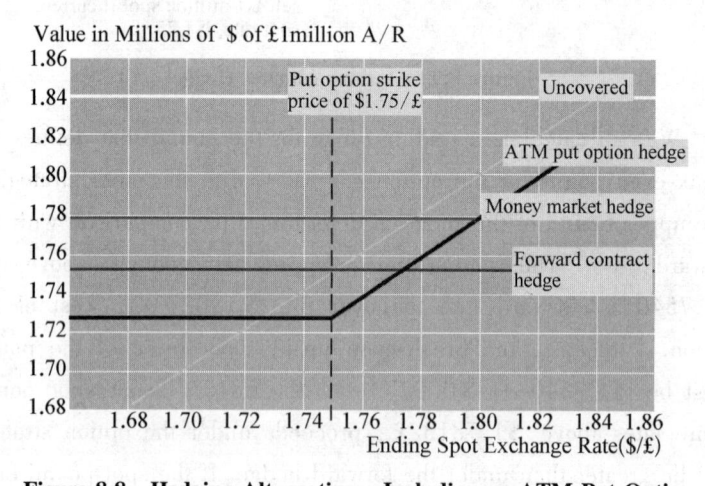

Figure 8.8 Hedging Alternatives, Including an ATM Put Option

If the firm does not hedge, it can expect $1,760,000 in three months (calculated at the expected spot rate of $1.76/£). However, this sum is at risk and might be greater or smaller. Under conditions when the forward rate is accepted as the most likely future spot rate, the expected results from an unhedged position are identical to the certain results from the forward hedge. Under such circumstances the advantage of hedging over remaining unhedged is the reduction of uncertainty.

The put option offers a unique alternative. If the exchange rate moves in the firm's favor, the option offers nearly the same upside potential as the unhedged alternative except for the upfront costs. If, however, the exchange rate moves against the firm, the put option limits the downside risk to net receipts of $1,722,746.

Foreign currency options have a variety of hedging uses beyond the one illustrated here. A put option is useful to construction firms or other exporters when they must submit a fixed-price bid in a foreign currency without knowing until some later date whether their bid is successful. A put option can be used to hedge the foreign exchange risk either for the bidding period alone or for the entire period of potential exposure if the bid is won. If the bid is rejected, the loss is limited to the cost of the option. In contrast, if the risk is hedged by a forward contract and the bid is rejected, the forward contract must be reversed or eventually fulfilled at an unknown potential loss or gain. The bidder has been holding what turned out to be an uncovered forward contract.

1.5 Management of an Account Payable

The management of an account payable, where the firm is required to make a foreign currency payment at a future date, is similar but not identical in form.

If the U.S. firm had a £1,000,000 account payable in 90 days, the hedging choices would appear as follows:

(1) Remain Unhedged. The U.S. firm could wait 90 days, exchange dollars for pounds at that time, and make its payment. If the firm expects the spot rate in 90 days to be $1.76/£, the payment would be expected to cost $1,760,000. This amount is, however, uncertain; the spot exchange rate in 90 days could be very different from that expected. 〔不对冲。〕

(2) Use Forward Market Hedge. Trident could buy £1,000,000 forward, locking in a rate of $1.7540/£ and a total dollar cost of $1,754,000. This is $6,000 less than the expected cost of remaining unhedged, and it is less risky. Therefore, it might be deemed preferable. 〔远期对冲。〕

(3) Use Money market hedge. The Money market hedge is distinctly different for a payable as opposed to a receivable. To implement a money market hedge in this case, Trident would exchange U.S. dollars spot and invest them for 90 days in a pound-denominated interest-bearing account. It would then use the principal and interest in British pounds at the end of the 90-day period to pay the £1,000,000 〔货币市场对冲。〕

account payable.

In order to ensure that the principal and interest exactly equal the £1,000,000 due in 90 days, the firm would discount the £1,000,000 by the pound investment interest rate of 8% per annum for 90 days (2%) in order to determine the pounds needed today:

$$\frac{£1,000,000}{1+(0.08\times 90/360)}= £980,392.16$$

This £980,392.16 needed today would require $1,729,411.77 at the current spot rate of $1.7640/£:

$$£980,392.16\times \$1,7640/£ = \$1,729,411.77$$

Finally, in order to compare the money market hedge outcome with the other hedging alternatives, the $1,729,411.77 cost today must be carried forward 90 days to the same future date as the other hedge choices. If the current dollar cost is carried forward at the firm's weighted average cost of capital (WACC) of 12%, the total future value cost of the money market hedge is

$$\$1,792,411.77\times [1+(0.12\times 90/360)] = \$1,781,294.12$$

This is higher than the forward hedge and therefore unattractive.

(4) Use Option Hedge. The firm could cover its £1,000,000 account payable by purchasing a call option on £1,000,000. A June call option on British pounds with a near at-the-money strike price of $1.75/£ would cost 1.5% (premium) or

$$£1,000,000\times 0.015\times \$1,7640/£ = \$26,460$$

This premium, regardless of whether the call option is exercised or not, will be paid up front. Its value carried forward 90 days at the WACC of 12%, as it was in the receivable example, would raise its end-of-period cost to $27,254.

If the spot rate in 90 days is less than $1.75/£, the option would be allowed to expire and the £1,000,000 for the payable would be purchased on the spot market. The total cost of the call option hedge if the option is not exercised is theoretically smaller than any other alternative (with the exception of remaining unhedged), because the option premium is still paid and lost.

If the spot rate in 90 days exceeds $1.75/£, the call option would be exercised. The total cost of the call option hedge if exercised is as follows:

Exercise call option (£ 1,000,000× $1.75/£)	$1,750,000
Call option premium (carried forward 90 days)	27,254
Total maximum expense of call option hedge	$1,777,254

The four hedging methods are summarized in Figure 8.9. The costs of the forward hedge and money market hedge are certain. The cost of using the call option hedge is calculated as a maximum, and the cost of remaining unhedged is highly uncertain.

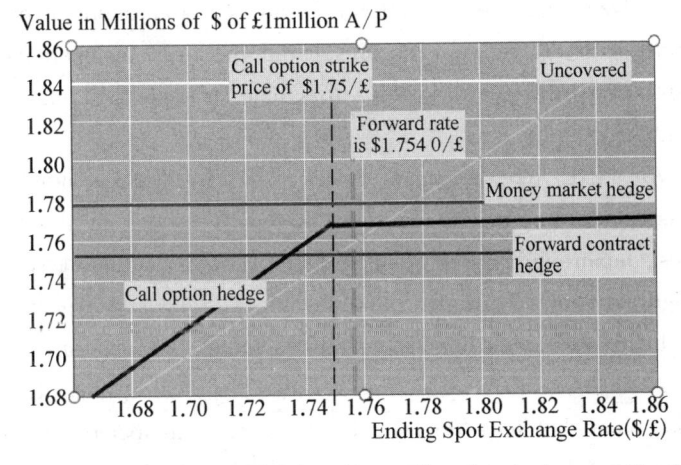

Figure 8.9 Valuation of Hedging Alternatives for an Account Payable

As with the firm's account receivable, the final hedging choice depends on the confidence of exchange rate expectations and willingness to bear risk. The forward hedge provides the lowest cost of making the account payable payment that is certain. If the dollar strengthens against the pound, ending up at a spot rate less than $1.75/£, the call option could potentially be the lowest cost hedge. Given an expected spot rate of $1.76/£, however, the forward hedge appears to be the preferred alternative.

2 Operating Exposure

It also called economic exposure, competitive exposure, or strategic exposure, measures the change in the present value of the firm resulting from any change in expected future operating cash flows of the firm caused by an unexpected change in exchange rates. The change in value depends on the effect of the exchange rate change on future sales volume, prices, and costs.

Transaction exposure and operating exposure exist because of

> 它也被称为经济风险、竞争风险或战略风险,衡量因汇率意外变化导致公司预期未来经营现金流的任何变化而导致的公司现值的变化。

unexpected changes in future cash flows. The difference between the two is that transaction exposure is concerned with future cash flows already contracted for, while operating exposure focuses on expected (not yet contracted for) future cash flows that might change because a change in exchange rates has altered international competitiveness.

2.1 Attributes of Operating Exposure

Measuring the operating exposure of a firm requires forecasting and analyzing all the firm's future individual transaction exposures together with the future exposures of all the firm's competitors and potential competitors worldwide. A simple example will clarify the point.

An MNE like Eastman Kodak (U.S.) has a number of transaction exposures at any time. Kodak has sales in the United States, Japan, and Europe and therefore posts a continuing series of foreign currency receivables (and payables). Sales and expenses that are already contracted for are traditional transaction exposures. Sales that are highly probable based on Kodak's historical business line and market share but have no legal basis yet are anticipated transaction exposures. (This term is used quite specifically in accounting for foreign exchange rate gains and losses.)

What if the analysis of the firm's exposure to exchange rate changes is extended even further into the future? What are the longer-term exposures of Kodak to exchange rate changes? Future exchange rate changes will not only alter the domestic currency value (U.S. dollars in this case) of the firms foreign currency cash flows, but also it will change the quantity of foreign currency cash flows generated. Any change in Kodak's cash flows in the future depends on how competitive it is in various markets. Kodak's international competitiveness will in turn be affected by the operating exposures of its major competitors like Fuji (Japan) and Agfa (Germany), The analysis of this longer term—where exchange rate changes are unpredictable and therefore unexpected—is the goal of operating exposure analysis.

2.1.1 Operating and Financing Cash Flows

The cash flows of the MNE can be divided into operating cash flows and financing cash flows. Operating cash flows arise from intercompany (between unrelated companies) and intracompany (between units of the same company) receivables and payables, rent and lease payments for the use of facilities and equipment, royalty and license fees for the use of technology and intellectual property, and assorted management fees for services provided. Financing cash flows are payments for the use of intercompany and intracompany loans (principal and interest) and stockholder equity (new equity investments and dividends). Each of these cash flows can occur at different time intervals, in different amounts, and in different currencies of denomination, and each has a different predictability of occurrence. We summarize cash flow possibilities in Figure 8.10 for an MNE which supports its foreign subsidiary.

Financial cash flows are cash flows related to the financing of the subsidiary Operating Cash Flow are cash flows related to the business activitiness of the subsidiary

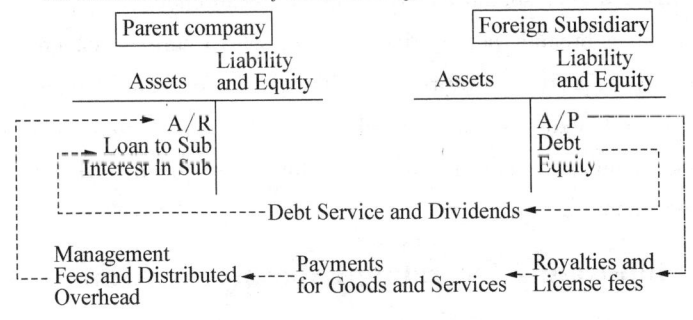

```
        Parent company                    Foreign Subsidiary
                    Liability                          Liability
          Assets    and Equity            Assets       and Equity
     ┌────────→ A/R                               A/P ──────────┐
     │  ┌── Loan to Sub                           Debt ─────┐   │
     │  │   Interest in Sub                       Equity    │   │
     │  │                                                   │   │
     │  └──────────────── Debt Service and Dividends ←──────┘   │
     │                                                          │
     │  Management                                              │
     └── Fees and Distributed ←── Payments ←── Royalties and ───┘
         Overhead                 for Goods and Services  License fees
```

Figure 8.10 Financial and Operating Cash Flows between Parent and Subsidiary

2.1.2 Expected versus Unexpected Changes in Cash Flow

Operating exposure is far more important for the long-run health of a business than changes caused by transaction or translation exposure.

However, operating exposure is inevitably subjective because it depends on estimates of future cash flow changes over an arbitrary time horizon. Thus, it does not spring from the accounting process but rather from operating analysis. Planning for operating exposure is a total management responsibility because it depends on the interaction of strategies in finance, marketing, purchasing, and production.

An expected change in foreign exchange rates is not included in the definition of operating exposure, because both management and investors should have factored this information into their evaluation of anticipated operating results and market value. From a management perspective, budgeted financial statements already reflect information about the effect of an expected change in exchange rates. For

> 对于企业的长期健康发展来说,经营风险远比交易或转换风险引起的变化更重要。

example, under equilibrium conditions the forward rate might be used as an unbiased predictor of the future spot rate. In such a case, management would use the forward rate when preparing the operating budgets, rather than assume the spot rate would remain unchanged.

Another example is that expected cash flow to amortize debt should already reflect the international Fisher effect. The level of expected interest and principal repayment should be a function of expected exchange rates rather than existing spot rates.

From an investor's perspective, if the foreign exchange market is efficient, information about expected changes in exchange rates should be widely known and thus reflected in a firm's market value. Only unexpected changes in exchange rates, or an inefficient foreign exchange market, should cause market value to change.

From a broader perspective, operating exposure is not only the sensitivity of a firm's future cash flows to unexpected changes in foreign exchange rates, but also its sensitivity to other key macroeconomic variables. This factor has been labeled as macroeconomic uncertainty.

2.2 Illustrating Operating Exposure: Trident

To illustrate the consequences of operating exposure, we use Trident's European subsidiary, Trident Europe.

Figure 8.11 presents the dilemma facing Trident Corporation as a result of an unexpected change in the value of the euro, the currency of economic consequence for the German subsidiary. Trident Corporation (U.S.) derives much of its reported profits (earnings and earnings per share—EPS—as reported to Wall Street) from its

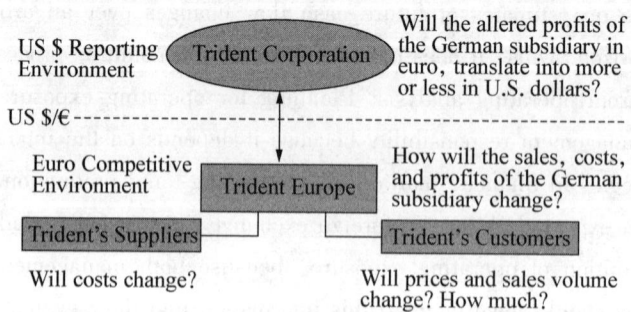

An unexpected depreciation in the value of the euro alters both the competitiveness of the subsidiary and the financial results, which are consolidated with the parent company.

Figure 8.11 Trident Corporation and Its European Subsidiary: Operating Exposure of the Parent and Its subsidiary

European subsidiary. If the euro unexpectedly falls in value, how will Trident Europe's revenues change (prices, in euro terms, and volumes)? How will its costs change (primarily input costs, in euro terms)? How will competitors respond? We explain the sequence of likely events over the short and medium run in the following section.

2.2.1 Base Case

Trident Europe manufactures in Germany from European material and labor. Half of production is sold within Europe for euros and half is expected to non-European countries. All sales are invoiced in euros, and accounts receivable are equal to one-fourth of annual sales. In other words, the average collection period is 90 days. Inventory is equal to 25% of annual direct costs. Trident Europe can expand or contract production volume without any significant change in per-unit direct costs or in overall general and administrative expenses. Depreciation on plant and equipment is € 600,000 per year, and the corporate income tax in Germany is 34%. The December 31, 2010, balance sheet and alternative scenarios are shown in Table 8.1.

Table 8.1 Trident Europe

Balance Sheet Information, End of Fiscal 2010			
Assets		Liabilities and Net Worth	
cash	€ 1,600,000	Accounts payable	€ 800,000
Accounts receivable	3,200,000	Short-term bank loan	1,600,000
Inventory	2,400,000	Long-term debt	1,600,000
Net plant and equipment	4,800,000	Common stock	1,800,000
		Retained earnings	6,200,000
Sum	12,000,000	Sum	12,000,000

Important Ratios to be Maintained and Other Date	
Accounts receivable, as percent of sales	25%
Inventory, as percent of annual direct costs	25%
cost of capital (annual discount rate)	20%
Income tax rate	34%

	STHZBase case	Case 1	Case 2	Case 3
Assumptions				
Exchange rate, $/€	1.2	1	1	1
Sales volume (units)	1,000,000	1,000,000	2,000,000	1,000,000
Sales price per unit	€ 12.80	€ 12.80	€ 12.80	€ 15.36
Direct cost per unit	€ 9.60	€ 9.60	€ 9.60	€ 9.60

continued

Annual cash flows before adjustments				
sales revenue	€ 12,800,000	€ 12,800,000	€ 25,600,000	€ 15,360,000
direct cost of goods sold	9,600,000	9,600,000	19,200,000	9,600,000
cash operating expense (fixed)	890,000	890,000	890,000	890,000
depreciation	600,000	600,000	600,000	600,000
pretax profit	€ 1,710,000	€ 1,710,000	€ 4,910,000	€ 4,270,000
income tax expense	581,400	581,400	1,669,400	1,451,800
profit after tax	€ 1,128,600	€ 1,128,600	€ 3,240,600	€ 2,818,200
add back depreciation	600,000	600,000	600,000	600,000
cash flow from operations, in euros	€ 1,726,600	€ 1,728,600	€ 3,840,600	€ 3,418,200
cash flow from operations, in dollars	€ 2,074,320	€ 1,728,600	€ 3,840,600	€ 3,418,200
Adjustments to working capital for 2011 and 2015 caused by changes in conditions				
Accounts receivables	€ 3,200,000	€ 3,200,000	€ 6,400,000	€ 3,840,000
inventory	2,400,000	2,400,000	4,800,000	2,400,000
sum	€ 5,600,000	€ 5,600,000	€ 11,200,000	€ 6,240,000
change from base conditions in 2011			€ 5,600,000	€ 640,000

year	Year-end cash flows			
1(2011)	$2,074,320	$1,728,600	($1,759,400)	$2,778,200
2(2012)	$2,074,320	$1,728,600	$3,840,600	$3,418,200
3(2013)	$2,074,320	$1,728,600	$3,840,600	$3,418,200
4(2014)	$2,074,320	$1,728,600	$3,840,600	$3,418,200
5(2015)	$2,074,320	$1,728,600	$9,440,600	$4,058,200
year	change in year-end cash flows from base conditions			
1(2011)	na	($345,720)	($3,833,720)	$703,880
2(2012)	na	($345,720)	$1,766,280	$1,343,880
3(2013)	na	($345,720)	$1,766,280	$1,343,880
4(2014)	na	($345,720)	$1,766,280	$1,343,880
5(2015)	na	($345,720)	$7,366,280	$1,983,880
	Present value of incremental year-end cash flows			
	na	($1,033,914)	$2,866,106	$3,742,892
	Base case	**Case 1**	**Case 2**	**Case 3**

We assume that on January 1, 2011, before any commercial activity begins, the euro unexpectedly drops 16.67% in value, from $1.2000/€ to $1.0000/€. If no devaluation had occurred, Trident Europe was expected to perform in 2011 as shown in the base case of

Table 8.1, generating a dollar cash flow from operations for Trident Corporation of $2,074,320.

Operating exposure depends on whether an unexpected change in exchange rates causes unanticipated changes in sales volume, sales prices, or operating costs. Following a euro devaluation, Trident Europe might choose to maintain its domestic sales prices constant in euro terms, or it might try to raise domestic prices because competing imports are now priced higher in Europe. The firm might choose to keep export prices constant in terms of foreign currencies, in terms of euros, or somewhere in between (partial pass-through). The strategy undertaken depends to a large measure on management's opinion about the price elasticity of demand. On the cost side, Trident Europe might raise prices because of more expensive imported raw material or components, or perhaps because all domestic prices in Germany have risen and labor is now demanding higher wages to compensate for domestic inflation.

Trident Europe's domestic sales and costs might also be partly determined by the effect of the euro devaluation on demand. To the extent that the devaluation, by making prices of German goods initially more competitive, stimulates purchases of European goods in import competing sectors of the economy as well as exports of German goods, German national income should increase. This assumes that the favorable effect of a euro devaluation on comparative prices is not immediately offset by higher domestic inflation. Thus, Trident Europe might be able to sell more goods domestically because of price and income effects and internationally because of price effects.

To illustrate the effect of various post-devaluation scenarios on Trident Europe's operating exposure, consider three simple cases:

Case 1: Devaluation; no change in any variable

Case 2: Increase in sales volume, other variables remain constant

Case 3: Increase in sales price, other variables remain constant.

To calculate the net change in present value under each of the scenarios, we will use a five-year horizon for any change in cash flow induced by the change in the dollar/euro exchange rate.

Case 1: Devaluation; No Change in Any Variable

Assume that in the five years ahead no changes occur in sales volume, sales price, or operating costs. Profits for the coming year in euros will be as expected, and cash flow from operations will be €1,728,600, as shown in Table 8.1. With a new exchange rate of

第一种情况:贬值,其他变量不变

$1.0000/€, this cash flow measured in dollars during 2011 will be

$$€1,728,600 × \$1.0000/€ = \$1,728,600.$$

Table 8.1 shows that the change in year-end cash flows from the base case is $345,720 for each of the next five years (2011—2015).

Table 8.1 shows that the discounted present value of this series of diminished dollar value cash flows is $1,033,914.

Case 2: Volume Increases: Other Variables Remain Constant

第二种情况:交易量增加,其他变量不变

Assume that sales within Europe double following the devaluation because German-made telecom components are now more competitive with imports. Additionally, export volume doubles because German-made components are now cheaper in countries whose currencies have not weakened. The sales price is kept constant in euro terms because management of Trident Europe has not observed any change in local German operating costs and because it sees an opportunity to increase market share.

Table 8.1 shows expected cash flow for the first year (2011) would be $3,840,600. This amount, however, is not available because a doubling of sales volume will require additional investment in accounts receivable and in inventory. Although a portion of this additional investment might be financed by increasing accounts payable, we assume additional working capital is financed by cash flow from operations.

At the end of 2011, accounts receivable will be equal to one-fourth of annual sales, or €6,400,000. This amount is twice receivables of €3,200,000 at the end of 2010, and the incremental increase of 3,200,000 must be financed from available cash. Year-end inventory would be equal to one-fourth of annual direct costs, or €4,800,000, an increase of €2,400,000 over the year-beginning level. Receivables and inventory together increase by €5,600,000. At the end of five years (2015), these incremental cash outflows will be recaptured because any investment in current assets eventually rolls back into cash.

Assuming no further change in volume, price, or costs, cash inflows for the five years would be as described in Table 8.1. In this instance, the devaluation causes a major drop in first-year cash flow from the $2,074,320 anticipated in 2011 without devaluation to a negative cash flow of $1,759,400. However, the remaining four years' cash flow is substantially enhanced by the operating effects of the devaluation. Over time, Trident Europe generates significantly more cash for its owners. The devaluation produces an operating gain over time, rather than an operating loss.

The reason that Trident Corporation is better off in Case 2 following the devaluation is that sales volume doubled while the per-unit dollar-equivalent sales price fell only 16.67%—the percent amount of the devaluation. In other words, the product faced a price elasticity of demand greater than one.

Case 3: Sales Price Increases; Other Variables Remain Constant

第三种情况:销售价格上升,其他变量不变

Assume the euro sales price is raised from € 12.80 to € 15.36 per unit to maintain the same U.S. dollar-equivalent price (the change offsets the depreciation of the euro). Assume further that volume remains constant in spite of this price increase; that is, customers expect to pay the same dollar-equivalent price, and local costs do not change.

Trident Europe is now better off following the devaluation than it was before because the sales price, which is pegged to the international price level, increased. However, volume did not drop. The new level of accounts receivable would be one-fourth of the new sales level of € 15,360,000 or € 3,840,000. an increase of € 640,000 over the base case. The investment in inventory is $2,400,000, which is the same as the base case because annual direct costs did not change.

Expected dollar cash flow in every year exceeds the cash flow of $2,074,320 that had been anticipated with no devaluation. The increase in working capital causes net cash flow to be only $2,778,200 in 2011, but thereafter the cash flow is $3,418,200 per year, with an additional $640,000 working capital recovered in the fifth year.

The key to this improvement is operating leverage. If costs are incurred in euros and do not increase after a devaluation, an increase in the sales price by the amount of devaluation will lead to sharply higher profits.

2.2.2 Other Possibilities

If any portion of sales revenues were incurred in other currencies, the situation would be different. Trident Europe might leave the foreign sales price unchanged, in effect raising the euro-equivalent price. Alternatively, it might leave the euro-equivalent price unchanged, thus lowering the foreign sales price in an attempt to gain volume. Of course, it could also position itself between these two extremes. Depending on elasticities and the proportion of foreign to domestic sales, total sales revenue might rise or fall.

If some or all raw material or components were imported and paid for in hard currencies, euro operating costs would increase after the devaluation of the euro. Another possibility is that local (not imported) euro costs would rise after a devaluation.

2.2.3 Measurement of Loss

Table 8.1 summarizes the change in expected year-end cash flows for the three cases and compares them with the cash flow expected should no devaluation occur (Base Case). These changes are then discounted by Trident Corporations assumed weighted average cost of capital of 20% to obtain the present value of the gain (loss) on operating exposure.

In Case 1, in which nothing changes after the euro is devalued, Trident Corporation incurs an operating loss with a present value of $1,033,914. In Case 2, in which volume doubled with no price change after devaluation, Trident Corporation experienced an operating gain with a present value of $2,866,106. In Case 3, in which the euro sales price was increased and volume did not change, the present value of the operating gain from devaluation was $3,742,892. An almost infinite number of combinations of volume, price, and cost could follow any devaluation, and any or all of them might take effect immediately after a evaluation or only after the passage of time.

2.3 Strategic Management of Operating Exposure

The objective of both operating and transaction exposure management is to anticipate and influence the effect of unexpected changes in exchange rates on a firm's future cash flows, rather than merely hoping for the best. To meet this objective, management can diversify the firms operating and financing base. Management can also change the firm's operating and financing policies.

The key to managing operating exposure at the strategic level is for management to recognize a disequilibrium in parity conditions when it occurs and to be prepositioned to react most appropriately. This task can best be accomplished if a firm diversifies internationally both its operating and its financing bases. Diversifying operations means diversifying sales. location of production facilities, and raw

---

经营和交易风险管理的目标都是预测和影响汇率的意外变化对公司未来现金流的影响，而不仅仅是期望最好的结果。为了实现这一目标，管理层可以使公司的经营和融资基础多样化，管理层也可以改变公司的经营和融资政策。

material sources. Diversifying the financing base means raising funds in more than one capital market and in more than one currency.

A diversification strategy permits the firm to react either actively or passively, depending on managements risk preference, to opportunities presented by disequilibrium conditions in the foreign exchange, capital, and product markets. Such a strategy does not require management to predict disequilibrium but only to recognize it when it occurs. It does require management to consider how competitors are prepositioned with respect to their own operating exposures. This knowledge should reveal which firms would be helped or hurt competitively by alternative disequilibrium scenarios.

2.3.1 Diversifying Operations

If a firm's operations are diversified internationally, management is prepositioned both to recognize disequilibrium when it occurs and to react competitively. Consider the case where purchasing power parity is temporarily in disequilibrium. Although the disequilibrium may have been unpredictable, management can often recognize its symptoms as soon as they occur. For example, management might notice a change in comparative costs in the firm's own plants located in different countries. It might also observe changed profit margins or sales volume in one area compared to another, depending on price and income elasticities of demand and competitors' reactions.

Recognizing a temporary change in worldwide competitive conditions permits management to make changes in operating strategies Management might make marginal shifts in sourcing raw materials, components, or finished products. If spare capacity exists, production runs can be lengthened in one country and reduced in another. The marketing effort can be strengthened in export markets where the firms products have become more price competitive because of the disequilibrium condition.

Even if management does not actively distort normal operations when exchange rates change, the firm should experience some beneficial portfolio effects. The variability of its cash flows is probably reduced by international diversification of its production, sourcing, and sales because exchange rate changes under disequilibrium conditions are likely to increase the firm's competitiveness in some markets while reducing it in others. In that case, operating exposure would be neutralized.

In contrast to the internationally diversified MNE, a purely domestic firm might be subject to the full impact of foreign exchange operating exposure even though it does not have foreign currency cash flows. For example, it could experience intense import competition in its domestic market from competing firms producing in countries with undervalued currencies.

A purely domestic firm does not have the option to react to an international disequilibrium condition in the same manner as an MNE. In fact, a purely domestic firm will not be positioned to recognize that a disequilibrium exists because it lacks comparative data from its own internal sources. By the time external data are available from published sources, it is often too late to react. Even if a domestic firm recognizes the disequilibrium, it cannot quickly shift production and sales into foreign markets in which it has had no previous presence.

2.3.2 Diversifying Financing

If a firm diversifies its financing sources, it will be prepositioned to take advantage of temporary deviations from the international Fisher effect. If interest rate differentials do not equal expected changes in exchange rates, opportunities to lower a firm's cost of capital will exist. However, to be able to switch financing sources, a firm must already be well known in the international investment community, with banking contacts firmly established. Once again, this is not an option for a domestic firm that has limited its financing to one capital market.

Although we recommend diversification as a strategy for foreign exchange risk management, such a strategy has a potentially favorable impact on other risks as well. In particular, it could reduce the variability of future cash flows due to domestic business cycles, provided these are not perfectly correlated with international cycles. It could increase the availability of capital, and reduce its cost, by diversifying such risks as restrictive capital market policies or government borrowing competition in the capital market. It could mitigate political risks such as expropriation, war, blocked funds, or unfavorable changes in laws that reduce or eliminate profitability. The list of advantages from international diversification can even be extended to such areas as spreading the risk of technological obsolescence and reducing portfolio risk in the context of the capital asset pricing model. Now we are verging on the diversification strategy thereof the capital asset pricing model.

Constraints exist that may limit the feasibility of a diversification strategy for foreign exchange risk management or one of the other risks just mentioned. For example, the technology of a particular industry may require such large economies of scale that it is not economically feasible to diversify production locations. Firms in this industry could still diversify sales and financing sources, however. On the other hand, a firm may be too small or too unknown to attract international equity investors or lenders. Yet it could at least diversify its sales internationally. Thus, a diversification strategy can be implemented only as far as is feasible.

2.4　Proactive Management of Operating Exposure

Operating and transaction exposures can be partially managed by adopting operating or financing policies that offset anticipated foreign exchange exposures. Six of the most commonly employed proactive policies are as follows:
- Matching currency cash flows
- Risk-sharing agreements
- Back-to-back or parallel loans
- Currency swaps
- leads and lags
- Reinvoicing centers

2.4.1　Matching Currency Cash Flows

One way to offset an anticipated continuous long exposure to a particular currency is to acquire debt denominated in that currency. Figure 8.12 demonstrates the exposure of a U.S. firm with continuing export sales to Canada. In order to compete effectively in Canadian markets, the firm invoices all export sales in Canadian

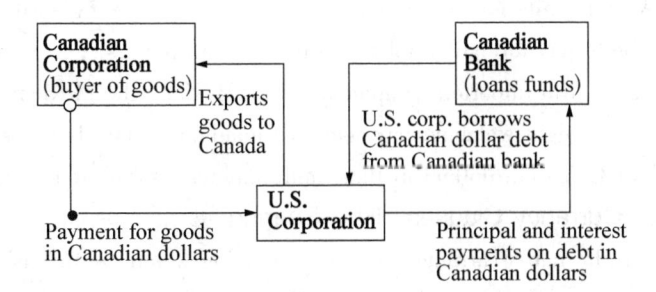

Exposure: The sale of goods to Canada creates a foreign currency exposure from the inflow of Canadian dollars.
Hedge: The Canadian dollar debt payments act as a financial hedge by requiring debt service, an outflow of Canadian dollars.

Figure 8.12　Matching: Debt Financing as a Financial Hedge

dollars. This policy results in a continuing receipt of Canadian dollars month after month. If the export sales are part of a continuing supplier relationship, the long Canadian dollar position is relatively predictable and constant. This endless series of transaction exposures could of course be continually hedged with forward contracts or other contractual hedges.

But what if the firm sought out a continual use, an outflow, for its continual inflow of Canadian dollars?

If the U.S. firm were to acquire part of its debt-capital in the Canadian dollar markets, it could use the relatively predictable Canadian dollar cash inflows from export sales to service the principal and interest payments on Canadian dollar debt and be cash flow matched. The U.S.-based firm has hedged an operational cash inflow by creating a financial cash outflow, and so it does not have to actively manage the exposure with contractual financial instruments such as forward contracts. This form of hedging, sometimes referred to as matching, is effective in eliminating currency exposure when the exposure cash flow is relatively constant and predictable over time.

The list of potential matching strategies is nearly endless. A second alternative would be for the U.S. firm to seek potential suppliers of raw materials or components in Canada as a substitute for U.S. or other foreign firms. The firm would then possess not only an operational Canadian dollar cash inflow, the receivable, but also a Canadian dollar operational cash out flow, a payable If the cash flows were roughly the same in magnitude and timing, the strategy would be a natural hedge. The term natural refers to operating-based activities of the firm.

A third alternative, often referred to as currency switching, would be to pay foreign suppliers with Canadian dollars. For example, if the U.S. firm imported components from Mexico, the Mexican firms themselves might welcome payment in Canadian dollars because they are short Canadian dollars in their multinational cash flow network.

2.4.2 Currency Clauses: Risk-Sharing

An alternative arrangement for managing a long-term cash flow exposure between firms with a continuing buyer-supplier relationship is risk-sharing. Risk-sharing is a contractual arrangement in which the buyer and seller agree to "share" or split currency movement impacts on payments between them. If the two firms are interested in a long-term relationship based on product quality and supplier reliability and not on the whims of the currency markets, a cooperative agreement to share the burden of currency risk management may be in order.

If Ford's North American operations import automotive parts from Mazda (Japan) every month, year after year, major swings in exchange rates can benefit one party at the expense of the other. Ford is a major stockholder of Mazda, but it does not exert control over its operations. Therefore, the risk-sharing agreement is particularly appropriate; transactions between the two are both intercompany and intracompany. A risk-sharing agreement solidifies the partnership. One potential solution would be for Ford and Mazda to agree that all purchases by Ford will be made in Japanese yen at the current exchange rate, as long as the spot rate on the date of invoice is between, say, ¥115/$ and ¥125/$. If the exchange rate is between these values on the payment dates, Ford agrees to accept whatever transaction exposure exists (because it is paying in a foreign currency) If, however, the exchange rate falls outside this range on the payment date, Ford and Mazda will share the difference equally.

For example, Ford has an account payable of ¥25,000,000 for the month of March. If the spot rate on the date of invoice is ¥110/$, the Japanese yen would have appreciated versus the dollar, causing Ford s costs of purchasing automotive parts to rise. Since this rate falls outside the contractual range, Mazda would agree to accept a total payment in Japanese yen which would result from a difference of ¥5/$ (¥115−¥110). Fords payment would be as follows:

$$\left[\frac{¥25,000,000}{¥115/\$ - \frac{¥5/\$}{2}}\right] = \frac{¥25,000,000}{¥112.5/\$} = \$222,222.22$$

Ford's total payment in Japanese yen would be calculated using an exchange rate of ¥112.50/$, and saves Ford $5,050.51 At a spot rate of ¥110/$, Ford's costs for March would be $227,272.73. The risk-sharing agreement between Ford and Mazda allows Ford to pay $222,222.22, a savings of $5,050.51 over the cost without risk-sharing (this "savings" is a reduction in an increased cost, not a true cost reduction). Both parties therefore incur costs and benefits from exchange rate movements outside the specified band. Note that the movement could just as easily have been in Mazda's favor if the spot rate had moved to ¥130/$.

The risk-sharing arrangement is intended to smooth the impact on both parties of volatile and unpredictable exchange rate movements. Of course, a sustained appreciation of one currency versus the other would require the negotiation of a new sharing agreement, but the ultimate goal of the agreement is to alleviate currency pressures on the continuing business relationship. Risk-sharing agreements like these have been in use for nearly 50 years on world markets. They became something of a rarity during the 1960s when exchange rates were relatively stable under the Bretton Woods Agreement. But with the return to floating exchange rates in the 1970s, firms with long-term customer-supplier relationships across borders have returned to some old ways of maintaining mutually beneficial long-term trade.

2.4.3 Back-to-Back Loans

A back-to-back loan, also referred to as a parallel loan or credit swap, occurs when two business firms in separate countries arrange to borrow each other's currency for a specific period of time. They return the borrowed currencies at an agreed terminal date. The operation is conducted outside the foreign exchange markets, although spot quotations may be used as the reference point for determining the amount of funds to be swapped. Such a swap creates a covered hedge against exchange loss, since each company, on its own books, borrows the same currency it repays. Back-to-back loans are also used at a time of actual or anticipated legal limitations on the transfer of investment funds to or from either country.

The structure of a typical back-to-back loan is illustrated in Figure 8.13. A British parent firm wanting to invest funds in its Dutch subsidiary locates a Dutch parent firm that wants to invest funds in the United Kingdom. Avoiding the exchange markets entirely, the British parent lends pounds to the Dutch subsidiary in the United Kingdom, while the Dutch parent lends euros to the British subsidiary in the Netherlands. The two loans would be for equal values at the current spot rate and for a specified maturity. At maturity the two separate loans would each be repaid to the original lender, again without any need to use the foreign exchange markets. Neither loan carries any foreign exchange risk, and neither loan normally needs the approval of any governmental body regulating the availability of foreign exchange for investment purposes.

> 背对背贷款,也称为平行贷款或信用互换,发生在两个不同国家的企业安排在一段特定的时间内互相借入对方的货币。

```
1. British firm wishes to          2. British firm identifies a Dutch
   invest funds in its Dutch          firm wishing to invest funds in its
   subsidiary                         British subsidiary
   ┌───────────────┐                  ┌───────────────┐
   │ British Parent│                  │ Dutch Parent  │
   │ Firm          │╲   Indirect    ╱ │ Firm          │
   └───────────────┘ ╲  Financing  ╱  └───────────────┘
   Direct loan        ╲           ╱   Direct loan
   in pounds           ╲         ╱    in euros
   ┌───────────────┐    ╲       ╱     ┌───────────────┐
   │ Dutch Firm's  │               │ British Firm's│
   │ British Subsidiary│               │ Dutch Subsidiary│
   └───────────────┘                  └───────────────┘
3. British firm loans British       4. British firm's Dutch
   pounds directly to the Dutch        subsidiary borrows euros
   firm's British subsidiary           from the Dutch parent
```

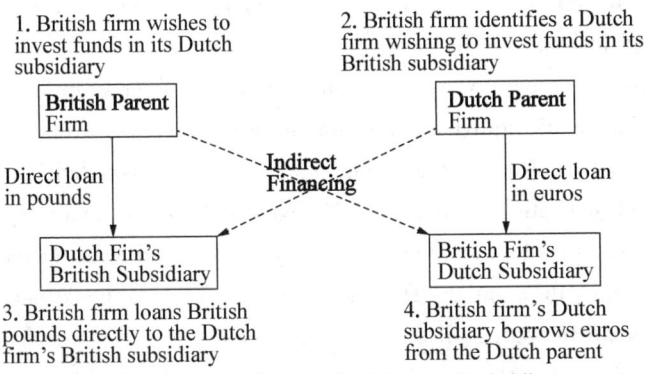

The back to back loan provides a method for parent subsidiary cross border financing without incurring direct currency exposure.

Figure 8.13 Using a Back-to-Back Loan for Currency Hedging

Parent company guarantees are not needed on the back-to-back loans because each loan carries the right of offset in the event of default of the other loan. A further agreement can provide for maintenance of principal parity in case of changes in the spot rate between the two countries. For example, if the pound dropped by more than, say, 6% for as long as 30 days. the British parent might have to advance additional pounds to the Dutch subsidiary to bring the principal value of the two loans back to parity. A similar provision would protect the British if the euro should weaken. Although this parity provision might lead to changes in the amount of home currency each party must lend during the period of the agreement, it does not increase foreign exchange risk, because at maturity all loans are repaid in the same currency loaned.

There are two fundamental impediments to widespread use of the back-to-back loan. First, it is difficult for a firm to find a partner, termed a counterparty, for the currency, amount, and timing desired. Second, a risk exists that one of the parties will fail to return the borrowed funds at the designated maturity-although this risk is minimized because party to the loan has, in effect, 100% collateral, albeit in a different currency. These vantages have led to the rapid development and wide use of the currency swap.

2.4.4 Currency Swaps

A currency swap resembles a back-to-back loan except that it does not appear on a firm's balance sheet. The term swap is widely used to describe a foreign exchange agreement between two parties to exchange a given amount of one currency for another and, after a period of time, to give back the original amounts swapped. Care

> 货币互换类似于背对背贷款,只是它不会出现在公司的资产负债表上。

should be taken to clarify which of the many different swaps is being referred to in a specific case.

In a currency swap, a firm and a swap dealer or swap bank agree to exchange an equivalent amount of two different currencies for a specified period of time. Currency swaps can be negotiated for a wide range of maturities up to at least 10 years. If funds are more expensive in one country than another, a fee may be required to compensate for the interest differential. The swap dealer or swap bank acts as a middleman in setting up the swap agreement.

A typical currency swap first requires two firms to borrow funds in the markets and currencies in which they are best known. For example, a Japanese firm would typically borrow yen on a regular basis in its home market. If, however, the Japanese firm were exporting to the United States and earning U.S. dollars, it might wish to construct a matching cash flow hedge, which would allow it to use the U.S. dollars earned to make regular debt service payments on U.S. dollar debt. If, however, the Japanese firm is not well known in the U.S. financial markets, it may have no ready access to U.S. dollar debt.

One way in which it could, in effect, borrow dollars, is to participate in a cross-currency swap (see Figure 8.14). The Japanese firm could swap its yen-denominated debt service payments with another firm that has U.S. dollar-debt service payments. This swap would have the Japanese firm "paying dollars" and "receiving yen." The Japanese firm would then have dollar debt service without actually borrowing U.S. dollars. Simultaneously, a U.S. corporation could actually be entering into a cross-currency swap in the opposite direction—"paying yen" and "receiving dollars." The swap dealer is a middleman.

Both the Japanese corporation and the U.S. corporation would like to enter into a cross currency swap that would allow them to use foreign currency cash inflows to service debt

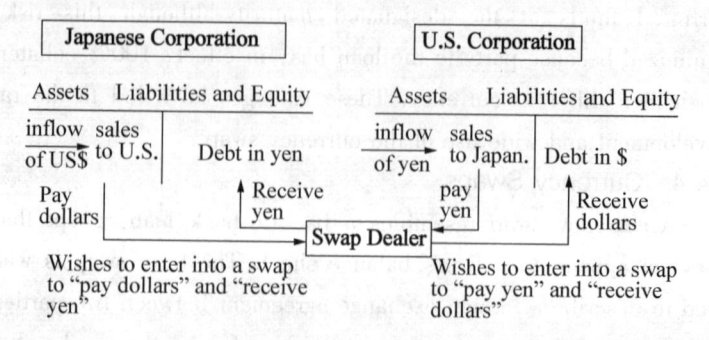

Figure 8.14 Using a cross-currency swap to hedge currency exposure

Swap dealers arrange most swaps on a blind basis, meaning that the initiating firm does not know who is, on the other side of the swap arrangement-the counterparty. The firm views the dealer or bank as its counterparty. Because the swap markets are dominated by the major money center banks worldwide, the counterparty risk is acceptable. Because the swap dealer's business is arranging swaps, the dealer can generally arrange for the currency, amount, and timing of the desired swap.

Accountants in the United States treat the currency swap as a foreign exchange transaction rather than as debt and treat the obligation to reverse the swap at some later date as a forward exchange contract. Forward exchange contracts can be matched against assets, but they are entered in a firm's footnotes rather than as balance sheet items. The result is that both translation and operating exposures are avoided, and neither a long-term receivable nor a long-term debt is created on the balance sheet. The risk of changes in currency rates to the implied collateral in a long-term currency swap can be treated with a clause similar to the maintenance-of-principal clause in a back-to-back loan. If exchange rates change by more than some specified amount, say 10%, an additional amount of the weaker currency might have to be advanced.

After being introduced on a global scale in the early 1980s, currency swaps have grown to be one of the largest financial derivative markets in the world.

2.4.5 Leads and Lags: Retiming the Transfer of Funds

Firms can reduce both operating and transaction exposure by accelerating or decelerating the timing of payments that must be made or received in foreign currencies.

> 企业可以通过加快或减缓必须以外币支付或接收的支付时间来降低运营和交易风险。

To lead is to pay early. A firm holding a soft currency or that has debts denominated in a hard currency will lead by using the soft currency to pay the hard currency debts as soon as possible. The object is to pay the currency debts before the soft currency drops in value. To lag is to pay late. A firm holding a hard currency and having debts denominated in a soft currency will lag by paying those debts late, hoping that less of the hard currency will be needed. If possible, firms will also lead and lag their collection of receivables, collecting soft foreign currency receivables early and collecting hard foreign currency receivables later.

Leading and lagging can be done between related firms (intracompany) or with independent firms (intercompany). Assuming that payments will be made eventually, leading or lagging always results in changing the cash and payables position of one firm, with the reverse effect on the other firm.

Intracompany Leads and Lags. Leading and lagging between related firms is more feasible because they presumably embrace a common set of goals for the consolidated group. Furthermore, the many periodic payments between units of an MNE provide opportunities for many types of leads or lags. Because opportunities for leading or lagging payments depend on the requirement for payments of this nature, the device is more readily adaptable to a company that operates on an integrated worldwide basis. If each unit functions as a separate and self-sufficient entity, the motivation for leading or lagging diminishes. In the case of financing cash flows with foreign subsidiaries, there is an additional motivation for early or late payments to position funds for liquidity reasons. For example, a subsidiary that is allowed to lag payments to the parent company is in reality borrowing from the parent.

Because the use of leads and lags is an obvious technique for minimizing foreign exchange exposure and for shifting the burden of financing, many governments impose limits on the allowed range. Terms allowed by governments are often subject to negotiation when a good argument can be presented. Thus, some limits are subject to exceptions. For example, in the past, Italy has placed no limit on export and import lags on trade payments with other OECD countries. However, a 180-day limit on export lags and a five-year limit on Import lags was applied to trade with non-OECD countries.

Intercompany Leads and Lags. Leading or lagging between independent firms requires the time preference of one firm to be imposed to the detriment of the other firm. For example, Trident Europe may wish to lead in collecting its Brazilian accounts receivable that are denominated in reals because it expects the reals to drop in value compared with the euro. But why should the Brazilian customers prepay their accounts payable? Credit in reals was part of the inducement for them to purchase from Trident Europe to begin with. The only way the Brazilians would be willing to pay their accounts payable early would be for the German creditor to offer a discount about equal to the forward discount on the reals or, in equilibrium, the difference between Brazilian and German interest rates for the period of prepayment. In equilibrium this "discount" would eliminate the benefit to Trident Europe of collecting the "soft" currency earlier.

2.4.6 Reinvoicing Centers

A reinvoicing center is a separate corporate subsidiary that serves as a type of middleman between the parent or related unit in one location and all foreign subsidiaries in a geographic region. Manufacturing subsidiaries sell goods to distribution subsidiaries of the same firm only by selling to a reinvoicing center, which in turn resells to the distribution subsidiary. Title passes to the reinvoicing center, but the physical movement of goods is direct from the manufacturing plant, in this case Trident USA, to the foreign subsidiary, Trident Brazil. Thus, the reinvoicing center handles paperwork but has no inventory.

As shown in Figure 8.15, the U.S. manufacturing unit of Trident Corporation invoices the firm's reinvoicing center-located within the corporate headquarters facilities in Los Angeles—in U.S. dollars. However, the actual goods are shipped directly to Trident Brazil. The reinvoicing center in turn resells to Trident Brazil in Brazilian reais. Consequentially, all operating units deal only in their own currency, and all transaction exposure lies with the reinvoicing center.

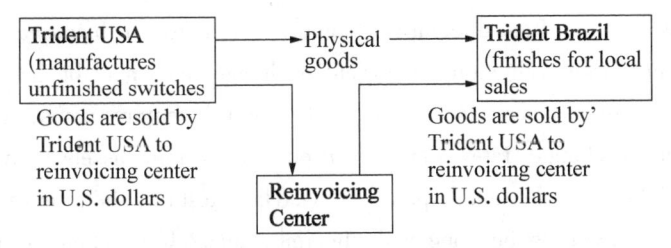

再投资中心是一个独立的公司子公司,为在某地的母公司或相关单位与其他区域所有的外国子公司之间充当一种中间人。制造子公司向同一公司的分销子公司销售商品,只能通过向再投资中心销售,再投资中心再向分销子公司销售。所有权转移到再投资中心,但货物的实际移动是直接从制造厂,在这种情况下是三叉戟美国公司到国外子公司——三叉戟巴西公司。因此,再投资中心处理文书工作,但没有库存。

```
Trident USA                                    Trident Brazil
(manufactures  ──Physical──▶ (finishes for local
unfinished switches)    goods              sales)

Goods are sold by              Goods are sold by'
Trident USA to                 Trident USA to
reinvoicing center             reinvoicing center
in U.S. dollars                in U.S. dollars
              ↘  Reinvoicing  ↗
                 Center
```

1. Trident USA ships goods directly to the Brazilian subsidiary.
2. The invoice by Trident USA which is denominated in U.S. dollars, is passed to the reinvoicing center.
3. The reinvoicing center takes legal title to the goods.
4. The reinvoicing center invoices Trident Brazil in Brazilian reals, repositioning the currency exposure from both operating units to the reinvoicing center.

Figure 8.15 Use of Reinvoicing Center

To avoid accusations of profit-shifting through transfer pricing, most reinvoicing centers resell at cost plus a small commission for their services. The resale price is frequently the manufacturer's price times the forward exchange rate for the date on which payment from the buyer is expected, although other combinations are possible. The commission covers the cost of the reinvoicing center, but does not shift profits away from operating subsidiaries.

3　Translation Exposure

It also called accounting exposure, it is the potential for accounting-derived changes in owner's equity to occur because of the need to "translate" foreign currency financial statements of foreign subsidiaries into a single reporting currency to prepare worldwide consolidated financial statements.

3.1　Overview of Translation

Translation in principle is quite simple. Foreign currency financial statements must be restated in the parent company's reporting currency for consolidation purposes. If the same exchange rate were used to remeasure each and every line item on the individual statement (income statement and balance sheet), there would be no imbalances resulting from the remeasurement. But if a different exchange rate were used for different line items on an individual statement, an imbalance would result.

Why would we use a different exchange rate in remeasuring different line items? It is because translation principles in many countries are often a complex compromise between historical and current market valuation. Historical exchange rates may be used for certain equity accounts, fixed assets, and inventory items, while current exchange rates may be used for current assets, current liabilities, income, and expense items. The question, then, is what—if anything—is to be done with the imbalance? It is taken to either current income or equity reserves.

Translation methods differ by country along two overall dimensions, as well as by individual account. One dimension is a difference in the way a foreign subsidiary is characterized based on its degree of independence of the parent firm. The second dimension is the definition of which currency is most important for the foreign subsidiary's operations.

3.1.1　Subsidiary Characterization

Today, most countries specify the translation method used by a foreign based on the subsidiary's business operations. For example, a foreign subsidiary's business can be categorized as either an integrated foreign entity or a self-sustaining foreign entity. An integrated foreign entity is one that operates as an extension of the parent company, with cash flows and general business lines that are highly interrelated with those of the parent. A self-sustaining foreign entity is one that operates in the local economic environment independent of the parent company. The differentiation is important to the logic of translation. A foreign subsidiary should be valued principally in terms of the currency that is the basis of its economic viability.

It is not unusual to find two different foreign subsidiaries of a single company that have different characters. For example, a U.S.-based manufacturer that produces subassemblies in the United States that are then shipped to a Spanish subsidiary for finishing, assembly, and resale in the European Union would likely characterize the Spanish subsidiary as an integrated foreign entity. The dominant currency of economic operation is likely the U.S. dollar. That same U.S. parent may, however, also own an agricultural marketing business in Venezuela, which has few cash flows or operations related to the U.S. parent company (or U.S. dollar). The Venezuelan subsidiary may purchase almost all materials and expend all costs of operations in Venezuelan bolivar, while selling exclusively in Venezuela. Because the Venezuelan subsidiary's operations are independent of its parent, and its functional currency is the Venezuelan bolivar, it would be classified as a self-sustaining foreign entity.

3.1.2 Functional Currency

A foreign subsidiary's functional currency is the currency of the primary economic environment in which the subsidiary operates and in which it generates cash flows. In other words, it is the dominant currency used by that foreign subsidiary in its day-to-day operations. It is important to note that the geographic location of a foreign subsidiary and its functional currency may be different. The Singapore subsidiary of a U.S. firm may find that its functional currency is the U.S. dollar (integrated subsidiary), the Singapore dollar (self-sustaining subsidiary), or a third currency such as the British pound (also a self-sustaining subsidiary).

3.2 Translation Methods

Two basic methods for the translation of foreign subsidiary financial statements are employed worldwide, the current rate method and the temporal method. Regardless of which method is employed, a

一家外国子公司的业务可以分为一体化式的外国实体或自负盈亏式的外国实体。一体化式外国实体是指作为母公司延伸经营的实体,其现金流和总体业务与母公司高度相关。自负盈亏式外国实体是指独立于母公司之外,在当地经济环境中运作的实体。这种区分对转换很重要。外国子公司的价值应该主要以其经济运作的基础货币来衡量。

外国子公司的功能货币是子公司运营和产生现金流的主要经济环境下的货币。换句话说,它是该外国子公司日常运营中使用的主导货币。需要注意的是,外国子公司的地理位置及其功能货币可能不同。美国公司的新加坡子公司可能会发现其功能货币是美元(一体化子公司)、新加坡元(自负盈亏式子公司)或第三种货币,如英镑(也是自负盈亏式子公司)。

translation method must not only designate at what exchange rate individual balance sheet and income statement items are remeasured, but also designate where any imbalance is to be recorded (typically either in current income or in an equity reserve account in the balance sheet). The significance of this decision is that imbalances passed through the income statement affect the firm's current reported income, while imbalances transferred directly to the balance sheet do not.

3.2.1 Current Rate Method

The current rate method is the most prevalent in the world today. Under this method, all financial statement line items are translated at the "current" exchange rate with few exceptions. Line items include the following:

- Assets and Liabilities. All assets and liabilities are translated at the current rate of exchange; that is, at the rate of exchange in effect on the balance sheet date.
- Income Statement Items. All items, including depreciation and cost of goods sold, are translated at either the actual exchange rate on the dates the various revenues, expenses, gains, and losses were incurred or at an appropriately weighted average exchange rate for the period.
- Distributions. Dividends paid are translated at the exchange rate in effect on the date of payment.
- Equity Items. Common stock and paid-in capital accounts are translated at historical rates. Year-end retained earnings consist of the original year-beginning retained earnings plus or minus any income or loss for the year.

Gains or losses caused by translation adjustments are not included in the calculation of consolidated net income. Rather, translation gains or losses are reported separately and accumulated in a separate equity reserve account (on the consolidated balance sheet) with a title such as cumulative translation adjustment (CTA). If a foreign subsidiary is later sold or liquidated, translation gains or losses of past years accumulated in the CTA account are reported as one component of the total gain or loss on sale or liquidation. The total gain or loss is reported as part of the net income or loss for the time period in which the sale or liquidation occurs. This is the subject of this chapter's Mini-Case.

The biggest advantage of the current rate method is that the gain or loss on translation does not pass through the income statement but goes directly to a reserve account. This eliminates the variability of reported earnings due to foreign exchange translation gains or losses. A second advantage of the current rate method is that the relative proportions of individual balance sheet accounts remain the same. Hence, the process of translation does not distort such balance sheet ratios as the current ratio or the debt-to-equity ratio. The main disadvantage of the current rate method is that it violates the accounting principle of carrying balance sheet accounts at historical cost. For example, foreign assets purchased with dollars and then recorded on a subsidiary's statements at their foreign currency historical cost are translated into dollars at a different rate. Thus, they are reported in the consolidated statement in dollars at something other than their historical dollar cost.

3.2.2 Temporal Method

Under the temporal method, specific assets and liabilities are translated at exchange rates consistent with the timing of the items creation. The temporal method assumes that a number of individual line item assets such as inventory, net plant and equipment are restated regularly to reflect market value. If these items were not restated but were instead carried at historical cost, the temporal method becomes the *monetary/nonmonetary* method of translation, a form of translation that is still used by a number of countries today. Line items include the following:

- Monetary assets (primarily cash, marketable securities, accounts receivable, and long-term receivables) are translated at current exchange rates.
- Monetary liabilities (primarily current liabilities and long-term debt) are translated at current exchange rates.
- Nonmonetary assets and liabilities (primarily inventory and fixed assets) are translated at historical rates.
- Income statement items are translated at the average exchange rate for the period, except for items such as depreciation and cost of goods sold that are directly associated with nonmonetary assets or liabilities. These accounts are translated at their historical rate.
- Distributions. Dividends paid are translated at the exchange rate in effect on the date of payment.
- Equity items. Common stock and paid-in capital accounts are

根据时态法,特定资产和负债按与项目创建时间一致的汇率进行换算。时态法假设一些单独的行项目资产,如库存、净厂房和设备定期重述,以反映市场价值。如果这些项目没有被重述,而是以历史成本进行,时态法就变成了货币/非货币的转换法:一种至今仍被许多国家使用的转换形式。行项目包括以下内容:

translated at historical rates. Year-end retained earnings consist of the original year-beginning retained earnings plus or minus any income or loss for the year, plus or minus any imbalance from translation, as explained next.

Under the temporal method, gains or losses resulting from remeasurement are carried directly to current consolidated income and not to equity reserves. Hence, foreign exchange gains and losses arising from the translation process do introduce volatility to consolidated earnings.

The basic advantage of the temporal method is that foreign nonmonetary assets are carried at their original cost in the parent's consolidated statement. In most countries, this approach is consistent with the original cost treatment of domestic assets of the parent firm. In practice, however, if some foreign accounts are translated at one exchange rate while others are translated at different rates, the resulting translated balance sheet will not balance. Hence, there is a need for a "plug" to remove what has been called the "dangling debit or credit." The true nature of the gain or loss created by use of such a plug is open to question. Unrealized foreign exchange gains or losses are included in quarterly primary earnings *per share* (EPS), thus increasing variability of reported earnings.

3.3 Translation Example: Trident Europe

Let us continue the example of Trident, focusing here on its European subsidiary. We will also illustrate translation by the temporal method in order to show the very arbitrary nature of a translation gain or loss. Selection of the accounting method is the major factor in determining the magnitude of gain or loss. The example that follows deals with balance sheet translation only. The somewhat more complex procedures for translating income statements are described in international accounting texts.

The functional currency of Trident Europe is the euro, and the reporting currency of its parent, Trident Corporation, is the U.S. dollar. Assume the following:

- Plant and equipment and long-term debt were acquired and common stock issued by Trident Europe sometime in the past when the exchange rate was $1.2760/€. Although the euro never traded at this rate against the dollar, the historic deutschemark rate in use at the time the initial investment was made must be converted to a "historic euro rate?" which, in effect, backdates euro rates against the deutschemark.

- Inventory currently on hand was purchased or manufactured during the immediately prior quarter when the average exchange rate was $1.2180/€. At the close of business on Monday, December 31, 2010, the current spot exchange rate was $1.2000/€.

The example will also look at the consequences had the euro strengthened by 10% overnight to $1.3200/€.

3.3.1 Current Rate Method

The top half of Table 8.2 illustrates translation loss using the current rate method. Assets and liabilities on the pre-depreciation balance sheet are translated at the current exchange rate of $1.1600/€. Capital stock is translated at the historical rate of $1.2760/€, and retained earnings are translated at a composite rate that is equivalent to having each past year's addition to retained earnings translated at the exchange rate in effect in that year.

Table 8.2 Trident Europe: Translation loss Just after deprecation of the Euro

	In Euros	Dec.31,2010 Just before depreciation		Jan.2,2011 Just after depreciation	
Current Rate Method					
Cash	€1,600,000	1.2000	$1,920,000	1.0000	$1,600,000
Accounts receivable	3,200,000	1.2000	3,840,000	1.0000	3,200,000
Inventory	2,400,000	1.2000	2,880,000	1.0000	2,400,000
Net plant and equipment	4,800,000	1.2000	5,760,000	1.0000	4,800,000
	€12,000,000		$14,400,000		$12,000,000
Accounts payable	€800,000	1.2000	€960,000	1.0000	€800,000
Short-term bank loan	1,600,000	1.2000	1,920,000	1.0000	1,600,000
Long-term debt	1,600,000	1.2000	1,920,000	1.0000	1,600,000
Common stock	1,800,000	1.2760	2,296,800	1.2760	2,296,800
Retained earnings	6,200,000	(a)	7,440,000	1.2(b)	7,440,000
Translation adjustment (CTA)	—	—	−136,800	—	−1,736,800
	€12,000,000		$14,400,000		$12,000,000
Temporal Method					
Cash	€1,600,000	1.2000	$1,920,000	1.0000	$1,600,000
Accounts receivable	3,200,000	1.2000	3,840,000	1.0000	3,200,000
Inventory	2,400,000	1.2180	2,923,000	1.2180	2,923,000
Net plant and equipment	4,800,000	1.2760	6,124,800	1.2760	6,124,800
	€12,000,000		$14,808,000		$13,848,000

continued

In Euros		Dec.31,2010		Jan.2,2011	
		Just before depreciation		Just after depreciation	
Accounts payable	€ 800,000	1.2000	$960,000	1.0000	$800,000
Short-term bank loan	1,600,000	1.2000	1,920,000	1.0000	1,600,000
Long-term debt	1,600,000	1.2000	1,920,000	1.0000	1,600,000
Common stock	1,800,000	1.2760	2,296,800	1.2760	2,296,800
Retained earnings	6,200,000	(a)	7,711,200	(b)	7,711,200
Translation gain (loss)	—	—	—	(c)	-160,000
	€ 12,000,000		$14,808,000		$13,848,000

(a) Dollar retained earnings before depreciation are the cumulative sum of additions to retained earnings of all prior years, translated at exchange rates in each year. See text for assumptions used in this example.

(b) Translated into dollars at the same rate as before depreciation of the euro.

(c) Under the temporal method, the translation loss of $160,000 would be closed into retained earnings via the income statement rather than left as a separate line item shown here. Hence, under the temporal method, ending retained earnings would actually be $7,711,200 - $160,000 = $7,551,200

The sum of retained earnings and the cumulative translation adjustment (CTA) account must "balance" the liabilities and net worth section of the balance sheet with the asset side. For this hypothetical text example, we have assumed the two amounts used for the December 31, 2010, balance sheet. The assumption does not affect the final measure of the increase in the CTA account because the retained earnings account is carried over at whatever arbitrary amount is assigned for this example.

As shown in the top half of Table 8.2, the "just before depreciation" dollar translation reports an accumulated translation loss from prior periods of $136,800. This balance is the cumulative gain or loss from translating euro statements into dollars in prior years, and it had been carried separately in the CTA account Statements from 1998 and earlier would have originally been deutschemark statements, translated into euros after January 1, 1999, when the euro was introduced.

After the 16.67% depreciation, Trident Corporation translates assets and liabilities at the new exchange rate of $1.0000/€. Equity accounts, including retained earnings, are translated just as they were before depreciation, and as a result the cumulative translation loss increases to $1,736,800. The increase of $1,600,000 in this account (from a cumulative loss of $136,800 to a new cumulative loss of $1,736,800) is the translation loss measured by the current rate method.

This translation loss is a decrease in equity, measured in the parent's reporting currency, of net exposed assets. An exposed asset is an asset whose value drops with the depreciation of the functional currency and rises with an appreciation of that currency. Net exposed assets in this context means exposed assets minus exposed liabilities. Net exposed assets are positive ("long") if exposed assets exceed exposed liabilities. They are negative ("short") if exposed assets are smaller than exposed liabilities.

Exposure can be measured by creating a before-and-after translated balance sheet, as shown in Table 8.2. A simpler method is to multiply net exposed assets by the percentage amount of depreciation. We did this calculation for the current rate method in the left column of Table 8.3, which illustrates that a 16.67% depreciation of the euro means that net exposed assets of $9,600,000 lose 16.67% of their value, a translation loss of $1,600,000.

Table 8.3   Trident Europe: Translation Loss or Gain: Comparison of Current Rate and Temporal Methods

Panel A: Depreciation of the Euro, from $1.2000/€ to $1.0000/€(−16.67%)		
	Current Rate Method	Temporal Method
Exposed Assets		
cash	$1,920,000	$1,920,000
Accounts receivable	3,840,000	3,840,000
Inventory	2,880,000	not expresed
Net plant and equipment	5,760,000	not expresed
Total exposed assets ("A")	$14,400,000	$5,760,000
Exposed Liabilities		
Accounts payable	$960,000	$960,000
Short-term bank loan	1,920,000	1,920,000
Long-term debt	1,920,000	1,920,000
Total exposed liabilities ("L")	$4,800,000	$4,800,000
Gain (loss) if euro depreciates		
Net exposed assets ("A"−"L")	$9,600,000	$960,000
Times amount of depreciation	×(0.1667)	×(0.1667)
Translation gain (loss)	$ −1,600,000	$ −160,000
Panel B: Appreciation of the Euro, from $1.2000/$ to $1.3200/$ (+10.00%)		
Gain (loss) if euro appreciates		
Net exposed assets ("A"+"L")	$9,600,000	$960,000
Times amount of appreciation	×0.1	×0.1
Translation gain (loss)	$960,000	$96,000

Suppose instead that the euro had appreciated. If, by the end of the year, the euro had appreciated from $1.2000/€ to $1.3200/€, the appreciation would be 10%. The effect of this appears in Panel B of Table 8.5, which starts with the same net exposed assets calculated in Panel A. Under the current rate method, the U.S. parent would have a translation gain of $960.000.

3.3.2 Temporal Method

Translation of the same accounts under the temporal method shows the arbitrary nature of any gain or loss from translation. This is illustrated in the bottom half of table 8.3. Monetary assets and monetary liabilities in the predepreciation euro balance sheet are translated at the current rate of exchange, but other assets and the equity accounts are translated at their historic rates. For Trident Europe, the historical rate for inventory differs from that for net plant and equipment because inventory was acquired more recently.

Under the temporal method, translation losses are not accumulated in a separate equity account but passed directly through each quarter's income statement. Thus, in the dollar balance sheet translated before depreciation, retained earnings were the cumulative result of earnings from all prior years translated at historical rates in effect each year, plus translation gains or losses from all prior years. In table 8.3, no translation loss appears in the predepreciation dollar balance sheet because any losses would have been closed to retained earnings.

The effect of the 16.67% depreciation is to create an immediate translation loss of $160,000. This amount is shown. as a separate line item in table 8.3 in order to focus attention on it for this textbook example. Under the temporal method, this translation loss of $160,000 would pass through the income statement, reducing reported net income and reducing retained earnings. Ending retained earnings would in fact be $7,711,200 minus $160,000. or $7,551,200. Other countries using the temporal method do not necessarily require gains and losses to pass through the income statement.

When translation loss is viewed in terms of changes in the value of exposed accounts, as shown in the right column of table 8.3, the loss under the temporal method is 16.67% of net exposed assets of $960,000, or $160,000. If the euro should appreciate 10%, the translation gain to the U.S. parent would be $96,000, as shown at the bottom of the right column in table 8.3.

> 在时态法下对相同账户的转换显示了转换后收益或损失的独特性。表8.3的下半部分对此进行了说明。预贬值欧元资产负债表中的货币资产和货币负债按当前汇率折算,但其他资产和权益账户按历史汇率折算。对于三叉戟欧洲公司,库存的历史汇率不同于净厂房和设备,因为库存是最近获得的。

3.3.3 Managerial Implications

In table 8.2 and table 8.3, translation loss or gain is larger under the current rate method because inventory and net plant and equipment, as well as all monetary assets, are deemed exposed. When net exposed assets are larger, gains or losses from translation are also larger.

The managerial implications of this fact are very important. If management expects a foreign currency to depreciate, it could minimize translation exposure by reducing net exposed assets. If management anticipates an appreciation of the foreign currency, it should increase net exposed assets to benefit from a gain.

Depending on the accounting method of the moment, management might select different assets and liabilities for reduction or increase. Thus, "real" decisions about investing and financing might be dictated by which accounting technique is required, when in fact the method of reporting should be neutral in its influence on operating and financing decisions.

这一点对管理来说非常重要。如果管理层预期一种外币会贬值，它可以通过减少净风险资产来最大限度地减少折算风险；如果管理层预期外汇会升值，它应该增加净风险资产，以从中获益。

3.4 Comparing Translation Exposure with Operating Exposure

In table 8.4 translation gains or losses in the event of a currency depreciation are compared with the operating gains or losses, Table 8.1. Obviously, translation gains or losses can be quite different from operating gains or losses, not only in magnitude but also in sign (a gain or loss). A manager focusing only on translation losses, in a situation such as Trident Europe, might avoid doing business in Germany because of the likelihood of such a loss. The manager might fear losing a bonus tied to reported profits, or possibly losing a job if the investment in Germany were made and the income statement reported severe translation losses back to the home office.

Operating exposure presents an entirely different view of the same situation. As summarized in table 8.4, Germany and Europe became more (not less) desirable location for investment because of the operating consequences that followed depreciation in two of the three cases shown here. This illustrates the importance of focusing decisions primarily on the operating consequences of changes in exchange rates and only secondarily on the accounting-based measurements of performance.

经营风险呈现出对相同情况的完全不同的看法。如表8.4所总结的，德国和欧洲成为更理想的投资地点，因为在此处显示的三种情况中，有两种情况下折旧后会产生经营后果。这说明了将决策重点主要放在汇率变化的经营后果上的重要性，其次才是基于会计的业绩衡量。

Table 8.4 Comparison of Translation Exposure with Operating Exposure, Depreciation of Euro from $1.2000/€ to $1.0000/€ for Trident Europe

Exposure	Amount	Gain or Loss
Translation Exposure (Exhibits 8.15 and 8.16)	($1,600,000)	Loss on translation
Temporal method	($160,000)	Loss on translation
Operating Exposure (in present value terms; Exhibit 12.3)		
Case 1: Depreciation of euro	($1,033,914)	loss on operations
Case 2: Volume doubles	$2,866,106	Gain on operations
Case 3: Sales price increases	$3,742,892	Gain on operations

3.5 Managing Translation Exposure

The main technique to minimize translation exposure is called a balance sheet hedge. Some firms have attempted to hedge translation exposure in the forward market. Such action amounts to speculating in the forward market in the hope that a cash profit will be realized to offset the noncash loss from translation. Success depends on a precise prediction of future exchange rates, for such a hedge will not work over a range of possible future spot rates. In addition, such a hedge will increase the tax burden, since the profit from the forward hedge (speculation) is taxable, but the translation loss does not reduce taxable income.

3.5.1 Balance Sheet Hedge Defined

A balance sheet hedge requires an equal amount of exposed foreign currency assets and liabilities on a firms consolidated balance sheet. If this can be achieved for each foreign currency, net translation exposure will be zero. A change in exchange rates will change the value of exposed liabilities in an equal amount but in a direction opposite to the change in value of exposed assets. If a firm translates by the temporal method, a zero net exposed position is called monetary balance. Complete monetary balance cannot be achieved under the current rate method because total assets would have to be matched by an equal amount of debt, but the equity section of the balance sheet must still be translated at historic exchange rates.

The cost of a balance sheet hedge depends on relative borrowing costs. If foreign currency borrowing costs, after adjusting for foreign exchange risk, are higher than parent currency borrowing costs, the

转换风险最小化的主要技术被称为资产负债表对冲。一些公司试图对冲远期市场的转换风险。这种行为相当于在期货市场上投机,希望能实现现金利润来抵消非现金损失。成功取决于对未来汇率的精确预测,因为这种对冲不会在未来一系列可能的即期汇率上奏效。此外,这种套期保值将增加税收负担,因为远期套期保值(投机)的利润是应纳税的,但折算损失不会减少应纳税收入。正如全球金融实践8.3中所说明的,套期保值转换在总体上仍然很有争议。

balance sheet hedge is costly, and *vice versa*. Normal operations, however, already require decisions about the magnitude and currency denomination of specific balance sheet accounts. Thus, balance sheet hedges are a compromise in which the denomination of balance sheet accounts is altered, perhaps at a cost in terms of interest expense or operating efficiency, to achieve some degree of foreign exchange protection.

3.5.2 Balance Sheet Hedge Illustrated

To illustrate a balance sheet hedge, let us return to the translation exposure previously identified for Trident Europe and its parent, Trident Corporation. Earlier data from table 8.3 is restated in a different format in table 8.5.

Trident Europe expects the euro to drop 16.67% in value from its year-beginning value to a new exchange rate of $1.0000/€. Under the current rate method, the expected loss is 16.67% of the exposure of $9,600,000, or $1,600,000. Under the temporal method, the expected loss is 16.67% of the exposure of $960,000, or $160,000.

To achieve a balance sheet hedge, Trident Corporation must either 1) reduce exposed euro assets without simultaneously reducing euro liabilities or 2) increase euro liabilities without simultaneously increasing euro assets. One way to do this is to exchange existing euro cash for dollars. If Trident Europe does not have large euro cash balances, it can borrow euros and exchange the borrowed euros for dollars. Another subsidiary could borrow euros and exchange them for dollars. That is, the essence of the hedge is for the parent or any of its subsidiaries to create euro debt and exchange the proceeds for dollars.

Table 8.5 Trident Europe, Balance Sheet Exposure

	Balance Sheet Accounts	Current Rate Exposure	Temporal Exposure
Assets			
cash	€ 1,600,000	€ 1,600,000	€ 1,600,000
Accounts receivable	3,200,000	3,200,000	3,200,000
Inventory	2,400,000	2,400,000	
Net plant and equipment	4,800,000	4,800,000	
Total assets	€ 12,000,000		
Exposed assets		€ 12,000,000	€ 4,800,000
Liabilities and Capital			
Accounts payable	€ 800,000	€ 800,000	€ 800,000
Short-term bank debt	1,600,000	1,600,000	1,600,000
Long-term debt	1,600,000	1,600,000	1,600,000
Capital stock	1,800,000		

	Balance Sheet Accounts	Current Rate Exposure	Temporal Exposure
Retained earnings	6,200,000		
Total liabilities and net worth	€ 12,000,000		
Exposed liabilities		€ 4,000,000	€ 4,000,000
Net exposed assets in euros		€ 8,000,000	€ 800,000
Times exchange rate ($/€)		×1.2000	×1.2000
Net exposed assets in dollars		€ 9,600,000	€ 960,000
Times amount of devaluation		×0.1667	×0.1667
Expected translation gain (loss)		($1,600,000)	($160,000)

continued

Current Rate Method. Under the current rate method, Trident Europe should borrow as much as € 8,000,000. The initial effect of this first step is to increase both an exposed asset (cash) and an exposed liability (notes payable) on the balance sheet of Trident Europe, with no immediate effect on net exposed assets. The required follow-up step can take two forms: 1) Trident Europe can exchange the acquired euros for U.S. dollars and hold those dollars itself or 2) it can transfer the borrowed euros to Trident Corporation, perhaps as a euro dividend or as repayment of intracompany debt. Trident Corporation could then exchange the euros for dollars. In some countries, of course, local monetary authorities will not allow their currency to be so freely exchanged.

Another possibility would be for Trident corporation or a sister subsidiary to borrow the euros, thus keeping the euro debt entirely off Trident Europe's books However, the second step is still essential to eliminate euro exposure: the borrowing entity must exchange the euros for dollars or other unexposed assets. Any such borrowing should be coordinated with all other euro borrowings to avoid the possibility that one subsidiary is borrowing euros to reduce translation exposure at the same time as another subsidiary is repaying euro debt. (Note that euros can be "borrowed," by simply delaying repayment of existing euro debt; the goal is to increase euro debt, not borrow in a literal sense.)

Temporal Method. If translation is by the temporal method, only the much smaller amount of € 800,000 need be borrowed. As before, Trident Europe could use the proceeds of the loan to acquire U.S. dollars. However, Trident Europe could also use the proceeds to acquire inventory or fixed assets in Europe. Under the temporal method these assets are not regarded as exposed and do not drop in dollar value when the euro depreciates.

3.5.3 When Is a Balance Sheet Hedge Justified?

If a firm's subsidiary is using the local currency as the functional currency, the following circumstances could justify when to use a balance sheet hedge:

- The foreign subsidiary is about to be liquidated, so that the value of its CTA would be realized.
- The firm has debt covenants or bank agreements that state the firm's debt/equity ratios will be maintained within specific limits.
- Management is evaluated on the basis of certain income statement and balance sheet measures that are affected by translation losses or gains.
- The foreign subsidiary is operating in a hyperinflationary environment.

If a firm is using the parent's home currency as the functional currency of the foreign subsidiary, all transaction gains/losses are passed through to the income statement. Hedging this consolidated income to reduce its variability may be important to investors and bond rating agencies.

3.5.4 Choice between Minimizing Transaction or Translation Exposure

Management will find it almost impossible to offset both translation and transaction exposure at the same time Reduction of one exposure usually changes the amount of the other exposure. For example, the easiest way to offset translation exposure is to require the parent and all subsidiaries to denominate all exposed assets and liabilities in the parent's reporting currency. For U.S. firms and their subsidiaries, all assets and liabilities would be held in dollars. Such firms would have no translation exposure, but each subsidiary would have its own transaction exposure.

To illustrate, assume that a U.S. parent company instructs its Japanese subsidiary to bill an export to the parent in dollars. The account receivable on the Japanese subsidiary's books is shown as the yen equivalent of the dollar amount, and yen profit is recorded at the time of sale. If, before the parent pays dollars to the Japanese subsidiary, the yen appreciates 5%, the parent still pays only the contracted dollar amount. The Japanese subsidiary receives 5% fewer yen than were expected and booked as profit. Hence, the Japanese subsidiary will experience a 5% foreign exchange loss on its dollar-denominated accounts receivable. Lower yen profit will eventually be translated into lower dollar profit when the subsidiary's income statement is consolidated with that of the parent. Eventually the consolidated U.S-based MNE will show a foreign exchange loss-in dollars!

Similar reasoning will show that if a firm chooses to eliminate transaction exposure translation exposure might even be increased. The easiest way to be rid of sure is to require the parent and all subsidiaries to denominate all accounts subject to transaction exposure in its local currency. Thus, every subsidiary would avoid transaction gains or losses. However, each subsidiary would be creating net translation exposure by being either long or short in terms of local currency-exposed assets or liabilities. The consolidated financial statement of the parent firm would show translation exposure in each local currency.

As a general matter, firms seeking to reduce both types of exposure usually reduce transaction exposure first. They then recalculate translation exposure (which may have changed), and decide if any residual translation exposure can be reduced without creating more transaction exposure. Taxes complicate the decision to seek protection against transaction or translation exposure. Transaction losses are normally considered "realized" losses and are therefore deductible from pretax income. However, translation losses are only "paper" losses, involving no cash flows, and are not deductible from pretax income. It is highly debatable whether protective techniques that necessitate cash payments, and so reduce net cash flow, should be incurred to avoid noncash losses.

Summary

- MNEs encounter three types of currency exposure: 1) transaction exposure, 2) operating exposure, and 3) translation exposure.
- Transaction exposure measures gains or losses that arise from the settlement of financial obligations whose terms are stated in a foreign currency.
- Operating exposure, also called economic exposure measures the change in the present value of the firm resulting from any change in

future operating cash flows of the firm caused by an unexpected change in exchange rates.

- Translation exposure is the possibility that accounting-derived changes in owner's equity will occur because of the need to "translate" foreign currency financial statements of foreign subsidiaries into a single reporting currency to prepare worldwide consolidated financial statements.
- Transaction exposure arises from 1) purchasing or selling on credit goods or services whose prices are stated in foreign currencies; 2) borrowing or lending fund when repayment is to be made in a foreign currency; 3) being a party to an unperformed forward foreign exchange contract; and 4) otherwise acquiring assets or liabilities denominated in foreign currencies.
- Transaction exposure can be managed by contractual techniques that include forward. futures, money market, and option hedges.
- Risk management in practice requires a firm's treasury department to identify its goals Is treasury a cost center or profit center?
- Operating exposure measures the change in value of the firm that results from changes in future operating cash flows caused by an unexpected change in exchange rates.
- Strategies for the management of operating exposure emphasize the structuring of firm operations in order to create matching streams of cash flows by currency. This is termed natural hedging.
- Contractual approaches (that is, options and forwards) have occasionally been used to hedge operating exposure but are costly and possibly ineffective.
- Proactive policies include matching currency of cash flow, currency risk-sharing clauses, back-to-back loan structures, and cross-currency swap agreements.
- Translation exposure results from translating foreign currency denominated statements of foreign subsidiaries into the parents reporting currency so the parent can prepare consolidated financial statements, Translation exposure is the potential for loss or gain from this translation process.
- The two basic procedures for translation used in most countries today are the current rate method and the temporal method.
- Translation gains and losses can be quite different from operating gains and losses, not only in magnitude but in sign. Management may need to determine which is of greater significance prior to

deciding which exposure is to be managed first.
- The main technique for managing translation exposure is a balance sheet hedge. This calls for having an equal amount of exposed foreign currency assets and liabilities.

Exercises

1. What does the word translation mean? Why is translation exposure sometimes called accounting exposure?
2. In the context of preparing consolidated financial statements, are the words translate and convert synonyms?
3. What is the central problem in consolidating the financial statements of a foreign subsidiary?
4. What is the difference between a self-sustaining foreign subsidiary and an Integrated foreign subsidiary?
5. What is a functional currency? What is a nonfunctional currency?
6. What are the major differences in translating assets between the current rate method and the temporal method?
7. What are the major differences in translating liabilities between the current rate method and the temporal method?
8. Why do unexpected exchange rate changes contribute to operating exposure, but expected exchange rate changes do not?
9. Operating exposure has other names. What are they, and what do the words in these names suggest about the nature of operating exposure?
10. What is macroeconomic uncertainty and how does it relate to measuring operating exposure?

Chapter 9
FDI: Political Risks

The requirement of Learning
- Understanding the classification of Political risks.
- Understanding the defines of Firm-specific risks, Country-specific risks and Global-specific risks.
- How to Assess Political Risk.
- Understanding the most important type of governance risk arises from a goal conflict between bona fide objectives of governments and private firms.
- Understanding the main tools used to manage goal conflict are to negotiate an investment agreement; to purchase investment insurance and guarantees; and to modify operating strategies in production, logistics, marketing, finance, organization, and personnel.
- Understanding the main country-specific risks are transfer risk, known as blocked funds, and certain cultural and institutional risks.

In addition to business and foreign exchange risks, foreign direct investment faces political risks.

1 Defining Political Risk

Political risk refers to the possibility of bringing economic losses to multinational enterprises due to unexpected changes in political factors in international investment activities. For example, the political events in the host country or the changes in the political relations between the host country and other countries may affect the interests of multinational corporations. Although political risk and political instability are related, they are different phenomena. Instability is a characteristic of the environment, and the risk is how to affect the determination of enterprises. Therefore, political fluctuations that do not affect the operating conditions of enterprises are not the political risks of enterprises' foreign direct investment.

For an MNE to identify, measure, and manage its political risks, it must define and classify these risks. Figure 9.1 classifies the political risks facing MNEs as being firm-specific, country-specific,

政治风险是指在国际投资活动中，由于未能预期到的政治因素变化而给跨国企业带来经济损失的可能性。

or global-specific.

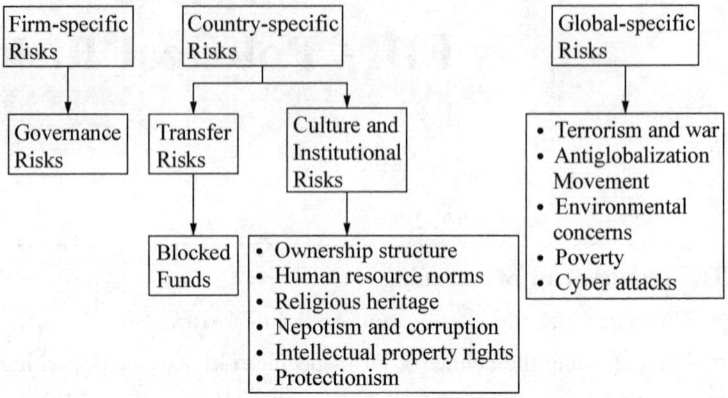

```
Firm-specific        Country-specific                          Global-specific
Risks                Risks                                     Risks
   │                  │      │                                    │
   ▼                  ▼      ▼                                    ▼
Governance       Transfer   Culture and                    • Terrorism and war
Risks            Risks      Institutional                  • Antiglobalization
                            Risks                            Movement
                    │         │                            • Environmental
                    ▼         ▼                              concerns
                Blocked    • Ownership structure           • Poverty
                Funds      • Human resource norms          • Cyber attacks
                           • Religious heritage
                           • Nepotism and corruption
                           • Intellectual property rights
                           • Protectionism
```

Figure 9.1   Classification of Political Risks

- Firm-specific risks, also known as micro risks, are those political risks that affect the MNE at the project or corporate level. Governance risk, due to goal conflict between an MNE and its host government, is the main political firm-specific risk.
- Country-specific risks, also known as macro risks, are those political risks that also affect the MNE at the project or corporate level but originate at the country level. The two main political risk categories at the country level are transfer risk and cultural and institutional risks. Transfer risk concerns mainly the problem of blocked funds, but also peripherally sovereign credit risk. Cultural and institutional risks spring from ownership structure, human resource norms, religious heritage, nepotism and corruption, intellectual property rights, and protectionism.
- Global-specific risks are those political risks that affect the MNE at the project or corporate level but originate at the global level. Examples are terrorism, the anti-globalization movement, environmental concerns, poverty, and cyber-attacks.

This method of classification differs sharply from the traditional method that classifies risks according to the disciplines of economics, finance, political science, sociology, and law.

2   Assessing Political Risk

How can multinational firms anticipate government regulations that, from the firm's perspective, are discriminatory or wealth depriving?

Normally a twofold approach is utilized: At the macro level, prior to undertaking foreign direct investment, firms attempt to assess a host country's political stability and attitude toward foreign investors. At the micro level, firms analyze whether their firm-specific activities are likely to conflict with host-country goals as evidenced by existing regulations. The most difficult task, however, is to anticipate changes in host-country goal priorities, new regulations to implement reordered priorities, and the likely impact of such changes on the firm's operations.

2.1 Predicting Firm-specific Risk (Micro Risk)

From the viewpoint of the MNE, assessing the political stability of a host country is only the first step, since the real objective is to anticipate the effect of political changes on activities of a specific firm. Indeed, different foreign firms operating within the same country may have very different degrees of vulnerability to changes in host-country policy or regulations. One does not expect a Kentucky Fried Chicken franchise to experience the same risk as a Ford manufacturing plant.

> 从跨国公司的角度看,评估东道国的政治稳定性只是第一步,因为真正的目标是预测政治变化对特定企业活动的影响。

The need for firm-specific analyses of political risk has led to a demand for tailor-made studies undertaken in-house by professional political risk analysts. This demand is heightened by the observation that outside professional risk analysts rarely even agree on the degree of macro-political risk that exists in any set of countries.

In-house political risk analysts relate the macro risk attributes of specific countries to the particular characteristics and vulnerabilities of their client firms. Mineral extractive firms, manufacturing firms, multinational banks, private insurance carriers, and worldwide hotel chains are all exposed in fundamentally different ways to politically inspired restrictions. Even with the best possible firm-specific analysis, MNEs cannot be sure that the political or economic situation will not change. Thus, it is necessary to plan protective steps in advance to minimize the risk of damage from unanticipated changes.

2.2 Predicting Country-Specific Risk (Macro Risk)

Macro political risk analysis is still an emerging field of study. Political scientists in academia, industry, and government study country risk for the benefit of multinational firms, government foreign policy decision makers, and defense planners.

> 宏观政治风险分析仍然是一个新兴的研究领域。

Political risk studies usually include an analysis of the historical stability of the country in question, evidence of present turmoil or dissatisfaction, indications of economic stability, and trends in cultural and religious activities. Data are usually assembled by reading local newspapers, monitoring radio and television broadcasts, reading publications from diplomatic sources, tapping the knowledge of outstanding expert consultants, contacting other business persons who have had recent experience in the host country, and finally conducting on-site visits.

Despite this impressive list of activities, the prediction track record of business firms, the diplomatic service, and the military has been spotty at best. When one analyzes trends, whether in politics or economics, the tendency is to predict an extension of the same trends into the future.

Despite the difficulty of predicting country risk, the MNE must still attempt to do so in order to prepare itself for the unknown. A number of institutional services provide updated country risk ratings on a regular basis.

2.3 Predicting Global-Specific Risk

Predicting global-specific risk is even more difficult than predicting the other two types of political risk. Nobody predicted the surprise attacks on the World Trade Center and the Pentagon in the United States on September 11, 2001. On the other hand, the aftermath of this attack—the war on global terrorism, increased U.S. homeland security, and the destruction of part of the terrorist network in Afghanistan was predictable. Nevertheless, we have come to expect future surprise terrorist attacks. U.S.-based MNEs are particularly exposed to not only Al Qaeda but also to other unpredictable groups willing to use terror or mob action to promote such diverse causes as anti-globalization, environmental protection, and even anarchy.

Since there is a great need to predict terrorism, we can expect to see a number of new indices, similar to country-specific indices, but devoted to ranking different types of terrorist threats, their locations, and potential targets.

3 Firm-Specific Risks

The firm-specific risks that confront MNEs include foreign

exchange risks and governance risks. We focus our discussion here on governance risks.

3.1 Governance Risks

Governance risk is the ability to exercise effective controlover an MNE's operations within a country's legal and political environment. For an MNE, however, governance is a subject similar in structure to consolidated profitability—it must be addressed for the individual business unit and subsidiary, as well as for the MNE as a whole.

治理风险是指在一个国家的法律和政治环境下,对跨国公司的运营实施有效控制的能力。

The most important type of governance risk for the MNE on the subsidiary level arises from a goal conflict between bona fide objectives of host governments and the private firms operating within their spheres of influence. Governments are normally responsive to a constituency of their citizens. Firms are responsive to a constituency of their owners and other stakeholders. The valid needs of these sets of constituents need not be the same, but governments set the rules. Consequently, governments impose constraints on the activities of private firms as part of their normal administrative and legislative functioning.

Historically, conflicts between objectives of MNEs and host governments have arisen over such issues as the firms impact on economic development, perceived infringement on national sovereignty, foreign control of key industries, sharing or non-sharing of ownership and control with local interests, impact on a host country's balance of payments, influence on the foreign exchange value of its currency, control over export markets, use of domestic versus foreign executives and workers, and exploitation of national resources. Attitudes about conflicts are often colored by views about free enterprise versus state socialism, the degree of nationalism or internationalism present, or the place of religious views in determining appropriate economic and financial behavior.

The best approach to goal conflict management is to anticipate problems and negotiate understandings ahead of time. Different cultures apply different ethics to the question of honoring prior contracts, especially when they were negotiated with a previous administration. Nevertheless, pre-negotiation of all conceivable areas of conflict provides a better basis for a successful future for both parties than does overlooking the possibility that divergent objectives will evolve over time. Preparation often includes negotiating investment agreements, buying investment insurance and guarantees, and designing risk-reducing operating strategies to be used after the foreign investment decision has been made.

3.1.1 Negotiating Investment Agreements

An investment agreement spells out specific rights and responsibilities of both the foreign firm and the host government. The presence of MNEs is as often sought by development-seeking host governments as a particular foreign location sought by an MNE. All parties have alternatives and so bargaining is appropriate.

> 投资协议规定了外国公司和东道国政府的具体权利和责任。

An investment agreement should define policies on financial and managerial issues, including the following:

- The basis on which fund flows, such as dividends, management fees, royalties, patent fees, and loan repayments, may be remitted
- The basis for setting transfer prices
- The right to export to third-country markets
- Obligations to build, or fund, social and economic overhead projects, such as schools, hospitals, and retirement systems
- Methods of taxation, including the rate, the type, and the means by which the rate base is determined
- Access to host-country capital markets, particularly for long-term borrowing
- Permission for 100% foreign ownership versus required local ownership (joint venture) participation
- Price controls, if any, applicable to sales in the host-country markets
- Requirements for local sourcing versus import of raw materials and components
- Permission to use expatriate managerial and technical personnel, and to bring them and their personal possessions into the country free of exorbitant charges or import duties
- Provision for arbitration of disputes
- Provisions for planned divestment, should such be required, indicating how the going concern will be valued and to whom it will be sold.

3.1.2 Investment Insurance and Guarantees: OPIC

> 跨国公司有时可以通过投资保险和担保计划将政治风险转移给母国的公共机构。

MNEs can sometimes transfer political risk to a home-country public agency through an investment insurance and guarantee program. Many developed countries have such programs to protect investments by their nationals in developing countries.

The U. S. investment insurance and guarantee program is managed by the government-owned Overseas Private Investment Corporation (OPIC). OPIC's stated purpose is to mobilize and facilitate the participation of U. S. private capital and skills in the economic and social progress of less-developed friendly countries and areas, thereby complementing the developmental assistance of the United States. OPIC offers insurance coverage for four separate types of political risk, which have their own specific definitions for insurance purposes:

- *Inconvertibility* is the risk that the investor will not be able to convert profits, royalties, fees, or other income, as well as the original capital invested, into dollars.
- *Expropriation* is the risk that the host government takes a specific step that for one year prevents the investor or the foreign subsidiary from exercising effective control over use of the property.
- *War, revolution, insurrection, and civil strife* coverage applies primarily to the damage of physical property of the insured, although in some cases inability of a foreign subsidiary to repay a loan because of a war may be covered.
- *Business income* coverage provides compensation for loss of business income resulting from events of political violence that directly cause damage to the assets of a foreign enterprise.

3.1.3 Operating Strategies after the FDI Decision

Although an investment agreement creates obligations on the part of both foreign investor and host government, conditions change and agreements are often revised in the light of such changes. The changed conditions may be economic, or they may be the result of political changes within the host government. The firm that sticks rigidly to the legal interpretation of its original agreement may well find that the host government first applies pressure in areas not covered by the agreement and then possibly reinterprets the agreement to conform to the political reality of that country. Most MNEs, in their own self-interest, follow a policy of adapting to changing host-country priorities whenever possible.

虽然投资协议给外国投资者和东道国政府双方都带来了义务,但条件会发生变化,协议往往会根据这种变化进行修订。

The essence of such adaptation is, anticipating host-country priorities and making the activities of the firm of continued value to the host country. Such an approach assumes the government acts rationally in seeking its country's self-interest and is based on the idea that the firm should initiate reductions in goal conflict. Future bargaining position can be enhanced by careful consideration of policies in production, logistics, marketing, finance, organization, and personnel.

Local Sourcing. Host governments may require foreign firms to purchase raw material and components locally as a way to maximize value-added benefits and to increase local employment. From the viewpoint of the foreign firm trying to adapt to host-country goals, local turmoil may shut down the operation and such issues as quality control, high local prices because of lack of economies of scale, and unreliable delivery schedules become important. Often the MNE lowers political risk only by increasing its financial and commercial risk.

Facility Location. Production facilities may be located so as to minimize risk. The natural location of different stages of production may be resource-oriented, footloose, or market-oriented. Oil, for instance, is drilled in and around the Persian Gulf, Russia, Venezuela, and Indonesia. No choice exists for where this activity takes place. Refining, on the other hand, is footloose: A refining facility can be moved easily to another location or country. Whenever possible, oil companies have built refineries in politically safe countries, such as Western Europe, or small islands (such as Singapore or Curacao), even though costs might be reduced by refining nearer the oil fields. They have traded reduced political risk and financial exposure for possibly higher transportation and refining costs.

Control of Transportation. Control of transportation has been an important means to reduce political risk. Oil pipelines that cross national frontiers, oil tankers, ore carriers, refrigerated ships, and railroads have all been controlled at times to influence the bargaining power of nations and companies.

Control of Technology. Control of key patents and processes is a viable way to reduce political risk. If a host country cannot operate a plant because it does not have technicians capable of running the process, or of keeping up with changed technology, abrogation of an investment agreement with a foreign firm is unlikely. Control of technology works best when the foreign firm is steadily improving its technology.

Control of Markets. Control of markets is a common strategy to

> 本地采购。东道国政府可能会要求外国公司在当地购买原材料和零部件,以此来最大限度地提高附加值和增加当地就业。从试图适应东道国目标的外国公司的角度来看,当地的动荡可能会导致业务中断,质量控制、由于缺乏规模经济而导致的当地高价以及不可靠的交货时间表等问题变得很重要。通常,跨国公司只有通过增加其金融和商业风险来降低政治风险。

enhance a firms bargaining position. As effective as the OPEC cartel was in raising the price received for crude oil by its member countries in the 1970s, marketing was still controlled by the international oil companies. OPEC'S need for the oil companies limited the degree to which its members could dictate terms. In more recent years OPEC members have established some marketing outlets of their own, such as Kuwait's extensive chain of Q8 gas stations in Europe.

Control of export markets for manufactured goods is also a source of leverage in dealings between MNEs and host governments. The MNE would prefer to serve world markets from sources of its own choosing, basing the decision on considerations of production cost, transportation, tariff barriers, political risk exposure, and competition. The selling pattern that maximizes long-run profits from the viewpoint of the worldwide firm rarely maximizes exports, or value added, from the perspective of the host countries. Some will argue that if the same plants were owned by local nationals and were not part of a worldwide integrated system, more goods would be exported by the host country. The contrary argument is that self-contained local firms might never obtain foreign market share because they lack economies of scale on the production side and are unable to market in foreign countries.

Brand Name and Trademark Control. Control of a brand name or trademark can have an effect almost identical to that of controlling technology. It gives the MNE a monopoly on something that may or may not have substantive value but quite likely represents value in the eyes of consumers. Ability to market under a world brand name is valuable for local firms and thus represents an important bargaining attribute for maintaining an investment position.

Thin Equity Base. Foreign subsidiaries can be financed with a thin equity base and a large proportion of local debt. If the debt is borrowed from locally owned banks, host-government actions that weaken the financial viability of the firm also endanger local creditors.

Multiple-Source Borrowing. If the firm must finance with foreign source debt, it may borrow from banks in a number of countries rather than just from home country banks. If, for example, debt is owed to banks in Tokyo, Frankfurt, London, and New York, nationals in a number of foreign countries have a vested interest in keeping the borrowing subsidiary financially strong. If the multinational is U.S.-owned, a fallout between the United States and the host government is

多源借款。

less likely to cause the local government to move against the firm if it also owes funds to these other countries.

4 Country-Specific Risks

Country-specific risks affect all firms, domestic and foreign, that are resident in a host country. Figure 9.2 presents a taxonomy of most of the contemporary political risks and firm strategies that emanate from a specific country location. The main country-specific political risks are *transfer risk and cultural and institutional risks*.

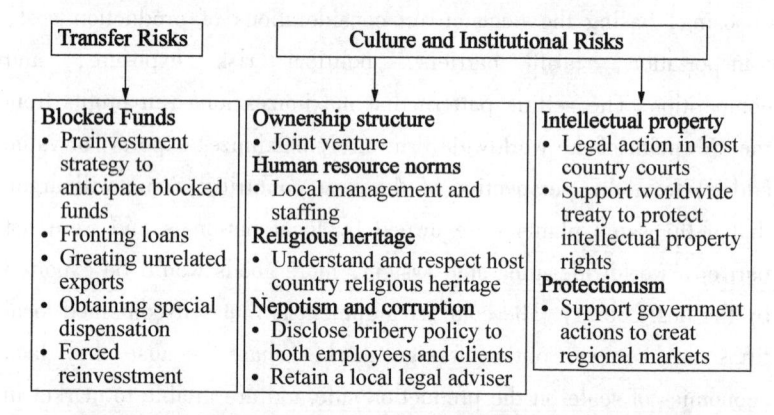

Transfer Risks	Culture and Institutional Risks	
Blocked Funds • Preinvestment strategy to anticipate blocked funds • Fronting loans • Greating unrelated exports • Obtaining special dispensation • Forced reinvesstment	**Ownership structure** • Joint venture **Human resource norms** • Local management and staffing **Religious heritage** • Understand and respect host country religious heritage **Nepotism and corruption** • Disclose bribery policy to both employees and clients • Retain a local legal adviser	**Intellectual property** • Legal action in host country courts • Support worldwide treaty to protect intellectual property rights **Protectionism** • Support government actions to creat regional markets

Figure 9.2 Management Strategies for Country-Specific Risks

4.1 Transfer Risk: Blocked Funds

Transfer risk is defined as limitations on the MNE's ability to transfer funds into and out of a host country without restrictions. When a government runs short of foreign exchange and cannot obtain additional funds through borrowing or attracting new foreign investment, it usually limits transfers of foreign exchange out of the country, a restriction known as blocked funds.

In theory, this does not discriminate against foreign-owned firms because it applies to everyone; in practice, foreign firms have more at stake because of their foreign ownership. Depending on the size of a foreign exchange shortage, the host government might simply require approval of all transfers of funds abroad, thus reserving the right to set a priority on the use of scarce foreign exchange in favor of necessities rather than luxuries. In severe cases, the government might make its currency nonconvertible into other currencies, thereby fully blocking transfers of funds abroad. In between these positions are policies that restrict the size and timing of dividends, debt amortization, royalties.

MNEs can react to the potential for blocked funds at three stages:
- Prior to making an investment, a firm can analyze the effect of blocked funds on expected return on investment, the desired local financial structure, and optimal links with subsidiaries.
- During operations a firm can attempt to move funds through a variety of repositioning techniques.
- Funds that cannot be moved must be reinvested in the local country in a manner that avoids deterioration in their real value because of inflation or exchange depreciation.

4.1.1 Pre-investment Strategy to Anticipate Blocked Funds

Management can consider blocked funds in their capital budgeting analysis. Temporary blockage of funds normally reduces the expected net present value and internal rate of return on a proposed investment. Whether the investment should nevertheless be undertaken depends on whether the expected rate of return, even with blocked funds, exceeds the required rate of return on investments of the same risk class. Pre-investment analysis also includes the potential to minimize the effect of blocked funds by financing with local borrowing instead of parent equity, swap agreements, and other techniques to reduce local currency exposure and thus the need to repatriate funds. Sourcing and sales links with subsidiaries can be predetermined so as to maximize the potential for moving blocked funds.

4.1.2 Moving Blocked Funds

What can a multinational firm do to transfer funds out of countries having exchange or remittance restrictions? At least six popular strategies are used:
- Providing alternative conduits for repatriating funds
- Transferring pricing goods and services between related units of the MNE.
- Leading and lagging payments
- Using fronting loans
- Creating unrelated exports
- Obtaining special dispensation

Fronting Loans. A fronting loan is a parent-to-subsidiary loan channeled through a financial intermediary, usually a large international bank. Fronting loans differ from parallel or back-to-back loans. The latter are offsetting loans between commercial businesses arranged outside the banking system. Fronting loans are sometimes

前置贷款。

referred to as link financing.

In a direct intracompany loan, a parent or sister subsidiary loans directly to the borrowing subsidiary, and at a later date the borrowing subsidiary repays the principal and interest. In a fronting loan, by contrast, the "lending" parent or subsidiary deposits funds in, say, a London bank, and that bank loans the same amount to the borrowing subsidiary in the host country. From the London bank's point of view the loan is risk-free, because the bank has 100% collateral in the form of the parents deposit. In effect the bank fronts for the parent—hence the name fronting loan. Interest paid by the borrowing subsidiary to the bank is usually slightly higher than the rate paid by the bank to the parent, allowing the bank a margin for expenses and profit.

The bank chosen for the fronting loan is usually in a neutral country, away from both the lender's and the borrower's legal jurisdiction. Use of fronting loans increases chances for repayment should political turmoil occur between the home and host countries. Government authorities are more likely to allow a local subsidiary to repay a loan to a large international bank in a neutral country than to allow the same subsidiary to repay a loan directly to its parent. To stop payment to the international bank would hurt the international credit image of the country, whereas to stop payment to the parent corporation would have minimal impact on that image and might even provide some domestic political advantage.

Creating Unrelated Exports. Another approach to blocked funds that benefits both the subsidiary and host country is the creation of unrelated exports. Because the main reason for stringent exchange controls is usually a host country's persistent inability to earn hard currencies, anything an MNE can do to create new exports from the host country helps the situation and provides a potential means to transfer funds out.

Some new exports can often be created from present productive capacity with little or no additional investment, especially if they are in product lines related to existing operations. Other new exports may require reinvestment or new funds, although if the funds reinvested consist of those already blocked, little is lost in the way of opportunity costs.

Special Dispensation. If all else fails and the multinational firm is investing in an industry that is important to the economic development of the host country, the firm may bargain for special dispensation to repatriate some portion of the funds that otherwise would be blocked.

Firms in "desirable" industries such as telecommunications, semiconductor manufacturing, instrumentation, pharmaceuticals, or other research and high-technology industries may receive preference over firms in mature industries. The amount of preference received depends on bargaining among the informed parties, the government and the business firm, either of which is free to back away from the proposed investment if unsatisfied with the terms.

Self—Fulfilling Prophecies. In seeking escape routes for blocked funds-or for that matter in trying to position funds through any of the techniques—the MNE may increase political risk and cause a change from partial blockage to full blockage.

自我实现的预言。

The possibility of such a self-fulfilling cycle exists any time a firm takes action that, no matter how legal, thwarts the underlying intent of politically motivated controls. In the statehouses of the world, as in the editorial offices of the local press and TV, MNEs and their subsidiaries are always a potential scapegoat.

Forced Reinvestment. If funds are indeed blocked from transfer into foreign exchange, they are by definition reinvested. Under such a situation the firm must find local opportunities that will maximize rate of return for a given acceptable level of risk. If blockage is expected to be temporary, the most obvious alternative is to invest in local money market instruments. Unfortunately, in many countries such instruments are not available in sufficient quantity or with adequate liquidity. In some cases, government treasury bills, bank deposits, and other short-term instruments have yields that are kept artificially low relative to local rates of inflation or probable changes in exchange rates. Thus, the firm often loses real value during the period of blockage.

强制再投资。

If short-or intermediate-term portfolio investments, such as bonds, bank time deposits, or direct loans to other companies, are not possible, investment in additional production facilities may be the only alternative. Often this investment is what the host country is seeking by its exchange controls, even if the existence of exchange controls is by itself counterproductive to the idea of additional foreign investment. Examples of forced direct reinvestment can be cited for Peru, where an airline invested in hotels and in maintenance facilities for other airlines; for Turkey, where a fish canning company constructed a plant to manufacture cans needed for packing the catch; and for Argentina, where an automobile company integrated vertically by acquiring a transmission manufacturing plant previously owned by a supplier.

If investment opportunities in additional production facilities are not available, funds may simply be used to acquire other assets expected to increase in value with local inflation. Typical purchases might be land, office buildings, or commodities that are exported to global markets. Even inventory stockpiling might be a reasonable investment, given the low opportunity cost of the blocked funds.

4.2 Country-Specific Risks: Cultural and Institutional Risks

When investing in some of the emerging markets, MNEs that are resident in the most industrialized countries face serious risks because of cultural and institutional differences. Among many such differences are the following:
- Differences in allowable ownership structures
- Differences in human resource norms
- Differences in religious heritage
- Nepotism and corruption in the host country
- Protection of intellectual property rights
- Protectionism

4.2.1 Ownership Structure

Historically, many countries have required that MNEs share ownership of their foreign subsidiaries with local firms or citizens. Thus, joint ventures were the only way an MNE could operate in some host countries. Prominent countries that used to require majority local ownership were Japan, Mexico, India, and Korea. This requirement has been eliminated or modified in more recent years by these countries and most others. However, firms in certain industries are still either excluded from ownership completely or must accept being a minority owner. These industries are typically related to national defense, agriculture, banking, or other sectors that are deemed critical for the host nation. Even the United States would not welcome foreign ownership of large key defense-related firms such as Boeing Aircraft.

4.2.2 Human Resource Norms

MNEs are often required by host countries to employ a certain proportion of host country citizens rather than staffing mainly with foreign expatriates. It is often very difficult to fire local employees due to host country labor laws and union contracts. This lack of flexibility to downsize in response to business cycles affects both MNEs and their local competitors. It also qualifies as a country-specific risk.

Cultural differences can also inhibit an MNE's staffing policies. For example, it is somewhat difficult for a woman manager to be accepted by local employees and managers in many Middle Eastern countries. The most extreme example of discrimination against women was highlighted in Afghanistan during the Taliban regime. Since the Taliban's downfall in late 2001. several women have been suggested for important government roles.

> 东道国经常要求多国企业雇用一定比例的东道国公民,而不是主要由外籍人员组成。

4.2.3 Religious Heritages

The current hostile environment for MNEs in some Middle Eastern countries such as Iran, Iraq, and Syria is being fed by some extremist Muslim clerics who are enraged about the continuing violence in Israel and the occupied Arab territories.

However, the root cause of these conflicts is a mixture of religious fervor for some and politics for others. Although it is popular to blame the Muslim religion for its part in fomenting the conflict, a number of Middle Eastern countries, such as Egypt, Saudi Arabia, and Jordan, are relatively passive when it comes to jihads-calls for Muslims to attack the infidels (Jews and Christians). Osama bin Laden's call for jihad against the United States has not generated any great interest on the part of moderate Muslims. Indeed, Turkey, a Muslim country, has had a secular government for many decades and it strongly supported efforts to rid the world of bin Laden.

Despite religious differences, MNES have operated successfully in emerging markets, especially in extractive and natural resource industries, such as oil, natural gas, minerals, and forest products. The main MNE strategy is to understand and respect the host country's religious traditions.

4.2.4 Nepotism and Corruption

MNEs must deal with endemic nepotism and corruption in a number of countries. Indonesia was famous for nepotism and corruption under the now deposed Suharto government. A number of African countries had a history of nepotism and corruption after they

> 跨国公司必须解决一些国家普遍存在的裙带关系和腐败问题。

threw out their colonial governments following World War II. Presently, one of the worst cases is that of Zimbabwe.

Bribery is not limited to emerging markets. It is also a problem in even the most industrialized countries, including the United States and Japan. In fact, the United States has an antibribery law that would imprison any U.S. business executive found guilty of bribing a foreign government official. This law was passed in reaction to an attempt by Lockheed Aircraft to bribe a Japanese Prime Minister.

Managing Bribery. MNEs are caught in a dilemma. Should they employ bribery if their local competitors use this strategy? The following are alternative strategies:

- Refuse bribery outright, or else demands will quickly multiply.
- Retain a local adviser to diffuse demands by local officials, customs agents, and other business partners.
- Do not count on the justice system in many emerging markets, because Western oriented contract law may not agree with local norms.
- Educate both management and local employees about whatever bribery policy the firm intends to follow.

4.2.5 Intellectual Property Rights

Rogue businesses in some host countries have historically infringed on *the intellectual property rights* of both MNEs and individuals. Intellectual property rights grant the exclusive use of patented technology and copyrighted creative materials. Examples of patented technology are unique manufactured products, processing techniques, and prescription pharmaceutical drugs. Examples of copyrighted creative materials are software programs, educational materials (textbooks), and entertainment products (music, film, and art).

MNES and individuals need to protect their intellectual property rights through the legal process. However, courts in some countries have historically not done a fair job of protecting intellectual property rights of anyone, much less of foreign MNEs. In those countries the legal process is costly and subject to bribery.

The agreement on Trade-Related Aspects of Intellectual Property Rights (TRIPS) to protect intellectual property rights has recently been ratified by most major countries. It remains to be seen whether host governments are strong enough to enforce their official efforts to stamp out intellectual piracy. Complicating this task is the thin line that exists between the real item being protected and look-alikes or

治理贿赂。

generic versions of the same item.

4.2.6 Protectionism

Protectionism is defined as the attempt by a national government to protect certain of its designated industries from foreign competition. Industries that are protected are usually related to defense, agriculture, and "infant" industries.

Defense. Even though the United States is a vocal proponent of open markets, a foreign firm proposing to buy Lockheed Missile Division or other critical defense suppliers would not be welcome. The same attitude exists in many other countries, such as France, which has always wanted to maintain an independent defense capability.

Agriculture. Agriculture is another sensitive industry. No MNE would be foolish enough to attempt to buy agricultural properties, such as rice operations, in Japan. Japan has desperately tried to maintain an independent ability to feed its population. Agriculture is the "Mother Earth" industry that most countries want to protect for their own citizens.

Infant Industries. The traditional protectionist argument is that newly emerging industries need protection from foreign competition until they can get firmly established. The infant industry argument is usually directed at limiting imports but not necessarily MNEs. In fact, most host countries encourage MNEs to establish operations in industries that do not presently exist in the host country. Sometimes the host country offers foreign MNEs infant-industry status for a limited number of years. This status could lead to tax subsidies, construction of infrastructure, employee training, and other aids to help the MNE get started. Host countries are especially interested in attracting MNEs that promise to export, either to their own foreign subsidiaries elsewhere or to unrelated parties.

Tariff Barriers. The traditional methods for countries to implement protectionist barriers were through tariff and nontariff regulations. Negotiations under the General Agreements on Tariffs and Trade (GATT) have greatly reduced the general level of tariffs over the past decades. This process continues today under the auspices of the WTO. However, many non-tariff barriers remain.

Nontariff Barriers. Nontariff barriers, which restrict imports by something other than a financial cost, are often difficult to identify because they are promulgated as health, safety, or sanitation requirements.

5 Global-Specific Risks

Global-specific risks faced by MNEs have come to the forefront in recent years. Figure 9.3 summarizes some of these risks and the strategies that can be used to manage them.

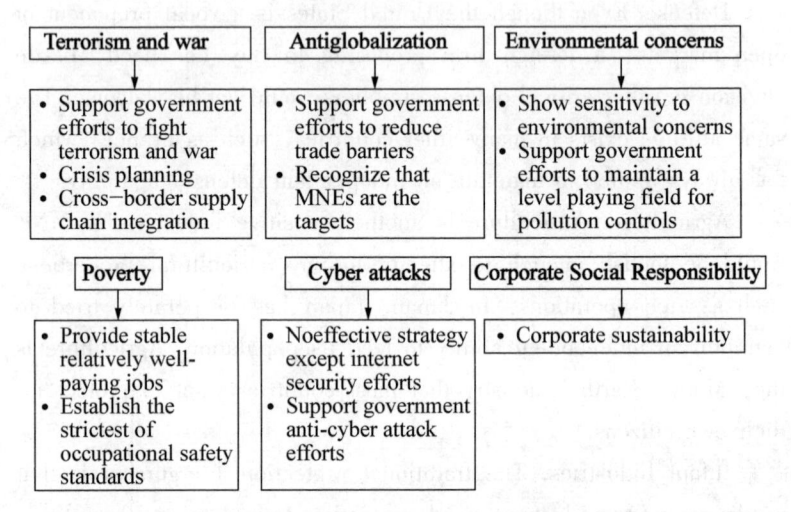

Terrorism and war	Antiglobalization	Environmental concerns
• Support government efforts to fight terrorism and war • Crisis planning • Cross-border supply chain integration	• Support government efforts to reduce trade barriers • Recognize that MNEs are the targets	• Show sensitivity to environmental concerns • Support government efforts to maintain a level playing field for pollution controls

Poverty	Cyber attacks	Corporate Social Responsibility
• Provide stable relatively well-paying jobs • Establish the strictest of occupational safety standards	• Noeffective strategy except internet security efforts • Support government anti-cyber attack efforts	• Corporate sustainability

Figure 9.3 Management Strategies for Global-Specific Risks

The most visible recent risk was, of course. the attack by terrorists on the twin towers of the World Trade Center in New York on September 11, 2001. Many MNEs had major operations in the World Trade Center and suffered heavy casualties among their employees.

In addition to terrorism, other global-specific risks include the anti-globalization movement, environmental concerns, poverty in emerging markets, and cyber-attacks on computer information systems.

5.1 Terrorism and War

Although the World Trade Center attack and its aftermath, the war in Afghanistan, and the war in Iraq have affected nearly everyone in the world, many other acts of terrorism have been committed in recent years, more terrorist acts are expected to occur in the future. Particularly exposed are the foreign subsidiaries of MNEs and their employees. As mentioned earlier, foreign subsidiaries are especially exposed to war, ethnic strife, and terrorism because they are symbols of their respective parent countries.

No MNE has the tools to avert terrorism. Hedging, diversification, insurance, and the like are not suited to the task, Therefore, MNEs must depend on governments to fight terrorism and protect their foreign subsidiaries (and now even the parent firm). In return, governments expect financial, material, and verbal support from MNEs to support antiterrorist legislation and proactive initiatives to destroy terrorist cells wherever they exist.

5.2　Crisis Planning

Resolving war and ethnic strife is beyond the ability of MNEs. Instead, they need to take defensive steps to limit the damage. Crisis planning has become a major activity for MNEs at both the foreign subsidiary and parent firm levels. Crisis planning means educating management and employees about how to react to various scenarios of violence. For example, MNE units must know how to stay in communication with each other: how to protect the MNE's property; how to escape the country; and how to protect themselves by maintaining a low profile.

5.3　Cross-Border Supply Chain Integration

The drive to increase efficiency in manufacturing has driven many MNEs to adopt just-in-time (JIT) near-zero inventory systems. Focusing on inventory velocity, the speed at which inventory moves through a manufacturing process, arriving only as needed and not before has allowed these MNEs to generate increasing profits and cash flows with less capital being bottled up in the production cycle. This finely tuned supply chain system, however, is subject to significant political risk if the supply chain extends across borders.

Supply Chain Interruptions. Consider the cases of Dell Computer, Ford Motor Company, Dairy queen, Apple Computer, Herman Miller, and The Limited in the days following the terrorist attacks of September 11, 2001. An immediate result of the event was the grounding of all aircraft into or out of the United States. Similarly, the land (Mexico and Canada) and sea borders of the United States were also shut down and not reopened for several days in some specific sites. Ford Motor Company shut down five of its manufacturing plants in the days following September 11 because of inadequate inventories of critical automotive inputs supplied from Canada. Dairy Queen experienced such significant delays in key

> 供应链中断。

confectionary ingredients that many of its stores were also temporarily closed.

Dell Computer, with one of the most highly acclaimed and admired virtually integrated supply chains, depends on computer parts and subassembly suppliers and manufacturers in Mexico and Canada to fulfill its everyday assembly and sales needs. In recent years, Dell has carried less than three full day's sales of total inventory-by cost-of-goods value. Suppliers are integrated electronically with Dell's order fulfillment system, and they deliver required components and subassemblies as sales demands require. But with the closure of borders and grounding of air freight, the company was brought to a near standstill because of its supply chains reliance on the ability to treat business units and suppliers in different countries as if they were all part of a single seamless political unit.

As a result of these newly learned lessons, many MNEs are now evaluating the degree of exposure their supply chains possess in regard to cross-border stoppages or other cross-border political events. These companies are not, however, about to abandon JIT. It is estimated that U.S. companies alone have saved more than \$ 1 billion a year in inventory carrying costs by using JIT methods over the past decade. This substantial benefit is now being weighed against the costs and risks associated with the post-September 11 supply chain interruptions.

To avoid suffering a similar fate in the future, manufacturers, retailers, and suppliers are now employing a range of tactics:

- Inventory Management. Manufacturers and assemblers are considering carrying more buffer inventory in order to hedge against supply and production-line disruptions. Retailers, meanwhile, should think about the timing and frequency of their replenishment. Rather than stocking up across the board, companies are focusing on the most critical parts to the product or service, and on those components that are uniquely available only from international sources.
- Sourcing. Manufacturers are now being more selective about where the critical inputs to their products come from. Although sourcing strategies will have to vary by location, firms are attempting to work more closely with existing suppliers to minimize cross-border exposures and reduce the potential costs with future stoppages.

- Transportation. Retailers and manufacturers alike are reassessing their cross-border shipping arrangements. For example, many inputs that currently are carried by passenger flights may be precluded from cohabitation on these flights in the future. Although the mode of transportation employed is a function of value, volume, and weight, many firms are now reassessing whether higher costs for faster shipment balance out the more tenuous their delivery under airline stoppages from labor, terrorist, or even bankruptcy disruptions in the future.

运输。

5.4 Anti-globalization Movement

During the past decade, there has been a growing negative reaction by some groups to reduced trade barriers and efforts to create regional markets, particularly to NAFTA and the European Union. NAFTA has been vigorously opposed by those sectors of the labor movement that could lose jobs to Mexico. Opposition within the European Union centers on loss of cultural identity, dilution of individual national control as new members are admitted over-centralization of power in a large bureaucracy in Brussels, and most recently the disappearance of individual national currencies in mid-2002, when the euro became the only currency in 12 of the 15 member nations.

The anti-globalization movement has become more visible following riots in Seattle during the 2001 annual meeting of the World Trade Organization. Anti-globalization forces were not solely responsible for these riots, or for subsequent riots in Quebec and Prague in 2001. other disaffected groups, such as environmentalists and even anarchists, joined in to make their causes more visible.

MNEs do not have the tools to combat anti-globalization movement. Indeed, they are blamed for fostering the problem in the first place. Once again, MNEs must rely on governments and crisis planning to manage these risks.

5.5 Environmental Concerns

MNEs have been accused of exporting their environmental problems to other countries. The accusation is that MNEs frustrated by pollution controls in their home country have relocated these activities to countries with weaker pollution controls, another accusation is that MNEs contribute to the problem of global warming. However, that accusation applies to all firms in all countries. It is based on the manufacturing methods employed by specific industries and on consumers' desire for certain products such as large automobiles and sport vehicles that are not fuel efficient.

Once again, solving environmental problems is dependent on governments passing legislation and implementing pollution control standards. In 2001, the Kyoto Treaty, which attempted to reduce global warming, was ratified by most nations, with the notable exception of the United States. However, the United States has promised to combat global warming using its own strategies. The United States objected to provisions in the worldwide treaty that allowed emerging nations to follow less restrictive standards, while the economic burden would fall on the most industrialized countries, particularly the United States.

5.6 Poverty

MNEs have located foreign subsidiaries in countries plagued by extremely uneven income one end of the spectrum is an elite class of well-educated, well-connected, and productive people. At the other end is a very large class of people living at or below the poverty level. They lack education, social and economic infrastructure, and political power.

MNEs might be contributing to this disparity by employing the elite class to manage their operations. On the other hand, MNEs are creating relatively stable and well-paying jobs for those who were otherwise unemployed and living below the poverty level. Despite being accused of supporting sweatshop conditions, MNEs usually compare favorably to their local competitors. For example, Nike, one of the targeted MNEs, usually pays better, provides more fringe benefits, maintains higher safety standards, and educates its workforce to allow personnel to advance up the career ladder. Of course, Nike cannot manage a country's poverty problems overall, but it can improve conditions for some people.

5.7 Cyber Attacks

The rapid growth of the Internet has fostered a whole new generation of scam artists and cranks who disrupt the usefulness of the World Wide Web. This is a domestic and an international problem. MNEs can face costly cyber-attacks because of their visibility and the complexity of their internal information systems.

At this time. we know of no uniquely international strategies that MNEs can use to combat cyber-attacks. MNEs are using the same strategies to manage foreign cyber-attacks as they use for domestic attacks. Once again, they must rely on governments to control cyber-attacks.

5.8 Corporate Social Responsibility

The first years of the twenty-first century have seen a rebirth in society's reflections on business. One of the most audible debates has been that regarding sustainable development, the principle that economic development today should not compromise the ability of future generations to achieve and enjoy similar standards of living.

Summary

- Political risks can be defined by classifying them on three levels: firm-specific, country-specific, and global-specific.
- Firm-specific risks, also known as micro risks, affect the MNE at the project or corporate level.
- Country-specific risks, also known as macro risks, he MNE at the project or corporate level but originate at the country level.
- Global-specific risks affect the MNE at the project or corporate level but originate at the global level.
- The main firm-specific risk is governance risk, The most important type of governance risk arises from a goal conflict between bona fide objectives of governments and private firms.
- The main tools used to manage goal conflict are to negotiate an investment agreement; to purchase investment insurance and guarantees; and to modify operating strategies in production, logistics, marketing, finance, organization, and personnel.
- The main country-specific risks are transfer risk, known as blocked funds, and certain cultural and institutional risks.
- Blocked funds can be managed by any of five strategies: 1) including blocked funds in their original capital budgeting analysis; 2) fronting loans; 3) creating unrelated exports; 4) obtaining special dispensation and 5) planning for forced reinvestment.
- Cultural and institutional risks emanate from host country policies

with respect to ownership structure, human resource norms, religious heritage, nepotism and corruption, intellectual property rights, and protectionism.

- The main global-specific risks are currently caused by terrorism and war, the anti-globalization movement environmental concerns, poverty, and cyber-attacks.
- In order to manage global-specific risks, an MNE should adopt a crisis plan to protect its employees and property and to secure its supply chain integrity. However, the MNE largely relies on government to protect its citizens and firms from global-specific threats.

Exercises

1. Governance Risk.
    a. What is meant by the term governance risk?
    b. What is the most important type of governance risk?

2. Investment Agreement. An investment agreement spells out the specific rights and responsibilities of a foreign firm and its host government. What are the main financial policies that should be included in an vestment agreement?

3. Investment Insurance and Guarantees (OPIC).
    a. What is OPIC?
    b. What types of political risks can OPIC insure against?

4. Operating Strategies after the FDI Decision. The following operating strategies, among others, are expected to reduce damage from political risk.
    Explain each one and how it reduces damage.
    a. Local sourcing
    b. Facility location
    c. Control of technology
    d. Thin equity base
    e. Multiple-source borrowing

5. Country-Specific Risk, Define the following terms:
    a. Transfer risk
    b. Blocked fund
    c. Sovereign credit risk

6. Blocked Funds. Explain the strategies used by an MNE to counter blocked funds.

7. **Cultural and Institutional Risks.** Identify and explain the main types of cultural and institutional risks. except protectionism.
8. **Strategies to Manage Cultural and Institutional Risks.** Explain the strategies used by an MNE to manage each of the cultural and institutional risks that you identified in question 9, except protectionism.
9. **Protectionism Defined.**
    a. Define protectionism and identify the industries that are typically protected.
    b. Explain the "infant industry" argument for protected.
10. **Managing Protectionism.**
    a. What are the traditional methods for countries to implement protectionism?
    b. What are some typical nontariff barriers to trade?
    c. How can MNEs overcome host-country protectionism?
11. **Global-Specific Risks.** What are the main types of political risks that are global in origin?
12. **Managing Global-Specific Risks.** What are the main strategies used by MNES to manage the global-specific risks you identified in question 13?
13. **U.S. anti-Bribery Law.** The United States has a law prohibiting U.S. firms from bribing foreign officials and business persons, even in countries where bribery is a normal practice. Some U.S. firms claim this place them at a disadvantage compared to host-country firms and other foreign firms that are not hampered by such a law. Discuss the ethics and practicality of the U.S. anti-bribery law.

Part IV

International Investment in China

Chapter 10
International Direct Investment in China

> **The requirement of Learning**
> - Knowing the growing studies on FDI in China.
> - Knowing the phases of FDI inflowing into China.
> - Knowing the meaning of round-tripping investments.
> - Knowing the status of Chinese inward FDI in the World FDI inflows.
> - Knowing the regional distribution of FDI within China.
> - Knowing the evolution of China's opening policies to FDI.
> - Familiar with the history of Chinese OFDI development.
> - Identify the determinants of Chinese OFDI.
> - Knowing the international strategies of Chinese firms and how these are influenced by domestic institutions and access to international networks.
> - Knowing the development stages of Chinese OFDI and its political and regulatory environment towards OFDI.
> - Knowing international Investment Strategy of Chinese MNEs.

1 FDI in China

Allowing FDI into its domestic economy is one of the most dramatic features of China's move from a planned economy towards a market economy. Since the passing, in late 1979, of the Equity Joint Venture Law which granted legal status to FDI in Chinese territory, China has gradually liberalized its FDI regime, and an institutional framework has been developed to regulate and facilitate such investments. The liberalization of the FDI regime together with the improved investment environment has greatly increased the confidence of foreign investors to invest in China. Consequently, FDI inflows into China increased rapidly after 1979, particularly during the early 1990s and after China's entry into the World Trade Organization (WTO) in 2001.

1.1 Why study FDI in China?

Owing to its fast growth and huge amount of inflows, FDI in China has received increasing attention both within China and abroad. There are several key reasons to study FDI in China.

First, China is the world's largest developing country and one of its fastest growing economies, with the annual real growth rate of gross domestic product (GDP) averaging around 10 percent for the 1980s—2010s. China's participation and growing role in the world economy, particularly after China's entry into the WTO, calls for a careful study of the pattern and process of China's internationalization. Undoubtedly, FDI in China's economy will play a very important and increasing role in the process of China's integration with the world economy. Therefore, studying FDI in China has a strategic significance not only for China but also for the whole world economy.

> 首先，中国是世界上最大的发展中国家，也是增长最快的经济体之一，20世纪80年代到21世纪10年代GDP实际增长率超10%。

Second, China has a particular political and economic environment. It is moving from a planned economy towards a market economy. Its experience with FDI is thus of relevance to many other developing countries, especially to the former socialist countries of Eastern Europe, not only because of the magnitude of FDI inflows it has attracted but also because the essential elements of the policy environment are replicated there.

> 第二，中国有特殊的政治和经济环境。

Third, China is the largest FDI recipient in the developing world. As a result, China has increasingly become more significant in influencing not only the flows of international FDI, but also the division of labor and specialization in global production. Therefore, studies of FDI cannot afford to ignore China.

> 第三，中国是发展中国家最大的FDI接受国。

Fourth, the fast growth rate of FDI inflows into China during the past three decades has caused increasing concern in other developing countries about their own efforts in attracting FDI inflows. Has the fast growth of FDI inflows into China caused a diversion of FDI away from other developing countries? One cannot answer this question without a careful study of the location determinants affecting FDI inflows and the relative performance of China in attracting FDI inflows as compared with other developing countries.

> 第四，过去三十年流入中国的外国直接投资的快速增长，引起了其他发展中国家对其吸引外国直接投资流入的关注。

Fifth, one of the prominent features of FDI in China is the overwhelming dominance of investments from developing source countries and economies, particularly from the overseas Chinese investors. The existing theories of FDI have been mainly drawn from

> 第五，中国外商直接投资的突出特点之一是主要由来自发展中国家和经济的投资主导，尤其是来自海外的中国投资者。

studies of developed source countries. Little work has been done on the investment behavior and characteristics of developing source countries. Fortunately, FDI in China provides a valuable opportunity for economists not only to test the adequacy of existing theories of FDI but also to compare the particular characteristics of developing source countries with developed source countries in their investment behavior.

Sixth, China, as the largest developing country with a huge amount of FDI inflows, provides a valuable case for the empirical study of spillovers of FDI on domestic firms' productivity and exports of developing countries. It is hypothesized that because FDI firms possess firm-specific ownership advantages, such as advanced technology and know-how, mature marketing and managerial skills, well-organized international distribution channels, coordinated relationships with suppliers and good reputation, FDI firms can compete locally with more informed domestic firms. Since both FDI firms and domestic firms can imitate each other in the same market, domestic firms are usually expected to increase their productivity and competitiveness in international markets. This positive impact of foreign presence on domestic firms' productivity and exports is referred to as 'spillovers of FDI', which is an important channel through which developing countries can close the technology gap with developed countries.

Finally, there is a considerable and a growing number of studies on FDI in China. These studies can be broadly classified into three groups. The first has mainly focused on China's FDI policies, legal and institutional framework, the impacts of trade and investment liberalization of China on FDI inflows and the characteristics of FDI in China. The second group has mainly focused on location determinants of FDI, sources of FDI and the impacts of China on FDI inflows into other countries. The third group has mainly focused on the impacts of FDI on China's economy.

1.2　FDI Inflows into China between 1979 and 2009

Since the reform and opening in 1980s, China has attracted a large amount of FDI inflows. As shown in Figure 10.1, the growth of FDI inflows into China from 1979 to 2009 can be broadly divided into three phases: the experimental phase from 1979 to 1991; the boom phase from 1992 to 2001; and the post-WTO phase from 2002 to 2009.

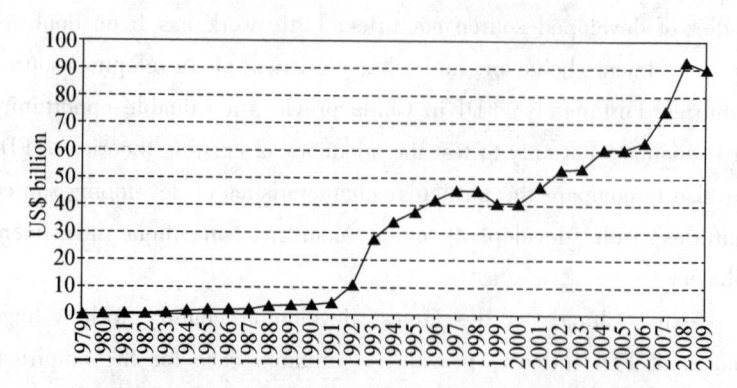

Figure 10.1 FDI inflows into China (current US$)

Note: The data do not include FDI inflows into the financial sector.
Sources: National Bureau of Statistics of China (various issues). China Statistical Yearbook, Beijing: China Statistics Press.

In the initial stage of the experimental phase, following the establishment of the four Special Economic Zones (SEZs) in Guangdong and Fujian provinces, accompanied by the special incentive policies for FDI offered by the Chinese government in these SEZs, FDI inflows into China were highly concentrated in Guangdong and Fujian provinces, and particularly in the four SEZs. For example, Guangdong and Fujian provinces absorbed more than 70 percent of total FDI inflows in 1983. However, since the Chinese government was very cautious about introducing FDI into its domestic economy, foreign investors were also cautious about making investments in China in the initial stage of China's opening up to the outside world. During this period, therefore, China's performance in attracting FDI inflows was not very impressive. The inflows of FDI were only US$0.11 billion in 1979 and US$0.64 billion in 1983, averaging US$0.35 billion annually.

In 1984, Hainan Island and 14 coastal cities across ten provinces were opened to FDI. As in the SEZs, a series of special economic policies were introduced in these open coastal cities. Consequently, in 1984 the inflows of FDI into China doubled the amount of those in 1983, reaching US$1.26 billion, indicating a new stage in attracting FDI inflows into China. The momentum of FDI inflows into China continued from 1984 to 1988. However, in 1989, mainly due to the Tiananmen event, the growth rate of FDI inflows into China fell sharply from 38 percent in 1988 to 6 percent in 1989. The downturn continued in 1990, until it recovered in 1991. During the period from 1984 to 1991, the Chinese government made a significant effort to attract FDI inflows. This included opening more and more areas and regions to FDI, such as the Yangzi River Delta, the Pearl River Delta, the Min Nan Delta, the Shanghai Pudong New Development Zone and the entire coastal areas, and introducing a series of laws and regulations to encourage FDI inflows. As a result, FDI inflows into China continued to increase in absolute terms during the whole period from 1984 to 1991.

The second phase began in 1992, when Deng Xiaoping made a tour to China's southern coastal economically opened areas and SEZs, and made a speech, which subsequently became famous. His aim was first to push China's overall economic reform process forward, and second to emphasize China's commitment to the open door policy and market-oriented economic reform in order to increase the confidence of foreign investors to invest in China. His speech explicitly declared his support for the successful economic development assisted by FDI in the economically opened areas and SEZs, and expressed a desire to see the pace of liberalization quickened. Deng Xiaoping's tour, which turned out to be a landmark, set the scene for China's move away from the uneven regional priority towards nationwide implementation of open policies for FDI. The Chinese government then adopted and implemented a series of new policies and regulations to encourage FDI inflows into China. The results were astounding. In 1992 the inflows of FDI into China reached US$11.01 billion, doubling the figure of 1991. In 1993 the inflows of FDI again doubled the figure of 1992, reaching US$27.52 billion. The high growth of FDI inflows continued during 1994 to 1996.

Foreign direct investment inflows slowed down after 1997 and declined in 1999 and 2000, followed by a moderate recovery in 2001. The slow-down from 1997 to 2000 could be explained by several factors. First, there was a slow-down in transfers of labor-intensive activities from neighboring Asian economies. In addition, the East Asian financial crisis weakened substantially the outward investment abilities of East and South-East Asian economies. As a result, FDI flows into China from East and South-East Asia declined substantially since 1997. Second, informal relationships and corruption still hinder many business transactions by foreigners. In addition, inefficient state-owned enterprises (SOEs) continue to dominate many key sectors of economy, especially the service sector. Third, there are still restrictions on FDI, such as on ownership shares, modes of entry, business operations, and regional and sectoral restrictions.

The third phase began in 2002 after China's entry into the WTO in 2001. China's accession to the WTO came at a critical time, when the country was facing difficulties sustaining a high level of FDI inflows. After China's accession to the WTO, with the implementation of its commitments and broader and deeper liberalization in trade and investment, FDI inflows presented an increasing trend. Foreign direct investment inflows increased from US$46.88 billion in 2001 to US$92.40 billion in 2008. However, because of the global financial and economic crisis, FDI inflows into China declined to US$90.03 billion in 2009.

According to the UNCTAD (2007), a significant share of FDI inflows into China is round-tripping, mainly via Hong Kong and more recently and increasingly via some tax-haven islands—Virgin Islands, Cayman Islands and Samoan Islands. Some estimates suggest that round-tripping inward FDI accounted for 25 percent of China's FDI inflows in 1992 and accounted for 40 percent of China's total FDI inflows during 1994 to 2001.

Round-tripping is driven by a number of incentives. In the case of China, preferential treatments offered for FDI are one of the main incentives for round-tripping FDI. Since the beginning of economic reform, the Chinese government has used tax incentives, tariff concessions and various preferential treatments intensively and selectively to attract FDI flowing into the designed areas and industries. These preferential treatments offered for FDI are the primary incentives for domestic firms to do round-tripping FDI.

Since China's accession to the WTO, China has gradually introduced national treatment of FDI firms. In March 2007 China passed the new corporate income tax law, unifying the corporate income tax rates for foreign and domestic enterprises at 25 percent. The unification of the corporate income tax rate and the elimination of preferential treatment of FDI firms will reduce the incentives for FDI round-tripping.

1.3 China's FDI Inflows in Global Perspective

Since the 1980s, world FDI inflows have experienced two massive waves of ups and downs. As shown in Figure 10.2, the first large increase of world FDI inflows started in the mid-1990s. World FDI inflows increased from US$331 billion in 1995 to US$1,393 billion in

2000. Following a sharp decline in 2001 to 2003, world FDI inflows increased again and experienced a period of high growth during 2003 to 2007, reaching a historical record of US$2,100 billion in 2007. However, the growing trend of world FDI inflows came to an end in 2008. World FDI inflows dropped sharply to US$1,771 billion, declining by 15.71 percent in 2008, and further dropped to US$1,114 billion in 2009, declining by 37.29 percent, caused by the global financial crisis, which was in turn triggered by the USA's subprime crisis which began in summer 2007 and led to a rapid deterioration of the global investment environment. However, as compared to the large fluctuations in world FDI inflows, FDI inflows into China have been relatively stable, presenting a steady growing trend with minor fluctuations.

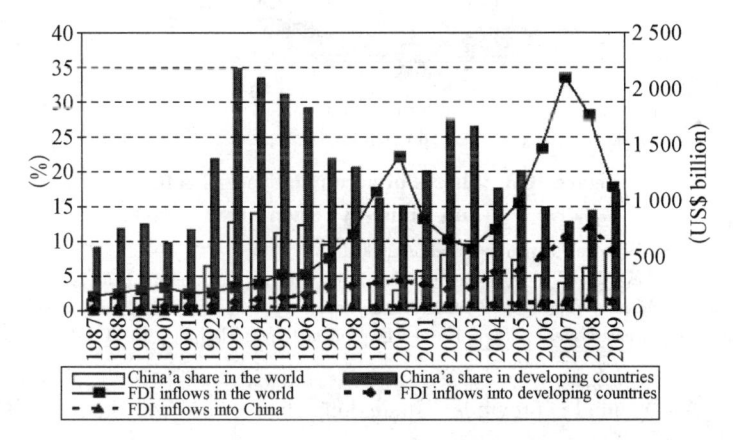

Figure 10.2 China's FDI inflows in global perspective (current US$)

Note: Data for China include FDI inflows into the financial sector after 2005.
Sources: Compiled from United Nations Conference on Trade and Development (various issues), World Investment Report, New York and Geneva: United Nations Publication.

What has been the position of China in world FDI inflows? As shown in Figure 10.2, during the 1980s China's share in FDI inflows in the world and in developing countries was around 2 percent and 11 percent respectively, with minor annual fluctuations. However, in the 1990s China's share in FDI inflows in the world and in developing countries increased dramatically, reaching 7.5 percent and 23 percent respectively. In the 2000s China's share in FDI inflows in the world and in developing countries declined slightly due to the massive increase in world FDI inflows during the period of 2004 to 2007. However, during the period from 2000 to 2009, China still accounted for 6 percent of total world FDI inflows and 17 percent of total FDI inflows into developing countries.

1.4　The Regional Distribution of FDI within China

By the end of 2008, as shown in Figure 10.3, FDI in China was overwhelmingly concentrated in the eastern region, which accounted for 86.26 percent of the total accumulative FDI inflows, while the central region and western region accounted for only 9.16 percent and 4.58 percent of the total respectively.

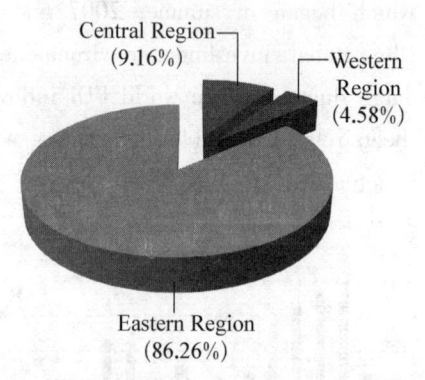

Figure 10.3　Shares of accumulative FDI inflows into China by region, 1983—2008

Note: The calculation is based on 2000 US$.
Sources: Compiled from National Bureau of Statistics of China (various issues), China Statistical Yearbook, Beijing: China Statistics Press; Ministry of Commerce of China (various issues), China Foreign Investment Report, Beijing: MOFCOM.

As a single province Guangdong has been the largest FDI recipient in China among all the provinces. Its share of accumulative FDI inflows from 1983 to 2005 was over a quarter of the national total (see Table 10.1), followed by Jiangsu (14.41 percent), Shanghai (8.94 percent), Shandong (8.44 percent), Fujian (7.99 percent), Liaoning (5.06 percent), Zhejiang (5.01 percent), Beijing (4.25 percent) and Tianjin (3.62 percent).

Table 10.1　Accumulative FDI inflows in China by region and selected provinces, 1983—2005

Regions	Accumulative FDI inflows 1983—2005 (US$ million)	Share 1983—2005(%)
Eastern Region	535,940	86.26
Guangdong	157,037	25.28
Jiangsu	89,519	14.41
Shanghai	55,545	8.94

Chapter 10 International Direct Investment in China

continued

Regions	Accumulative FDI inflows 1983—2005 (US$ million)	Share 1983—2005(%)
Shandong	52,428	8.44
Fujian	49,617	7.99
Liaoning	31,438	5.06
Zhejiang	31.589	5.01
Beijing	26,380	4.25
Tianjin	22,870	3.62
Central Region	56,902	9.16
Hubei	13,120	2.11
Hunan	10,551	1.70
Jiangxi	8,634	1.39
Henan	6,807	1.10
Western Region	28,462	4.58
Guangxi	8,748	1.41
Sichuan	5,844	0.94
Shaanxi	4,639	0.75
Chongqing	3,744	0.60
Provincial total	612,304	100.00

Sources: Chen chunlai, Foreign Direct Investment in China, 2011.

1.5 Who are the Major Investors in China?

Since 1979 more than 170 countries and economies have invested in China. However, of interest is to determine who are the major investors. By the end of 2008, as shown in Table 10.2, FDI in China was overwhelmingly dominated by developing countries and economies, which accounted for 75.38 percent of the total accumulative FDI inflows, while developed countries accounted for only 24.62 percent of the total. Among the developing countries and economies, as a group the Asian newly industrializing economies (NIEs) has been the largest investor, accounting for 56.64 percent of the total. Within the Asian NIEs, Hong Kong has held the dominant position, accounting for 41.75 percent of the total, followed by Taiwan (5.76 percent), South Korea (4.74 percent) and Singapore (4.39 percent). The four Association of South-East Asian Nations (ASEAN) economies accounted for 1.48 percent of the total.

One notable feature is the large shares held by the tax-haven economies. Foreign direct investment inflows into China from the tax-haven economies increased dramatically in the 1990s and particularly in the 2000s. As a result, their combined shares in total FDI inflows increased to 13.64 percent by the end of 2008. The Virgin Islands took the dominant position, accounting for 9.78 percent of the total, followed by the Cayman Islands (1.78 percent) and the Samoan Islands (1.30 percent).

Among the developed countries, Japan and the USA are the most important investors in China, accounting for 7.78 percent and 7.18 percent of the total, while the combined share of the European Union (15) was 7.19 percent. Apart from the UK, Germany, the Netherlands and France, whose shares are 1.89 percent, 1.76 percent, 1.06 percent and 1.03 percent respectively, no other individual developed country has contributed more than 1 percent of the total accumulative FDI inflows into China.

Table 10.2 Accumulative FDI inflows into China by developing and developed countries and economies, 1983—2008 (2000 US$)

	1983—2008	
	(US$ million)	(%)
Developing countries and economies	620,925	75.38
NIEs	466,542	56.64
Hong Kong	343,888	41.75
Taiwan	47,423	5.76
South Korea	39,043	4.74
Singapore	36,188	4.39
ASEAN(4)	12,225	1.48
Tax-haven economies	112,372	13.64
Other developing countries	29,787	3.62
Developed countries	202,814	24.62
Japan	64,114	7.78
USA	59,172	7.18
EU(15)	59,262	7.19
UK	15,561	1.89

Chapter 10 International Direct Investment in China

| | 1983—2008 ||
	(US$ million)	(%)
Germany	14,480	1.76
Netherlands	8,715	1.06
France	8.474	1.03
Other developed countries	20,266	2.46
Total	823,739	100.00

Sources: Chen chunlai, Foreign Direct Investment in China, 2011.

1.6 Sectoral Distribution of FDI in China

By the end of 2008, the sectoral distribution of FDI in China was characterized by a high concentration in the manufacturing sector. As shown in Figure 10.4, the manufacturing sector attracted 62.72 percent, the service sector attracted 34.74 percent, while the primary sector attracted only 2.54 percent of the total accumulative FDI inflows into China during the period from 1997 to 2008.

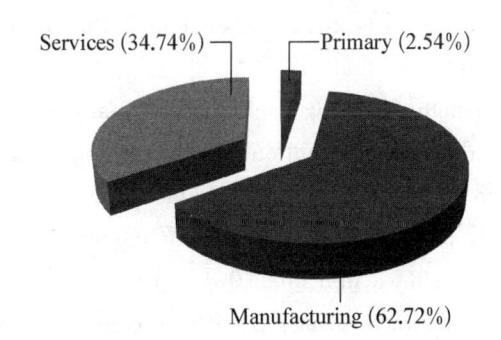

Figure 10.4 Sectoral distribution of accumulative FDI inflows in China, 1997—2008

Sources: Chen chunlai, Foreign Direct Investment in China, 2011.

How important are FDI firms in China's manufacturing sector? As shown in Table 10.3, in terms of total assets, the share of FDI firms in the manufacturing sector has increased from 18.93 percent in 1995 to 32.10 percent in 2008. In other words, one-third of the total assets of manufacturing sector were held by FDI firms in 2008. This is significant, especially when we take into account the large aggregate scale and overall fast growth rate of China's manufacturing sector in the last 30 years.

Table 10.3 Shares of FDI firms in manufacturing by total assets (%)

Sector	1995	2008
Labour intensive	25.19	33.79
Capital intensive	10.75	24.01
Technology intensive	22.04	42.15
Total	18.93	32.10

Sources: Chen chunlai, Foreign Direct Investment in China, 2011.

Among the three industry groups of manufacturing, FDI firms in the technology-intensive sector gained more share, and therefore more importance, than FDI firms in the labor-intensive sector and the capital-intensive sector in manufacturing. By 2008, the share of FDI firms in the technology-intensive sector reached 42.15 percent, increasing 20.11 percentage points compared with that in 1995. The share of FDI firms in the labor-intensive sector increased to 33.79 percent in 2008, rising by 8.60 percentage points above that in 1995. The share of FDI firms in the capital-intensive sector is still relatively low compared with those in the technology-intensive sector and the labor-intensive sector. However, it increased to 24.01 percent in 2008, rising by 13.26 percentage points over that in 1995.

Since the manufacturing sector is the main recipient of FDI inflows, its industrial distribution has special significance. In the early stage of FDI inflows into manufacturing, FDI firms were overwhelmingly concentrated in the labor-intensive sector. By the end of 1995, as shown in Table 10.4, in terms of the total assets of FDI firms in manufacturing, 50.91 percent were in the labor-intensive sector while only 21.71 percent and 27.38 percent were in the capital-intensive sector and the technology-intensive sector respectively.

Table 10.4 Industrial structure of FDI firms in manufacturing by total assets (%)

Sector	1995	2008
Labour intensive	50.91	31.11
Capital intensive	21.71	31.28
Technology intensive	27.38	37.61
Total	100.00	100.00

Sources: Chen chunlai, Foreign Direct Investment in China, 2011.

With the fast economic growth, high level of capital accumulation, large improvement in human capital development and technology progress, China's comparative advantage has changed rapidly. Though China still has strong comparative advantage in labor-intensive activities owing to its huge population and abundant labor supply, China has greatly increased its comparative advantages in capital-intensive and technology-intensive activities. As a result, FDI flows into Chinese manufacturing have gradually shifted from a high level of concentration in the labor-intensive sector towards increasing investment in the capital-intensive sector and the technology-intensive sector.

By the end of 2008, as shown in Table 9.4, the investment structure of FDI firms in Chinese manufacturing has changed fundamentally. The technology-intensive sector has become the most important and largest sector receiving FDI, and the capital-intensive sector has also surpassed the labor-intensive sector receiving FDI. In terms of the total assets of FDI firms, the shares of the technology-intensive sector and the capital-intensive sector have increased to 37.61 percent and 31.28 percent respectively, while the share of the labor-intensive sector has fallen to 31.11 percent.

1.7 The Contribution of FDI to China's Economy

In the FDI literature, FDI is believed to have played some major roles in the development process of a host country's economy, via capital formation, the creation of employment opportunities, promotion of international trade, technology transfer and spillovers to the domestic economy. Over the past three decades, China has attracted a huge amount of FDI inflows, and FDI firms have made some important impacts on China's economy.

1.7.1 Capital formation

How important have FDI inflows been in China's domestic capital formation? To evaluate the contribution of FDI to China's domestic capital formation, we use the share of FDI in China's total investment in fixed assets.

As shown in Figure 10.5, the share reached the highest level of 9 percent in 1996. Since then it fell to around 3.5 percent or less after 2000. This suggests that FDI made an important contribution to China's domestic capital formation during the 1990s. However, since 2000, the role of FDI in China's domestic capital formation has been declining. Nevertheless, for a large and fast-growing economy like China—average annual GDP growth around 10 percent for the past three decades—FDI has provided an important supplementary source of finance to its domestic capital formation.

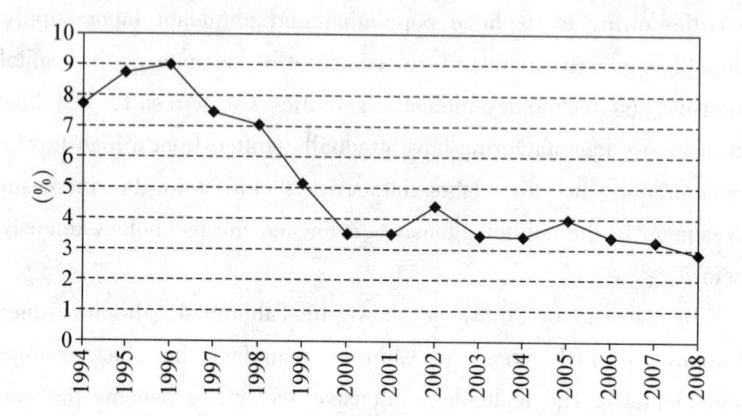

Figure 10.5 FDI inflows as a percentage of total investment in fixed assets in China, 1994—2008

Sources: Chen chunlai, Foreign Direct Investment in China, 2011.

1.7.2 Employment creation

In the developing countries, where capital is relatively scarce but labor is abundant, one of the most prominent contributions of FDI to the local economy is the creation of employment opportunities.

Figure 10.6 shows FDI firms' employment in the manufacturing sector during 1995 to 2008 and indicates that FDI firms' manufacturing employment increased significantly after 2001. While they employed 6.05 million workers or 8.9 percent of China's

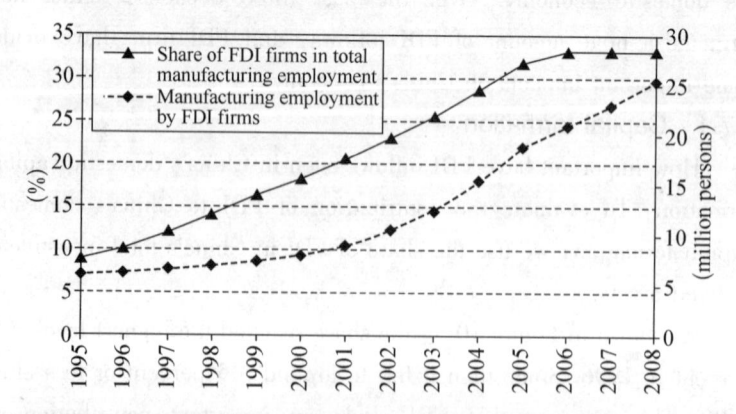

Figure 10.6 FDI firms' manufacturing employment in China, 1995—2008

Sources: Chen chunlai, Foreign Direct Investment in China, 2011.

manufacturing employment in 1995, the figures have increased to 25.45 million workers or 32.97 percent in 2008. In other words, by the end of 2008, FDI firms employed one-third of China's manufacturing labor force.

1.7.3 Export promotion

There is considerable evidence that FDI contributes to the growth of host countries' international trade. In the case of China, the most prominent contribution of FDI perhaps is expanding China's exports.

Figure 10.7 presents the export performance of FDI firms from 1980 to 2008. FDI firms' exports rose from US$0.01 billion in 1980 to US$119 billion in 2000 and to US$791 billion in 2008. As a result, the importance of FDI firms in China's exports has increased from only 0.05 percent in 1980 to 47.93 percent in 2000 and further to 58.30 percent in 2005, before falling slightly to 55.25 percent in 2008. One reason for this is that China's FDI policy has been deliberately biased towards export-oriented FDI. As a result, FDI firms have rapidly become a major exporting group.

Figure 10.7 FDI firms' export performance, 1980—2008 (current US$)

Sources: Chen chunlai, Foreign Direct Investment in China, 2011.

1.8 The Evolution of China's Opening Policies to FDI

1.8.1 Uneven Regional Opening Policies to FDI

Following the adoption of the 'open door policy' in late 1978 and the issue of the Equity Joint Venture Law in 1979, China established four SEZs, Shenzhen, Zhuhai, Xiamen and Shantou, located in Guangdong and Fujian Provinces in 1980. The creation of the four SEZs not only symbolized the beginning of China's economic reform but also constituted an integral part of the overall open door policy. However, the interesting question is why was it necessary to set up SEZs when China had decided to implement the open door policy nationwide?

First, one of the political purposes of the Chinese government to promote the SEZs lay in its strategic plans to resume sovereignty over Hong Kong, which is adjacent to Shenzhen, by 1997. It was believed that the SEZs could contribute positively to the peaceful handover of Hong Kong to China.

Second, the geographic proximity of the SEZs, which are the original home of many overseas Chinese, to Hong Kong, Macao, Taiwan and ASEAN, makes it possible for China to exploit national advantages by using the overseas Chinese business network to accumulate capital, productive technology and management skills, and to get access to the international market.

Third, at the very beginning of carrying out market-oriented economic reforms, the establishment of a small number of selected SEZs also served as a laboratory for China's overall economic reforms. The idea was to introduce the successful experience drawn from the actual practice of market-oriented economic reforms in a small number of SEZs into other areas and, meanwhile, to make it easily controlled if something went wrong by keeping the effects within bounds. In addition, from the perspective of their spatial diffusion effect, the establishment of the SEZs could be viewed as a pioneering effort for the more extensive operation of the uneven development strategy that was implemented in 1988.

Fourth, the creation of SEZs was also aimed at providing a favorable investment environment for foreign investors, while trying out preferential foreign investment policies to be implemented at a later stage in the rest of the country.

Finally, but equally important, was the reformers' strategic consideration of reducing possible political resistance from the conservatives against market-oriented economic reforms in order to carry out the overall economic reform scheme more smoothly and effectively.

Drawing on the experience of the export-processing zones established in Taiwan, South Korea, and other developing countries and economies, the SEZs in China have the multiple functions of free-trade zones and export-processing zones. The main objective of the

SEZ policy was to attract FDI by offering favorable terms and a good business climate.

As an initial experiment in the market-oriented economic reform, the SEZs were granted unique freedoms to manage and operate their economies on a market basis and were allowed to offer concessionary tax policies to foreign investors. Among the preferential policies for FDI firms in the SEZs, for example, all FDI firms were granted 15 percent reduction of income tax, and FDI firms engaged in production and scheduled to operate for a period of ten years or more were exempted from income tax in the first and second profit-making years and allowed a 50 percent reduction of income tax in the following three years.

The FDI firms were also granted exemption from income tax on the remitted share of profits, exemption from export duties and from import duties for equipment, instruments and apparatus for producing export products, and the easing of entry and exit formalities. With the establishment and implementation of a series of laws, regulations, and special open policies, especially those concerning FDI firms, the SEZs were granted the highest priority and freedom for economic development.

In addition to the concessionary tax policies for foreign investors, the four SEZs and their home provinces, Guangdong and Fujian, were also awarded financial subsidies in the form of fiscal and foreign exchange revenue contracts. Beginning in 1980, Guangdong and Fujian were awarded five-year fiscal contracts permitting them to retain almost all of the taxes and industrial profits generated by firms in their jurisdiction.

In contrast, the three provincial-level cities of Beijing, Tianjin and Shanghai were still required to turn over between 63 and 88 percent of their revenues. In terms of the special policy of foreign exchange retention, the SEZs were allowed to retain all of the hard currency they earned from trade, in contrast to the average of 25 percent allowed to other localities.

Guangdong and Fujian also were granted special foreign exchange retention rates higher than those for other provinces (Shirk, 1994). The special financial incentives for SEZs, Guangdong and Fujian provinces not only motivated local officials to develop their local economies in a profit-oriented manner, but also greatly facilitated the export expansion and overall rapid economic growth of the SEZs and Guangdong and Fujian provinces.

The economic success and the experience with FDI in the SEZs greatly increased the confidence of the Chinese government. However, owing to the small size and the specific location of the four SEZs, the desired diffusion effect was geographically limited. In addition, the pressure from other provinces in demanding the same special policies granted to SEZs increased.

In February 1984 when Deng Xiaoping visited Shenzhen, Zhuhai and Xiamen SEZs, he pointed out: "for us to establish SEZs and adopt open door policies, we must have a clear guiding ideology that is not to constrain but to release." He also said: "in addition to the existing SEZs, we can consider opening several more areas and port cities, such as Dalian and Qingdao. These areas will not be named SEZs but can apply some of the special policies implemented in SEZs." (Liu et.al., 1993).

In order to implement to Deng's speech, to prove further the government's commitment to the stability continuity and long-term nature of the open door policy, and to tap fully the comparative advantage in encouraging the inflows of FDI, advanced technology and management skills, in May 1984 the Chinese government announced the opening up and extension of the concept of SEZs to another 14 coastal cities and Hainan Island. These coastal open cities and the SEZs virtually form a coastal belt which, from a geographical viewpoint, is important not only for linkage with foreign markets but also for its wider connection with the massive domestic inland areas.

First, this coastal belt physically constitutes a significant portion of the pacific Rim, which makes it well positioned, from north to south, to attract FDI from Japan, South Korea, Taiwan and the South-East Asian countries, as well as from the USA, Canada and Europe. With their relatively more sophisticated existing labor force, technical capabilities and infrastructures, it was hoped that quicker, better and more sustainable returns in terms of capital formation, technological progress, structural transformation and overall economic development would be gained, and at lower cost (Wei, 1994).

The coastal open cities were permitted to offer tax incentives for FDI firms similar to, but less generous than, those offered in the SEZs. The coastal open cities, however, were encouraged to establish Economic and Technological Development Zones (ETDZs) that could offer terms as generous as those offered in the SEZs. The tax incentives offered to the FDI firms in the coastal open cities include mainly:

(1) 15% income tax reduction which is only to FDI firms that are technology or knowledge intensive and intend to develop energy, transportation and ports construction, to those that have an investment exceeding US$30 million with a low profit margin, or to those productive-type projects set up within the ETDZs;

(2) 20% income tax reduction that applies to those FDI firms that do not meet the foregoing requirements yet are involved in one of the categorized sectors, including machine building, electronics, metallurgy chemicals, building materials, light industry etc.

(3) Exemption from customs duties, import taxes and value-added tax with respect to production and management equipment, raw and semi-finished materials, components, spare parts and packaging materials for producing export products, and telecommunications and office equipment (Liu et al., 1993). These tax incentives plus the local government's infrastructure investments, in areas such as transport, water and electricity, telecommunications and special land use privileges, proved to be a great inducement to foreign investors.

In order to realize further the potential in attracting FDI and develop an externally oriented economy, in early 1988 another step towards expanding the open policies for FDI, termed the "coastal development strategy", was taken by the Chinese government to extend the open policy to the entire coastal areas, with a total population of over 200 million. With the implementation of the coastal development strategy, many special open zones were established in the coastal provinces and municipalities. In particular, Hainan Island became a province and China's fifth—and the largest—SEZ in April 1988, and later the concepts of SEZ and ETDZ were extended to the Shanghai Pudong New Economic and Technological Development Zone in June 1990.

The implementation of the uneven regional open strategy for FDI, from the SEZs to coastal cities and then to the entire coastal areas, has enabled the coastal region to gain more benefits than other regions, not only in the form of fiscal priority and foreign exchange earnings, but also in the acquisition of capital, technology, modern, management skills and the opportunity to access the international market. It is also true that there have been some beneficial effects on the inland economy. However, not only has the process of diffusion from the coastal region to the inland areas been slow, but also the outflow of skilled workers, technical personnel and capital from the inland areas to the coastal region has been increasing. Perhaps, more important is that the coastal region has been getting more freedom in economic decision-making from the central government than the inland regions.

Consequently, the gap in economic development and income level between the coastal region and the inland areas has enlarged since the late 1980s. To deal with these problems, in the 1990s the Chinese government gradually moved the implementation of the open policies for FDI towards a more level playing field throughout China.

1.8.2　Nationwide Implementation of Opening Policies to FDI

In the spring of 1992, during his famous tour to the southern coastal economically opened areas and SEZs, Deng Xiaoping explicitly declared his support for the successful economic development assisted by FDI and expressed a desire to see the pace of liberalization quickened. Consequently, the Chinese government reaffirmed the adherence of the open door policy and launched another massive drive to attract FDI. To facilitate the implementation of this policy, a series of measure with regard to FDI have been taken not only to address the existing unfair competition between the coastal and inland regions, but also to make more concessions to attract foreign investors.

First, the application of preferential policies to FDI will gradually shift from regional priority to accommodating national and local industrial development policies.

Second, 52 cities, including all the inland provincial capitals (except Lhasa in Tibet and Urumqi in Xinjiang) and the major cities along the Yangzi River, became open to foreign investor.

Third, more than 15 border cities and counties in the south-west, north-west, north and north-east of China were declared open border cities. Some were authorized to offer coastal FDI preferential policies, while others were mandated reopen or expand their existing border trade ties with neighboring countries or to set up Economic Development Zones (EDZs).

Fourth, some services industries, such as aviation, telecommunications, banking and retail trade, were opened to FDI participation in a limited and experimental fashion.

Fifth, to develop further foreign trade and processing industries in the Coastal areas, more duty-free zones are to be established.

Sixth, the government allows foreign business people, either those with an intention to set up FDI firms in a later stage or land developers, to buy land use rights for building infrastructure facilities, including residential, commercial, industrial and recreational real estate.

As a result, with the implementation of these new policies, during the first nine months of 1992, almost 2000 EDZs were set up, and a large proportion of them were located in inland areas.

The EDZ policy was extremely popular throughout China, since the local officials saw it not only as a way to gain access to international business but also as a means of gaining benefit and privilege. As a result, the establishment of EDZs created some unintended negative consequences, such as economic overheating, shortages of funds, energy, transport and raw materials, the appropriation of good farmland for factories, and competitive cutting of tax rates and land prices to attract of foreign investors. All of these led to the 1993 rectification of all existing EDZs and the requirement of central approval for all new EDZs in order to solve the above-mentioned problems and ensure the healthy development of FDI.

To boost economic growth and, therefore, to reduce the gap of economic development between the coastal region and the central and western regions, the Chinese government launched the "west development strategy" in 1998. According to the west development strategy, the areas include 12 provinces, municipality and autonomous regions, which are Sichuan, Chongqing, Guizhou, Yunnan, Gansu, Shanxi, Qinghai, Ningxia, Xinjiang, Tibet, Guangxi and Inner Mongolia, and two prefectures, which are Enshi of Hubei Province and Xiangxi of Hunan Province.

The west development strategy emphasizes infrastructure development, environmental protection, industrial structural readjustment, development of sciences and education, and economic reform and openness. To realize these goals, four concrete measures are to be implemented. First, the central government will dramatically increase investment in the central and western regions, especially to increase transfer payment from central government budget. Second, the central and western regions will increase the degree of openness and implement more open policies, especially open more areas and sectors to FDI.

Third, enterprises, especially FDI firms, in the coastal region are encouraged to invest and to do business in the central and western regions. Fourth, the central and western regions will enhance the development of sciences and education in order to attract and to improve human resources.

Undoubtedly, the west development strategy and the further opening up of the central and western regions not only provide great opportunities for foreign investors, but also will accelerate economic growth in the central and western regions.

Increasing Openness to FDI after WTO Accession. In December 2001, after 15 years of extensive negotiations, China entered the WTO. China's accession to the WTO is widely regarded as a major milestone in the development of the Chinese economy as well as the multilateral trading system. China made extensive commitments to the WTO to bring its economy into harmony with the rules of the WTO. In goods, China must progressively lower its tariffs and phase out non-tariff measures. China's simple average tariff rate dropped from 42.9% in 1992 to 15.3% at the beginning of 2002, and further reduced to 9.8% in 2010. In services, China made substantial commitments to the WTO to reduce restrictions on trade in services.

Among the WTO members, China made the most commitments in terms of the number of service sectors open to international trade and FDI. However, China is taking a step-by-step approach to implement its commitments. In most of the service sectors, especially in telecommunications, banking and insurance, wholesale and retail, storage and transportation, China will fulfill its commitments in three to five years after China's accession to the WTO. In FDI, China committed to comprehensively implement the Agreement on Trade Related Investment Measures (TRIMs) after entering into the WTO.

2 OFDI in China

2.1 Introduction

OFDI flows have steadily increased. Since 1979, a first peak was reached just after Deng Xiaoping revived the economic liberalization and reform process in 1992 and annual outflows jumped to USD 4.4bn (see Figure 10.8). Outflow levels remained on a relatively high level for an emerging economy and reached another peak of nearly USD 12bn in 2005 before significantly increasing to about USD 40bn and USD 43bn in 2008 and 2009, respectively.

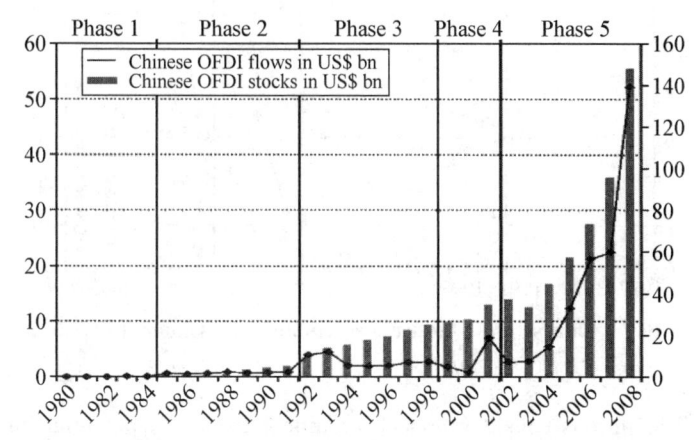

Figure 10.8 Chinese OFDI stocks and flows (1980 to 2008)
Source: UNCTAD (2010a).

To date, China has become one of the most important developing source countries for FDI in terms of absolute flow and stock figures (UNCTAD 2010a). UNCTAD reports that China's OFDI stock has been valued at nearly USD 150bn by the end of 2008. This places China behind economically more advanced East Asian countries like Hong Kong (special administrative region, SAR), Singapore and Taiwan but ahead of emerging countries from South American, West Asian and European transition economies such as Finland, the Republic of Korea, or Malaysia.

Although Chinese OFDI flows and stocks are generally relatively low compared to the USA or the UK, the development since the end of the 1970s nevertheless marks a significant departure from the former hostile business environment towards capitalistic forces.

The rise of China's OFDI stock is also evident in other areas. Chinese firms are increasingly active in acquiring international firms. Not only has the number and total value of the acquisitions risen, as Figure 10.9 illustrates, but also the proliferation of the target companies. Well-publicized purchases include the takeover of IBM's PC business (USA) by Lenovo in 2005, Nanjing Automobile's successful bidding competition with its domestic rival Shanghai Automotive Industry Corporation (SAIC) for MG Rover (UK) in 2004/05, or Geely's purchase of Sweden-based Volvo from Ford in 2010 (FT, 2005a, 2010).

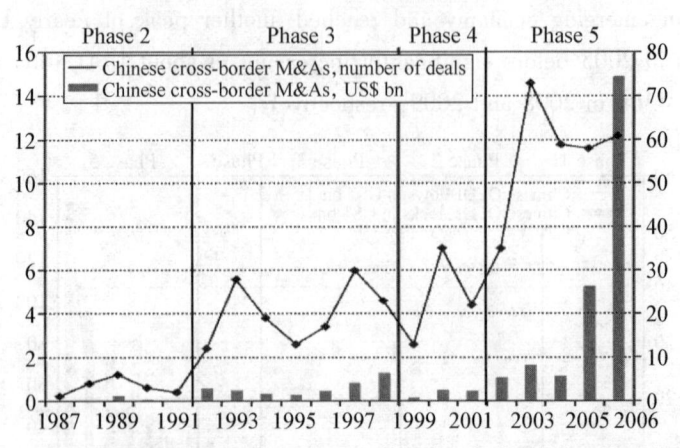

Figure 10.9   Chinese cross-border mergers and acquisitions (1987 to 2006)
Source: UNCTAD (2010a).

The serious consideration of a Chinese firm as a potential buyer of a leading automobile manufacturer exemplifies the perceived change in the quality and potential of China's OFDI. What this example however fails to identify or to explain are the drivers behind China's outbound surge.

It also raises the question of why Chinese firms are deemed capable of acquiring and managing a large Western multinational enterprise (MNE) when their firm-specific advantages and managerial capabilities are generally questioned.

The objectives of the research are to identify (i) the determinants of Chinese OFDI, (ii) the international strategies of Chinese firms and how these are influenced by (iii) domestic institutions and (iv) access to international networks.

The answers to these questions may help to find explanations for the observable phenomena and rumors around, for example, the acquisition of Chrysler. In so doing, theories on FDI and on MNE investment behavior which were developed from research focusing on industrialized country MNEs are tested for their applicability to a developing country context like the Chinese.

A positive finding is generally expected (UNCTAD 2006). Thus, first, a thorough analysis of the international investment strategies of the Chinese will shed some light on the determinants of Chinese OFDI and the drivers behind international acquisitions and the potentially rising investment in South East Asia and Africa. Work by Deng (2003), Wong and Chan (2003) and others has provided a first assessment of Chinese outbound investments. Investment in Africa occurs rather to access natural resources while access to technology is the driver for investments in industrialized countries, for example.

Second, companies are said to experience a sequence of stages in their internationalization during which they increase their commitment and psychic distance to the home market. This may not hold true for Chinese firms. Official Chinese statistics demonstrate that early Chinese OFDI was destined to psychic distant countries in North America and Oceania. Recently this pattern has changed and Hong Kong has become the main destination for Chinese investments. It may therefore be that Chinese firms rather follow a pattern identified for international new venture. Such firms invest in locations where there is a good business opportunity readily available (Oviatt and McDougall, 1994).

Third, to account for China's heritage of economic planning, which is still visible in the government's involvement today (Scott, 2002), and the continuous changes in the institutional environment since 1979, a special emphasis is placed on institutional theory. In this respect, Chinese OFDI is generally argued to have evolved in phases as is illustrated in the Figures 10.1(Ye, 1992; Wu and Chen, 2001; Wong and Chan, 2003). Each phase is defined by changes in the nature of Chinese OFDI mainly caused by advancements in the institutional environment and the administration and regulation concerning outbound investments. This comprises changes in the outward investment approval regime and the capability to pursue international business, among others. Capability in the Chinese context may not necessarily mean managerial capacity and technological advancement over competitors, but access to financial resources.

The possibility to internalize access to abundant funding may help Chinese firms to overcome competitive weaknesses and invest abroad to pursue objective other than purely profit-maximizing objectives. This is not to say that Chinese firms are not profit-maximizers. But there exists the likelihood that they invest in one country to gain access to resources which will then be exploited in a third country. The institutional realm is also of importance from another perspective. Not all Chinese firms were allowed at all times to pursue investments abroad. Liberalization of this policy and the consequential upcoming of a different breed of firms may change the nature of the determinants of Chinese OFDI. The impact of the changes is probably best illustrated in Figure 10.2. It shows major ups and downs in the annual value of cross-border acquisitions by Chinese firms at the brink of each phase. This hints that the domestic institutional environment may affect the international investment strategies of the Chinese. Taking better account of institutions therefore seems reasonable and could help to explain the steady growth and the very positive prospect of Chinese OFDI evidenced in the official Chinese data.

Fourth, a further not fully accounted element is the influence of Overseas Chinese on the investment decision-making. A large body of research has identified that Overseas Chinese played a very important role in re-integrating China into the world economy (Gao, 2003; Naughton, 2007) and that the Chinese government actively tries to retain strong linkages with Overseas Chinese whom have generally a strong affinity towards their ancestors home region (Liu, 2001). It therefore seems impertinent to include the extent to which the presence of Overseas Chinese in a host country takes a bridging role to the host market.

2.2 Phases of Chinese OFDI

Since 1979 and the implementation of China's "Open Door" policy, Chinese OFDI has increased steadily, especially after 2000. Chinese OFDI is generally argued to have developed in five distinctive phases. The classification follows changes in the geographical scope and adjustments in China's political and regulatory environment towards OFDI, namely the outward approval process. The key regulations issued during each of the five phases concerning OFDI are listed for each period. The five phases embrace the years 1979—1985, 1986—19991, 1992—1998, 1999—2001, and 2002 onwards.

2.2.1 "Open Door" Policy (1979—1985)

The introduction of the "Open Door" policy was an instrument for the Chinese government to create an institutional environment to attract foreign MNEs to China and to encourage Chinese companies to expand internationally.

The number of overseas subsidiaries established by trading companies prior to 1979 increased rapidly with the instigation of the 'Open Door' policy. By 1983 more than 100 foreign affiliates in mainly industrialized countries and a wide range of sectors were established. International joint ventures were, for example, established in the service sector such as banking and technical consultancy, and in trade-related activities (for example, manufacturing and resource development).

A successful early investor was **CITIC**. CITIC was established by the state Council in 1979 with the explicit goal to invest and diversify internationally. Sinotrans, the Chinese logistics company, established a subsidiary in the USA in 1980 and China National Metals and Minerals Import and Export Corp., the specialized trading company, opened offices in Hong Kong and the United Kingdom. By the end of 1985, China's OFDI stock had increased from USD 44mn in 1982 to around USD 900mn (UNCTAD, 2010a) (Table 10.6).

中信集团

Table 10.6 Geographical distribution of Chinese OFDI: accumulated stock (1979—2005)
(Period average stock in USD billion and % of period average)

	Phase 1 and 2 1979—92[a]	Phase 3 1992—98	Phase 4 1999—01	Phase 5 2002—05[b]
World (USD bn)	**1.21 bn**	**1.99 bn**	**3.78 bn**	**14.50 bn**
Develped economies	70%	59%	37%	23%
Europe	3%	3%	2%	5%
North America	41%	37%	24%	13%
Asia/Oceania	27%	20%	10%	6%
Developing economies	27%	35%	57%	71%
Other America	5%	7%	14%	9%
Asia/Oceania	18%	21%	26%	54%
Africa	4%	7%	16%	8%
Economies in tranition	3%	5%	5%	6%

Notes:
(a) The MOFCOM publication reports Chinese OFDI from onwards only. The figures in this column refer to the Phases 1 and 2 by inference as they represent accumulated figures.
(b) The latest available data are for the year 2005.
Sources: MOFCOM (varions years) *Almanac of China's Foreign Economic Relation and Trade* and MOFCOM (varions years) *China Conomic Yearbook*.

2.2.2 Government Encourages (1986—1991)

With the issuance of OFDI regulations by the MOFCOM in 1985, restrictive policies on OFDI eased in phase 2. Companies still had to undergo the administrative approval process, including the evaluation of sufficient financial and managerial capacity and evaluation of the foreign joint venture partner. Advancements in the technological and managerial standards of Chinese enterprises promoted the outward investment drive of the Chinese firms and of Chinese authorities at all levels. At the same time, international activities in more mature industries were encouraged by the Chinese government with the aim of profit maximization.

In 1989, **SAFE and MOFCOM** issued refined regulations on OFDI and increased the transparency of the documentations needed during the OFDI approval process. SAFE and MOFCOM also issued in 1989 the first regulation on the usage of foreign exchange earnings. In 1991, the **NDRC** issued circulars to strengthen the administration of outward investment projects and on the drafting and approval of project proposals and feasibility studies.

Following these policy changes, Chinese international investment projects rose from 185 during the first phase to 801 by the end of 1990 and 904 by the end of 1992 (table 10.2). A contributory factor to the increase could have been the opening of the approval process to SOEs other than the trading companies and to privately owned enterprises. The explicit inclusion of privately-owned firms in the MOFCOM directive is questionable. Private firms were for the first time domestically recognized as supplementing entities to SOEs in 1982.

2.2.3 Deng Xiaoping's Journey to the South (1992—1998)

In early 1992, Deng travelled to Southern China in an effort to express his support to economic reforms and openings. In response to this liberalization momentum, China's OFDI officially became part of the national economic development plan, local and provincial government authorities increasingly engaged in overseas businesses and allowed companies under their supervision to establish subsidiaries.

In light of the Asian crisis, MOFCOM again tightened the OFDI approval procedure and the screening and monitoring of outward investments. This policy was supported by SAFE and its local offices in 1998 which stopped approving foreign exchange for OFDI projects.

The investment project pattern of phase 3 is very similar to phase 2. Developing and transitional countries dominated with a share of 67 percent. The increase by 6 percentage points was caused by proportionally more investments in the transitional economies.

2.2.4　Pre-WTO Accession Adjustments and the 'Go Global' Policy (1999—2001)

During the years 1999 to 2001 of Chinese OFDI, the spatial distribution started to shift. The developing countries recorded, on average, a 22 percentage point larger FDI stock from China per year. This growth took place in Africa (+9 percentage points), Latin America and the Caribbean (+7), and South, East and Southeast Asia (+5). Accordingly, Chinese OFDI in developed countries declined relatively. Most significant were the drops in share for North America (-13 percentage points) and Asia/Oceania (-10). Considering that these figures reflect the stock of China's outward foreign direct investment, the actual flows to developing countries had been significantly higher than to developed countries over this period.

The distribution of investment projects supports this spatial shift. The investment numbers in developing and transitional countries rose by 5 percentage points to a share of 72 percent of total Chinese OFDI projects. In particular, the number of projects in Africa rose along with the investment value. By the end of 2001, Chinese companies had invested in 149 countries.

2.2.5　Accession to WTO and 'Go Global' Implementation

Since China's accession to the WTO in 2001, the business environment for Chinese enterprises has changed dramatically. WTO accession necessitates the gradual opening of once locally protected markets to comply with the accession protocol and the WTO's 'most favored nations' rule. Domestic enterprises in these markets and regions thus face successively increasing competition with Chinese and foreign-invested enterprises as well as with foreign exporters. The growing domestic competition forces Chinese companies, especially privately owned and smaller firms with little political support and protection, to consider new sustainable and profitable markets, both in China and abroad. This may stimulate Chinese OFDI flows.

Against this backdrop and in line with the 'go global' policy, the Chinese government has undertaken several initiatives to facilitate Chinese OFDI. First, the investment approval process has been decentralized to sub-national government authorities. Only investment in seven selected countries requires approval at national level (the relevant countries are not mentioned in any reference referring to this policy). Second, the government has simplified and abolished the feasibility study but emphasized market forces and the managerial capabilities of the investing enterprise instead. Third, control on international capital movement will be eased which should promote Chinese OFDI. Finally, enterprises are no longer required to deposit security at SAFE and are allowed to raise money on international finance markets.

In a recent statement to existing regulations on the OFDI approval process MOFCOM (2005) stated that Chinese firms are guided via the approval process to invest in a feasible project in an economically and politically stable host country which has concluded bilateral treaties with China on investment and taxation. The investment should also carry benefits for the firm and the domestic economy by: (1) promoting China's exports of goods and services; (2) enhancing the firm's technological capacity and R&D activities; (3) enabling the firm to create and establish an international brand. It has also been indicated that the formal approval process will evolve further over time into a pure registration and monitoring process, easing overseas investment further. These steps, from a system of micro to macro control mechanisms, have, *de jure*, significantly eased the internationalization of Chinese firms via OFDI.

2.3 The latest development of Chinese OFDI

Since authorities in China released the annual data in 2003, the average annual growth rate reached 31.2% between 2002 and 2017. In the past five years (2013—2017), China's outward FDI totaled $731.07 billion, accounting for 40.4% of the total foreign direct investment stock.

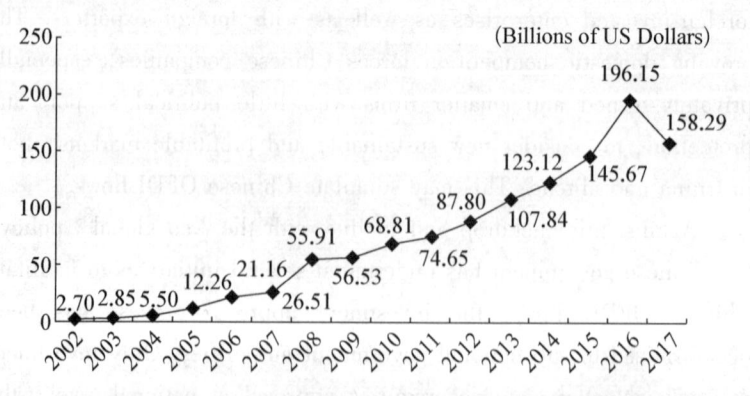

Figure 10.10 Outward FDI flows of China, 2002—2017

Sources: 2017 Statistical Bulletin of China's Outward Foreign Direct Investment.

Chapter 10　International Direct Investment in China

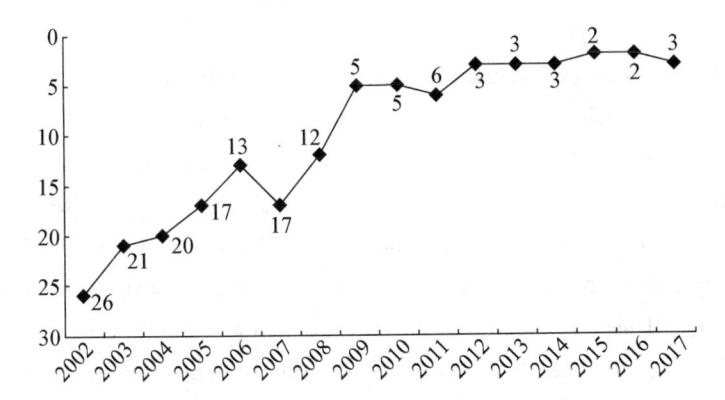

Figure 10.11　Rankings of China's OFDI in the World, 2002—2017

Sources: 2017 Statistical Bulletin of China's Outward Foreign Direct Investment.

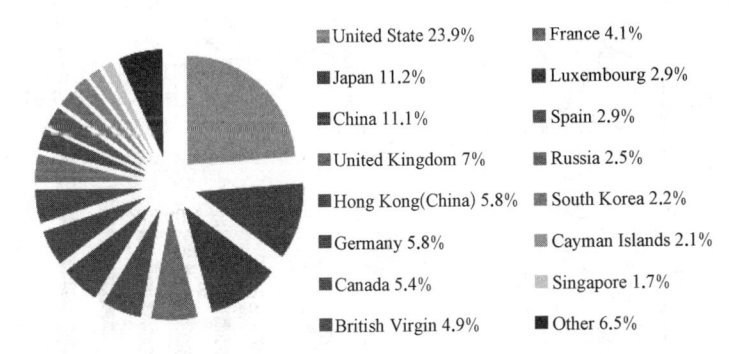

Figure 10.12　Share of FDI Flows from Major Global Economies

Sources: Data from other countries and regions are from UNCTAD's 2018 World Investment Report.

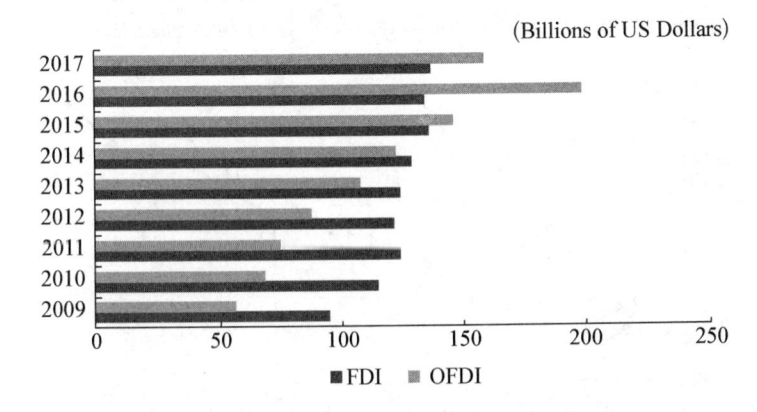

Figure 10.13　OFDI and FDI Comparison in China, 2009—2017

Sources: Data from other countries and regions are from UNCTAD's 2018 World Investment Report.

2.3.1 Characteristics of China's Outward FDI Stock by the End of 2017

2.3.1.1 The global ranking and share of China's outward FDI stock

By the end of 2017, China's outward FDI stock had reached $1809.04 billion, increased by $451.65 billion compared with the previous year and was 60.5 times the stock by the end of 2002. It accounted for 5.9% of the global stock, increased from 0.4% in 2002. It ranked second globally, only second to the United State ($7.8 trillion), up from 25th in 2002. In terms of scale, the stock from China by the end of 2017 were only equivalent to 23.2% of the United States and closer to the others in top six: Hong Kong, Germany, the Netherlands, and the United Kingdom.

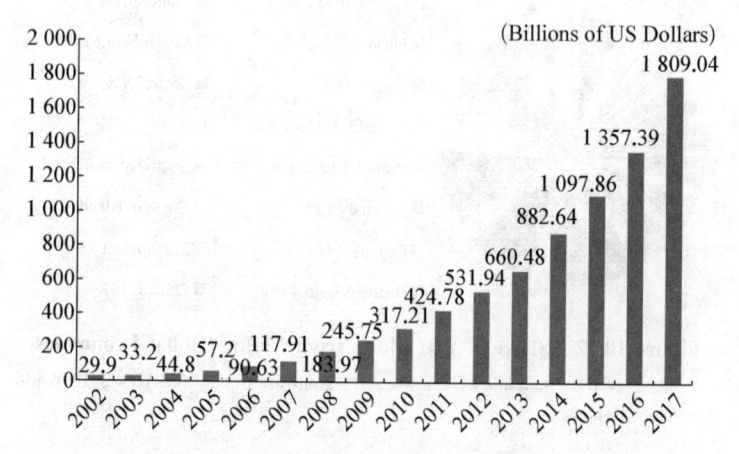

Figure 10.14　China's Outward FDI Stock, 2002—2017
Sources: 2017 Statistical Bulletin of China's Outward Foreign Direct Investment.

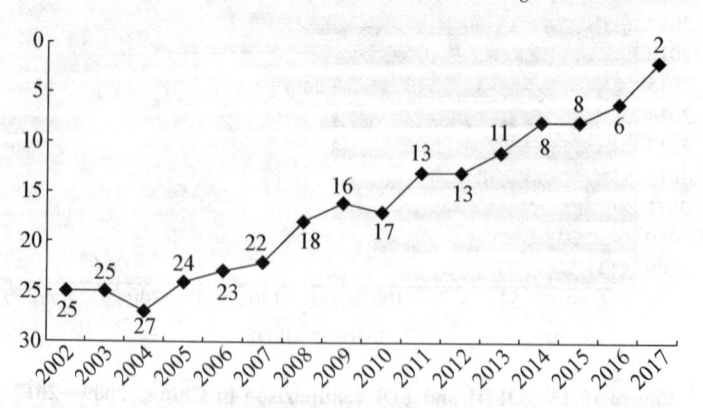

Figure 10.15　Global Ranking of China's Outward FDI Stock, 2002—2017
Sources: 2017 Statistical Bulletin of China's Outward Foreign Direct Investment.

Table 10.7 Top Ten Countries (Regions) as Sources of Global Outward FDI Stock, by the end of 2017 (Billions of US Dollars)

Ranking	Country (Region)	Stock by the End of 2017	Share in Global Total(%)
1	United States	7,799.0	25.3
2	China	1,809.0	5.9
3	Hong Kong	1.804.2	5.9
4	Germany	1,607.4	5.2
5	Netherlands	1,604.9	5.2
6	United Kingdom	1,531.7	5.0
7	Japan	1,520.0	4.9
8	Canada	1.487.1	4.8
9	France	1,451.7	4.7
10	Swirzerlan	1,271.8	4.1
	Total	21,886.7	71.0

Sources: Data on China's outward FDI in 2017 is based on Statistical Bulletin of China's Outward Foreign Direct Investment, and data on other countries (regions) is based on World Investment Report 2018 by UNCTAD

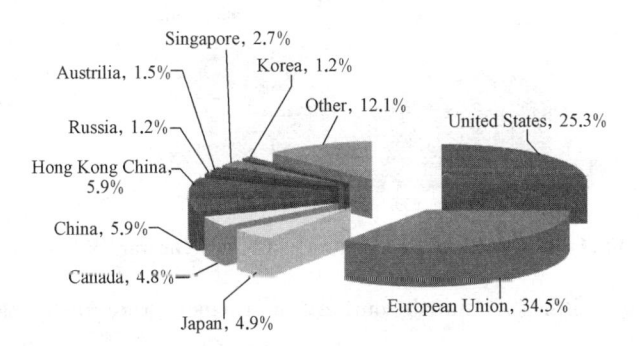

Figure 10.16 Proportions of OFDI Stock of Global Major Economies, by the end of 2017

2.3.2.2 Country (region) distribution

By the end of 2017, China's outward FDI had spread across 189 countries (regions), accounting for 80.8% of the total number of countries (regions) in the world. Compared with the previous year, investment to Belize was cancelled in 2017. By the end of 2017, China's outward FDI stock in Asia had reached $1,139.32 billion, accounting for 63% of the total. The stock were mainly concentrated in Hong Kong China, Singapore, Indonesia, Macau China, etc. In particular, Hong Kong China accounted for 86.1% of China's outward FDI in Asia. China's outward FDI stock in Latin America reached $386.89 billion, accounting for 21.4% of the total.

The stock were mainly concentrated in the Cayman Islands, British Virgin Islands, etc. In particular, China's accumulated outward FDI stock in the Cayman Islands and the British Virgin Islands amounted to $371.74 billion, accounting for 96.1% of the stocks in Latin America. China's outward FDI stock in Europe reached $110.86 billion, accounting for 6.1% of the total. The stocks were mainly concentrated in the UK, the Netherlands, etc. China's outward FDI stock in North America reached $86.91 billion, accounting for 4.8% of the total, the stock were mainly concentrated in the United States and Canada. China's outward FDI stock in Africa reached $43.3 billion, accounting for 2.4% of the total. The stock were mainly concentrated in South Africa, Congo (Kinshasa), etc. China's outward FDI stock in Oceania reached $41.76 billion, accounting for 2.3% of the total. The stock were mainly concentrated in Australia, New Zealand, etc.

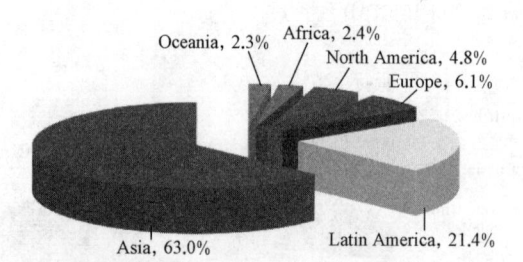

Figure 10.17　Geographical Distribution of China's Outward FDI stock, 2017

Four fifths of China's outward FDI stock were distributed in developing economies. By the end of 2017, China's outward FDI stock in developing economies had reached $1,552.42 billion, accounting for 85.8% of the total. In particular, the stock in Hong Kong China reached $981.27 billion, accounting for 63.2% of the total stock among developing economies and the stocks in ASEAN countries reached $89.01 billion, accounting for 5.7% of the total. The stock in developed economies reached $229.13 billion, accounting for 12.7% of the total. In particular, the European Union received $86.02 billion, accounting for 37.5% of the total investment stock in developed economies. The United States received $67.38 billion, accounting for 29.4% of the total.

Table 10.8 China's Outward FDI Stock in Developed Countries (Regions), by the end of 2017

Economy	Stock (Billions of US Dollars)	Share(%)
European Union	86.02	37.5
United States	67.38	29.4
Australia	36.18	15.8
Canada	10.94	4.8
Bermuda	8.59	3.8
Switzerland	8.11	3.5
Israel	4.15	1.8
Japan	3.20	1.4
New Zealand	2.49	1.1
Norway	2.08	0.9
Total	229.13	100.0

By the end of 2017, China's outward FDI stock in transition economies had reached $27.49 billion, accounting for 1.5% of the total stock. In particular, Russia received $13.87 billion, accounting for 50.5% of the total stock in the transition economies.

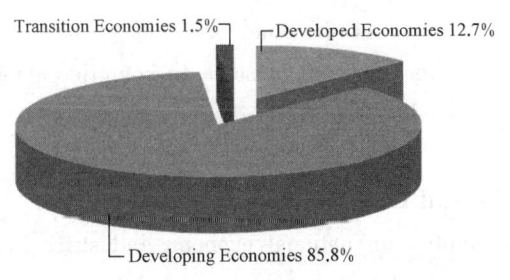

Figure 10.18 Structure of China's Outward FDI Stock in Economies, by the end of 2017

Table 10.9 Top 20 Countries (Regions) as Destinations of China's Outward FDI Stock, by the End of 2017

No.	Country (Region)	Stock (Billions of US Dollars)	Share (%)
1	Hong Kong China	981.27	54.2
2	Cayman Islands	249.68	13.8
3	British Virgin Islands	122.06	6.7
4	United States	67.38	3.7
5	Singapore	44.57	2.5
6	Australia	36.18	2.0
7	United Kingdom	20.32	1.1

continued

No.	Country (Region)	Stock (Billions of US Dollars)	Share (%)
8	Netherlands	18.53	1.0
9	Luxembourg	13.94	0.8
10	Russia	13.87	0.8
11	Germany	12.16	0.7
12	Canada	10.94	0.6
13	Indonesia*	10.54	0.6
14	Macao China	9.68	0.5
15	Bermuda	8.59	0.5
16	Switzerland	8.11	0.5
17	Kazakhstan	7.56	0.4
18	South Africa	7.47	0.4
19	Sweden	7.31	0.4
20	Laos	6.65	0.4
	Total	**1,656.80**	**91.6**

By the end of 2017, China's outward FDI stock in top 20 countries (regions) as destinations had accumulated to $1,656.80 billion, accounting for 91.6% of the total stock of China's outward FDI. China's outward direct investment stock in countries along "the Belt and Road" had reached $154.40 billion, accounting for 8.5% of the total.

2.3.2.3 Industrial Distribution

(1) Distribution in national economy industries by the end of 2017, China's outward FDI stock had spread in all industries of the national economy. In particular, six industries received over a hundred of billion dollars, with information transmission, software and IT services sector being newly added compared to the end of previous year. The Leasing and Business Services sector remained the highest and received $615.77 billion, accounting for 34.1% of the total stock, including foreign investment activities with investment control as its main purpose.

In particular, the stock of the equipment manufacturing reached $64.29 billion, accounting for 45.8% of the total stock in the manufacturing sector. The investment to the manufacture of automobiles, the manufacture of computer, telecommunications and other electronic equipment, and the manufacture of chemical raw material and chemical products have each reached over $10 billion. The stock in six sectors above amount to total $1561.86 billion, accounting for 86.3% of the total.

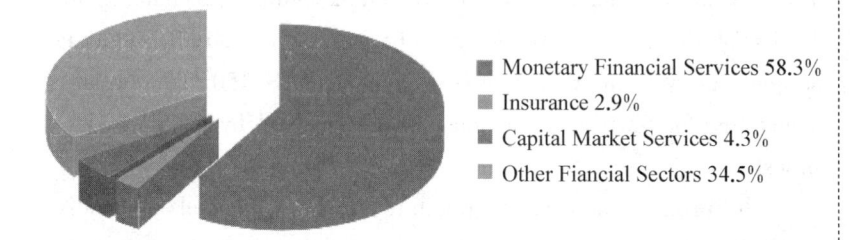

- Monetary Financial Services 58.3%
- Insurance 2.9%
- Capital Market Services 4.3%
- Other Fiancial Sectors 34.5%

Figure 10.19 Structure of China's Outward FDI Stock in the Financial Sector, by the end of 2017

(Billions of US Dollars)

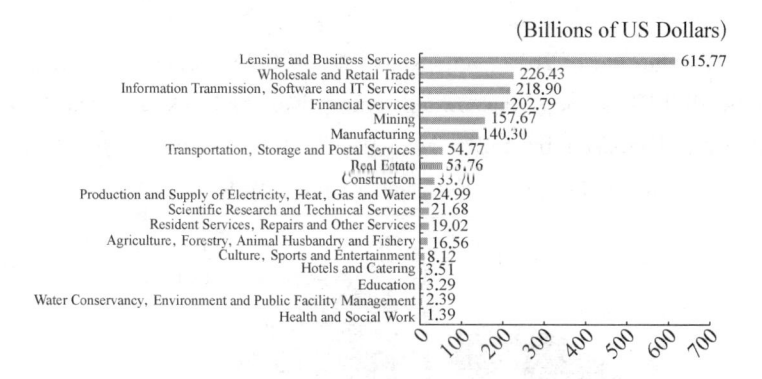

Leasing and Business Services	615.77
Wholesale and Retail Trade	226.43
Information Tranmission, Software and IT Services	218.90
Financial Services	202.79
Mining	157.67
Manufacturing	140.30
Transportation, Storage and Postal Services	54.77
Real Estate	53.76
Construction	33.70
Production and Supply of Electricity, Heat, Gas and Water	24.99
Scientific Research and Techinical Services	21.68
Resident Services, Repairs and Other Services	19.02
Agriculture, Forestry, Animal Husbandry and Fishery	16.56
Culture, Sports and Entertainment	8.12
Hotels and Catering	3.51
Education	3.29
Water Conservancy, Environment and Public Facility Management	2.39
Health and Social Work	1.39

Figure 10.20 Industrial Distribution of China's Outward FDI Stock, by the End of 2017

Locational distributions of industries show that the industries that received China's direct investment in each region were highly concentrated.

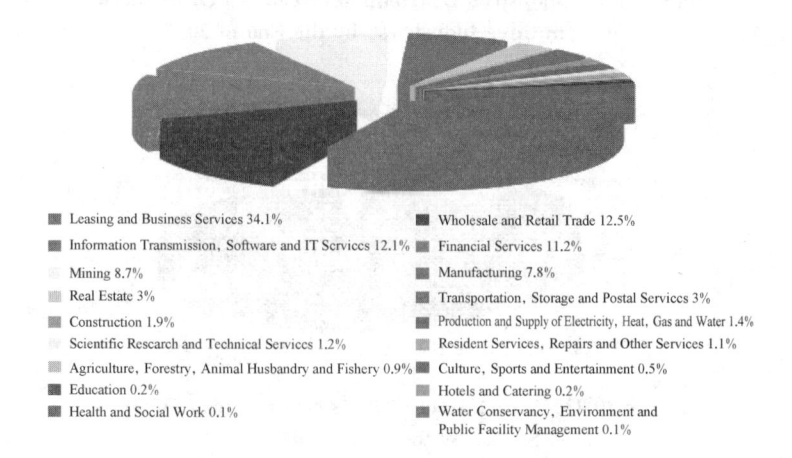

- Leasing and Business Services 34.1%
- Wholesale and Retail Trade 12.5%
- Information Transmission, Software and IT Services 12.1%
- Financial Services 11.2%
- Mining 8.7%
- Manufacturing 7.8%
- Real Estate 3%
- Transportation, Storage and Postal Services 3%
- Construction 1.9%
- Production and Supply of Electricity, Gas and Water 1.4%
- Scientific Research and Technical Services 1.2%
- Resident Services, Repairs and Other Services 1.1%
- Agriculture, Forestry, Animal Husbandry and Fishery 0.9%
- Culture, Sports and Entertainment 0.5%
- Education 0.2%
- Hotels and Catering 0.2%
- Health and Social Work 0.1%
- Water Conservancy, Environment and Public Facility Management 0.1%

Figure 10.21 Industry Distribution of China's Outward FDI Stock, by the End of 2017

(2) Distribution in three industries by the end of 2017, 79.8% of China's outward direct investment had been received by the tertiary industry (i.e. service industry), amounting to $1,443.93 billion. The secondary industry received $353.32 billion, accounting for 19.5% of the total. In particular, the mining industry (excluding supplementary mining activities) received $150.57 billion, accounting for 42.6% of the total stocks received by the secondary industry.

The primary industry (agriculture, forestry, animal husbandry and fishery but excluding related service activities) received $11.79 billion, accounting for 0.7% of the total outward FDI stock of China.

2.3.2.4 Distribution by domestic investor's business registration type

By the end of 2017, among the $1,606.25 billion non-financial outward FDI stock, state-owned enterprises had taken a share of 49.1%, decreased by 5.2% compared with the previous year, and that of the non-state enterprises had reached 50.9%.

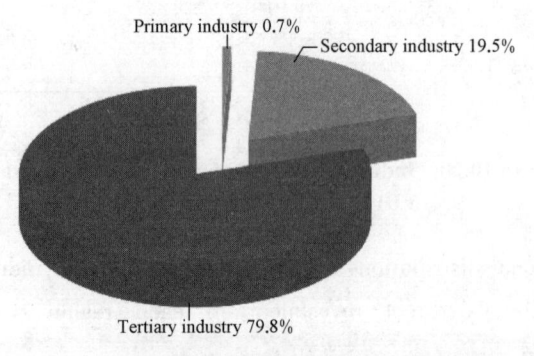

Figure 10.22 Industrial Distribution of China's OFDI Stock in three Industries, by the End of 2017

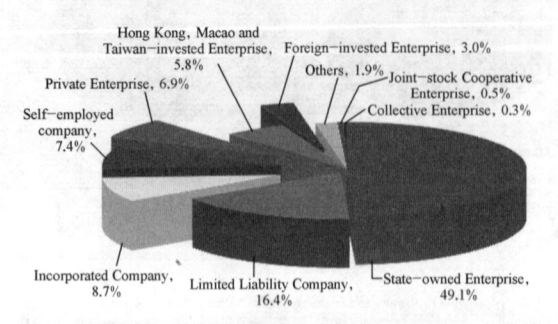

Figure 10.23 Structure of China's Non-financial OFDI Stock, by the End of 2017

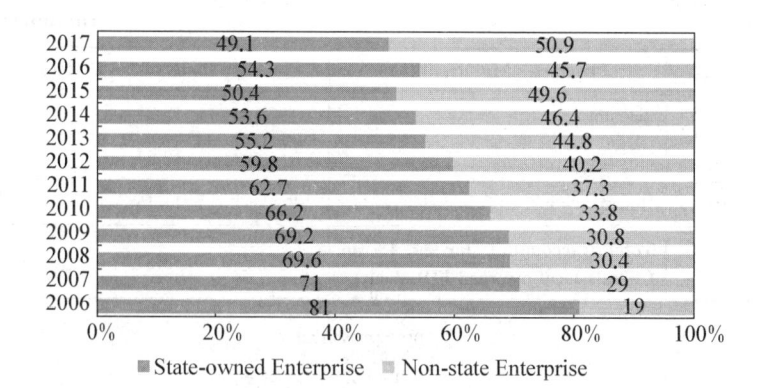

Year	State-owned Enterprise	Non-state Enterprise
2017	49.1	50.9
2016	54.3	45.7
2015	50.4	49.6
2014	53.6	46.4
2013	55.2	44.8
2012	59.8	40.2
2011	62.7	37.3
2010	66.2	33.8
2009	69.2	30.8
2008	69.6	30.4
2007	71	29
2006	81	19

Figure 10.24 Proportions of State-owned Enterprises and Non-state Enterprises in China's Outward FDI Stock, 2006—2017

2.3.2.5 Provincial distribution

By the end of 2017, non-financial outward FDI stock by local enterprises had reached $727.46 billion, accounting for 45.3% of China's total non-financial outward FDI stock, increased by 0.9% compared with the previous year. In particular, $611.52 billion came from eastern China, accounting for 84.1% of the total. $53.08 billion came from western China, accounting for 7.3% of the total. $41.55 billion came from central China, accounting for 5.7% of the total. $21.31 billion came from three provinces in northeastern China, accounting for 2.9% of the total. Guangdong was the largest province as the source of outward FDI stock with $189.71 billion, followed by Shanghai with 112 billion. Among the five cities separately listed on the state plan, Shenzhen ranked first with $140.47 billion, accounting for 74% of Guangdong's outward FDI stock. Qingdao ranked second with $13.09 billion, accounting for 27.4% of Shandong's stock.

Table 10.11 Top Ten Provinces as Sources of China's OFDI stock, by the End of 2017

No.	Province (Municipality)	Stock (Billions of US Dollars)
1	Guangdong	189.71
2	Shanghai	112.00
3	Zhejiang	98.39
4	Beijing	64.84
5	Shandong	47.79
6	Jiangsu	40.32
7	Tianjin	23.54

continued

No.	Province (Municipality)	Stock (Billions of US Dollars)
8	Liaoning	13.25
9	Fujian	12.67
10	Hunan	11.16
	Total (accounting for 84.4% of China's local outward FDI stock)	613.67

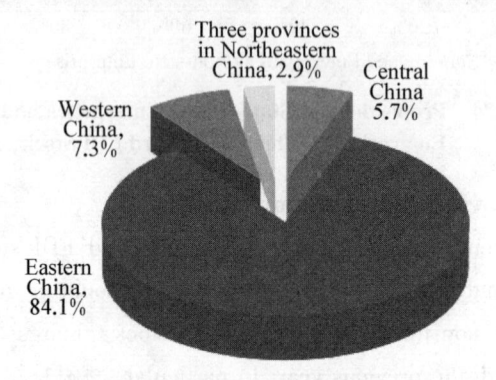

Fig. 10.25 Regional Weightings of China's OFDI Stock by Local Enterprises, by the End of 2017

2.3.2 China's Outward FDI to Major Economies in the World

In 2017, outward FDI flows from Mainland China to major economies in the world were illustrated in table 10.12.

Table 10.12 China's OFDI to Major Economies in the World, 2017 (Billions of US Dollars)

Economy	Flows Amount	Year-on-Year Growth Rate (%)	Share(%)	Stock Amount	Share(%)
Hong Kong China	91.153	−20.2	57.6	981.266	54.2
ASEAN	14.119	37.4	8.9	89.014	4.9
European Union	10.267	2.7	6.5	86.015	4.8
United States	6.425	−62.2	4.0	67.381	3.7
Australia	4.242	1.3	2.7	36.175	2.0
Russia	1.548	19.7	1.0	13.872	0.8
Total	127.754	−18.6	80.7	1,273.723	70.4

2.3.3 Structure of China's Outward Foreign Direct Investors

By the end of 2017, the structure of China's OFDI were shown in figure 10.26 and figure 10.27.

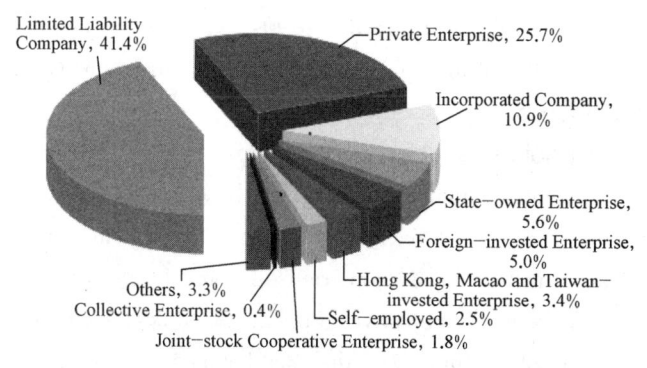

Figure 10.26 Structure of Domestic Investors, by Registration Type, by the End of 2017

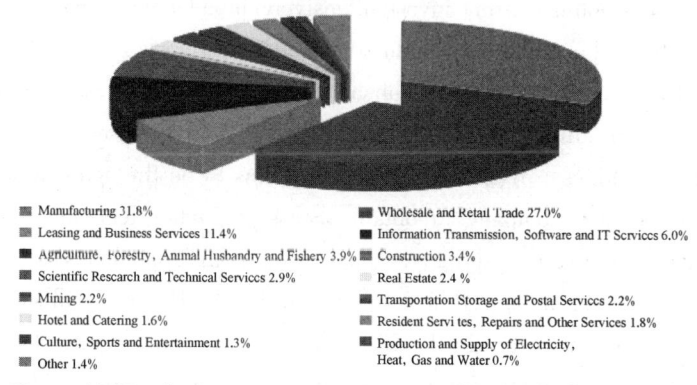

- Manufacturing 31.8%
- Leasing and Business Services 11.4%
- Agriculture, Forestry, Animal Husbandry and Fishery 3.9%
- Scientific Research and Technical Services 2.9%
- Mining 2.2%
- Hotel and Catering 1.6%
- Culture, Sports and Entertainment 1.3%
- Other 1.4%
- Wholesale and Retail Trade 27.0%
- Information Transmission, Software and IT Services 6.0%
- Construction 3.4%
- Real Estate 2.4%
- Transportation Storage and Postal Services 2.2%
- Resident Services, Repairs and Other Services 1.8%
- Production and Supply of Electricity, Heat, Gas and Water 0.7%

Figure 10.27 Structure of Domestic Investors, by the End of 2017

2.4 International Investment Strategy of China's OFDI

2.4.1 Market-seeking

Chinese companies have invested internationally in order to access and develop new markets as domestic markets have become increasingly competitive and saturated, especially after 2000. The international diversification of business interests by Chinese firms is supported by the Chinese government to spur their growth and competitiveness. One reason is the on-going economic integration of China into the world economy and heightened domestic competition following China's World Trade Organization accession in 2001.

Moreover, the domestic growth of Chinese firms is constrained by an insufficient distribution and logistics network, market saturation and regional market protection in some industry sectors. Market-seeking investment behavior has also seen Chinese firms re-orientate their FDI strategy towards developing countries in Asia and Africa. The Chinese investments in these countries are argued to be small-scale and food companies by China Metallurgical Import and Export

Corporation and CITIC during the 1990s, and by the acquisition of Canada-based PetroKaz by China National Petroleum Corporation (CNPC) in 2005.

2.4.2 Technology-seeking FDI

International technology-seeking FDI by Chinese MNEs is argued to be unique in some respect. Such an investment type occurs predominantly in advanced industrialized countries, such as Europe and the USA, with the objective to obtain technologies either through the acquisition of a company or the establishment of a subsidiary in a cluster region. Although this sounds sensible, it is new that developing country firms invest offensively in advanced countries to close the technology-gap to industrial leaders.

Chinese firms have established more than 600 research and development affiliates in the USA as of 2002. The most common entry mode by Chinese MNEs in this respect seems to be the acquisition of a host country company to obtain access to higher technology and management practice quickly. Haier used both approaches to gain access to new, advanced technology. In 1999, Haier established a new refrigerator factory in the USA but acquired a refrigerator factory from a leading European manufactured in Italy in 2001. Chinese companies which access foreign technology by acquisition tend to transfer the technology and other tangible assets back to China to strengthen their production facilities; foreign markets are subsequently serviced through exports with products made to higher specifications. One of the most prominent examples of such a transfer is the acquisition of MG Rover by Nanjing Automobile Corporation (NAC). Although NAC has kept some production facilities in the UK, major parts of the production line have been transferred to Nanjing where production commenced in 2007 and will serve as a blueprint for a subsequent third production line said to be opened in the USA in 2008.

2.4.3 Strategic asset-seeking FDI

Strategic asset-seeking motives seem to be a driving force behind investments in the USA and Europe, although it is not necessarily confined to these regions. The acquisition of typically insolvent European and US firms is aimed at acquiring an established brand, advanced technology and management know-how, and access to distribution channels and customers seems to play an ever-increasing role in the firm's strategy to build-up and strengthen their firm-specific advantages.

2.4.4 Efficiency-seeking FDI

Efficiency-seeking FDI is said to be of minor importance for MNEs from other developing countries. This seems to be the case for Chinese firms as well. There are two explanations for the absence of this FDI motive. First, Chinese MNEs hardly coordinate international supply chains which they could re-organize to benefit from different factor prices. Second, China possesses abundant low-cost labor and cheap land, so Chinese MNEs may rather relocate their production within China than moving abroad.

Summary

- There is a considerable and a growing number of studies on FDI in China. These studies can be broadly classified into three groups.
- The growth of FDI inflows into China from 1979 to 2009 can be broadly divided into three phases: the experimental phase from 1979 to 1991; the boom phase from 1992 to 2001; and the post-WTO phase from 2002 to 2009.
- There has long been an issue of 'round-tripping' of FDI in the case of China.
- During the period from 2000 to 2009, China accounted for 6 percent of total world FDI inflows and 17 percent of total FDI inflows into developing countries.
- The distribution of inward FDI among China's regions and provinces has been very uneven.
- In the FDI literature, FDI is believed to have played some major roles in the development process of a host country's economy, via capital formation, the creation of employment opportunities, promotion of international trade, technology transfer and spillovers to the domestic economy.
- The objectives of the research are to identify (i) the determinants of Chinese OFDI, (ii) the international strategies of Chinese firms and how these are influenced by (iii) domestic institutions and (iv) access to international networks.
- There are five phases of Chinese outward direct investment, which embrace the years 1979—1985, 1986—19991, 1992—1998, 1999—2001, and 2002 onwards.

Exercises

1. Why study FDI in China?
2. Describe the mainly stages of FDI in China.
3. Describe the mainly effects of FDI in China.
4. What is the "round-tripping" of FDI?
5. Describe the regional distribution of FDI in China.
6. Describe the sectoral distribution of FDI in China.
7. What were the contribution of FDI to China's economy?
8. Describe the mainly international investment strategy of Chinese MNEs.

Chapter 11
International Portfolio Investment in China

Learning requirements
- Understand the participation of foreign investors in China's equity and bond investment.
- Learn about the history of Chinese companies listing overseas.
- Understand the differences of A-shares, B-shares, H-shares, and red chips.
- Understand the main model of overseas listing of Chinese enterprises.
- Learn about QFII and RQFII systems.
- Understanding the ShenKong Tong and HuKong Tong systems.
- Understand the operating mechanism of Hulun Tong.
- Learn about the QDII system.
- Learn about sovereign wealth funds.
- Understand panda bonds and dim sum bonds.

1 Overview

China is becoming increasingly important in global financial markets, reflecting the growth of its financial markets relative to the size of the real domestic economy (Figure 11.1, panel 1) and the fast-growing real economy itself, with its rising ratio to world GDP. The figure's right panel shows that Chinese bond market capitalization stood at about 1 percent of global GDP at the start of the 2000s, but had reached 9 percent by the end of 2017.

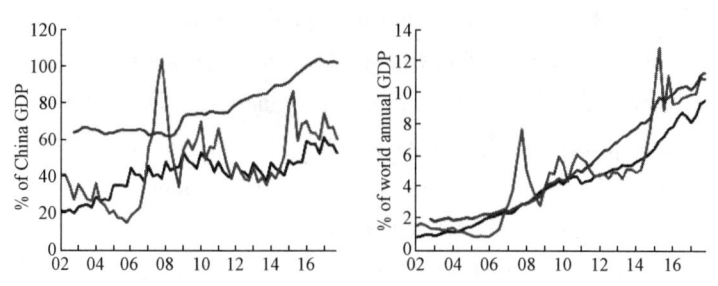

Figure 11.1 China's bond and stock market capitalization and bank assets

Sources: CEIC; IMF, World Economic Outlook; and IMF staff calculations.

At the same time, foreign participation in China's stock and bond markets has risen, although it remains relatively low compared with international peers. Helped by landmark reforms in Chinese financial markets (such as the Shanghai-Hong Kong and Shenzhen-Hong Kong Stock Connect Programs), as well as by the inclusion of Chinese equities in the MSCI index, foreign participation in the Chinese stock market increased slightly in recent years (see Figure 11.2).

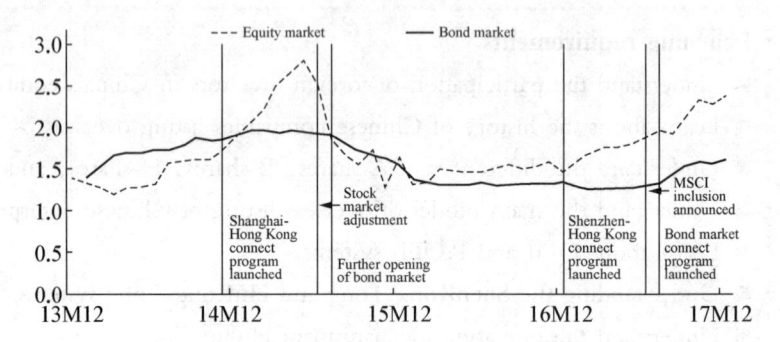

Figure 11.2　Foreign participation in China's stock and bond markets (assets held by overseas entities as % of market size)

Sources: CEIC; People's Bank of China; and IMF staff calculations.

Foreign equity holdings are about 2.4 percent of total Chinese equity market capitalization. Foreign participation in Chinese bond markets is similarly small, just about 1.6 percent of the total value of bonds outstanding, with that share being stable in recent years.

In contrast, as shown in Figure 11.3 (panel1), foreign participation in the stock markets of the United States (about 35 percent in 2017), Korea (33 percent), Japan (17 percent), and India (16 percent) is much more important than in China. The evidence is similar for the bond market (Figure 11.3, panel 2), with China substantially below its peers in foreign bond-market participation.

Limited foreign participation in China's financial markets is also visible in IMF Balance of Payments data, highlighting the wide scope for further external integration of those markets. The international investment position of China as of 2015 showed that its liabilities to foreigners (claims of nonresidents on Chinese residents) were about 40 percent of domestic GDP (Figure 11.4, panel 1), substantially below the levels of the United States (about 160 percent of GDP), Japan (115 percent), as well as Korea (65 percent) and India (55 percent).

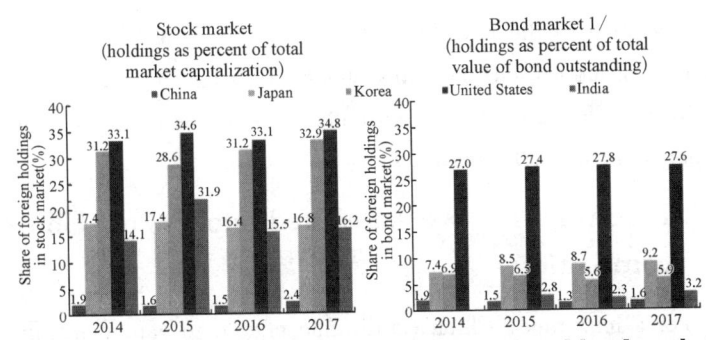

Figure 11.3 Foreign participation in China's stock and bond markets

Sources: Bank of Japan; CEIC; Financial Supervisory Service; Financial Supervisory Service, Korea; Haver Analytics; Ministry of Finance, Japan; People's Bank of China; Reserve Bank of India; SIMFA; U.S. Department of Treasury; and IMF staff calculations.

1/Data for India only includes government securities.

The composition of these liabilities across countries also reflects the scope for further integration of China in both equity and, especially, bond markets. The share of portfolio equity and bonds is just 1/5 of total Chinese external liabilities, a much lower share than for the United States (3/4 of total external liabilities), Japan (3/5 of total external liabilities), Korea (3/5 of total external liabilities), and India (2/5 of total external liabilities). A similar picture (Figure 11.4, panel 2) prevails on the asset side (Chinese residents' holdings of foreign assets), highlighting the still modest external diversification of Chinese wealth, especially of portfolio equity and debt.

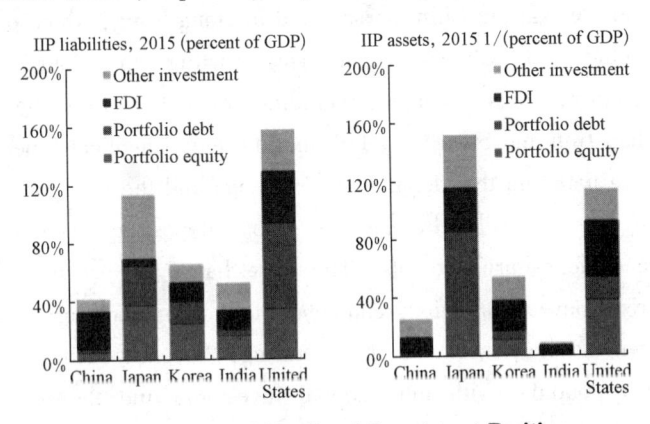

Figure 11.4 International Investment Position

Sources: Lane and Milesi-Ferretti (2017); IMF, BOP Statistics; and IMF staff calculations. 1/ Net of reserves.

2 Foreign investors invest in Chinese stocks

As of 2019, as China's capital account and capital markets are not fully open to the outside world, foreign investors are subject to certain restrictions on their investment in China's equity market. Specifically, foreign investors currently invest in the equity of Chinese companies in the following ways:

2.1 Investing in overseas-listed stocks of Chinese companies

For a long time, China's utilization of foreign capital mainly by attracting foreign direct investment, the establishment of Sino-foreign joint ventures, foreign borrowing and direct issuance of bonds, there are high financing costs and bear foreign exchange rate risks and other problems. Since 1992, in order to explore more flexible, convenient and beneficial ways to attract foreign investment, the concept of direct listing of enterprises overseas has been put on the agenda.

2.1.1 The history of Chinese companies listing abroad

The history of overseas listing of Chinese enterprises has mainly gone through the following stages:

Phase 1 (1993—1994): Debut in International Market

第一阶段：国际市场上试水

In 1993, Chinese companies first appeared in overseas stock markets. China Securities Regulatory Commission was established at the end of 1992, and then approved the first batch of companies to be listed overseas. On June 29th, 1993, Tsingtao Brewery, the first mainland company in China, was listed in Hong Kong, which opened the prelude of Chinese enterprises' listing in Hong Kong. Subsequently, 8 companies including Shanghai Petrochemical, Maanshan Iron and Steel Co., Ltd. and Yizheng Chemical Fiber Co., Ltd. were listed on the global stock exchange and the new york Stock Exchange respectively through the global depositary receipts and American depositary receipts. The first batch of overseas listed enterprises have two obvious characteristics: first, most of them are state-owned enterprises after restructuring; Secondly, these stocks were very popular with international investors, and the prosperity didn't fade until 1994. On the one hand, they were affected by the Mexican financial crisis at the end of 1994, but more importantly, their financial statements were not good.

Phase 2 (1994—Jun.1996): Overseas listing of infrastructure companies

第二阶段：基建公司海外上市

Shortly after the first wave triggered by manufacturing stocks subsided, the second batch of Chinese stocks appeared on Wall Street again. The overseas listing was mainly based on Chinese infrastructure, such as Huaneng Power, China Eastern Airlines, China Southern Airlines and Datang Power Generation. With the growth of China's national economy, the government stepped up efforts to develop the infrastructure industry. Overseas investors believed that China's infrastructure industry was relatively weak at that time, and China's per capita air mileage, per capita electricity consumption and per capita energy consumption all lagged behind developed countries, so this industry has broad development space and great growth potential for investment in this area. However, the government began to carry out macro-control in 1994 and 1995, and many projects were forced to slow down or stop construction. Most of the listed companies were deeply affected, and the profitability of the companies was not good. The published annual report made investors disappointed. The infrastructure field is vicious competition, such as the civil aviation industry, with too many imported aircraft, excess operating capacity of aircraft and discounted air tickets, resulting in a total loss of the civil aviation industry. Coupled with the adjustment of domestic interest rates and tax rates and the influence of market rumors, investment institutions have sold the shares of these companies one after another, and the market performance has since entered a trough.

Phase 3 (Jun. 1996—Oct.1997): Red chips

The third wave of China's oversea stocks was in the form of red chips which began at the end of 1996 and ended in the East Asian financial turmoil in October 1997.

The so-called red-chip stocks are the stocks issued by window companies that invest in Hong Kong with a certain department or a certain level of government as the background. In actual distinction, the shares issued by companies that have the largest controlling stake (usually more than 30%) directly or indirectly affiliated with relevant departments or enterprises in mainland China and registered and listed in Hong Kong are generally classified as red-chip stocks. According to FTSE Russell, there are four main criteria for a firm to be classified as a red chip:

> ➢ Chinese government-affiliated organizations must own at least 35% of the company. These organizations may include the government of the People's Republic of China, Chinese provincial governments, municipal governments in China, and Chinese state-owned enterprises.

> More than 55% of the firm's revenue must come from the People's Republic of China, or the firm must have over 55% of its assets in China.
> The firm must be incorporated outside of mainland China.
> The company's stock must be listed on the Hong Kong Stock Exchange.

There were several factors to attract overseas investors for the red chips: First, they benefited from the rapid development of China's economy as "China concept"; Second, the red chip company is registered in Hong Kong and operated by the local management in Hong Kong. It has a good operating environment and convenient financing, and can grasp the pulse of the market more correctly and develop its business more pertinently; Third, with the strong support of the Chinese government, these enterprises are either backed by the industry or backed by strong local governments to obtain high-quality and unconventional asset that can lead to rapid development of enterprises; Finally, it is related to the general environment of Hong Kong's return to China.

However, with the sudden outbreak of the Asian financial crisis at the end of 1997, the Hong Kong stock market plummeted, and its popularity was extremely depressed. In addition, the performance of red chips was poor, and many stocks fell below the issue price. After the upsurge of red chips subsided, foreign capital markets closed the door to Chinese stocks for 15 months.

Phase 4 (Oct. 1997—Feb. 2000): High-Tech and Network

The development of information Internet technology set off a climax at the end of the last century, and the words about network economy, eyeball economy, attention economy and new economy came to the fore. The nature of high-risk, high-return has attracted a lot of venture capital, and the NASDAQ stock market boom has fueled investor enthusiasm for such stocks. China Net, Century Yonglian, Sina, Sohu, Netease, Hexun, 8848 and a number of high-tech and Internet-characterized enterprises also seize the opportunity to list on the NASDAQ stock market, forming the fourth wave of overseas listings.

But the internet myth was shattered in 2000 and the NASDAQ market nearly collapsed. The decline in the new economy has dragged down the pace of economic growth across the United States, the global economy has been in the doldrums, the value of global equity markets has shrunk.

Phase 5 (Feb. 2000—): Large state-owned enterprises

The Chinese enterprises listing aboard in this stage were large enterprises with monopoly industries represented by petroleum and telecommunications, such as China Unicom, Sinopec and CNOOC, etc. With the new situation of joining WTO, the government was ready to form some internationally competitive large companies and enterprise groups in key areas and key industries of the national economy, making it truly the backbone of China's economy and the main force to participate in international competition. Against this backdrop, large state-owned enterprises, once China's economic leader, had become the darlings of the stock market again after years of market snubbing. With PetroChina and Unicom listed in the U.S. A, the scale of overseas listed enterprises was growing, and had been involved in some of the overall industry transformation. The transformation of listed companies is becoming more and more thorough, and the management's stock option incentive mechanism was generally introduced, which was welcomed by overseas investors. In addition, some group companies are also in the formation and listing preparation, such as railway, banking, civil aviation, nonferrous metals and other industries.

第五阶段：大型国有企业海外上市

2.1.2 The main modes and procedures for Chinese enterprises to list abroad

The main overseas listing of Chinese enterprises is listed on the Stock Exchange of Hong Kong, the New York Stock Exchange and the NASDAQ stock market of the United States. In addition, some companies also choose to list on the London Stock Exchange, Hong Kong GEM, Singapore Stock Exchange, Singapore Stock Auto Quote Market, US counter market, Canadian GEM, Vancouver Stock Exchange, European Second Market, EU Stock Auto Quote Market and other places. The main mode of Chinese enterprises listing abroad include:

(1) IPO

Domestic enterprises issued and listed directly on overseas exchanges, such as H shares, N shares and S shares. there are some difficulties for IPO owing to the differences of political, economical and cultural factors of the two countries. First, the laws are different, they had been established and managed by the Chinese basic laws, such as the Company Law, Securities Law, etc., but if they listed abroad, they must comply with the legal requirements of other country. Second, the accounting standards between countries are different. When domestic enterprises go overseas to list, they must prepare the financial statements in accordance with China's accounting standards, but also in accordance with the accounting standards of the place of listing, it will increase the accounting costs of the company. Third, it is very complicated for the approval procedure. When a domestic enterprise goes overseas to list, it must first apply to the relevant departments of the Chinese government and the CSRC, after being approved, it begin to reform shareholding system and reviewed by the CSRC, and then submit a securities registration application and preparation registration form to the securities authority of the place of listing, it is a long operating time and complicated procedures.

(2) Buy a shell and go public

Chinese enterprises acquire a company that has been listed on overseas securities markets by means of cash or stock exchange, that is, all or part of the "shell" company' shares, and then injected into the assets and business of domestic enterprises, in order to achieve the purpose of indirect overseas listing. The advantage of shell listing is that it can avoid domestic restrictions on overseas listing and the complicated procedures of applying for, registration, offering, listing, etc., avoiding the differences between different countries in terms of system, accounting system and relevant laws, and it has some advantages, such as simple procedure, lower cost, less time, etc. Because of these advantages, it is also a more popular way to go public. Of course, there are some problems: First, the choice of the target shell company. Given the acquisition costs and risks, it is not easy for choosing a satisfying shell company. Second, the issue of taxation, the shell company under takeover is actually a subsidiary of a domestic enterprise, there may be a double tax problem. Double taxation reduces the profit of domestic companies. Third, the financing capacity. Domestic enterprises inject domestic enterprises' assets into shell companies and go public indirectly through shell companies through acquisition of target companies and directional allotment of shares. However, if domestic enterprises need to issue new shares through shell companies, there is still a cost problem of issuing new shares for financing.

(3) Shell-making listing

Shell-making listing means that domestic enterprises register a holding company overseas, and then the holding company overseas is listed on the overseas securities market, and the funds raised are invested in domestic enterprises, so as to achieve the purpose of indirect listing of domestic enterprises overseas. Overseas holding companies have close ties with domestic enterprises in terms of property rights and personnel, and the registered places of overseas holding companies are generally in the places to be listed or countries or regions with similar political, economic, cultural and legal backgrounds in the places to be listed, so as to obtain listing status. After the overseas holding company obtains the listing status, domestic enterprises can raise funds through shell companies.

(4) Convertible Bond Listing

Convertible bonds are issued by companies, which stipulate that bondholders can convert these bonds into a certain number of common shares of the issuing company within a certain time in the future as stipulated in the bond terms. Convertible bond is a kind of credit bond, which does not need special mortgage to support its issuance. The issuing company pays its debt with its credit guarantee and takes the form of contract as debt certificate.

(5) Depository Receipt Listing

Depository Receipt is a kind of negotiable securities issued in the form of certificates, which is generally issued by American banks and represents the transferable certificates of one or more non-American issuers' equity shares deposited in the custodian bank of the original issuing country. According to its distribution scope, it can be divided into: American depositary receipts are issued to American investors; Global depositary receipts are issued to global investors.

2.1.3 Meaning of Overseas Listing of Chinese Enterprises

(1) Strengthen the introduction of foreign capital and broaden the financing channels of enterprises. Capital is of great strategic significance to the rapidly growing developing countries. The large amount of capital brought by overseas listing has become an important part of the introduction of foreign capital in China and played an important role in China's economic growth. As far as micro-enterprises are concerned, the shortage of funds has always been a big problem that puzzles the development of Chinese enterprises. Large state-owned enterprises, through the reorganization of shareholding system, issued H shares and N shares abroad, which solved the urgent need of development funds, improved the capital structure and enhanced the

加强了外资引进,拓宽了企业的筹资渠道。

comparative competitive advantage, thus greatly strengthening the sustainable development ability of enterprises.

(2) Promote the reform of Chinese enterprises and accelerated the pace of perfecting the corporate governance structure and modern enterprise system. For the first time, Chinese enterprises are required to set up a joint stock limited company according to the laws and regulations of the place where they are listed, and build a mixed economic enterprise with foreign participation. After listing to attract foreign shareholders, foreign shareholders will protect their investors according to the company's articles of association, requiring the company to earnestly fulfill its obligations promised by the company's articles of association and disclose information in a timely and accurate manner, which forms an external constraint to a certain extent. Under such pressure, most overseas listed companies are able to conduct business according to international practices and international rules, and their business behavior is gradually standardized.

(3) Accelerate the process of internationalization of Chinese enterprises. The overseas listing of domestic enterprises not only provides an information platform for foreign enterprises to understand domestic enterprises, but also creates a good beginning for domestic enterprises to move towards the international capital market. Overseas listing has significantly increased the overseas popularity of these companies. At the same time, overseas listed companies have attracted the attention of many international securities analysts, who deliver market quotes and analysis reports to all parts of the world every day, and the image of Chinese enterprises has been more and more deeply imprinted in the minds of international investors and enterprises in the same industry.

China's overseas listed enterprises not only establish their international image, but also start their own international operation by means of overseas listing, from international capital operation to international industrial operation. CNOOC, for example, has successfully acquired nine companies of Ripso in Indonesia through the standardized operation of the international capital market, and has become the operator of some of them, thus realizing the internationalization of enterprises. In addition, the overseas listing process has also promoted the market-oriented transformation of government industry policies to a certain extent. For example, the overseas listing of Sinopec has directly contributed to the liberalization of domestic refined oil prices that have been controlled for many years.

2.2 QFII and RQFII

2.2.1 QFII

QFII is an acronym for Qualified Foreign Institutional Investor. As a system, it means that the relevant administrative departments in China allow approved foreign institutional investors to convert foreign currency into RMB under certain supervision and restrictions, and invest in the local securities market through special accounts; Investors' capital gains, dividends and other profits can only be remitted to China after approval. As a transitional and low-risk model, QFII is playing a unique role in the gradual opening of China's securities market.

China's QFII system has the following characteristics:
- The introduction of QFII system is a leap-forward development in one step. According to the general international experience, the opening of the capital market has to go through two stages. In the first stage, an "overseas fund" (Taiwan model) or an "open international trust fund" (Korean model) can be established first; At this stage, it took 7 years in Taiwan and 11 years in South Korea. China has bypassed the first stage and achieved one step at a time, and its advantage of backwardness is immeasurable.
- The main scope of QFII access is expanded and the requirements are improved. In order to strengthen supervision and control, countries and regions in emerging capital markets generally specify what types of foreign institutional investors can enter their own countries or regions by enumerating. In addition, they have strict requirements on the amount of registered capital, financial status and operating period of QFII. On the contrary, China's recognition of QFII subject scope is relatively broad, and foreign investors are given more autonomy. However, in order to ensure the stability and healthy development of the domestic securities market, our country has further improved the requirements of registered capital, financial status, operating period and other indicators.

2.2.2 RQFII(RMB Qualified Foreign Institutional Investors)

RQFII refers to qualified foreign investors in RMB and R stands for RMB. RQFII can invest foreign exchange settlement within the approved quota in the domestic securities market. The liberalization of stock market investment in RQFII accelerates the internationalization of RMB.

RQFII pilot was launched in December 2011, and the initial participating institutions were limited to domestic fund management companies and Hong Kong subsidiaries of securities companies. In December last year, the CSRC, the central bank and the SAFE decided to increase the RQFII investment quota by 200 billion yuan, bringing the total amount of pilot projects to 270 billion yuan. In March 2013, the China Securities Regulatory Commission, the central bank and the foreign exchange bureau jointly issued the revised Pilot Measures for Domestic Securities Investment by Qualified Foreign Institutional Investors in RMB, allowing more overseas financial institutions to invest RMB funds raised offshore in the domestic capital market, while relaxing the restrictions on RQFII investment scope.

There has a large amount of RMB deposits in Hang kong, and there are not many investment outlets. Every time RMB funds are released, although the returns are not considerable, retail investors have responded enthusiastically. The introduction of RQFII not only helps to broaden the investment channels of RMB staying in Hong Kong, but also helps to enhance the liquidity of capital market. Since the promulgation of QFII at the end of 2002, Foreign institutions keep applying for QFII, and always keep their enthusiasm for A-share market.

2.3 Interconnection mechanism

2.3.1 Shanghai—Hong Kong Stock Connect and Shenzhen—Hong Kong Stock Connect

As the first real interconnection mechanism, Shanghai—Hong Kong Stock Connect was officially approved at the opening ceremony of Boao Forum on April 10, 2014. On November 17, 2014, the pilot stock interconnection mechanism between Shanghai and Hong Kong was officially opened to investors under the intense preparation of the two places for more than six months. Based on the experience of Shanghai—Hong Kong Stock Connect, the connection between A-share market and Hong Kong stock market will be further strengthened, and Shenzhen—Hong Kong Stock Connect is imperative. On August 16, 2015, the State Council officially approved the Shenzhen—Hong Kong Stock Connect Implementation Plan; On November 19 th, the Hong Kong Stock Exchange and the Shenzhen Stock Exchange jointly conducted a simulation test of the Shenzhen—Hong Kong Stock Connect transaction; On December 5th, Shenzhen—Hong Kong Stock Connect officially opened to investors for stock trading between the two places.

On April 11, 2018, Shanghai—Hong Kong Stock Connect and Shenzhen—Hong Kong Stock Connect were expanded again, and the daily limit was tripled on the original basis. In fact, before the expansion, the utilization rate of daily limit of Shanghai—Hong Kong Stock Connect was mostly below 50%, and that of Shenzhen—Hong Kong Stock Connect was only about 20%. The main purpose of the expansion was to respond to MSCI requirements and promote A shares to enter the MSCI index. On June 1, 2018, A-shares were successfully incorporated into MSCI, and the proportion of A-shares was constantly increasing, which contributed to Shanghai—Hong Kong Stock Connect and Shenzhen—Hong Kong Stock Connect.

Shanghai—Hong Kong Stock Connect, Shenzhen—Hong Kong Stock Connect, QFII and RQFII are the main ways for foreign investors to invest in domestic capital markets. The differences between them are as follows:

➢ Investment targets: The investment targets of Shanghai—Hong Kong Stock Connect and Shenzhen—Hong Kong Stock Connect are limited to the stocks specified in the two markets, and participate in margin financing and securities lending within the limited scope, but cannot participate in the issuance and subscription of stocks and bonds. QFII and RQFII can invest in common stocks, preferred stocks, bonds, funds, stock index futures, asset-backed securities and other products, and can participate in the issuance of new shares, additional issuance, allotment of shares, subscription of convertible bonds and bond issuance, but cannot participate in margin financing and securities lending.

➢ Investment quota: China Securities Regulatory Commission and Hong Kong Securities Regulatory Commission jointly signed the Joint Announcement of Shenzhen—Hong Kong Stock Connect, announcing the total cancellation of

Shanghai—Hong Kong Stock Connect. The daily quota of Shanghai Stock Connect and Shenzhen Stock Connect (trading northward) is 13 billion yuan, The daily quota of Hong Kong Stock Connect (trading southward) is 10.5 billion yuan. As of the end of December, 2017, the total approved rate of QFII was USD 97.159 billion, and that of RQFII was RMB 605.062 billion. The maximum investment quota of a single QFII institution is USD 5 billion, and there is no limit to the investment quota of a single RQFII institution.

➢ Approval process: Shanghai Stock Exchange and Shenzhen Stock Exchange have set a limit of not less than 500,000 yuan in total assets of securities accounts and capital accounts for individual investors participating in Hong Kong Stock Connect transactions, and there are no restrictions on institutional investors. Hong Kong Stock Exchange has no restrictions on investors participating in Shanghai Stock Connect and Shenzhen Stock Connect. Therefore, the approval of Shanghai—Hong Kong Stock Connect and Shenzhen—Hong Kong Stock Connect is relatively simple, and investors can submit a declaration to the exchange through the local securities company. However, the single quota of QFII and RQFII needs to be approved by China Securities Regulatory Commission and State Administration of Foreign Exchange, and the approval process is long, which usually takes 3—6 months.

➢ Fund management: The funds of Shanghai—Hong Kong Stock Connect and Shenzhen—Hong Kong Stock Connect are managed in a closed path. After the daily transaction, the funds will return to the local capital account and not stay at the exchange location, so there will be no exchange loss or cash flow pressure. However, QFII and RQFII must be exchanged for RMB before they are put into the market, and they are bound by the State Administration of Foreign Exchange when they are remitted, so it is inconvenient to return funds.

➢ Transaction costs: Compared with the cost of investing in A shares, Shanghai Stock Connect and Shenzhen Stock Connect have lower costs than QFII and RQFII. Compared with the cost of investing in Hong Kong stocks, the cost of Hong Kong Stock Connect is higher than QFII and RQFII. The emergence of interconnection mechanism is to balance the market price difference between mainland and Hong Kong stocks in a basket of heavyweights, and to provide a convenient channel for small-scale institutional investors and some individual investors. The emergence of QFII and RQFII is to introduce large-scale overseas funds to support the development of domestic capital market, and expect overseas institutional investors with long-term investment and value investment as their main investment ideas to improve the structure of A-share investors.

2.3.2　HuLun Tong

"Huluntong" was formally proposed as the seventh China-UK economic and financial dialogue held on September 21st, 2015. Since then, the CSRC and the Stock Exchange have actively promoted the feasibility study of "Huluntong". In March 2016, the two sides reached a preliminary consensus on the principles and framework of cooperation. The 8th China-UK Economic and Financial Dialogue affirmed the staged achievements of the joint feasibility study of Huluntong, and supported the research and preparation of relevant operational systems and arrangements. "Huluntong" has entered a new stage.

On November 2, 2018, Shanghai Stock Exchange disclosed the relevant supporting business rules of Huluntong. On December 8, 2018, the brokerage business of Huluntong was tested for customs clearance. On January 22, 2019, the director of the Shanghai Financial Work Bureau said at the press conference of the Shanghai Municipal Government that Shanghai has made full preparations and will work well with Beijing and other central units to promote Huluntong as soon as possible in the new year. Up to now, the Shanghai Stock Exchange has filed with four institutions, namely CITIC CLSA UK, haitong international UK Limited, China International Capital Corporation (UK) Limited and Barclays Bank, the UK cross-border conversion agency of Huluntong global depositary receipts.

"Huluntong" realizes the interconnection between the two markets through the cross-border conversion mechanism between depositary receipts and basic securities. "Huluntong" includes

"沪伦通"

eastward business and westward business, that is, China Depositary Receipts of listed companies on the Stock Exchange and Global Depositary Receipts of A-share listed companies on the Stock Exchange.

2.4 Foreign investor invest in China's Bond

2.4.1 Overview

Chinese bonds outstanding at the end of 2017 were high in absolute terms, with a stock of about $11 trillion at the end of 2017 (Figure 11.5), more than Korea (about $2 trillion), similar to Japan ($12 trillion), but not comparable yet with the euro area ($20 trillion) or the United States ($41 trillion).

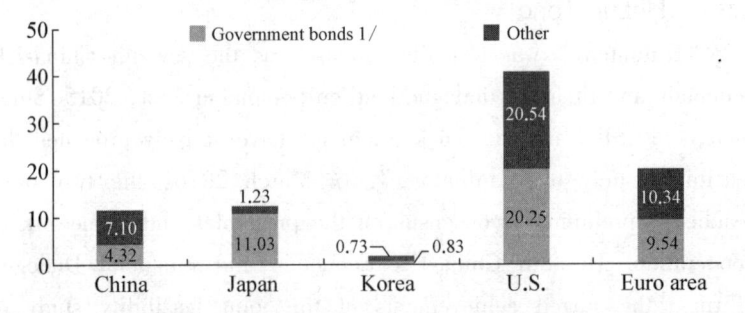

Figure 11.5 Total value of bond outstanding, end 2017 (USD trillions)

Sources: People's Bank of China; European Central Bank; Bank of Japan; Financial Supervisory Service, Korea; Bank of Korea; SIFMA. 1/Government bonds cover bonds issued by the general government (central, state and local government accounts, social security funds and non-market non-profit institutions controlled and mainly financed by government units).

Unlike Japan, Korea, and even the euro area and the United States, the issuers of Chinese bonds are more concentrated in the non-government sector (although for China that includes important state-owned enterprises and various government-sponsored vehicles). Nonetheless, most foreign holdings of Chinese bonds are concentrated in government instruments.

This situation resembles Japan's and Korea's, but is far from those of the United States, India, and euro area countries such as Germany, where nonresidents contribute a substantial fraction of the private sector's bond financing. In this context, further liberalization of the bond market in China could help the private sector diversify funding, improve liquidity, and lengthen borrowing maturities. (Figure 11.6)

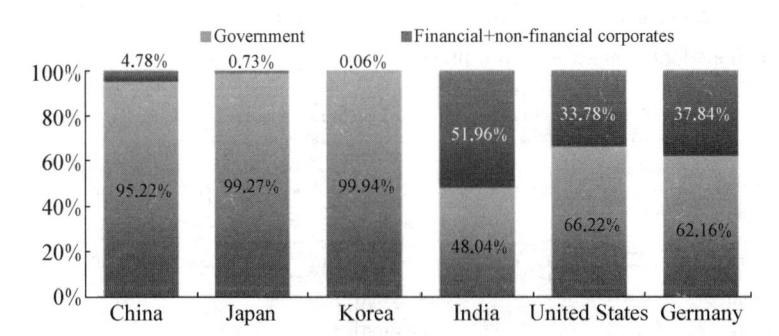

Figure 11.6 Breakdown of foreign holdings by type of bonds, 2016 (percent of total)

Sources: U.S. Department of Treasury; Haver Analytics; Deutsche Bundesbank; Bank of Japan; Financial Supervisory Service, Korea; Reserve Bank of India; National Securities Depository, India; and IMF staff calculations.

In terms of pricing, the evolution of the Chinese bond yield curve reflects higher nominal yields than either U.S. or euro area bonds, as well as a degree of co-movement in the evolution of Chinese yields relative to those countries despite China's closed capital account. Figure 11.7 depicts the bond yields at the end of April 2018, as well as the yield curve before the beginning of monetary normalization in the United States in December 2015 (dashed lines in Figure 11.7).

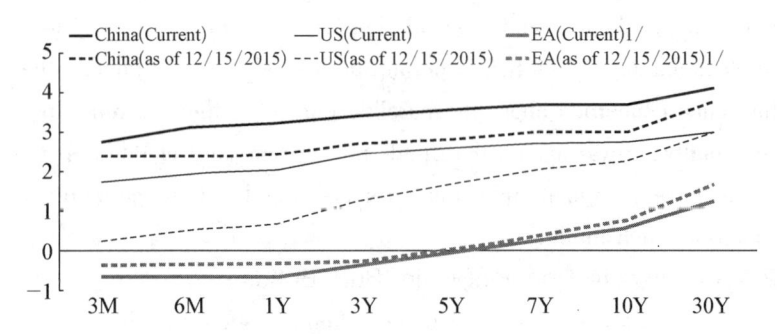

Figure 11.7 Yield curve of government bonds (percent)
Source: Bloomberg L.P. 1/: Based on Euro Area AAA-rated government bonds.

Synchronized yield developments between China and the rest of the world do not necessarily imply the existence of big cross-currency arbitrage opportunities, both because of remaining capital controls and the relatively high cost of hedging currency risk. Figure 11.8 captures the relative hedged yield differentials between similar Chinese and U.S. government bonds, using either onshore or offshore forwards. The hedged China-foreign yield differentials are not as positive as the unhedged ones, especially when using non-deliverable offshore forwards (green lines in Figure 11.8). Comparing covered twelve-month with three-month differentials, shorter maturity investments hedged onshore look somewhat more attractive to foreign investors.

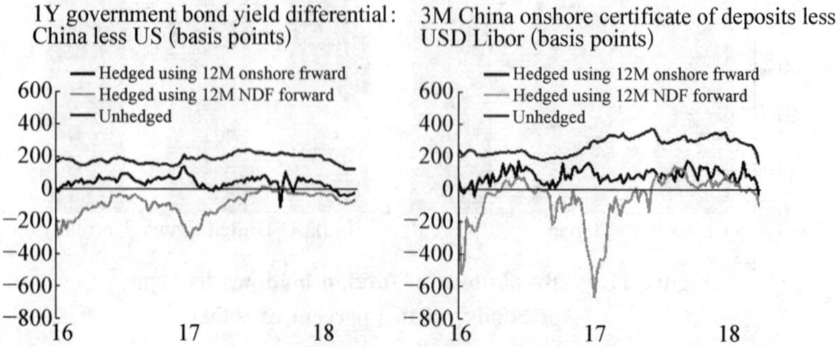

Figure 11.8 FX-hedged and unhedged yield differentials
Sources: CFETS, Bloomberg L.P.; and IMF staff calculations.

2.4.2 Panda bonds

> 熊猫债券是由非中国发行人发行、以人民币计价的债券, 在中国境内出售。

A Panda bond is a Chinese renminbi-denominated bond from a non-Chinese issuer, sold in the People's Republic of China. The first two Panda bonds were issued in October 2005 on the same day by the International Finance Corporation and the Asian Development Bank. Their terms were 1.13 billion yuan of 10-year bonds at a 3.4% yield and 1 billion yuan of 10-year bonds at a 3.34% yield. The Chinese government had been negotiating for several years about implementation details before permitting the sale of such bonds; they had been concerned about the possible effects on their currency peg. Eventually, it was agreed that funds raised from sales of Panda bonds would have to remain in China; issuers would not be permitted to repatriate such funds.

2.4.3 Offshore RenMenBi Dim Sum Bonds

The market for dim sum bonds (bonds issued outside of China and denominated in Chinese renminbi) in Hong Kong SAR has expanded since 2011, underpinned by policies promoting external use of the renminbi and liberalization of two-way renminbi fund flows between onshore and offshore markets, before peaking in 2015. Key driving forces for the attractiveness of the market include the need from foreign companies for offshore renminbi funds to support businesses in the onshore market and from mainland firms for external financing to support outward direct investment (ODI) conducted through Hong Kong SAR. The role of the dim sum bond market as an alternative renminbi fund raising platform for international and mainland issuers helps promote external use of the currency by global firms and investors attracted by its high accessibility. Indeed, the market has played an important role in price discovery and intermediating renminbi funds between onshore and offshore markets. Accordingly, policymakers must understand the major factors driving the dim sum bond market to formulate appropriate policy to foster the development of the offshore renminbi bond market. In this spirit, this chapter reviews the structure of the dim sum bond market, including its issuer profile and key features of dim sum bonds. It identifies factors driving issuance, and suggests that economic growth, offshore-onshore yield differentials, the use of the renminbi funds raised, the effective and forward exchange rate of renminbi, and mainland policy factors are key determinants of net issuance of dim sum bonds in the offshore market.

3 China's Indirect Investment abroad

3.1 QDII

3.1.1 Introduction

QDII is the acronym of "Qualified Domestic Institutional Investors", that is, qualified domestic institutional investor, which refers to an institutional arrangement established in a country under the conditions that RMB capital is not convertible and the capital market is not open, and approved by the relevant departments of the country to allow domestic institutions to invest in securities investment business such as stocks and bonds in overseas capital markets under control. The direct purpose of setting up the system is to "further open the capital account, create more foreign exchange demand, make the RMB exchange rate more balanced and market-oriented, and encourage more domestic enterprises to go abroad, thereby reducing trade surplus and capital account surplus", which is directly manifested in allowing domestic investors to directly participate in foreign markets and obtain global market benefits.

QDII system was first proposed by Hong Kong government departments. Like CDR (depositary receipt) and QFII, QDII system will be an expedient measure for opening up the mainland capital market under foreign exchange control, so as to allow domestic investors to invest in overseas capital markets when capital account items are not fully opened. QDII can accumulate experience for the orderly opening of China's capital market and will play a positive role in cultivating institutional investors in the Mainland. Especially for Hong Kong's capital market, it may be just a drop in the bucket for the Hong Kong market with a market value of nearly HK \$3.4 trillion.

The design of the QDII system mainly involves three aspects: the qualification of investors, the monitoring of access to funds, the licensed investment of securities varieties and proportion limits.

3.1.2 The difference between QDII and traditional offshore finance

Traditional commercial banks' overseas financial management business on behalf of customers refers to a business in which commercial banks approved by the CBRC issue overseas financial products priced in RMB to domestic residents and purchase the raised RMB funds to purchase foreign exchange for overseas financial products. After the investment principal and income are remitted back to China, the commercial bank will settle the foreign exchange and pay it to the domestic residents in RMB. There is no doubt that QDII system, as a specific system when RMB capital account is not open, will die after RMB is fully opened. At the same time, QDII shows signs of further opening up compared with the traditional overseas financial management business on behalf of customers. Generally speaking, the differences between QDII and traditional overseas financial management mainly include:

(1) Different types of investable securities

Traditional banks can invest in overseas fixed-income products on behalf of customers, but cannot directly invest in stocks and their structured products, commodity derivatives, and bonds and bills below BBB level. QDII allows mainland residents to invest in overseas capital markets in foreign exchange. According to the Trial Measures for the Administration of Overseas Securities Investment in qualified domestic institutional investor issued by CSRC, there is no upper limit on the proportion of stock investment, and financial derivatives investment is allowed.

Traditional bank valet offshore banking business may invest in fixed income products overseas, but may not invest directly in stocks and their structured products, commodity derivatives, and BBB-grade bonds and notes. QDII allows mainland residents to invest in foreign exchange in overseas capital markets, and according to the SFC's Pilot Measures for the Administration of Foreign Securities Investment by Qualified Domestic Institutional Investors, there is no cap on the proportion of equity investment, and financial derivatives investments are also permitted.

(2) Risk

In QDII business, there is a relationship between clients and banks, in which banks only invest and manage clients' funds, and collect management fees from them, and the investors themselves bear the profits and losses. In traditional wealth management products, the relationship between individuals and banks is a counterparty, and individuals buy products designed by banks. Up to now, no cases of loss of principal have been heard. Besides exchange rate risk, QDII investment also has systematic risk and non-systematic risk in capital market. Compared with overseas financial management on behalf of clients, QDII investment is more risky, and the actual return due may be negative.

(3) Return

Due to the different types and proportions of investable financial products, the expected income of QDII is generally higher than that of overseas wealth management products on behalf of banks. In contrast, the traditional bank's overseas wealth management business generally does not exceed its preset maximum rate of return. Different kinds of QDII funds have different yields. The income of QDII mainly depends on the investment variety and investment area. Generally speaking, most of the QDII products of banks invest in fixed-income financial products such as bonds and monetary instruments in overseas capital markets. The proportion of investment stocks generally does not exceed 50%, so the income is relatively stable but relatively low; The QDII products of the fund are mostly invested in overseas stock markets, and the proportion of QDII investment stocks of some funds can reach 100% (for example, Southern Global Selected Allocation Securities Investment Fund), so the expected return will be relatively high. QDII investing in emerging markets is expected to have a higher rate of return due to the good growth of emerging markets; QDII invested in mature markets is expected to have lower returns due to the high stability and limited growth of mature markets.

(4) Different currencies issued

Traditional banks manage overseas wealth on behalf of customers, raising RMB funds from domestic institutions and individuals, and banks invest in overseas fixed-income products by purchasing foreign exchange. Overseas investment by QDII requires domestic institutions and individuals to have foreign exchange. If investors do not have foreign exchange, they need to purchase foreign exchange before they can invest. In addition, QDII can't avoid RMB exchange rate risk by certain means, just like traditional overseas wealth management business.

3.1.3 Major Risks for QDII

(1) Markets

Overseas investment is affected by many factors, such as macroeconomic conditions, fiscal, monetary and tax policies, social laws and regulations, etc., which make the income of overseas investment face uncertainty.

(2) Industry

Economic cycles, industrial policies, fiscal and monetary policies and other factors in various countries have an important impact on the development of the industry. Moreover, in the global economic development environment, the development opportunities and risks of different industries are different in different periods, and the ups and downs of industries have an important impact on QDII performance.

(3) Interest rate

Investment is affected by the rate of return caused by the fluctuation of interest rates in financial markets of various countries. Interest rates are one of the important means for central banks to regulate and control, and their changes will affect many aspects.

(4) Exchange rate

When investors invest in the world, the final rate of return depends not only on the rate of return calculated in local currency, but also on the change of exchange rate between foreign currency and local currency. Under the condition of floating exchange rate in major regions of the world, this risk is even greater.

(5) Politics

Foreign governments are very wary of the influx of Chinese QDII, fearing that these funds will pose a threat to Chinese enterprises and may introduce some policies to restrict investment behavior.

In addition, in the investment yield of products, we should look at whether the yield is floating or guaranteed. If it is floating income, see how likely it is to be realized. For example, it is linked to a financial instrument. Guess its future trend, and then analyze which grade of floating income is larger.

3.2 Sovereign wealth funds

3.2.1 Introduction

Sovereign Wealth, corresponding to private wealth, refers to the public wealth accumulated by a country's government through specific tax and budget allocation, renewable natural resources income and balance of payments surplus, which is controlled and dominated by the government and usually held in foreign currency. Sovereign Wealth Funds (SWFs) is a new word coined by international investment banks in 2005, but it is not a new thing, which appeared as early as 1950s. In 1953, Kuwait used its oil export revenue to set up Kuwait Investment Bureau to invest in international financial markets. In 1956, British gilbert islands, a western Pacific island country, also created a SWFs with its phosphate-rich bird droppings export income. When the bird droppings are exhausted, the investment portfolio value of SWFs in the islands reaches 520 million US dollars, which is about 9 times of the annual GDP of the islands.

Generally speaking, SWFs has two remarkable characteristics: one is owned, controlled and dominated by the government, and the other is to pursue the goal of maximizing returns after risk adjustment. From the perspective of funding sources of SWFs, it can be formed by a government through specific tax and budget allocation, or accumulated by means of resource export income or non-resource trade surplus, but it is usually inseparable from how to manage excess foreign exchange reserves: Taking Asia as an example, oil-producing countries in the Middle East, China and Southeast Asian countries have accumulated a large amount of US dollar foreign exchange reserves. If only for the purpose of maintaining external payment functions and maintaining currency stability, Asian countries do not need so much foreign exchange reserves; From the perspective of economic efficiency, excessive holding of foreign exchange reserves with low yield is also a waste of financial resources. Therefore, the surplus foreign exchange reserves are gradually no longer invested in traditional highly liquid assets, but converted into sovereign investment funds, and through expert management, a wider range of investment tools are selected and a more effective asset portfolio is constructed to obtain high returns after risk adjustment.

According to the statistics of London International Financial

> 所谓主权财富（Sovereign Wealth），与私人财富相对应，是指一国政府通过特定税收与预算分配、可再生自然资源收入和国际收支盈余等方式积累形成的，由政府控制与支配的，通常以外币形式持有的公共财富。

Services Authority (IFSL) in March 2009, the assets managed by global sovereign wealth funds in 2008 were as high as 3.9 trillion US dollars, an increase of 18% over 2007. Among them, oil-producing countries in the Middle East owned 45% of global sovereign wealth funds, and other Asian regions accounted for about one third. The main source of funds for these sovereign wealth funds is the export of resource commodities such as oil, totaling 2.5 trillion US dollars; In addition, the funds from official foreign exchange reserves, government budget surplus, pension reserve and privatization income are $1.4 trillion.

3.2.2 China's sovereign wealth funds

Since the global financial crisis in 2008, SWFs' investments have resulted in national security concerns of host countries because SWFs continue to expand rapidly and have become increasingly active in real-time strategic transactions. Given this background, China, which has the biggest SWF in the world, is facing severe challenges of energy resources shortages while its plan is to accomplish social and economic development goals. Energy security is a key driving force of the energy investment policy of China's SWFs. This makes the SWF investments more complicated and more politically sensitive. The combination of sovereign rights and the strategic importance of energy also makes geopolitics more complicated and brings more uncertainty to SWF investments.

At 10:00 on September 29, 2007, China Investment Corporation (hereinafter referred to as CIC) was formally established in Beijing. As a wholly state-owned company, CIC has a registered capital of US$200 billion and is responsible for managing China's foreign exchange reserves of US$200 billion. Since March, 2007, CIC has been making preparations, and its foreign exchange investment business is mainly overseas financial portfolio products. Previously, CIC had invested US$3 billion in Blackstone, the largest private equity investment fund in the United States.

The sources of funds for sovereign wealth funds include four categories:

- ❖ The surplus of foreign exchange reserves is mainly in five major countries and regions in Asia, such as Singapore, Malaysia, South Korea, Taiwan and Hong Kong (see the list of foreign exchange reserves of various countries).
- ❖ Foreign exchange surplus of natural resources export,

including foreign trade surplus of natural resources such as oil, natural gas, copper and DIA, mainly represented by countries in the Middle East and Latin America.
- ❖ Relying on international aid funds, represented by Uganda's poverty aid fund.
- ❖ Issue special treasury bonds, represented by China.

Sovereign wealth funds and official foreign exchange reserves are owned by the state, which belong to national sovereign wealth in a broad sense and have similar sources. But there are still differences:

- ❖ Official foreign exchange reserves are reflected in the balance sheet of assets and liabilities of the central bank, while the former has independent balance sheet and other corresponding financial statements besides the balance sheet of assets and liabilities of the central bank.
- ❖ The operation and changes of official foreign exchange reserve assets are closely related to a country's balance of payments and exchange rate policy, while sovereign wealth funds are generally not necessarily and directly related to a country's balance of payments and exchange rate policy.
- ❖ The change of official foreign exchange reserve assets has monetary policy effect, that is, other conditions remain unchanged, the increase or decrease of central bank's foreign exchange reserve assets will cause a country's money supply to increase or decrease through the change of monetary base. The changes of sovereign wealth funds usually do not have monetary effects.
- ❖ Central banks usually adopt a conservative and prudent attitude in the management of foreign exchange reserves, and pursue maximum liquidity and security, while sovereign wealth funds usually implement active management, which can sacrifice certain liquidity and bear greater investment risks, so as to achieve the goal of maximizing investment returns.

Summary

- ■ At present, foreign investors have the following ways to invest in the equity of China's enterprises: by investing in China's enterprises listed stocks overseas to invest.

- The main overseas listing of China's enterprises can be divided into 5 stages.
- The main modes of overseas listing of China's enterprises are: initial public offering mode, shell listing model, shell listing model, convertible bond listing model, depository receipt listing model.
- QFII and RQFII, as a transitional, low-risk model, are playing a unique role in the gradual opening of China's securities market.
- Both the Shanghai—HongKong Stock Exchange and Shenzhen—HongKong link have a significant role in promoting the development of capital markets in the Mainland and Hong Kong, and the interconnection mechanism can strengthen the links between the capital markets of the two places and promote the two-way opening of the capital markets of the two places.
- "HuLun tong" through the depository receipts and the cross-border conversion mechanism between the basic securities to achieve the interconnection between the two markets.
- QDII is different from traditional offshore finance.
- Sovereign Wealth, corresponding to private wealth, refers to public wealth, which is accumulated by a government through specific tax and budgetary allocations, renewable natural resource income and balance-of-payments surplus, which is controlled and controlled by the government and is usually held in foreign currency.
- On September 29, 2007, at 10 a.m., China Investment Corporation, China Investment Corporation, China's sovereign wealth fund, was officially listed in Beijing.

Exercises

1. What is the difference between sovereign wealth funds and official foreign exchange reserves?
2. What are the main risks to QDII?
3. What are the main differences between QDII and traditional offshore finance?
4. What is the difference between QDII and QFII?
5. What does R mean in RQFII?
6. Shanghai—Hong Kong Stock Connect, Shenzhen—Hong Kong Pass and QFII and RQFII mechanism are the main ways for foreign investors to invest in domestic capital markets, what is the

difference between the two?
7. How does the introduction of QFII system affect the development of China's securities market?
8. What are the main problems of Chinese companies listing abroad?
9. What is the point of Chinese companies listing abroad?
10. What are the main modes of listing of Chinese companies abroad?
11. What is the difference between H-shares and red chips?

REFERENCES

1. Arnott, D. (2004). The Meaning of a Slender Risk Premium. *Financial Analysts Journal*, Vol.60, No.2:6-8.
2. Arnott, D. & Bernstein, P. L. (2002). What Risk Premium is Normal?. *Financial Analyst Journal*, Vol.58, No.2: 64-85.
3. Asness, S. (2003). Fight the Fed Model. *Journal of Portfolio Management*, Vol 30, No.1: 11-24.
4. Bailey, E. & David Zapol. (2005). Venture Capital and Global Health. *Financing Global Health Ventures Discussion Paper*. www.commonscapital.com/ downloads/Venture-Capital-and Global Health. pdf.
5. Bessembinder, Hendrik, & Kalok Chan. (1998). Market Effciency and the Returns to Technical Analysis. *Financial Management*. Vol.27, No.2: 5-17.
6. Bruno Solnik, Dennis Mcleavey. International investments（第五版）. 北京：中信出版社, 2007 年.
7. Edwin J. Elton, Martin J. Gruber, Stephen J. Brown. Modern Portfolio Theory and Investment Analysis (7th Edition). 北京：机械工业出版社, 2008 年.
8. David K.Eiteman, Arthur I. Stonehill, Michael H. Moffett. 跨国金融与财务（第 11 版）. 北京：北京大学出版社, 2009 年.
9. Michael G., McMillan, Jerald E., Pinto, Wendy L., Pirie. (2011). *Investments: Principles of Portfolio and Equity Analysis*. John Wiley & Sons, Inc.
10. Zvi Bodie, Alex Kane, Alan Marcus. Investments（第 9 版）. 北京：机械工业出版社, 2015 年.